The Complete Apocrypha

OF THE

ETHIOPIAN

BIBLE

20 Missing Books In The Protestant Canon Of
Ge'ez Bible in English Version.

Includes Enoch, Giants, Watchers, Angels And Sirach.

ANCIENT HOLY

W R I T I N G S

EXCLUSIVE BONUS!

We're thrilled you've chosen this book, and we want to extend an EXCLUSIVE INVITATION to you!

This book participates in the **"Exclusive Book Club Program"** 📚 - a unique initiative that rewards YOU for doing what you love - Discover 🕵️, Read 📖, and Share 💬 thoughts about new books you didn't know about!

🔎 **LEARN MORE, JOIN THE PROGRAM TO RECEIVE ADDITIONAL BONUS RESOURCES!** 🔍

🎯 **SCAN THE QR CODE BELOW NOW TO GET FREE ACCESS!** 🎯

The Complete Apocrypha Of The Ethiopian Bible – Contents

Introduction - Guide To Apocryphal Writings

Protestants use the term *apocryphal* to name books that were included in the Old Testament of the Septuagint but not in the Old Testament of the Masoretic Text.

If we pick up the Protestant Bible, we notice 66 books. Precisely 39 from the Old Testament and 27 from the New Testament. What most people miss is that there are other books in the Old Testament. We are talking about the so-called apocryphal, *deuterocanonical* books.

Apocryphal means *hidden*, not in a negative sense as one might think but in the strict definition of *secondary*. Protestants did not remove these books from their Bibles but removed them from their classical Old Testament position and placed them in a separate section between the Old and New Testaments. They called this section the *Apocryphal books* because of their dubious canonicity.

Apocryphal is a term used mostly by Protestants, while Roman Catholics call these books deuterocanonical, that is, *secondary canon* precisely. Let us then emphasize that the Apocrypha were not *excommunicated* from the King James Version of the Bible or any other Protestant Bible of the Reformation era. The Septuagint, on the other hand, is a Greek translation of the Old Testament dating from about the second century B.C. At the same time, the Masoretic Text is the modern Hebrew version of the Old Testament from the eighth century A.D. We note that the Septuagint and the Masoretic Text had older Jewish origins. The Septuagint was centuries older than Christianity and had been the popular version of the Old Testament for Jews at the time of Christ and the apostles.

However, beginning in the fifth century CE, Jews preferred the proto-Masoretic family of texts, while Christians continued to use the Septuagint. This eventually led to Jewish accusations of using a corrupted Old Testament by Christians. Partly out of ignorance of Greek Old Testament history, Christians came to use the proto-Masoretic text as the basis for the Old Testament, but the extra books of the Septuagint were retained in the canon of the time. From the data we have, there is no certainty of considering it "*God's Word*"; however, the signature of the narrating prophets is there, and it is undeniable. The Apocrypha was included in all Reformation-era Bibles, and Protestants continued to read them, but because of their questionable status, they did not use them to derive doctrine. None of them condemned the use or reading of the Books and in fact, did not exclude them from the Bible. The Books precisely were included in the Luther Bible, the Geneva Bible, the Bishop's Bible, the King James Bible and others. But as time went on, books were read less and less. In the 19th century, various translations, such as the King James Bible, began to be produced without these "*secondary*" texts. The Ethiopian church was never against the presentation of these books; everyone, including the Jews of Ethiopia and Ethiopian Christians, considered the presence of these writings legitimate without ever questioning them. Gathered in this book are the books excluded from the Protestant canon of the 66 traditional biblical texts that, for convenience, we will call the *restricted canon*, such as *The Book of Enoch* or ancient Ethiopian books of the prophet Enoch, the *3 Meqabyan*, *The Wisdom of Solomon* and all those unique texts of the canons of the ancient Ethiopian Bible, one of the earliest and oldest ever.

The initial language of these ancient writings was *Ge'ez*; this edition readily translated into English except for some parts in the lyrics Rastafari version of Jamaica Patos like the Meqabyan. You can only find these books in Catholic and Eastern Orthodox Bibles, especially the Meqabyan in the Ethiopian Orthodox Testament and the beta Israel Masnada Kedus biblical canon. Ge'ez is the language also called *"Classical Ethiopian"* and translated into English in this edition which has apocryphal texts of Ethiopian origin also present, in the minority, in the King James version.

Why none of these books are continued in other Christian or Jewish traditions is a mystery. The only plausible explanation is the difficulty of linguistic translation of the Greek and Hebrew versions. If we take Enoch and his testament, then, for example, one must know that for most of the history of the Church in Asia and Europe, Enoch was unknown. James Bruce, a Scotsman, brought him to light in 1773 when up to that time, only Ethiopia had survived. The work, *The Book of Enoch*, was later, in fact translated into English by Sir R.H. Charles in 1893. It was never considered by Protestants and also the other books that follow in this collection and never instead considered controversial by orthodox Christians.

It has never been considered by Protestants and the other books that follow in this collection and never instead regarded as controversial by Orthodox Christians. It is not a heretical text as the Gnostic texts are, but it is still considered an unpopular text by Protestants. For all other considerations, we leave the discussion to you.

This edition aims to make possible the dissemination of the texts and to give cues for interpretation to those who want to study the documents of history.

Happy reading.

The Wisdom Of Solomon

Wis.1

[1] Love righteousness, ye that be judges of the earth: think of the Lord with a good heart, and in simplicity of heart seek him.

[2] For he will be found of them that tempt him not; and sheweth himself unto such as do not distrust him.

[3] For froward thoughts separate from God: and his power, when it is tried, reproveth the unwise.

[4] For into a malicious soul wisdom shall not enter; nor dwell in the body that is subject unto sin.

[5] For the holy spirit of discipline will flee deceit, and remove from thoughts
that are without understanding, and will not abide when unrighteousness cometh in.

[6] For wisdom is a loving spirit; and will not acquit a blasphemer of his words: for God is witness of his reins, and a true beholder of his heart, and a hearer of his tongue.

[7] For the Spirit of the Lord filleth the world: and that which containeth all things hath knowledge of the voice.

[8] Therefore he that speaketh unrighteous things cannot be hid: neither shall vengeance, when it punisheth, pass by him.

[9] For inquisition shall be made into the counsels of the ungodly: and the sound of his words shall come unto the Lord for the manifestation of his wicked deeds.

[10] For the ear of jealousy heareth all things: and the noise of murmurings is not hid.

[11] Therefore beware of murmuring, which is unprofitable; and refrain your tongue from backbiting: for there is no word so secret, that shall go for nought: and the mouth that belieth slayeth the soul.

[12] Seek not death in the error of your life: and pull not upon yourselves destruction with the works of your hands.

[13] For God made not death: neither hath he pleasure in the destruction of the living.

[14] For he created all things, that they might have their being: and the generations of the world were healthful; and there is no poison of destruction in them, nor the kingdom of death upon the earth:

[15] For righteousness is immortal:

[16] But ungodly men with their works and words called it to them: for when they thought to have it their friend, they consumed to nought, and made a covenant with it, because they are worthy to take part with it.

Wis.2

[1] For the ungodly said, reasoning with themselves, but not aright, Our life is short and tedious, and in the death of a man there is no remedy: neither was there any man known to have returned from the grave.

[2] For we are born at all adventure: and we shall be hereafter as though we had never been: for the breath in

our nostrils is as smoke, and a little spark in the moving of our heart:

[3] Which being extinguished, our body shall be turned into ashes, and our spirit shall vanish as the soft air,

[4] And our name shall be forgotten in time, and no man shall have our works in remembrance, and our life shall pass away as the trace of a cloud, and shall be dispersed as a mist, that is driven away with the beams of the sun, and overcome with the heat thereof.

[5] For our time is a very shadow that passeth away; and after our end there is no returning: for it is fast sealed, so that no man cometh again.

[6] Come on therefore, let us enjoy the good things that are present: and let us speedily use the creatures like as in youth.

[7] Let us fill ourselves with costly wine and ointments: and let no flower of the spring pass by us:

[8] Let us crown ourselves with rosebuds, before they be withered:

[9] Let none of us go without his part of our voluptuousness: let us leave tokens of our joyfulness in every place: for this is our portion, and our lot is this.

[10] Let us oppress the poor righteous man, let us not spare the widow, nor reverence the ancient gray hairs of the aged.

[11] Let our strength be the law of justice: for that which is feeble is found to be nothing worth.

[12] Therefore let us lie in wait for the righteous; because he is not for our turn, and he is clean contrary to our doings: he upbraideth us with our offending the law, and objecteth to our infamy the transgressings of our education.

[13] He professeth to have the knowledge of God: and he calleth himself the child of the Lord.

[14] He was made to reprove our thoughts.

[15] He is grievous unto us even to behold: for his life is not like other men's, his ways are of another fashion.

[16] We are esteemed of him as counterfeits: he abstaineth from our ways as from filthiness: he pronounceth the end of the just to be blessed, and maketh his boast that God is his father.

[17] Let us see if his words be true: and let us prove what shall happen in the end of him.

[18] For if the just man be the son of God, he will help him, and deliver him from the hand of his enemies.

[19] Let us examine him with despitefulness and torture, that we may know his meekness, and prove his patience.

[20] Let us condemn him with a shameful death: for by his own saying he shall be respected.

[21] Such things they did imagine, and were deceived: for their own wickedness hath blinded them.

[22] As for the mysteries of God, they kn ew them not:

neither hoped they for the wages of righteousness, nor discerned a reward for blameless souls.

[23] For God created man to be immortal, and made him to be an image of his own eternity.

[24] Nevertheless through envy of the devil came death into the world: and they that do hold of his side do find it.

Wis.3

[1] But the souls of the righteous are in the hand of God, and there shall no torment touch them.

[2] In the sight of the unwise they seemed to die: and their departure is taken for misery,

[3] And their going from us to be utter destruction: but they are in peace.

[4] For though they be punished in the sight of men, yet is their hope full of immortality.

[5] And having been a little chastised, they shall be greatly rewarded: for God proved them, and found them worthy for himself.

[6] As gold in the furnace hath he tried them, and received them as a burnt offering.

[7] And in the time of their visitation they shall shine, and run to and fro like sparks among the stubble.

[8] They shall judge the nations, and have dominion over the people, and their Lord shall reign for ever.

[9] They that put their trust in him shall understand the truth: and such as be faithful in love shall abide with him: for grace and mercy is to his saints, and he hath care for his elect.

[10] But the ungodly shall be punished according to their own imaginations, which have neglected the righteous, and forsaken the Lord.

[11] For whoso despiseth wisdom and nurture, he is miserable, and their hope is vain, their labours unfruitful, and their works unprofitable:

[12] Their wives are foolish, and their children wicked:

[13] Their offspring is cursed. Wherefore blessed is the barren that is undefiled, which hath not known the sinful bed: she shall have fruit in the visitation of souls.

[14] And blessed is the eunuch, which with his hands hath wrought no iniquity, nor imagined wicked things against God: for unto him shall be given the special gift of faith, and an inheritance in the temple of the Lord more acceptable to his mind.

[15] For glorious is the fruit of good labours: and the root of wisdom shall never fall away.

[16] As for the children of adulterers, they shall not come to their perfection, and the seed of an unrighteous bed shall be rooted out.

[17] For though they live long, yet shall they be nothing regarded: and their last age shall be without honour.

[18] Or, if they die quickly, they have no hope, neither comfort in the day of trial.

[19] For horrible is the end of the unrighteous generation.

Wis.4

[1] Better it is to have no children, and to have virtue: for the memorial thereof is immortal: because it is known with God, and with men.

[2] When it is present, men take example at it; and when it is gone, they desire it: it weareth a crown, and triumpheth for ever, having gotten the victory, striving for undefiled rewards.

[3] But the multiplying brood of the ungodly shall not thrive, nor take deep rooting from bastard slips, nor lay any fast foundation.

[4] For though they flourish in branches for a time; yet standing not last, they shall be shaken with the wind, and through the force of winds they shall be rooted out.

[5] The imperfect branches shall be broken off, their fruit unprofitable, not ripe to eat, yea, meet for nothing.

[6] For children begotten of unlawful beds are witnesses of wickedness against their parents in their trial.

[7] But though the righteous be prevented with death, yet shall he be in rest.

[8] For honourable age is not that which standeth in length of time, nor that is measured by number of years.

[9] But wisdom is the gray hair unto men, and an unspotted life is old age.

[10] He pleased God, and was beloved of him: so that living among sinners he was translated.

[11] Yea speedily was he taken away, lest that wickedness should alter his understanding, or deceit beguile his soul.

[12] For the bewitching of naughtiness doth obscure things that are honest; and the wandering of concupiscence doth undermine the simple mind.

[13] He, being made perfect in a short time, fulfilled a long time:

[14] For his soul pleased the Lord: therefore hasted he to take him away from among the wicked.

[15] This the people saw, and understood it not, neither laid they up this in their minds, That his grace and mercy is with his saints, and that he hath respect unto his chosen.

[16] Thus the righteous that is dead shall condemn the ungodly which are living; and youth that is soon perfected the many years and old age of the unrighteous.

[17] For they shall see the end of the wise, and shall not understand what God in his counsel hath decreed of him, and to what end the Lord hath set him in safety.

[18] They shall see him, and despise him; but God shall laugh them to scorn: and they shall hereafter be a vile carcase, and a reproach among the dead for evermore.

[19] For he shall rend them, and cast them down headlong, that they shall be speechless; and he shall shake them from the foundation; and they shall be utterly laid waste, and be in sorrow; and their memorial shall perish.

[20] And when they cast up the accounts of their sins, they shall come with fear: and their own iniquities shall convince them to their face.

Wis.5

[1] Then shall the righteous man stand in great boldness before the face of such as have afflicted him, and made no account of his labours.

[2] When they see it, they shall be troubled with terrible fear, and shall be amazed at the strangeness of his salvation, so far beyond all that they looked for.

[3] And they repenting and groaning for anguish of spirit shall say within themselves, This was he, whom we had sometimes in derision, and a proverb of reproach:

[4] We fools accounted his life madness, and his end to be without honour:

[5] How is he numbered among the children of God, and his lot is among the saints!

[6] Therefore have we erred from the way of truth, and the light of righteousness hath not shined unto us, and the sun of righteousness rose not upon us.

[7] We wearied ourselves in the way of wickedness and destruction: yea, we have gone through deserts, where there lay no way: but as for the way of the Lord, we have not known it.

[8] What hath pride profited us? or what good hath riches with our vaunting brought us?

[9] All those things are passed away like a shadow, and as a post that hasted by;

[10] And as a ship that passeth over the waves of the water, which when it is gone by, the trace thereof cannot be found, neither the pathway of the keel in the waves;

[11] Or as when a bird hath flown through the air, there is no token of her way to be found, but the light air being beaten with the stroke of her wings and parted with the violent noise and motion of them, is passed through, and therein afterwards no sign where she went is to be found

[12] Or like as when an arrow is shot at a mark, it parteth the air, which immediately cometh together again, so that a man cannot know where it went through:

[13] Even so we in like manner, as soon as we were born,

began to draw to our end, and had no sign of virtue to shew; but were consumed in our own wickedness.

[14] For the hope of the Godly is like dust that is blown away with the wind; like a thin froth that is driven away with the storm; like as the smoke which is dispersed here and there with a tempest, and passeth away as the remembrance of a guest that tarrieth but a day.

[15] But the righteous live for evermore; their reward also is with the Lord, and the care of them is with the most High.

[16] Therefore shall they receive a glorious kingdom, and a beautiful crown from the Lord's hand: for with his right hand shall he cover them, and with his arm shall he protect them.

[17] He shall take to him his jealousy for complete armour, and make the creature his weapon for the revenge of his enemies.

[18] He shall put on righteousness as a breastplate, and true judgment instead of an helmet.

[19] He shall take holiness for an invincible shield.

[20] His severe wrath shall he sharpen for a sword, and the world shall fight with him against the unwise.

[21] Then shall the right aiming thunderbolts go abroad; and from the clouds, as from a well drawn bow, shall they fly to the mark.

[22] And hailstones full of wrath shall be cast as out of a stone bow, and the water of the sea shall rage against them, and the floods shall cruelly drown them.

[23] Yea, a mighty wind shall stand up against them, and like a storm shall blow them away: thus iniquity shall lay waste the whole earth, and ill dealing shall overthrow the thrones of the mighty.

Wis.6

[1] Hear therefore, O ye kings, and understand; learn, ye that be judges of the ends of the earth.

[2] Give ear, ye that rule the people, and glory in the multitude of nations.

[3] For power is given you of the Lord, and sovereignty from the Highest, who shall try your works, and search out your counsels.

[4] Because, being ministers of his kingdom, ye have not judged aright, nor kept the law, nor walked after the counsel of God;

[5] Horribly and speedily shall he come upon you: for a sharp judgment shall be to them that be in high places.

[6] For mercy will soon pardon the meanest: but mighty men shall be mightily tormented.

[7] For he which is Lord over all shall fear no man's person, neither shall he stand in awe of any man's greatness: for he hath made the small and great, and careth for all alike.

[8] But a sore trial shall come upon the mighty.

[9] Unto you therefore, O kings, do I speak, that ye may learn wisdom, and not fall away.

[10] For they that keep holiness holily shall be judged holy: and they that have learned such things shall find what to answer.

[11] Wherefore set your affection upon my words; desire them, and ye shall be instructed.

[12] Wisdom is glorious, and never fadeth away: yea, she is easily seen of them that love her, and found of such as seek her.

[13] She preventeth them that desire her, in making herself first known unto them.

[14] Whoso seeketh her early shall have no great travail: for he shall find her sitting at his doors.

[15] To think therefore upon her is perfection of wisdom: and whoso watcheth for her shall quickly be without car.

[16] For she goeth about seeking such as are worthy of her, sheweth herself favourably unto them in the ways, and meeteth them in every thought.

[17] For the very true beginning of her is the desire of discipline; and the care of discipline is love;

[18] And love is the keeping of her laws; and the giving heed unto her laws is the assurance of incorruption;

[19] And incorruption maketh us near unto God:

[20] Therefore the desire of wisdom bringeth to a kingdom.

[21] If your delight be then in thrones and sceptres, O ye kings of the people, honour wisdom, that ye may reign for evermore.

[22] As for wisdom, what she is, and how she came up, I will tell you, and will not hide mysteries from you: but will seek her out from the beginning of her nativity, and bring the knowledge of her into light, and will not pass over the truth.

[23] Neither will I go with consuming envy; for such a man shall have no fellowship with wisdom.

[24] But the multitude of the wise is the welfare of the world: and a wise king is the upholding of the people.

[25] Receive therefore instruction through my words, and it shall do you good.

Wis.7

[1] I myself also am a mortal man, like to all, and the offspring of him that was first made of the earth,

[2] And in my mother's womb was fashioned to be flesh in the time of ten months, being compacted in blood, of the seed of man, and the pleasure that came with sleep.

[3] And when I was born, I drew in the common air, and fell upon the earth, which is of like nature, and the first voice

which I uttered was crying, as all others do.

[4] I was nursed in swaddling clothes, and that with cares.

[5] For there is no king that had any other beginning of birth.

[6] For all men have one entrance into life, and the like going out.

[7] Wherefore I prayed, and understanding was given me: I called upon God, and the spirit of wisdom came to me

[8] I preferred her before sceptres and thrones, and esteemed riches nothing in comparison of her.

[9] Neither compared I unto her any precious stone, because all gold in respect of her is as a little sand, and silver shall be counted as clay before her.

[10] I loved her above health and beauty, and chose to have her instead of light: for the light that cometh from her never goeth out.

[11] All good things together came to me with her, and innumerable riches in her hands.

[12] And I rejoiced in them all, because wisdom goeth before them: and I knew not that she was the mother of them.

[13] I learned diligently, and do communicate her liberally: I do not hide her riches.

[14] For she is a treasure unto men that never faileth: which they that use become the friends of God, being commended for the gifts that come from learning.

[15] God hath granted me to speak as I would, and to conceive as is meet for the things that are given me: because it is he that leadeth unto wisdom, and directeth the wise.

[16] For in his hand are both we and our words; all wisdom also, and knowledge of workmanship.

[17] For he hath given me certain knowledge of the things that are, namely, to know how the world was made, and the operation of the elements:

[18] The beginning, ending, and midst of the times: the alterations of the turning of the sun, and the change of seasons:

[19] The circuits of years, and the positions of stars:

[20] The natures of living creatures, and the furies of wild beasts: the violence of winds, and the reasonings of men: the diversities of plants and the virtues of roots:

[21] And all such things as are either secret or manifest, them I know.

[22] For wisdom, which is the worker of all things, taught me: for in her is an understanding spirit holy, one only, manifold, subtil, lively, clear, undefiled, plain, not subject to hurt, loving the thing that is good quick, which cannot be letted, ready to do good,

[23] Kind to man, steadfast, sure, free from care, having all power, overseeing all things, and going through all understanding, pure, and most subtil, spirits.

[24] For wisdom is more moving than any motion: she passeth and goeth through all things by reason of her pureness.

[25] For she is the breath of the power of God, and a pure influence flowing from the glory of the Almighty: therefore can no defiled thing fall into her.

[26] For she is the brightness of the everlasting light, the unspotted mirror of the power of God, and the image of his goodness.

[27] And being but one, she can do all things: and remaining in herself, she maketh all things new: and in all ages entering into holy souls, she maketh them friends of God, and prophets.

[28] For God loveth none but him that dwelleth with wisdom.

[29] For she is more beautiful than the sun, and above all the order of stars: being compared with the light, she is found before it.

[30] For after this cometh night: but vice shall not prevail against wisdom.

Wis.8

[1] Wisdom reacheth from one end to another mightily: and sweetly doth she order all things.

[2] I loved her, and sought her out from my youth, I desired to make her my spouse, and I was a lover of her beauty.

[3] In that she is conversant with God, she magnifieth her nobility: yea, the Lord of all things himself loved her.

[4] For she is privy to the mysteries of the knowledge of God, and a lover of his works.

[5] If riches be a possession to be desired in this life; what is richer than wisdom, that worketh all things?

[6] And if prudence work; who of all that are is a more cunning workman than she?

[7] And if a man love righteousness her labours are virtues: for she teacheth temperance and prudence, justice and fortitude: which are such things, as en can have nothing more profitable in their life.

[8] If a man desire much experience, she knoweth things of old, and conjectureth aright what is to come: she knoweth the subtilties of speeches, and can expound dark sentences: she foreseeth signs and wonders, and the events of seasons and times.

[9] Therefore I purposed to take her to me to live with me, knowing that she would be a counsellor of good things, and a comfort in cares and grief.

[10] For her sake I shall have estimation among the

multitude, and honour with the elders, though I be young.

[11] I shall be found of a quick conceit in judgment, and shall be admired in the sight of great men.

[12] When I hold my tongue, they shall bide my leisure, and when I speak, they shall give good ear unto me: if I talk much, they shall lay their hands upon their mouth.

[13] Moreover by the means of her I shall obtain immortality, and leave behind me an everlasting memorial to them that come after me.

[14] I shall set the people in order, and the nations shall be subject unto me.

[15] Horrible tyrants shall be afraid, when they do but hear of me; I shall be found good among the multitude, and valiant in war.

[16] After I am come into mine house, I will repose myself with her: for her conversation hath no bitterness; and to live with her hath no sorrow, but mirth and joy.

[17] Now when I considered these things in myself, and pondered them in my heart, how that to be allied unto wisdom is immortality;

[18] And great pleasure it is to have her friendship; and in the works of her hands are infinite riches; and in the exercise of conference with her, prudence; and in talking with her, a good report; I went about seeking how to take her to me.

[19] For I was a witty child, and had a good spirit.

[20] Yea rather, being good, I came into a body undefiled.

[21] Nevertheless, when I perceived that I could not otherwise obtain her, except God gave her me; and that was a point of wisdom also to know whose gift she was; I prayed unto the Lord, and besought him, and with my whole heart.

Wis.9

[1] O God of my fathers, and Lord of mercy, who hast made all things with thy word,

[2] And ordained man through thy wisdom, that he should have dominion over the creatures which thou hast made,

[3] And order the world according to equity and righteousness, and execute judgment with an upright heart:

[4] Give me wisdom, that sitteth by thy throne; and reject me not from among thy children:

[5] For I thy servant and son of thine handmaid am a feeble person, and of a short time, and too young for the understanding of judgment and laws.

[6] For though a man be never so perfect among the children of men, yet if thy wisdom be not with him, he shall be nothing regarded.

[7] Thou hast chosen me to be a king of thy people, and a judge of thy sons and daughters:

[8] Thou hast commanded me to build a temple upon thy holy mount, and an altar in the city wherein thou dwellest, a resemblance of the holy tabernacle, which thou hast prepared from the beginning.

[9] And wisdom was with thee: which knoweth thy works, and was present when thou madest the world, and knew what was acceptable in thy sight, and right in thy commandments.

[10] O send her out of thy holy heavens, and from the throne of thy glory, that being present she may labour with me, that I may know what is pleasing unto thee.

[11] For she knoweth and understandeth all things, and she shall lead me soberly in my doings, and preserve me in her power.

[12] So shall my works be acceptable, and then shall I judge thy people righteously, and be worthy to sit in my father's seat.

[13] For what man is he that can know the counsel of God? or who can think what the will of the Lord is?

[14] For the thoughts of mortal men are miserable, and our devices are but uncertain.

[15] For the corruptible body presseth down the soul, and the earthy tabernacle weigheth down the mind that museth upon many things.

[16] And hardly do we guess aright at things that are upon earth, and with labour do we find the things that are before us: but the things that are in heaven who hath searched out?

[17] And thy counsel who hath known, except thou give wisdom, and send thy Holy Spirit from above?

[18] For so the ways of them which lived on the earth were reformed, and men were taught the things that are pleasing unto thee, and were saved through wisdom.

Wis.10

[1] She preserved the first formed father of the world, that was created alone, and brought him out of his fall,

[2] And gave him power to rule all things.

[3] But when the unrighteous went away from her in his anger, he perished also in the fury wherewith he murdered his brother.

[4] For whose cause the earth being drowned with the flood, wisdom again preserved it, and directed the course of the righteous in a piece of wood of small value.

[5] Moreover, the nations in their wicked conspiracy being confounded, she found out the righteous, and preserved him blameless unto God, and kept him strong against his tender compassion toward his son.

[6] When the ungodly perished, she delivered the righteous

man, who fled from the fire which fell down upon the five cities.

[7] Of whose wickedness even to this day the waste land that smoketh is a testimony, and plants bearing fruit that never come to ripeness: and a standing pillar of salt is a monument of an unbelieving soul.

[8] For regarding not wisdom, they gat not only this hurt, that they knew not the things which were good; but also left behind them to the world a memorial of their foolishness: so that in the things wherein they offended they could not so much as be hid.

[9] Rut wisdom delivered from pain those that attended upon her.

[10] When the righteous fled from his brother's wrath she guided him in right paths, shewed him the kingdom of God, and gave him knowledge of holy things, made him rich in his travels, and multiplied the fruit of his labours.

[11] In the covetousness of such as oppressed him she stood by him, and made him rich.

[12] She defended him from his enemies, and kept him safe from those that lay in wait, and in a sore conflict she gave him the victory; that he might know that goodness is stronger than all.

[13] When the righteous was sold, she forsook him not, but delivered him from sin: she went down with him into the pit,

[14] And left him not in bonds, till she brought him the sceptre of the kingdom, and power against those that oppressed him: as for them that had accused him, she shewed them to be liars, and gave him perpetual glory.

[15] She delivered the righteous people and blameless seed from the nation that oppressed them.

[16] She entered into the soul of the servant of the Lord, and withstood dreadful kings in wonders and signs;

[17] Rendered to the righteous a reward of their labours, guided them in a marvellous way, and was unto them for a cover by day, and a light of stars in the night season;

[18] Brought them through the Red sea, and led them through much water:

[19] But she drowned their enemies, and cast them up out of the bottom of the deep.

[20] Therefore the righteous spoiled the ungodly, and praised thy holy name, O Lord, and magnified with one accord thine hand, that fought for them.

[21] For wisdom opened the mouth of the dumb, and made the tongues of them that cannot speak eloquent.

Wis.11

[1] She prospered their works in the hand of the holy prophet.

[2] They went through the wilderness that was not inhabited, and pitched tents in places where there lay no way.

[3] They stood against their enemies, and were avenged of their adversaries.

[4] When they were thirsty, they called upon thee, and water was given them out of the flinty rock, and their thirst was quenched out of the hard stone.

[5] For by what things their enemies were punished, by the same they in their need were benefited.

[6] For instead of of a perpetual running river troubled with foul blood,

[7] For a manifest reproof of that commandment, whereby the infants were slain, thou gavest unto them abundance of water by a means which they hoped not for:

[8] Declaring by that thirst then how thou hadst punished their adversaries.

[9] For when they were tried albeit but in mercy chastised, they knew how the ungodly were judged in wrath and tormented, thirsting in another manner than the just.

[10] For these thou didst admonish and try, as a father: but the other, as a severe king, thou didst condemn and punish.

[11] Whether they were absent or present, they were vexed alike.

[12] For a double grief came upon them, and a groaning for the remembrance of things past.

[13] For when they heard by their own punishments the other to be benefited, they had some feeling of the Lord.

[14] For whom they respected with scorn, when he was long before thrown out at the casting forth of the infants, him in the end, when they saw what came to pass, they admired.

[15] But for the foolish devices of their wickedness, wherewith being deceived they worshipped serpents void of reason, and vile beasts, thou didst send a multitude of unreasonable beasts upon them for vengeance;

[16] That they might know, that wherewithal a man sinneth, by the same also shall he be punished.

[17] For thy Almighty hand, that made the world of matter without form, wanted not means to send among them a multitude of bears or fierce lions,

[18] Or unknown wild beasts, full of rage, newly created, breathing out either a fiery vapour, or filthy scents of scattered smoke, or shooting horrible sparkles out of their eyes:

[19] Whereof not only the harm might dispatch them at once, but also the terrible sight utterly destroy them.

[20] Yea, and without these might they have fallen down with one blast, being persecuted of vengeance, and scattered abroad through the breath of thy power: but thou hast ordered all things in measure and number and weight.

[21] For thou canst shew thy great strength at all times when thou wilt; and who may withstand the power of thine arm?

[22] For the whole world before thee is as a little grain of the balance, yea, as a drop of the morning dew that falleth down upon the earth.

[23] But thou hast mercy upon all; for thou canst do all things, and winkest at the sins of men, because they should amend.

[24] For thou lovest all the things that are, and abhorrest nothing which thou hast made: for never wouldest thou have made any thing, if thou hadst hated it.

[25] And how could any thing have endured, if it had not been thy will? or been preserved, if not called by thee?

[26] But thou sparest all: for they are thine, O Lord, thou lover of souls.

Wis.12

[1] For thine incorruptible Spirit is in all things.

[2] Therefore chastenest thou them by little and little that offend, and warnest them by putting them in remembrance wherein they have offended, that leaving their wickedness they may believe on thee, O Lord.

[3] For it was thy will to destroy by the hands of our fathers both those old inhabitants of thy holy land,

[4] Whom thou hatedst for doing most odious works of witchcrafts, and wicked sacrifices;

[5] And also those merciless murderers of children, and devourers of man's flesh, and the feasts of blood,

[6] With their priests out of the midst of their idolatrous crew, and the parents, that killed with their own hands souls destitute of help:

[7] That the land, which thou esteemedst above all other, might receive a worthy colony of God's children.

[8] Nevertheless even those thou sparedst as men, and didst send wasps, forerunners of thine host, to destroy them by little and little.

[9] Not that thou wast unable to bring the ungodly under the hand of the righteous in battle, or to destroy them at once with cruel beasts, or with one rough word:

[10] But executing thy judgments upon them by little and little, thou gavest them place of repentance, not being ignorant that they were a naughty generation, and that their malice was bred in them, and that their cogitation would never be changed.

[11] For it was a cursed seed from the beginning; neither didst thou for fear of any man give them pardon for those things wherein they sinned.

[12] For who shall say, What hast thou done? or who shall withstand thy judgment? or who shall accuse thee for the nations that perish, whom thou made? or who shall come to stand against thee, to be revenged for the unrighteous men?

[13] For neither is there any God but thou that careth for all, to whom thou mightest shew that thy judgment is not unright.

[14] Neither shall king or tyrant be able to set his face against thee for any whom thou hast punished.

[15] Forsomuch then as thou art righteous thyself, thou orderest all things righteously: thinking it not agreeable with thy power to condemn him that hath not deserved to be punished.

[16] For thy power is the beginning of righteousness, and because thou art the Lord of all, it maketh thee to be gracious unto all.

[17] For when men will not believe that thou art of a full power, thou shewest thy strength, and among them that know it thou makest their boldness manifest.

[18] But thou, mastering thy power, judgest with equity, and orderest us with great favour: for thou mayest use power when thou wilt.

[19] But by such works hast thou taught thy people that the just man should be merciful, and hast made thy children to be of a good hope that thou givest repentance for sins.

[20] For if thou didst punish the enemies of thy children, and the condemned to death, with such deliberation, giving them time and place, whereby they might be delivered from their malice:

[21] With how great circumspection didst thou judge thine own sons, unto whose fathers thou hast sworn, and made covenants of good promises?

[22] Therefore, whereas thou dost chasten us, thou scourgest our enemies a thousand times more, to the intent that, when we judge, we should carefully think of thy goodness, and when we ourselves are judged, we should look for mercy.

[23] Wherefore, whereas men have lived dissolutely and unrighteously, thou hast tormented them with their own abominations.

[24] For they went astray very far in the ways of error, and held them for gods, which even among the beasts of their enemies were despised, being deceived, as children of no understanding.

[25] Therefore unto them, as to children without the use of reason, thou didst send a judgment to mock them.

[**26**] But they that would not be reformed by that correction, wherein he dallied with them, shall feel a judgment worthy of God.

[**27**] For, look, for what things they grudged, when they were punished, that is, for them whom they thought to be gods; [now] being punished in them, when they saw it, they acknowledged him to be the true God, whom before they denied to know: and therefore came extreme damnation upon them.

Wis.13

[**1**] Surely vain are all men by nature, who are ignorant of God, and could not out of the good things that are seen know him that is: neither by considering the works did they acknowledge the workmaster;

[**2**] But deemed either fire, or wind, or the swift air, or the circle of the stars, or the violent water, or the lights of heaven, to be the gods which govern the world.

[**3**] With whose beauty if they being delighted took them to be gods; let them know how much better the Lord of them is: for the first author of beauty hath created them.

[**4**] But if they were astonished at their power and virtue, let them understand by them, how much mightier he is that made them.

[**5**] For by the greatness and beauty of the creatures proportionably the maker of them is seen.

[**6**] But yet for this they are the less to be blamed: for they peradventure err, seeking God, and desirous to find him.

[**7**] For being conversant in his works they search him diligently, and believe their sight: because the things are beautiful that are seen.

[**8**] Howbeit neither are they to be pardoned.

[**9**] For if they were able to know so much, that they could aim at the world; how did they not sooner find out the Lord thereof?

[**10**] But miserable are they, and in dead things is their hope, who call them gods, which are the works of men's hands, gold and silver, to shew art in, and resemblances of beasts, or a stone good for nothing, the work of an ancient hand.

[**11**] Now a carpenter that felleth timber, after he hath sawn down a tree meet for the purpose, and taken off all the bark skilfully round about, and hath wrought it handsomely, and made a vessel thereof fit for the service of man's life;

[**12**] And after spending the refuse of his work to dress his meat, hath filled himself;

[**13**] And taking the very refuse among those which served to no use, being a crooked piece of wood, and full of knots, hath carved it diligently, when he had nothing else to do, and formed it by the skill of his understanding, and fashioned it to the image of a man;

[**14**] Or made it like some vile beast, laying it over with vermilion, and with paint colouring it red, and covering every spot therein;

[**15**] And when he had made a convenient room for it, set it in a wall, and made it fast with iron:

[**16**] For he provided for it that it might not fall, knowing that it was unable to help itself; for it is an image, and hath need of help:

[**17**] Then maketh he prayer for his goods, for his wife and children, and is not ashamed to speak to that which hath no life.

[**18**] For health he calleth upon that which is weak: for life prayeth to that which is dead; for aid humbly beseecheth that which hath least means to help: and for a good journey he asketh of that which cannot set a foot forward:

[**19**] And for gaining and getting, and for good success of his hands, asketh ability to do of him, that is most unable to do any thing.

Wis.14

[**1**] Again, one preparing himself to sail, and about to pass through the raging waves, calleth upon a piece of wood more rotten than the vessel that carrieth him.

[**2**] For verily desire of gain devised that, and the workman built it by his skill.

[**3**] But thy providence, O Father, governeth it: for thou hast made a way in the sea, and a safe path in the waves;

[**4**] Shewing that thou canst save from all danger: yea, though a man went to sea without art.

[**5**] Nevertheless thou wouldest not that the works of thy wisdom should be idle, and therefore do men commit their lives to a small piece of wood, and passing the rough sea in a weak vessel are saved.

[**6**] For in the old time also, when the proud giants perished, the hope of the world governed by thy hand escaped in a weak vessel, and left to all ages a seed of generation.

[**7**] For blessed is the wood whereby righteousness cometh.

[**8**] But that which is made with hands is cursed, as well it, as he that made it: he, because he made it; and it, because, being corruptible, it was called god.

[**9**] For the ungodly and his ungodliness are both alike hateful unto God.

[**10**] For that which is made shall be punished together with him that made it.

[**11**] Therefore even upon the idols of the Gentiles shall there be a visitation: because in the creature of God they are become an abomination, and stumblingblocks to the souls of men, and a snare to the feet of the unwise.

[12] For the devising of idols was the beginning of spiritual fornication, and the invention of them the corruption of life.

[13] For neither were they from the beginning, neither shall they be for ever.

[14] For by the vain glory of men they entered into the world, and therefore shall they come shortly to an end.

[15] For a father afflicted with untimely mourning, when he hath made an image of his child soon taken away, now honoured him as a god, which was then a dead man, and delivered to those that were under him ceremonies and sacrifices.

[16] Thus in process of time an ungodly custom grown strong was kept as a law, and graven images were worshipped by the commandments of kings.

[17] Whom men could not honour in presence, because they dwelt far off, they took the counterfeit of his visage from far, and made an express image of a king whom they honoured, to the end that by this their forwardness they might flatter him that was absent, as if he were present.

[18] Also the singular diligence of the artificer did help to set forward the ignorant to more superstition.

[19] For he, peradventure willing to please one in authority, forced all his skill to make the resemblance of the best fashion.

[20] And so the multitude, allured by the grace of the work, took him now for a god, which a little before was but honoured.

[21] And this was an occasion to deceive the world: for men, serving either calamity or tyranny, did ascribe unto stones and stocks the incommunicable name.

[22] Moreover this was not enough for them, that they erred in the knowledge of God; but whereas they lived in the great war of ignorance, those so great plagues called they peace.

[23] For whilst they slew their children in sacrifices, or used secret ceremonies, or made revellings of strange rites;

[24] They kept neither lives nor marriages any longer undefiled: but either one slew another traiterously, or grieved him by adultery.

[25] So that there reigned in all men without exception blood, manslaughter, theft, and dissimulation, corruption, unfaithfulness, tumults, perjury,

[26] Disquieting of good men, forgetfulness of good turns, defiling of souls, changing of kind, disorder in marriages, adultery, and shameless uncleanness.

[27] For the worshipping of idols not to be named is the beginning, the cause, and the end, of all evil.

[28] For either they are mad when they be merry, or prophesy lies, or live unjustly, or else lightly forswear themselves.

[29] For insomuch as their trust is in idols, which have no life; though they swear falsely, yet they look not to be hurt.

[30] Howbeit for both causes shall they be justly punished: both because they thought not well of God, giving heed unto idols, and also unjustly swore in deceit, despising holiness.

[31] For it is not the power of them by whom they swear: but it is the just vengeance of sinners, that punisheth always the offence of the ungodly.

Wis.15

[1] But thou, O God, art gracious and true, longsuffering, and in mercy ordering all things,

[2] For if we sin, we are thine, knowing thy power: but we will not sin, knowing that we are counted thine.

[3] For to know thee is perfect righteousness: yea, to know thy power is the root of immortality.

[4] For neither did the mischievous invention of men deceive us, nor an image spotted with divers colours, the painter's fruitless labour;

[5] The sight whereof enticeth fools to lust after it, and so they desire the form of a dead image, that hath no breath.

[6] Both they that make them, they that desire them, and they that worship them, are lovers of evil things, and are worthy to have such things to trust upon.

[7] For the potter, tempering soft earth, fashioneth every vessel with much labour for our service: yea, of the same clay he maketh both the vessels that serve for clean uses, and likewise also all such as serve to the contrary: but what is the use of either sort, the potter himself is the judge.

[8] And employing his labours lewdly, he maketh a vain god of the same clay, even he which a little before was made of earth himself, and within a little while after returneth to the same, out when his life which was lent him shall be demanded.

[9] Notwithstanding his care is, not that he shall have much labour, nor that his life is short: but striveth to excel goldsmiths and silversmiths, and endeavoureth to do like the workers in brass, and counteth it his glory to make counterfeit things.

[10] His heart is ashes, his hope is more vile than earth, and his life of less value than clay:

[11] Forasmuch as he knew not his Maker, and him that inspired into him an active soul, and breathed in a living spirit.

[12] But they counted our life a pastime, and our time here a market for gain: for, say they, we must be getting every way, though it be by evil means.

[13] For this man, that of earthly matter maketh brittle

vessels and graven images, knoweth himself to offend above all others.

[14] And all the enemies of thy people, that hold them in subjection, are most foolish, and are more miserable than very babes.

[15] For they counted all the idols of the heathen to be gods: which neither have the use of eyes to see, nor noses to draw breath, nor ears to hear, nor fingers of hands to handle; and as for their feet, they are slow to go.

[16] For man made them, and he that borrowed his own spirit fashioned them: but no man can make a god like unto himself.

[17] For being mortal, he worketh a dead thing with wicked hands: for he himself is better than the things which he worshippeth: whereas he lived once, but they never.

[18] Yea, they worshipped those beasts also that are most hateful: for being compared together, some are worse than others.

[19] Neither are they beautiful, so much as to be desired in respect of beasts: but they went without the praise of God and his blessing.

Wis.16

[1] Therefore by the like were they punished worthily, and by the multitude of beasts tormented.

[2] Instead of which punishment, dealing graciously with thine own people, thou preparedst for them meat of a strange taste, even quails to stir up their appetite:

[3] To the end that they, desiring food, might for the ugly sight of the beasts sent among them lothe even that, which they must needs desire; but these, suffering penury for a short space, might be made partakers of a strange taste.

[4] For it was requisite, that upon them exercising tyranny should come penury, which they could not avoid: but to these it should only be shewed how their enemies were tormented.

[5] For when the horrible fierceness of beasts came upon these, and they perished with the stings of crooked serpents, thy wrath endured not for ever:

[6] But they were troubled for a small season, that they might be admonished, having a sign of salvation, to put them in remembrance of the commandment of thy law.

[7] For he that turned himself toward it was not saved by the thing that he saw, but by thee, that art the Saviour of all.

[8] And in this thou madest thine enemies confess, that it is thou who deliverest from all evil:

[9] For them the bitings of grasshoppers and flies killed, neither was there found any remedy for their life: for they were worthy to be punished by such.

[10] But thy sons not the very teeth of venomous dragons overcame: for thy mercy was ever by them, and healed them.

[11] For they were pricked, that they should remember thy words; and were quickly saved, that not falling into deep forgetfulness, they might be continually mindful of thy goodness.

[12] For it was neither herb, nor mollifying plaister, that restored them to health: but thy word, O Lord, which healeth all things.

[13] For thou hast power of life and death: thou leadest to the gates of hell, and bringest up again.

[14] A man indeed killeth through his malice: and the spirit, when it is gone forth, returneth not; neither the soul received up cometh again.

[15] But it is not possible to escape thine hand.

[16] For the ungodly, that denied to know thee, were scourged by the strength of thine arm: with strange rains, hails, and showers, were they persecuted, that they could not avoid, and through fire were they consumed.

[17] For, which is most to be wondered at, the fire had more force in the water, that quencheth all things: for the world fighteth for the righteous.

[18] For sometime the flame was mitigated, that it might not burn up the beasts that were sent against the ungodly; but themselves might see and perceive that they were persecuted with the judgment of God.

[19] And at another time it burneth even in the midst of water above the power of fire, that it might destroy the fruits of an unjust land.

[20] Instead whereof thou feddest thine own people with angels' food, and didst send them from heaven bread prepared without their labour, able to content every man's delight, and agreeing to every taste.

[21] For thy sustenance declared thy sweetness unto thy children, and serving to the appetite of the eater, tempered itself to every man's liking.

[22] But snow and ice endured the fire, and melted not, that they might know that fire burning in the hail, and sparkling in the rain, did destroy the fruits of the enemies.

[23] But this again did even forget his own strength, that the righteous might be nourished.

[24] For the creature that serveth thee, who art the Maker increaseth his strength against the unrighteous for their punishment, and abateth his strength for the benefit of such as put their trust in thee.

[25] Therefore even then was it altered into all fashions, and was obedient to thy grace, that nourisheth all things, according to the desire of them that had need:

[26] That thy children, O Lord, whom thou lovest, might

know, that it is not the growing of fruits that nourisheth man: but that it is thy word, which preserveth them that put their trust in thee.

[27] For that which was not destroyed of the fire, being warmed with a little sunbeam, soon melted away:

[28] That it might be known, that we must prevent the sun to give thee thanks, and at the dayspring pray unto thee.

[29] For the hope of the unthankful shall melt away as the winter's hoar frost, and shall run away as unprofitable water.

Wis.17

[1] For great are thy judgments, and cannot be expressed: therefore unnurtured souls have erred.

[2] For when unrighteous men thought to oppress the holy nation; they being shut up in their houses, the prisoners of darkness, and fettered with the bonds of a long night, lay there exiled from the eternal providence.

[3] For while they supposed to lie hid in their secret sins, they were scattered under a dark veil of forgetfulness, being horribly astonished, and troubled with [strange] apparitions.

[4] For neither might the corner that held them keep them from fear: but noises [as of waters] falling down sounded about them, and sad visions appeared unto them with heavy countenances.

[5] No power of the fire might give them light: neither could the bright flames of the stars endure to lighten that horrible night.

[6] Only there appeared unto them a fire kindled of itself, very dreadful: for being much terrified, they thought the things which they saw to be worse than the sight they saw not.

[7] As for the illusions of art magick, they were put down, and their vaunting in wisdom was reproved with disgrace.

[8] For they, that promised to drive away terrors and troubles from a sick soul, were sick themselves of fear, worthy to be laughed at.

[9] For though no terrible thing did fear them; yet being scared with beasts that passed by, and hissing of serpents,

[10] They died for fear, denying that they saw the air, which could of no side be avoided.

[11] For wickedness, condemned by her own witness, is very timorous, and being pressed with conscience, always forecasteth grievous things.

[12] For fear is nothing else but a betraying of the succours which reason offereth.

[13] And the expectation from within, being less, counteth the ignorance more than the cause which bringeth the torment.

[14] But they sleeping the same sleep that night, which was indeed intolerable, and which came upon them out of the bottoms of inevitable hell,

[15] Were partly vexed with monstrous apparitions, and partly fainted, their heart failing them: for a sudden fear, and not looked for, came upon them.

[16] So then whosoever there fell down was straitly kept, shut up in a prison without iron bars,

[17] For whether he were husbandman, or shepherd, or a labourer in the field, he was overtaken, and endured that necessity, which could not be avoided: for they were all bound with one chain of darkness.

[18] Whether it were a whistling wind, or a melodious noise of birds among the spreading branches, or a pleasing fall of water running violently,

[19] Or a terrible sound of stones cast down, or a running that could not be seen of skipping beasts, or a roaring voice of most savage wild beasts, or a rebounding echo from the hollow mountains; these things made them to swoon for fear.

[20] For the whole world shined with clear light, and none were hindered in their labour:

[21] Over them only was spread an heavy night, an image of that darkness which should afterward receive them: but yet were they unto themselves more grievous than the darkness.

Wis.18

[1] Nevertheless thy saints had a very great light, whose voice they hearing, and not seeing their shape, because they also had not suffered the same things, they counted them happy.

[2] But for that they did not hurt them now, of whom they had been wronged before, they thanked them, and besought them pardon for that they had been enemies.

[3] Instead whereof thou gavest them a burning pillar of fire, both to be a guide of the unknown journey, and an harmless sun to entertain them honourably.

[4] For they were worthy to be deprived of light and imprisoned in darkness, who had kept thy sons shut up, by whom the uncorrupt light of the law was to be given unto the world.

[5] And when they had determined to slay the babes of the saints, one child being cast forth, and saved, to reprove them, thou tookest away the multitude of their children, and destroyedst them altogether in a mighty water.

[6] Of that night were our fathers certified afore, that assuredly knowing unto what oaths they had given

credence, they might afterwards be of good cheer.

[7] So of thy people was accepted both the salvation of the righteous, and destruction of the enemies.

[8] For wherewith thou didst punish our adversaries, by the same thou didst glorify us, whom thou hadst called.

[9] For the righteous children of good men did sacrifice secretly, and with one consent made a holy law, that the saints should be like partakers of the same good and evil, the fathers now singing out the songs of praise.

[10] But on the other side there sounded an ill according cry of the enemies, and a lamentable noise was carried abroad for children that were bewailed.

[11] The master and the servant were punished after one manner; and like as the king, so suffered the common person.

[12] So they all together had innumerable dead with one kind of death; neither were the living sufficient to bury them: for in one moment the noblest offspring of them was destroyed.

[13] For whereas they would not believe any thing by reason of the enchantments; upon the destruction of the firstborn, they acknowledged this people to be the sons of God.

[14] For while all things were in quiet silence, and that night was in the midst of her swift course,

[15] Thine Almighty word leaped down from heaven out of thy royal throne, as a fierce man of war into the midst of a land of destruction,

[16] And brought thine unfeigned commandment as a sharp sword, and standing up filled all things with death; and it touched the heaven, but it stood upon the earth.

[17] Then suddenly visions of horrible dreams troubled them sore, and terrors came upon them unlooked for

[18] And one thrown here, and another there, half dead, shewed the cause of his death.

[19] For the dreams that troubled them did foreshew this, lest they should perish, and not know why they were afflicted.

[20] Yea, the tasting of death touched the righteous also, and there was a destruction of the multitude in the wilderness: but the wrath endured not long.

[21] For then the blameless man made haste, and stood forth to defend them; and bringing the shield of his proper ministry, even prayer, and the propitiation of incense, set himself against the wrath, and so brought the calamity to an end, declaring that he was thy servant.

[22] So he overcame the destroyer, not with strength of body, nor force of arms, but with a word subdued him that punished, alleging the oaths and covenants made with the fathers.

[23] For when the dead were now fallen down by heaps one upon another, standing between, he stayed the wrath, and parted the way to the living.

[24] For in the long garment was the whole world, and in the four rows of the stones was the glory of the fathers graven, and thy Majesty upon the daidem of his head.

[25] Unto these the destroyer gave place, and was afraid of them: for it was enough that they only tasted of the wrath.

Wis.19

[1] As for the ungodly, wrath came upon them without mercy unto the end: for he knew before what they would do;

[2] How that having given them leave to depart, and sent them hastily away, they would repent and pursue them.

[3] For whilst they were yet mourning and making lamentation at the graves of the dead, they added another foolish device, and pursued them as fugitives, whom they had intreated to be gone.

[4] For the destiny, whereof they were worthy, drew them unto this end, and made them forget the things that had already happened, that they might fulfil the punishment which was wanting to their torments:

[5] And that thy people might pass a wonderful way: but they might find a strange death.

[6] For the whole creature in his proper kind was fashioned again anew, serving the peculiar commandments that were given unto them, that thy children might be kept without hurt:

[7] As namely, a cloud shadowing the camp; and where water stood before, dry land appeared; and out of the Red sea a way without impediment; and out of the violent stream a green field:

[8] Wherethrough all the people went that were defended with thy hand, seeing thy marvellous strange wonders.

[9] For they went at large like horses, and leaped like lambs, praising thee, O Lord, who hadst delivered them.

[10] For they were yet mindful of the things that were done while they sojourned in the strange land, how the ground brought forth flies instead of cattle, and how the river cast up a multitude of frogs instead of fishes.

[11] But afterwards they saw a new generation of fowls, when, being led with their appetite, they asked delicate meats.

[12] For quails came up unto them from the sea for their contentment.

[13] And punishments came upon the sinners not without former signs by the force of thunders: for they suffered justly according to their own wickedness, insomuch as they used a more hard and hateful behaviour toward strangers.

[14] For the Sodomites did not receive those, whom they knew not when they came: but these brought friends into bondage, that had well deserved of them.

[15] And not only so, but peradventure some respect shall be had of those, because they used strangers not friendly:

[16] But these very grievously afflicted them, whom they had received with feastings, and were already made partakers of the same laws with them.

[17] Therefore even with blindness were these stricken, as those were at the doors of the righteous man: when, being compassed about with horrible great darkness, every one sought the passage of his own doors.

[18] For the elements were changed in themselves by a kind of harmony, like as in a psaltery notes change the name of the tune, and yet are always sounds; which may well be perceived by the sight of the things that have been done.

[19] For earthly things were turned into watery, and the things, that before swam in the water, now went upon the ground.

[20] The fire had power in the water, forgetting his own virtue: and the water forgat his own quenching nature.

[21] On the other side, the flames wasted not the flesh of the corruptible living things, though they walked therein; neither melted they the icy kind of heavenly meat that was of nature apt to melt.

[22] For in all things, O Lord, thou didst magnify thy people, and glorify them, neither didst thou lightly regard them: but didst assist them in every time and place.

The Book Of Meqabyan (In Lyric Rastafari Version of Jamaican Patois)

I MEQABYAN

Chapter 1

[1] There were one man whose name are called Tseerutsaydan an who love sin ~ him would boast ina him horses abundance an him troops firmness beneath him authority.

[2] Him had many priests who serve him idols whom him worship an fe whom him bow an sacrifice sacrifice by night an by daylight.

[3] But ina him heart dullness it would seem fe him that them give him firmness an Power.

[4] An ina him heart it would seem fe him that them give him authority ina all him Rule.

[5] An again ina formation time it would seem fe him that them give him all the desired authority also.

[6] An him would sacrifice sacrifice fe them day an night.

[7] Him appointed priests who serve him idols.

[8] While them ate from that defouled sacrifice - them would tell him pretendin that the idols eat night an day.

[9] Again them would mek other persons diligent like unto them - that them might sacrifice sacrifice an eat. An again them would mek other persons diligent that them might sacrifice sacrifice - an sacrifice sacrifice like unto them.

[10] But him would trust ina him idols that don't profit nor benefit.

[11] By him timeframe bein small - an ina him heart dullness - it would seem fe him that them Irated him - that them feed him an that them crown him ~ it would seem fe him that them Irated him - fe Seythan have deafened him reasonin lest him know him Irator Who Irated him bringin from not livin toward livin - or lest him with him kindreds know him Irator Who Irated him bringin from not livin toward livin - that them might go toward *Gehannem* of Fiyah foriva - it bein judged pon them with him who call them gods without them bein gods.

[12] As them aren't never well whenever - it are due that him might call them dead ones.

[13] As Seythan authority that mislead them will lodge ina that idol image - an as him will tell them them reasonin accord - an as him will reveal fe them like unto them loved - him will judge pon the idols wherein them believed an wherein 'Adam childran trust - whose reasonin were like unto ashes.

[14] An them will marvel pon the time them sight up that him fulfilled what them thought fe them - an them will do him accord fe him reachin up til them sacrifice them dawta childran an them male childran birthed from them nature - up til them spill them dawta childran an male childran blood that were clean.

[15] Them didn't sadden them - fe Seythan have savoured him sacrifice fe them fe fulfill them evil accord - that him might lower them toward *Gehannem* like unto him - where there are no exits up til Iternity - where him will raceive tribulation.

[16] But that Tseerutsaydan were arrogant ~ him had fifty idols worked ina males pattern an twenty worked ina dawtaz pattern.

[17] An him would boast ina those idols that have no benefit ~ him would totally glorify them while him sacrificed sacrifice mornin an evenin.

[18] An him would command persons that them might sacrifice sacrifice fe the idols - an him would eat from that defouled sacrifice - an him would command other persons that them might eat from the sacrifice ~ him would especially provoke fe evil.

[19] Him had five houses worked fe him beaten worked idols that were iron an brass an lead.

[20] An him ornamanted them ina silver an gold ~ him veiled curtains around the houses fe them an planted a tent fe them.

[21] Him appointed keepers fe them there ~ him would Itinually sacrifice forty fe him idols - ten fattened oxen - ten sterile cows - ten fattened sheep ewes - ten barren goats - with birds that have wings.

[22] But it would seem fe him that him idols ate ~ him would present fe them fifty *feeqen* of grapes an fifty dishes of wheat kneaded with oil.

[23] An him told him priests: - "Tek an give them ~ mek mi irators eat what mi slaughtered fe them - an mek them drink the grape mi presented fe them ~ as fe if it aren't enough fe them - mi will add fe them."

[24] An him would command all that them might eat an drink from that defouled sacrifice.

[25] But ina him evil malice him would send him troops who visit ina all the kingdom - that as it were there were one who neither sacrifice nor bow - them might separate an know an bring him - an might punish him by fiyah an by sword before him - that them might plunder him money an might burn him house ina fiyah - that them might downstroy all him money him had pon him.

[26] "Fe them are kind an great ones - an fe them have Irated wi ina them charity - an mi will show punishmant an tribulation fe him unless him worshipped mi irators an sacrificed sacrifice fe mi irators.

[27] An mi will show him punishmant an tribulation - fe them have Irated Earth an Heaven an the sea that were wide an moon an Sun an stars an rains an winds an all that live ina this world fe be food an fe be satiety fe wi."

[28] But persons who worship them shall be punished ina firm tribulation - an them won't be nice fe them.

Chapter 2

[1] There were one man birthed from the tribe of Binyam whose name are called Meqabees;

[2] him had three childran who were handsome an totally warriors ~ them had bein iloved alongside all persons ina that Midyam an Miedon country that are Tseerutsaydan Rule.

[3] An like unto the king commanded them pon the time him found them: - "Don't unu bow fe Tseerutsaydan irators? How about don't unu sacrifice sacrifice?

[4] But if unu refuse - wi will seize an tek unu toward the king - an wi will downstroy all your money like unto the king commanded."

[5] These youts who were handsome replied fe him sayin - "As fe Him fe Whom InI bow - there are InI Faada Irator Who Irated Earth an Heaven an what are within she - an the sea - moon an Sun an clouds an stars ~ Him are the True Irator Whom InI worship an ina Whom InI believe."

[6] An these the king youts are four - an them servants who carry shield an spear are a hundred.

[7] An pon the time them loved that them might seize these hola ones - them escaped from them hands and there are none who touched them ~ as those youts are totally warriors ina Power - them went seizin shields an them spears.

[8] An there were from them one who strangle an kill panther - an at that time him would strangle it like unto a chicken.

[9] An there were one from them who kill a lion with one rock or strikin at one time with a stick.

[10] An there were one from them who kill a hundred persons - strikin ina formation time with one sword - an them name an them hunt were thus ~ it were called ina all Babilon an Mo`ab countries.

[11] An them were warriors ina Power - an them had a thing bein iloved an comeliness.

[12] An again them features comeliness were wondrous - however becau them worshipped JAH an becau them didn't fear death - it are them reasonin comeliness that surpass all.

[13] An pon the time them frightened the troops - there are none who could able fe seize them - but them who were warriors escaped proceedin toward a lofty mountain.

[14] An those troops returned toward the city an shut the fortress gate ~ them terrorized the people sayin - "Unless unu brought those warriors the Meqabyans - wi will burn your city ina fiyah - an wi will send toward the king an downstroy your country."

[15] An at that time the country persons - rich an poor ones an dawtaz an males - a child whose faada an mother dead pon him an old dawtaz - everyone proceeded an shouted together - an them straightened them necks toward the mountain an shouted toward them sayin - "Don't downstroy InI - an don't downstroy InI country pon InI."

[16] At that time them wept together - an them feared - arisin from JAH.

[17] Returnin them faces Eastward an streachin forth them hands them begged toward JAH together - "Lord - should InI refuse these men who demolished Thy Command an Thy LAW?

[18] Yet him believed ina silver an gold an ina the stone an wood that a person hands worked - but InI don't love that InI might hear that criminal word - who didn't believe Thy LAW" them said.

[19] When Thou are the Irator Who save an Who kill - him mek him ras self like unto them Irated him also ~ as fe him - him are who spill a person blood an who eat a person flesh.

[20] But InI don't love that InI might sight up that criminal face nor hear him word" them said.

[21] "However if Thou commanded InI - InI will go toward him ~ becau InI believe ina Thee-I - InI will pass an give InI bodies fe death - an pon the time him said 'Sacrifice sacrifice fe mi irators' - InI won't hear that criminal word.

[22] But InI believed Thee-I - Lord Who examine kidneys an reasonins - InI Faadas Irator - 'Abriham an Yis'haq an Ya`iqob who did Thy Accord an lived firmed up ina Thy LAW.

[23] Thou examine a person reasonin an help the sinner an the righteous one - an there be none hidden from Thee-I - an him who took refuge are revealed alongside Thee-I.

[24] But InI have no other Irator apart from Thee-I.

[25] That InI might give InI bodies fe death becau Thy glorified Name - however be Power an Firmness an a Shelter fe InI ina this Work that InI are ruled fe Thee-I.

[26] An pon the time 'Isra'iel entered toward Gibts country Thou heard Ya`iqob plea - an now glorified God - InI beg Thee-I."

[27] An pon the time the two men whose features were quite handsome were sight up fe them standin before them - pon the time fiyah swords that frighten like unto lightnin

alit an cut them necks an killed them - at that time them arose bein well like unto formerly.

[28] Them features comeliness became totally handsome an them shone more than Sun - an them became more handsome than formerly.

Chapter 3

[1] Like unto unu sight up before unu these the Most I JAH slaves - 'Abya - Seela - Fentos who dead an arose - unu have that unu might arise likewise after unu dead - an your faces shall shine like unto the Sun ina the Kingdom of Heaven.

[2] An them went with those men an raceived martyrdom there.

[3] At that time them begged - them praised - an them bowed fe JAH ~ death didn't frighten them an the king punishmant didn't frighten them.

[4] An them went toward those youts an became like unto a sheep that have no evil - yet them didn't frighten them - an pon the time them arrived toward them - them seized an beat them an bound an whipped them - an them delivered them toward the king an stood them before him.

[5] An the king answered fe them sayin - "How won't unu stubborn ones sacrifice sacrifice an bow fe mi irators?"

[6] Those bredren who were cleansed from sin - who were honoured an chosen an Irie - an who shine like unto a jewel whose value were wondrous - Seela an 'Abya an Fentos answered fe him ina one word.

[7] Them told that king who were a plague - "As fe InI - InI won't bow nor sacrifice fe defouled idols that have no knowledge nor reasonin."

[8] An again them told him - "InI won't bow fe idols that were silver an gold that a person hand worked - that were stone an wood - that have no reasonin nor soul nor knowledge - that don't benefit them friends nor harm them enemies."

[9] An the king answered fe them sayin - "Why do unu do thus - an as them know who insult them an who wrong them - why do unu insult the glorified irators?"

[10] Them answered fe him sayin - "As them are like unto a trifle alongside InI - as fe InI - InI will insult them an won't glorify them."

[11] An the king answered fe them sayin - "Mi will punish unu like unto your Work evil measure ~ mi will downstroy your features comeliness with whippin an firm tribulation an fiyah.

[12] An now tell mi whether unu will give or won't give sacrifice fe mi irators - as fe if this didn't happen - mi will punish unu by sword an by whippin."

[13] Them answered fe him sayin - "As fe InI - InI won't sacrifice sacrifice nor bow fe defouled idols" - an the king commanded them that them might beat them with a fat stick - an again that them might whip them with a whip - an after it - that them might splinter them up til them inner organs were sight up.

[14] An after this them bound an made them while ina jail house up til him counsel by money that punish an kill them.

[15] Without niceness them took an bound them a firm imprisonmant ina prison house - an them sat ina prison house three nights an three daylights.

[16] An after this third day the king commanded that a Proclamation speaker might turn an that counselors an nobles - country elders an officials - might be gathered.

[17] An pon the time the king Tseerutsaydan sat ina square - him commanded that them might bring those honoured ones - Seela an 'Abya an Fentos ~ them stood before him bein wounded an bound.

[18] An the king told them - "When unu sat these three days - are there really the returnin that unu returned - or are unu ina your former evil?"

[19] An those honoured JAH Souljahs answered fe him sayin - "As fe that InI were cruel - InI won't agree that InI might worship the idols filled of sin an evil that thou check up."

[20] An that criminal vexed an commanded that them might stand them up ina lofty place an might renew them wounds ~ them blood flowed pon Earth.

[21] An again him commanded that them might burn them with a torch lamp an might char them flesh - an him servants did like unto him commanded them - an those honoured men told him - "Thou who forgot JAH LAW - speak ~ InI reward shall abound ina the measure whereby thou multiply InI punishmant."

[22] An again him commanded that them might bring an send pon them bears an tigers an lions that were evil beasts before them eat them food that them might totally eat them flesh with them bones.

[23] An him commanded persons who keep the beasts that them might send the beasts pon them - an them did like unto him commanded them - an them bound those honoured martyrs feet - an again them maliciously beat an bound them with tent-stakes.

[24] An those beasts were flung over them while them roared - an pon the time them arrived toward the martyrs them hailed an bowed fe them.

[25] Them returned toward them keepers while them roared - an them frightened them keepers ~ them took them toward the square up til them delivered them toward before the king.

[26] An them killed seventy five men from the criminals army there.

[27] Many persons panicked - the one anguishin pon the one ina fear - up til the king quit him throne an fled - an them seized the beasts with difficulty an took them toward them lodgin.

[28] Seela an 'Abya an Fentos two bredren came an released them from the imprisonmant them bound them an told them - "Come mek InI flee lest these skeptics an criminals find InI.

[29] An those martyrs answered them bredren sayin - "It aren't procedure that InI might flee after InI set up fe testimony ~ as it were unu had feared - go fleein."

[30] An those them likkle bredren said - "InI will stand with unu before the king - an if unu dead InI will dead with unu."

[31] An after this the king were pon him lordship hall balcany an sight up that these honoured men were released an that all the five bredren stood together ~ those chiefs who work an punish troops questioned that them were bredren an told the king - an the king vexed an shouted like unto a wilderness boar.

[32] An up til the king counseled by money that punish all the five bredren - him commanded that them might seize an add them ina prison house ~ them placed them ina prison house bindin ina firm imprisonmant without niceness with a hollow stalk.

[33] An the king Tseerutsaydan said - "These youts who erred wearied mi ~ what should these men reasonin firm up? an them Work evil are like unto them Power firmness ~ if mi say - "Them will return" - them will mek them reasonin evil.

[34] An mi will bring the hardship pon them like unto them Work evil measure - an mi will burn them flesh ina fiyah that it might be charred ash - an pon that mi will scattar them flesh ash like unto dust pon mountains."

[35] An after him spoke this him waited three days an commanded that them might bring those honoured men - an pon the time those honoured men approached him commanded that them might burn a fiyah within the great pit oven - an that them might add within it a malice Work that flame the fiyah an whereby them boil a yat - the fat an soapberries - sea foam an resin an the sulfur.

[36] An pon the time fiyah flamed ina the pit the messengers went toward the king when them said - "Wi did what thou commanded wi - send the men who will be added."

[37] An him commanded that them might receive an cast them ina the fiyah pit - an the youts did like unto the king commanded them - an pon the time those honoured men entered toward the fiyah them gave them souls fe JAH.

[38] An when the persons who cast them sight up - Angels raceived an took them souls toward the Garden where Yis'haq an 'Abriham an Ya`iqob are - where Irie Ites are found.

Chapter 4

[1] An pon the time that criminal sight up that them dead - him commanded that them might burn them flesh ina fiyah up til it are ash an that them might scattar them ina wind - but the fiyah couldn't able fe burn the corpse hair from them corpses side - an them sent them forth from the pit.

[2] An again them flamed fiyah over them iginnin from mornin up til evenin ~ it didn't burn them ~ them said - "An now come mek wi cast them corpses seaward."

[3] An them did like unto the king commanded them ~ them cast them pon the sea ~ even if them cast them seaward addin great stones an iron hearthstones an a millstone whereby a donkey grind by turnin - there are no sinkin that the sea sank them ~ as JAH Spirit of Support have lodged ina them - them floated pon the sea yet them didn't sink ~ it failed him fe downstroy them by all the malice that were provoked pon them.

[4] "As this them death have made weary more than them Life - mek mi cast them corpses fe beasts that them might eat them - yet what will mi do?" him said.

[5] An the youts did like unto him commanded them ~ vultures an beasts didn't touch them corpses ~ birds an vultures veiled them with them wings from burnin ina Sun an the five martyrs corpses sat fourteen days.

[6] An pon the time them sight them up - them bodies shone up like unto Sun - an Angels incircled them corpses like unto light incircle the Tent.

[7] Him counseled counsel ~ him lacked what him do - an after this him dug a grave an buried the five martyrs corpses.

[8] An when that king who forgot JAH LAW had reclined pon a bed at night the five martyrs were sight up fe him standin before him at night vexin an seizin swords.

[9] As it have seemed fe him that them entered toward him house at night ina crime - pon the time him awoke from him slumber him feared an loved that him might flee from the bedchamber toward the hall - an as it have seemed fe him that them kill him seemin that them committed crime pon him - him feared an him knees trembled.

[10] Becaudis thing him said - "Mi lords - what do unu love? as fe mi - what should mi do fe unu?"

[11] Them answered fe him sayin - "Aren't InI whom thou killed burnin ina fiyah an InI whom thou commanded that them might cast pon the sea? As JAH have kept InI bodies becau InI believed ina Him - it failed thee fe downstroy InI ~ as a person who believed ina Him won't perish - mek glory an praise due fe JAH - an InI also who believed ina Him didn't shame ina the tribulation.

[12] "As mi didn't know that a punishmant like unto this will find mi - what reward should mi give unu becau the stead wherefore mi did a evil thing pon unu?

[13] An now separate fe mi the reward mi give unu - lest unu tek mi body ina death an lest unu lower mi body toward *See'ol* when mi are ina Life.

[14] As mi have wronged unu - forgive mi mi sin - becau it were your Faada JAH LAW Niceness" him told them.

[15] An those honoured martyrs answered fe him sayin - "Becau the stead wherefore thou did a evil thing pon InI - as fe InI - InI won't pay thee a evil thing ~ as JAH are Who bring hardship pon a soul - as fe Him Who will pay thee hardship - there are JAH.

[16] However InI were sight up fe thee bein revealed that InI were well fe thy timeframe bein small an becau thy reasonin deafness ~ as fe it seemin fe thee that thou killed InI - thou prepared welfare fe InI.

[17] But thy idols priests an thou will downscend toward *Gehannem* where are no exits foriva.

[18] Woe fe thy idols fe whom thou bow havin quit bowin fe JAH Who Irated unu when unu were scorned like unto spit - an fe unu who worship them - an unu don't know JAH Who Irated unu bringin from not livin toward livin ~ aren't unu who are sight up today like unto smoke an tomorrow who perish?"

[19] An the king answered fe them sayin - "What will unu command mi that mi might do fe unu all that unu loved?"

[20] "It are fe save thy ras self lest thou enter toward the *Gehannem* of Fiyah - yet it aren't fe save InI ras selves who teach thee.

[21] Fe your idols are silver an gold - stone an wood - that have no reasonin nor soul knowledge - that a person hand worked.

[22] But them don't kill ~ them don't save ~ them don't benefit them friend ~ them don't harm them enemy ~ them don't downbase ~ them don't honour ~ them don't mek wealthy ~ them don't impoverish ~ them mislead unu by demons authority - who don't love that the one from persons might be saved - yet them don't uproot nor plant.

[23] Them especially don't love that the persons like unto unu might be saved from death - unu dull-hearted ones fe whom them seem that them irated unu - when unu are who worked them.

[24] As Seythans an demons authority have lodged ina them - them shall return a thing fe unu like unto unu loved - that it might drown unu within the sea of *Gehannem*.

[25] But thou - quit this thy error an mek this also be InI reward becau InI dead stead - that InI might benefit InI souls worshippin InI Irator JAH" them told him.

[26] But him were alarmed an would totally astony - an as all five have been sight up fe him drawin them swords - him feared - an becaudis thing him bowed fe them.

[27] "Hence mi knew that after dead ones who were dust dead them will really arise ~ as fe mi - only a likkle had remained fe mi fe dead."

[28] After this them were hidden from before that king face ~ from that day onward that Tseerutsaydan who are totally arrogant quit burnin them corpses.

[29] As them have misled them many eras - him would be Irie ina him idols an him reasonin error - an him misled many persons like unto him up til them quit followin ina Worship JAH Who Irated them - yet it aren't only him who erred.

[30] An them would sacrifice them dawta childran an them male childran fe demons - yet them work a seducin an downsturbance that are them reasonin accord - that them faada Seythan taught them that him might mek the seducin an downsturbance that JAH don't love.

[31] Them marry them mothers - an them abuse them aunts an them sistren ~ them abuse them bodies while them worked all that resemble this filthy Work ~ as Seythan have firmed up those crooked persons reasonin - them said - "Wi won't return."

[32] But that Tseerutsaydan - who don't know him Irator - were totally arrogant - an him would boast ina him idols.

[33] If them say - "How will JAH give the Kingdom fe the persons who don't know Him ina LAW an ina Worship?" - them will totally return toward Him ina repentance ~ as Him test them thus - it are becaudis.

[34] But if them totally return ina repentance Him would love them - an Him would keep them Kingdom - but if them refuse a fiyah will punish them ina Fiyah of *Gehannem* foriva.

[35] But it would be due a king fe fear him Irator JAH like unto him lordship fame - an it would be due a judge fe be ruled fe him Irator while him judged goodly judgemant like unto him Rule fame.

[36] An it would be due elders an chiefs an envoys an petty kings fe be commanded fe them Irator like unto them lordship abundance measure.

[37] As Him are Heaven an Earth Lord Who Irated all the Iration - becau there are no other Irator ina Heavan nor Earth who impoverish an mek rich - Him are Who honour an downbase.

Chapter 5

[1] "The one warrior from the sixty warriors were proud ~ JAH made him body Iginnin from him foot up til him head fe swell with one spoon of sulphur ~ him dead ina one plague.

[2] An again Keeram who built a iron bed were proud arisin from him powerfulness abundance - an JAH hid him ina death.

[3] An again Nabukedenetsor were proud sayin - 'There are no other king without mi - an mi are Irator who mek the Sun rise ina this world' - an him said thus arisin from him arrogance abundance.

[4] An JAH separated from persons an sent him toward a wilderness seven years - an him made him fortune with Heaven birds an wilderness beasts up til him knew that JAH were Who Irated him.

[5] An pon the time him knew Him ina worship - Him again returned him toward him kingdom ~ who are it who weren't of Earth - bein boldly proud pon JAH Who Irated him?

[6] How about who are it demolished HIM LAW an Him Order an whom Earth didn't swallow?

[7] An thou Tseerutsaydan love that thou might be proud pon thy Irator - an again thou have that Him might downstroy thee like unto them - an might lower thee toward a grave arisin from thy arrogance.

[8] An again after them entered toward *See'ol* where are tooth grindin an mournin - that were darkness fulfillmant - thou have that Him might lower thee toward the deep pit *Gehannem* where are no exits foriva.

[9] As fe thou - thou are a man who will dead and be demolished tomorrow like unto arrogant kings who were like unto thee - who quit this world livin.

[10] As fe InI - InI say - 'Thou are demolished ruins - but thou aren't JAH - fe JAH are Who Irated Earth an Heaven an thee.'

[11] Him downbase arrogant ones ~ Him honour them who were downbased ~ Him give firmness fe persons who wearied.

[12] Him kill well ones ~ Him raise up the persons who were Earth - who dead buried ina grave.

[13] An Him send slaves forth free ina Life from sin rulership.

[14] O king Tseerutsaydan - why do thou boast ina thy defouled idols who have no benefit?

[15] But JAH Irated Earth an Heaven an great seas ~ Him Irated moon an Sun - an Him prepared eras.

[16] Man graze toward him field - an him while when him plough up til it dusk - an Heaven stars live firmed up by Him Word.

[17] An Him call all ina Heaven ~ there are nothing done without JAH knowin it.

[18] Him commanded Heaven Angels that them might serve Him an might praise Him glorified Name - an Angels are sent toward all persons who inherit Life.

[19] Rufa'iel who were a servant were sent toward Thobeet - an him saved Thobya from death ina Ragu'iel country.

[20] Hola Meeka'iel were sent toward Giediewon that him might draw him attention by money that him downstroy 'Iloflee persons; an him were sent toward the prophet Mussie pon the time him made 'Isra'iel cross 'Eritra sea.

[21] As only JAH have said him led them - there were no different idol with them.

[22] An Him sent them forth toward crops pon Earth.

[23] An Him fed them Him plantation grain ~ as Him have totally loved them - Him cherished them feedin the honey that firmed up like unto a rock.

[24] An that thou might totally keep Him kindreds by what are due - an that thou might do JAH Accord Who Irated thee - Him crowned thee givin Itority pon the four kingdoms.

[25] Fe Him have crowned thee makin loftier than all - an thy Irator totally crowned thee that thou might love JAH.

[26] An it are procedure that thou might love thy Irator JAH like unto Him loved thee - like unto Him trusted thee pon all the people - an thou - do JAH Accord that thy era might abound ina this world an that Him might live with thee ina Support.

[27] An do JAH Accord that Him might stand fe thee bein a Guardian pon thy enemies - an that Him might seat thee pon thy throne - an that Him might hide thee ina him Wing of Support.

[28] As fe if thou don't know - JAH chose an crowned thee pon 'Isra'iel like unto Him chose Sa'ol fron 'Isra'iel childran when him kept him faada donkeys - an Him crowned him pon him kindreds 'Isra'iel - an him sat with 'Isra'iel pon him throne.

[29] An Him gave him a lofty fortune separatin from him kindreds ~ JAH crowned thee pon Him kindreds ~ as fe henceforth onward - check - keep Him kindreds.

[30] As JAH have Ipointed thee over them that thou might kill an might save - keep them ina evil thing - them who work a goodly thing an them who work a evil thing pon a goodly thing" him told him.

[31] "An as JAH have Ipointed thee pon all that thou might do Him Accord be it while thou whipped or while thou saved - pay them evil Work - them who work goodly Work an them who work goodly Work an evil Work.

[32] Fe thou are a slave of JAH Who rule all ina Heaven - an thou - do JAH Accord that Him might do thy accord fe thee ina all thou thought an ina all thou begged while thou wheedled before Him.

[33] There are none who rule Him - but Him rule all.

[34] There are none who Ipoint Him - but Him Ipoint all.

[35] There are none who dismiss Him - but Him dismiss all.

[36] There are none who reproach Him - but Him reproach all.

[37] There are none who mek Him diligent - but Him mek all diligent ~ as Heaven an Earth rulership are fe Him - there are none who escape from Him Itority; all are revealed alongside Him - yet there are none hidden from Him Face.

[38] Him sight up all - but there are none who sight Him up ~ Him hear the person priah who pray toward Him sayin 'Save I' - fe Him have Irated man ina Him Pattern - an Him accept him plea.

[39] As Him are a King Who live up til the Iternity - Him feed all from Him unchangin Nature.

Chapter 6

[1] As Him crown fe true the kings who do Him Accord - the kings wrote a straight thing becau Him.

[2] As them have done JAH Accord - Him shall shine up ina Light that aren't examined Yis'haq an 'Abriham an Ya`iqob - Selomon an Daweet an Hiziqyas lodgins ina the Garden where are all beautiful kings whose lodgin were Light.

[3] Heaven Hall are what totally shone - yet Earth halls aren't like unto Heaven Hall ~ it floor - whose features are silver an gold an jewel features - are clean.

[4] An it features that totally shine are unexamined by a person reasonin ~ Heaven Hall are what shine like unto jewels.

[5] Like unto JAH knew - Who were a Nature Knower - the Heaven Hall that Him Irated are what a person reasonin don't examine an what shine ina total Light ~ it floor - that were worked ina silver an gold - ina jewels - ina white silk an ina blue silk - are clean.

[6] It are quite totally beautiful like unto this.

[7] Righteous ones who firmed up ina religion an virtue are who shall inherit it ina JAH Charity an fe Pardon.

[8] An there are welfare Water that flow from it - an it totally shine like unto Sun - an there are a Light tent within it - an it are incircled by grace perfume.

[9] A Garden fruit that were beautiful an Iloved - whose features an taste were different - are around the house - an

there are a oil an grape place there - an it are totally beautiful - an it fruit fragrance are sweet.

[10] When a fleshly bloodly person enter toward it - him soul would have separated from him flesh from the Irie Ites abundance that are ina it arisin from it fragrance flavour.

[11] Beautiful kings who did JAH Accord shall be Irie there ~ them honour an them place are known ina the Kingdom of Heaven that live firmed up foriva - where welfare are found.

[12] Him showed that them lordship pon Earth were famed an honoured - an that them lordship ina Heaven were famed an honoured; them shall be honoured an lofty ina Heaven like unto them honour them an bow fe them ina this world ~ if them work goodly Work ina this world them shall be Irie.

[13] But kings who were evil ina them Rule an them kingdoms that JAH gave them - them don't judge fe true by what are due ~ as them have ignored the destitute an poor ones cries - them don't judge Truth an save the refugee an the wronged child whose faada an mother dead pon him.

[14] Them don't save destitute an poor ones from the wealthy hand that rob them ~ them don't divide an give from them food an satta them who hungered - an them don't divide an give from them drink an give fe drink the persons who thirsted - an them didn't return them ears toward the poor one cry.

[15] An Him shall tek them toward *Gehannem* that were a dark endin ~ pon the time that lofty Day arrived pon them when JAH shall come - an pon the time Him wrath were done pon them like unto Daweet spoke ina him Praises 'Lord - don't chastise I ina Thy Judgemant an don't admonish I ina Thy chastisemant' - them problems an them downbasemant shall abound like unto them fame abundance measure.

[16] When nobles an kings are who rule this world ina this world - there are persons who didn't keep thy law.

[17] But JAH Who rule all are there ina Heaven ~ all persons souls an all persons welfare have been seized by Him Itority ~ Him are Who give honour fe persons who glorify Him - fe Him totally rule all - an Him love the persons who love Him.

[18] As Him are Earth an Heaven Lord - Him examine an know what kidneys transported an what a reasonin thought - an fe a person who begged toward Him with a pure reasonin - Him shall give him him plea reward.

[19] Him shall downstroy powerful ones arrogance - who work evil Work pon the child whose mother an faada dead pon him - an pon old dawtaz.

[20] It aren't by thy Power that thou seized this kingdom ~ it aren't by thy bein able that thou sat pon this throne ~ Him loved fe test thee thus that it be possible fe thee fe rule like unto Sa'ol who ruled him kindreds ina that season - an Him seated thee pon a kingdom throne - yet it aren't by thy Power that thou seized this kingdom ~ it are when Him test thee like unto Sa'ol who ignored the prophet Samu'iel word an JAH Word an didn't serve him army nor 'Amalieq king - yet it aren't by thy bein able that thou seized this kingdom.

[21] An JAH told the prophet Samu'iel - Go - an as them have saddened I by demolishin LAW an worshippin the idols an bowin fe the idol an by them mosques an by all them hated Works without benefit - tell Sa'ol - 'Go toward 'Amalieq country an downstroy them hosts an all the kings Iginnin from persons up til livestock.'

[22] Pon them who saddened JAH - becaudis thing Him sent Sa'ol that him might downstroy them.

[23] But him saved them king from death - an him saved many livestock an beauties an dawtaz an handsome youts from death ~ As him have scorned I thing an as him didn't hear I Command - becaudis thing - JAH told the prophet Samu'iel - Go an divide him kingdom.

[24] Becau him stead - Inoint `Issiey child Daweet that him might reign pon 'Isra'iel.

[25] But pon him adjourn a demon who will strangle an cast him.

[26] As him have refused if I-man gave him a kingdom that him might do I Accord - pon the time him refused I fe do I Accord I-man dismissed him from him kingdom that are due him - but thou - go an tell him sayin - 'Will thou thus ignore JAH Who crowned thee pon Him kindreds 'Isra'iel - Who seated thee pon Him Lordship Throne?'

[27] But thou - tell him - 'Thou didn't know JAH Who gave around this much honour an famousness' Him told him.

[28] An the prophet Samu'iel went toward the king Sa'ol an entered toward him sittin at a dinnertable - an when 'Amalieq king 'Agag had sat pon him left.

[29] 'Why did thou totally ignore JAH Who commanded thee that thou might downstroy the livestock an persons?' him told him.

[30] An at that time the king feared an arose from him throne an tellin Samu'iel 'Return fe wi' him seized him clothes - an Samu'iel refused fe return ~ Samu'iel clothes were torn.

[31] An Samu'iel told Sa'ol - 'JAH divided thy kingdom.'

[32] An again Sa'ol told Samu'iel before the people - 'Honour mi an atone mi sin fe mi before JAH that Him might forgive mi' ~ an as him have feared JAH Word Who Irated him - but as him didn't fear the king who dead - Samu'iel refused fe return ina him word.

[33] Becaudis thing him pierced 'Amalieq king 'Agag before him swallowed what him chewed.

29

[34] An a demon seized that Sa'ol who demolished the LAW of JAH - an becau Him were the King of Kings Who rule all - JAH struck pon him head a king who worked sin - fe it don't shame him.

[35] Fe Him are all the Iration Lord Who dismiss all the nobles an kings Itority who don't fear Him - but there are none who rule Him.

[36] Like unto Him spoke sayin - Daweet kindred shall go while it were famed an honoured - but Sa'ol kindred shall go while it were downbased - Him downstroyed kingdom from him child an from Sa'ol.

[37] Becau it saddened Him - an becau Him downstroyed the criminals who saddened Him by them evil Work - JAH revenged an downstroyed Sa'ol kindred childran - fe a person who don't revenge JAH enemy - him are JAH enemy.

[38] When it are possible fe him fe revenge an downstroy - an when him have Itority - a person who don't revenge an downstroy the sinner an don't revenge an downstroy a person who don't keep JAH LAW - as him are JAH enemy - Him downstroyed Sa'ol kindred childran.

Chapter 7

[1] An whether thou be a king or a ruler - what important thing are thou?

[2] Aren't it JAH Who Irated thee bringin from not livin toward livin - that thou might do Him Accord an might live firmed up by Him Command an might fear Him Judgemant? Like unto thou vex pon thy slaves an governed over them - all likewise there are also JAH Who vex pon thee an govern over thee.

[3] Like unto thou beat without niceness persons who worked sin - all likewise there are also JAH Who will strike thee an lower thee toward *Gehannem* where are no exits up til Iternity.

[4] Like unto thou whip him who weren't ruled fe thee an didn't bring a tribute fe thee - fe what are it that thou don't introduce a tribute fe JAH?

[5] As Him are Who Irated thee in order that thou love that them might fear thee - an Who crowned thee pon all the Iration that thou might keep Him kindreds fe true - fe what are it that thou don't fear thy Irator JAH?

[6] Judge by what are due an fe true like unto JAH Ipointed thee - yet don't sight up a face an favour fe small nor great ~ whom will thou fear without Him? keep Him Worship an the Nine Commands.

[7] Like unto Mussie commanded 'Isra'iel childran sayin - 'I-man presented Water an fiyah fe thee-I ~ add thy hand toward what thou loved' - don't go neither rightward nor leftward.

[8] Hear Him Word that I-man tell thee - that thou might hear Him Word an might do Him Command - lest thou say - 'She are beyond the sea or beyond the deep or beyond the river ~ who will bring fe mi that mi might sight she up an might hear Him Word an might do Him Command?'

[9] Lest thou say - 'Who will proceed toward Heaven again an lower that JAH Word fe mi that mi might hear an do she?' - JAH Word are what approached - check - fe thou fe teach she with thy mouth an give alms by she with thy hand.

[10] An thou didn't hear thy Irator JAH unless thou heard Him Book - an thou didn't love Him nor keep Him Command unless thou kept Him LAW.

[11] An thou have that thou might enter toward *Gehannem* foriva - an unless thou loved Him Command - an unless thou did JAH Accord - Who honoured an famed thee separatin from all thy kindreds that thou might keep them fe true - thou have that thou might enter toward *Gehannem* foriva.

[12] Him made thee above all - an Him crowned thee pon all Him kindreds that thou might rule Him kindreds fe true by what are due while thou thought of thy Irator Name Who Irated thee an gave thee a kingdom.

[13] There are them whom thou whip from persons who wronged thee - an there are him whom thou pardon while thou thought of JAH Work - an there are him fe whom thou judge by what are due straightenin up thy reasonin.

[14] An don't favour havin sight up a face pon the time them argued before thee ~ as Earth physique are thy money - don't accept a bribe that thou might pardon the sinner person an wrong the clean person.

[15] If thou did Him Accord - JAH shall multiply thy era ina this world fe thee - but if thou sadden Him - Him will diminish thy era.

[16] Think that thou will rise after thou dead - an that thou will be examined standin before Him pon all the Work thou worked whether it be goodly or evil.

[17] If thou work goodly Work - thou will live ina Garden ina the Kingdom of Heaven - ina houses where kind kings live an where Light filled. Fe JAH don't shame thy lordship authority - but if thou work evil Work - thou will live ina *See'ol Gehannem* where evil kings live.

[18] But pon the time thou sight up thy bein feared famousness - thy warriors award - thy hangin shield an spear - an pon the time thou sight up thy horses an thy troops beneath thy authority an them who beat drum an persons who play pon a harp before thee...

[19] But pon the time thou sight up all this - thou mek thy reasonin lofty - an thou firm up thy collar of reasonin - an thou don't think of JAH Who gave thee all this honour -

however pon the time Him told thee - Quit all this - thou aren't who quit it.

[20] Fe thou have totally neglected the Ipointmant Him Ipointed thee - an Him shall give thy lordship fe another.

[21] As death shall suddenly come pon thee - an as Judgemant shall be done ina Resurrection time - an as all man Work shall be examined - Him shall totally investigate an judge pon thee.

[22] There are none who will honour this world kings - fe becau Him were Truth Judge - ina Judgemant time poor an wealthy will stand together. This world nobles crowns wherein them boast shall fall.

[23] Judgemant are prepared - an a soul shall quake ~ at that time sinners an righteous ones Work shall be examined.

[24] An there are none who shall be hidden. Pon the time a dawta arrived fe birthin - an pon the time the fetus ina she belly arrived fe bein birthed - like unto she cyaan prevent she womb - Earth also cyaan prevent she lodgers that are pon she ~ she will return.

[25] An like unto clouds cyaan prevent rain lest them tek an rain toward the place JAH commanded them - fe JAH Word have Irated all bringin from not livin toward livin - an fe JAH Word again have introduced all toward a grave; an all likewise - after Resurrection time arrived - it aren't possible fe be that dead persons won't rise.

[26] Like unto Mussie spoke sayin - 'It are by Words that proceed from JAH Tongue - yet it aren't only by grain that a person are saved'; an JAH Word again shall arouse all persons from graves.

[27] Check - it were known that dead persons shall arise by JAH Word.

[28] An again JAH said thus ina Repeatin Law becau persons who were nobles an kings who do Him Accord - As the day have arrived when them are counted fe downstruction - I-man shall revenge an downstroy them pon the day when Judgemant are judged an at the time when them feet stumble Him said.

[29] An again JAH told persons who know Him Judgemant - Know know that I-man were your Irator JAH - an that I-man kill an I-man save.

[30] I-man chastise ina the tribulation an I-man pardon ~ I-man lower toward *See'ol* an again I-man send forth toward the Garden - an there are none who shall escape from I Itority Him told them.

[31] JAH said thus becau nobles an kings who didn't keep Him LAW - As Earthly kingdoms are a passin - an as them pass from mornin up til evenin - keep I Order an I LAW that unu might enter toward the Kingdom of Heaven that live firmed up foriva Him said.

[32] Fe JAH callin Righteous ones are fe glory - an sinners fe tribulation ~ Him will mek the sinner wretched but will honour righteous ones.

[33] Him will dismiss the person who didn't do Him Accord - but Him will Ipoint the person who did Him Accord.

Chapter 8

[1] Hear I - mek I tell thee the thing whereby dead persons shall arise ~ them shall plant a plant an be fertile an grapes shall send forth vines ~ as JAH shall bring the fruit 'imhibe 'albo ~ them shall cast wine from it.

[2] Overstand that that plant thou planted were small - but that she sent forth tips fruit an leaves today.

[3] JAH give she root fe drink from Earth an Water - from both.

[4] But Him feed she wood from fiyah an wind ~ roots give leaves Water fe drink - an Earth give firmness fe woods.

[5] But the soul that JAH Irated mek them bear fruit amidst them - an dead persons arisin are likewise.

[6] Pon the time soul were separated from flesh - as each of them ras selves have gone - Him said - Gather souls from the four natures - from Earth an Water - wind an fiyah.

[7] But Earth nature lived firmed up ina she nature an became Earth - an Water nature lived firmed up ina she nature an became Water.

[8] An wind nature lived firmed up ina she nature an became wind - an fiyah nature lived firmed up ina she nature an became a hot fiyah.

[9] But a soul that JAH separated from flesh returned toward she Irator ~ up til Him raise she up inited with flesh pon the time Him loved - Him place she ina Garden ina the place Him loved.

[10] Him place righteous souls ina Light house ina Garden - but that Him might send way sinners souls - Him also place them ina darkness house ina *See'ol* up til the time when Him loved.

[11] JAH told the prophet Hiziq'iel - Call souls from the four corners - that them might be gathered an be one limb.

[12] Pon the time Him spoke ina one Word sayin thus - the souls were gathered from the four corners.

[13] An Water nature brought verdure - an again fiyah nature brought fiyah.

[14] An again Earth nature brought Earth - an wind nature brought wind.

[15] An JAH brought a soul from the Garden place where Him placed it ~ them were gathered by one Word - an a Resurrection were made.

[16] An again I-man shall show thee the example that are alongside thee ~ the day dusk ~ thou sleep ~ the night dawn

- an thou rise from thy beddin - but pon the time thou slept it are thy death example.

[17] An pon the time thou awoke it are thy arisin example - but the night when all persons sleep whose physiques were dark - fe darkness have covered them - are this world example.

[18] But the mornin light - when darkness are eliminated an when light are ina all the world an when persons arise an graze toward the field - are dead persons example.

[19] An this Kingdom of Heaven where man are renewed are like unto this ~ dead persons Resurrection are like unto this ~ as this world are passin - it are the night example.

[20] An like unto Daweet spoke sayin - 'Him placed Him example ina Sun' - as Sun shine pon the time it rose - it are a Kingdom of Heaven example.

[21] An like unto Sun shine ina this world today - pon the time Kristos come Him shall shine like unto Sun ina Kingdom of Heaven that are new ~ as Him have said - I-man am a Sun that don't set an a Torch that aren't extinguished - Him JAH are she Light.

[22] An Him shall quickly arouse the dead persons again ~ I-man shall bring one example fe thee again from thy food that thou sow an whereby thou are saved - an whether it be a wheat kernel or a barley kernel or a lentil kernel or all man seeds sown pon Earth - there are none that grow unless it were demolished an rotten.

[23] An like unto the person flesh thou sight up - pon the time it were demolished an rotten - Earth eat stoutness with the hide.

[24] An pon the time Earth ate it stoutness it grow bein around a kernel seventh ~ JAH give a cloud that seized rain like unto Him loved - an roots grow pon Earth an send forth leaves.

[25] An if she were demolished an rotten she cyaan grow - but after she grew she send forth many buds.

[26] An by JAH Accord fruit are given fe those buds that grew - an Him clothe it stoutness ina straw.

[27] Sight up like unto the measure that the seed kernel thou sowed abounded - yet the silver an the leaf - the ear an the straw aren't counted fe thee.

[28] Don't be a dull one who don't know - an sight up thy seed that it abounded - an all likewise - think that dead persons shall raceive the arisin that them will arise - an them hardship like unto them Work.

[29] Hear I - that if thou sow wheat - it won't grow bein barley - nor bein wheat if thou sow barley - an mek I tell thee again that it won't grow ~ if thou sow wheat will thou gather barley? If thou sow watercress will thou gather linseed?

[30] How about from plants kind - if thou plant figs will it really grow fe thee bein nuts? How about if thou plant almonds - will it grow fe thee bein grapes?

[31] If thou plant the sweet fruit will it grow fe thee bein bitter? How about if thou plant the bitter fruit - are it possible fe it fe be sweet?

[32] How about all likewise - if a sinner dead are it possible fe arise bein righteous ina Resurrection time? How about if a righteous person dead - are it possible fe arise bein a sinner ina Resurrection time? Every one shall raceive him hardship like unto him Work - yet him will raceive him hardship like unto him sin an him hand Work - yet there are none who will be canvicted by him companion sin.

[33] A highland tree are planted an it send forth long branches ~ it will totally dry up ~ yet unless Heaven rained rain it leaves won't be verdant.

[34] An the cedar will be uprooted from it roots unless summer rain alit pon it.

[35] An all likewise - dead persons won't arise unless welfare dew alit fe them bein commanded from JAH.

Chapter 9

[1] Unless highland mountains an Gielabuhie regions rained a pardon rain fe them bein commanded from JAH - them won't grow grass fe beasts an animals.

[2] An 'Elam mountains an Gele`ad mountains won't give verdant leaves fe sheeps an goats - nor fe oribi an animals ina wilderness - nor fe ibexes an hartebeest.

[3] An likewise - pardon an dew bein commanded from JAH didn't alight fe doubters an criminals who made error an crime a money beforehand ~ dead persons won't arise ~ an Deemas an Qophros who worship idols an dig roots an work an instigate a thing...

[4] An them who dig roots an practice sorcery an mek persons battle...

[5] An them who lust havin departed from LAW - an Miedon an 'Atiena persons who believe ina them idols - an them who play an sing fe them while them beat violins an drums an strummed harps - them won't arise unless pardon dew alit fe them bein commanded from JAH.

[6] These are who will be canvicted pon the day when dead persons arise an when Definite Judgemant are done - yet persons who save them ras selves an who lust ina them hands Work - them err by them idols.

[7] Thou wasteful of heart dull one - do it seem fe thee that dead persons won't arise?

[8] Pon the time a trumpet were blown by the Angels Chief Hola Meeka'iel tongue - that dead ones arise then - as thou

won't remain ina grave without arisin - don't think a thing that are thus.

[9] Hills an mountains shall be level an shall be a cleared path.

[10] An Resurrection shall be done fe all fleshly ones.

Chapter 10

[1] However if it weren't thus - it are that former persons might be buried ina them faadas grave Iginnin from 'Adam - Iginnin from Siet an 'Abiel - Siem an Noh - Yis'haq an 'Abriham - Yosief an Ya`iqob - an 'Aron an Mussie - yet fe what are it that them didn't love that them might be buried ina another place?

[2] Aren't it fe them fe arise together with them cousins ina Resurrection time? How about aren't it lest them bones be counted with evil ones an pagans bones - them who worship idols? Fe what are it that them didn't love that them might be buried ina another place?

[3] But thou - don't mislead thy reasonin while thou said - 'How will dead persons arise after them dead - them who were buried ina one grave bein tens of thousands an whose bodies were demolished an rotten?'

[4] An pon the time thou sight up toward a grave - thou speak this ina thy reasonin dullness while thou said - 'A whole fistful of Earth won't be found ~ how will dead persons arise?'

[5] Will thou say the seed thou sowed won't grow? Even the seed thou sowed shall grow.

[6] An all likewise - the souls JAH sowed shall quickly arise - as Him have Irated man ina Him Truth bringin from not livin toward livin - Him shall arouse them quickly by Him Word that save ~ Him won't delay Him arousin.

[7] An as Him have again returned him from livin - toward a grave ina death - what about aren't it possible fe Him again fe return from death toward Life?

[8] Savin an liftin up are possible fe JAH.

Chapter 11

[1] 'Armon perished an she fortress were demolished ~ as JAH have brought the hardship pon them like unto them evil an the Work them worked by them hands - persons who worship the idols ina 'Edomyas an Zablon shall be downbased at that time ~ as JAH have approached - Who shall canvict them who worked ina them infancy an didn't quit up til them aged - becau them idols an them evil - Seedona an Theeros shall weep..

[2] Becau them worked sin an seducin fornication an worshipped idols - becaudis thing JAH shall revenge an downstroy them ~ fe them didn't live firmēd up ina them Irator JAH Command - an Yihuda dawta childran shall be wretched.

[3] She lived firmed up ina killin prophets an ina Irie Ites - yet as she didn't live firmed up ina the Nine Laws an the Worship - pon the time when dead ones arise - 'Iyerusaliem sin shall be revealed.

[4] At that time JAH shall examine she ina Him Nature Wisdom ~ Him will revenge an downstroy she pon all she sin that she worked ina she infancy era ~ she didn't quit workin she sin Iginnin from she beauty era up til she age.

[5] She entered toward a grave an became dust like unto she former faadas who lived firmed up ina them sin - an ina Resurrection time Him shall revenge an downstroy persons who demolished JAH LAW.

[6] It shall be judged pon them - fe Mussie have spoken becau them sayin - 'Them LAW lodgin - them reasonins - became Sedom law lodgin.'

[7] An them kindred are Gemorra kindred - an them law are what downstroy - an them Work are evil.

[8] An them law are snake poison that downstroy - an viper poison that downstroy from alongside that.

Chapter 12

[1] 'Iyerusaliem child - as this thy sin are like unto Gemorra an Sedom sin - 'Iyerusaliem child - this are thy tribulation that were spoken by a prophet.

[2] An thy tribulation are like unto Gemorra an Sedom tribulation - an them law lodgin reasonin firmed up ina adultery an arrogance.

[3] Aside from adultery an arrogance rain - pardon an humility rain didn't rain from them reasonins by money that them Law reasonin lodgin are fertile - apart from spillin man blood an robbin an forgettin them Irator JAH.

[4] An them didn't know them Irator JAH - apart from them evil Work an them idols - an them are Irie ina them hands Work - an them lust pon males an pon livestock.

[5] As them eye of reasonin have been blinded lest them sight up secrets - an as them ears have deafened lest them hear or do JAH Accord that Him love - them didn't know JAH ina them Work - an them reasonins are like unto Sedom law lodgin. An them kindred - Gemorra grapes kindred that bear sweet fruit.

[6] An if them examine them Work - it are poison that kill - fe it have firmed up ina curse Iginnin from the day when it were worked - an fe it grounation have been ina downstruction era.

[7] As them Law lodgin - them reasonins - have firmed up ina sin Work - as them bodies have firmed up ina Seythan burnin Work fe build sin - them Law lodgin - them reasonins - have no goodly Work everytime.

[8] An pon the time him shame an were baptise (by one who is led) it were fe chastisemant an downstruction - an him will firm up the persons who drank an them reasonins - an him will mek them who downstroy I - disgustin persons who distanced from JAH.

[9] Fe them have lived firmed up ina them Work that were evil - an him will mek them Deeyablos lodgin - an eatin what were sacrificed fe the idols have been begun ina the House of 'Isra'iel - an she proceed toward the mountains an the trees.

[10] An she worship the idols that peoples ina she area worship - an she dawta childran an she male childran fe demons who don't know goodly Work separatin from evil.

[11] An them spill clean blood ~ them gush an spill grapes from Sedom fe the idols foriva.

[12] An she glorify an worship the Dagwon that the 'Iloflans worship - an she sacrifice fe him from she flocks an she fattened cows - that she might be Irie ina demons laziness that them taught she fe sacrifice fe them - an ina them gushin an spillin the grapes - an that she might do them accord.

[13] She sacrifice fe him that she might be Irie in demons laziness that them taught she lest she know she Irator JAH Who feed she at each time an Who cherished an raised she Iginnin from she infancy up til she beauty - an again up til she age - an again up til she age day when she dead.

[14] An again I-man shall revenge an canvict him ina Resurrection time - an as she didn't return toward I LAW - an as she didn't live firmed up ina I Command - she time when she live ina *Gehannem* shall be up til Iternity.

[15] If them were Irators fe true - mek she idols arise with she an downscend toward *Gehannem* an save she pon the time I-man vexed an downstroyed she - an pon the time I-man distanced all the priests of the idols who lust with she.

[16] Like unto she made sin an insult pon the Hola Items an pon I Lodgin the Temple - I-man made she wretched by all this.

[17] When them told she - 'Check - this are JAH kindred - an she are 'Isra'iel Irator JAH Lodgin - an the famous King country 'Iyerusaliem who were separate from them who were separate - she are the Most I JAH Name Lodgin' - I-man made she wretched like unto she saddened I Name that were called ina she.

[18] She boast ina I that she were I slave an that I-man were she Lord ~ she wink pon I like unto a criminal - yet she aren't who fear I an do I Accord like unto I bein she Lord.

[19] Them became a obstacle pon she fe mislead that them might distance she from I - yet she are ruled fe other idols who don't feed she nor clothe she.

[20] She sacrifice sacrifice fe them - an she eat the sacrifice - an she spill blood fe them - an she gush an drink from the grapes fe them ~ she smoke up ishence fe them - an she mek the ishence fragrance smell fe them ~ she idols command she - an she are commanded fe them.

[21] An again she sacrifice she dawta childran an she male childran fe them - an as she present praises fe them becau them Love - she are Irie ina the thing she spoke by she tongue an ina she hands Work.

[22] Woe fe she pon the day when Definite Judgemant are done - an woe fe she idols whom she love an inite;
an she shall downscend with them toward *Gehannem* beneath *See'ol* - where the worm don't slumber an the fiyah aren't extinguished.

[23] Woe fe thee wretched 'Iyerusaliem child - fe thou have quit I Who Irated thee an have worshipped different idols.

[24] An I-man shall bring the hardship pon thee like unto thy Work ~ as thou have saddened I - an as thou have ignored I Word - an as thou didn't work goodly Work - I-man shall canvict thee toward thy pretensions.

[25] Fe thou have saddened I Word - an fe thou didn't live firmed up ina I LAW whereby thou swore with I - that thou might keep I LAW an that I-man might live with thee ina Support an might save thee from all who fight thee - an also that thou might keep I Order that I-man commanded thee - an I-man shall ignore thee an won't quickly save thee from the tribulation.

[26] Thou didn't keep all this - an I-man ignored thee ~ as I-man have created thee - an as thou didn't keep I Command nor I Word - I-man shall canvict thee ina Judgemant time - an I-man honoured thee that thou might be I kin.

[27] An like unto Gemorra an Sedom were separated from I - thou were separated from I.

[28] An I-man judged an downstroyed them - an like unto Sedom an Gemorra were separated from I - thou separated from I - an now like unto I-man vexed an downstroyed them - I-man vexed an downstroyed thee ~ as thou are from Sedom an Gemorra kindred whom I-man downstroyed - I-man downstroyed thee ~ as them whom I-man Irated have saddened I by goin toward a youtmon wife an by lustin without LAW - with animals an males like unto arrivin with dawtaz - I-man downstroyed them name invocation from this world lest them live ina them Irie Ites.

[29] There are no fearin JAH ina them faces Iginnin from a infant up til a elder ~ them help him ina all them evil Work - yet Him don't vex pon each one that them might quit

workin she ~ as them Work are evil - them are sated of sin an iniquity.

[30] All evil Work - robbery an arrogance an greed - are prepared ina them reasonins.

[31] An becaudis thing JAH ignored them an downstroyed them countries - an them are there that Him might burn them with fiyah up til them root grounation perish ~ them totally perished up til the Iternity - yet Him didn't mek even one from them remain.

[32] As them have firmed up ina sin - them shall wait ina downstruction foriva up til the Day of Advent when Definite Judgemant are done - fe them have saddened I with them evil Work - an I-man won't pardon them nor forgive them.

[33] An I-man ignored them ~ fe thou won't find a reason pon the time I-man vexed an seized thee becau all thy Work were robbery an sin - adultery an greed an speakin lies - all error Work an the obstacle that I-man don't love - an thou 'Iyerusaliem child who were wretched - pon the day when Judgemant are done thou will be seized ina Judgemant like unto them.

[34] I-man had made thee fe honour - but thou downbased thy ras self ~ I-man had called thee I money - but thou became fe another.

[35] I-man had betrothed thee fe honour - but thou became fe Deeyablos - an I-man shall revenge an downstroy thee like unto thy evil Work.

[36] Becau thou didn't hear all I Word - an becau thou didn't keep the Command I-man commanded thee pon the time I-man loved thee - I-man shall multiply an bring firm vengeance pon thee - fe I-man am JAH Who Irated thee - an I-man shall judge pon all sinners like unto thee - an pon the day when Judgemant are done I-man shall bring the hardship pon them like unto them evil Work.

[37] As thou didn't keep I Word - an as thou have ignored I Judgemant - I-man shall canvict thee with them.

[38] Woe fe unu - Gemorra an Sedom - who have no fearin JAH ina your reasonin.

[39] All likewise - woe fe thy sista 'Iyerusaliem child pon whom it shall be judged together with thee ina Fiyah of *Gehannem* - fe unu will downscend together toward *Gehannem* that were prepared fe unu - where are no exits foriva - an woe fe all sinners who worked thy sin.

[40] As unu didn't keep I Command nor I Word - thou an she who didn't keep I Command nor I Word shall downscend toward *See'ol* together pon the day when Judgemant are judged.

[41] But kind persons who kept I Command an I Word shall eat the money that sinner persons accumulated - an like unto JAH commanded - kind persons shall share the loot that evil persons captured - an kind persons shall be totally Irie.

[42] But wrongdoers an sinner persons shall weep - an them shall be sad becau all them sin that them wronged havin departed from I Command.

[43] Him who keep I Word an live firmed up ina I Command - him are who find I blessin an are honoured alongside I.

[44] All person who keep I Word an live firmed up ina I Command shall eat the fatness found from Earth - an shall live havin entered toward the Garden where enter kind kings who have straight reasonins.

Chapter 13

[1] As them shall be wretched an perish by I wrath pon the time I-man seized them - woe fe Theeros an Seedona an all Yihuda country regions who mek them ras selves arrogant today.

[2] Conquerin JAH said thus ~ Him have said - Deeyablos child who are totally arrogant shall be birthed from them - the False *Messeeh* who fe a Truth thing are she enemy - who firm up him collar of reasonin - who boast an don't know him Irator - an Him said - Woe fe them - an JAH Who rule all said - I-man made him fe I anger pattern that I-man might be revealed ina him Power.

[3] An this Qifirnahom Semarya an Geleela an Demasqo an Sorya an 'Akeya an Qophros an all Yordanos region are kindreds who firmed up them collars of reasonin - who live firmed up ina them sin - an whom death shadow an darkness covered - fe Deeyablos have covered them reasonins ina sin - an fe them are commanded fe that arrogant Deeyablos - an them didn't return toward fearin JAH.

[4] At that time woe fe persons who are commanded fe demons an who sacrifice sacrifice ina them name fe them ~ as them have denied JAH Who Irated them - them resemble animals without minds - fe the False *Messeeh* who forgot JAH LAW an are Deeyablos child shall set up him image ina all the places (fe him have said 'Mi are a god') - an him shall be Irie ina him reasonin accord - ina him hand Work an ina robbery an all the sins an perfidy an iniquity - ina robbery an all the adulteries that a person work.

[5] Fe becau it were counted alongside JAH that him work this - the era are known that them work sin.

[6] Sun shall darken an moon shall be blood - an stars shall be shaken from Heaven - all the Work shall pass by the miracles that JAH shall bring ina Fulfillmant Era that Him might mek Earth pass - an that Him might mek all pass who live ina sin of persons who live within she.

[7] As JAH have been proud pon the Iration Him Irated - an as Him have quickly made all Him loved ina one iwa - the Lord death shall downstroy a small enemy Deeyablos.

[8] Fe JAH Who rule all have said - I-man shall judge an downstroy - but after Advent - Deeyablos have no authority.

[9] An pon the day when him were seized by I anger - him shall downscend toward *Gehannem* - fe which him mek application an where firm tribulation are ~ as him will tek all who are with him toward chastisemant an downstruction an perfidy - becau I-man were Who send forth from *Gehannem* an Who introduce toward *Gehannem* - him will downscend toward *Gehannem*.

[10] As Him give firmness an Power fe weak persons - an again as Him give weakness fe powerful an firm persons - mek a powerful one not boast ina him Power.

[11] As Him are a Ruler - an as Him judge an save the wronged persons from the persons hands who wrong them - Him will return the grudge of the widows an the child whose faada an mother dead pon him.

[12] Woe fe thee who boast an firm up thy collar of reasonin - fe whom it seem that I-man won't rule thee nor judge an downstroy thee - fe ina him boastin an him arrogance him have said - 'Mi will streach mi throne ina stars an Heaven - an mi will be like unto JAH Who are lofty.'

[13] An like unto Him spoke sayin - How Deeyablos fell from Heaven - him who shine like unto a mornin star that were Irated precedin all - woe fe thee.

[14] An thou dared an spoke this ina thy arrogance - an thou didn't think of JAH Who totally Irated thee by Him Itority ~ why did thou boast thy ras self that thou downscend toward *Gehannem* ina thy reasonin firmness?

[15] Thou were downbased separate from all Angels like unto thee - fe them praise them Irator with a humbled reasonin becau them knew that Him were Who Irated them from fiyah an wind - an fe them don't depart from Him Command - an fe them keep them reasonins from perfidy lest them totally depart from Him Command.

[16] But thou did a firm perfidy ina thy reasonin arrogance ~ thou became a wretched man separate from thy companions - fe thou have cherished all the sin an iniquity - robbery an perfidy whereby persons who forgot JAH LAW an sinners like unto thee live firmed up - them who are from thy kindred an commit crime like unto thee - an who live firmed up by thy command an thy accord whereby thou teach sin.

[17] Woe fe thee - fe the demons thou misled ina thy malice an thou will downscend toward *Gehannem* together.

[18] O unu JAH childran who erred by that misleadin criminal Deeyablos - woe fe unu ~ as unu have erred like unto him by the money that him taught unu an that him hosts taught unu
- unu will downscend toward *Gehannem* together - where are no exits foriva.

[19] An formerly when JAH slave Mussie were there - unu saddened JAH by the Water where argumant were made an pon Korieb - an by 'Amalieq an pon Mount Seena.

[20] An moreover pon the time unu sent scouts toward Kene`an - pon the time them told unu this sayin 'The path are far - an them ramparts an them fortresses that reach up til Heaven are firm - an warriors live there' - unu vexed that unu might return towad Gibts country where unu work worrisome Work - an unu saddened JAH Word.

[21] Unu didn't think of JAH Who firmed unu up from the tribulation - an Who did great miracles ina Gibts - an Who led unu by Him Angel Itority. Him would veil unu ina cloud by day lest the Sun burn unu an Him would shine a column of fiyah fe unu by night lest your feet stumble ina darkness.

[22] An pon the time the army an Fer`on frightened unu - unu totally cried toward Mussie - an Mussie totally cried toward JAH - an Him lodged ina Him Angel an kept unu lest unu meet with Fer`on.

[23] But Him introduced them toward 'Eritra ina tribulation ~ JAH led only 'Isra'iel - fe Him have said - An there were no different idol with them - but Him buried them enemies ina sea at one time - an Him didn't preserve none who flee from them.

[24] An Him made 'Isra'iel cross amidst the sea by foot ~ there are no tribulation that found them arisin from the Gibtsans ~ Him delivered them toward Mount Seena - an there Him fed them *menna* forty eras.

[25] As 'Isra'iel childran sadden JAH everytime - Him did all this goodly thing fe them an them neglected fe worship JAH.

[26] Them placed evil ina them reasonins Iginnin from them childhood up til them age - fe JAH Mouth have spoken thus ina *'Oreet* where the faadas birth were written ~ as Him have spoken sayin - 'Adam childran reasonin are ash - an all them Work are toward robbery an them run toward evil ~ there are none from them who love straight Work - apart from gatherin a person money ina violence an swearin ina lie an wrongin companions an robbin an stealin - them placed evil ina them reasonins.

[27] An all go toward evil Work ina the era when them live ina Life ~ 'Isra'iel childran who demolished JAH LAW totally saddened JAH Iginnin from Antiquity up til fufillmant era.

Chapter 14

[1] An pon the time JAH downstroyed Qayen childran - kindreds who preceded - ina downstruction Water becau them sin - Him baptised Earth ina Water of Downstruction - an Him cleansed she from all Qayel childran sin.

[2] As Him have said - I-man were sad becau I-man Irated man - Him downstroyed all wrongdoers ~ Him didn't preserve apart from eight persons ~ Him downstroyed all ~ after this Him multiplied them an them filled Earth ~ them shared them faada 'Adam inheritance.

[3] But Noh swore with JAH a oath ~ them swore a oath with JAH lest JAH again downstroy Earth ina Downstruction Water - an lest Noh childran eat what deceased nor what lodged dead - lest them worship different idols apart from JAH Who Irated them - an that Him might be a Love Faada fe them - an lest Him downstroy them at one time ina them vain sin - an lest Him prevent them the first an the spring rain - an that Him might give fe livestock an persons them food at each time - that Him might give them the grass an the grain fruit an plants - an that them might work goodly Work ina all that JAH love.

[4] An after Him gave them this Order - 'Isra'iel childran saddened JAH by them sin ~ them didn't live firmed up ina Him LAW like unto them faadas Yis'haq an 'Abriham an Ya`iqob who didn't demolish them Irator JAH LAW.

[5] An Iginnin from the small up til the great - those 'Isra'iel childran who didn't keep JAH LAW are crooked ina them Work.

[6] An whether them be them priests or them chiefs or them scribes - everyone demolish JAH LAW.

[7] Them don't live firmed up ina JAH Order an Him LAW that Mussie commanded them ina Repeatin Law sayin - 'Love thy Irator JAH ina thy complete body an thy complete reasonin.'

[8] Them don't firm up ina JAH Order an Him LAW that Mussie commanded them ina book where LAW were written sayin - 'Love thy companion like unto thy body - an don't worship him idols that were different - an don't go toward a youtmon wife ~ don't kill a soul ~ don't steal.

[9] An don't witness ina lie - an be it him donkey or be it him ox - don't love thy companion money nor all that thy bredda bought.'

[10] However after him commanded them all this - 'Isra'iel childran who were evil return toward treachery an sin - robbery an iniquity - toward a youtmon wife an toward lies an stealin an worshippin idols.

[11] 'Isra'iel childran saddened JAH pon Korieb by workin a cow that graze toward grass ~ them bowed sayin - 'Check - these are wi irators who sent wi forth from Gibts.'

[12] An them were Irie ina them hand Work ~ if them ate an drank an satta - them arose fe sing.

[13] As JAH have told him sayin - Thy kindreds whom thou sent forth from Gibts country where rulership are - them have proceeded from LAW an wronged - an them worked a cow image an bowed fe the idol - becaudis thing Mussie vexed an alit from Seena mountain.

[14] While Mussie vexed pon him kindreds - him alit with him canfidante 'Iyasu - an pon the time 'Iyasu heard - him said - 'Check - I-man hear warriors voice ina 'Isra'iel camp.'

[15] An Mussie told 'Iyasu - 'It are when 'Isra'iel play havin drunk the unboiled wine - yet as fe a warrior voice - it aren't' - an him alit an broke them image an totally crushed it up til it were like unto dust ~ him mixed it within the Water that 'Isra'iel childran drink beside the mountain.

[16] An after this him commanded the priests that them might slay one another becau the sin them worked before JAH.

[17] Them knew that defyin JAH surpass killin them an killin them faadas - an them did like unto him commanded them.

[18] An Mussie told them - 'Becau unu saddened JAH Who fed unu an cherished unu an Who sent unu forth from a rulership house an Who bequeathed fe unu the inheritance that Him swore fe your faadas that Him might give fe them an fe them childran after them - becaudis thing unu made JAH Irie.'

[19] Fe them go toward sin an a evil thing - an them didn't quit saddenin JAH there.

[20] Them aren't like unto them faadas Yis'haq an 'Abriham an Ya`iqob who made JAH Irie with them goodly Work that Him might give them what are pon Earth an what Him prepared fe persons who love Him ina Heaven Iginnin from them infancy up til them youthood an up til them age ~ them aren't like unto 'Abriham an Yis'haq an Ya`iqob who made Him Irie with them Work that Him might give them a Earth of inheritance where Irie Ites are found ina this world - an a garden that mek Irie - prepared fe kind persons ina hereafter world - what Him prepared fe 'Abriham an Yis'haq an Ya`iqob who made JAH Irie when them were ina Life an who love Him - Whom a eye didn't sight up nor a ear hear an Who aren't thought of ina reasonin.

[21] An them childran who denied JAH an were evil an who live firmed up ina them reasonin accord - them didn't hear JAH Command - Him Who fed them an cherished them an kept them Iginnin from them infancy.

[22] Them didn't think of JAH - Who sent them forth from Gibts land an saved them from brick Work an a firm rulership.

[23] But them totally saddened Him - an Him would arouse peoples ina them area pon them - an them would arise pon them ina enmity an also tax them like unto them loved.

Chapter 15

[1] An at that time Midyam persons arose pon them ina enmity - an them aroused them armies pon 'Isra'iel that them might fight them - an them king name are called 'Akrandis ~ him quickly gathered many armies ina Keeliqyas an Sorya an Demasqo.

[2] An campin beyond Yordanos him sent messengers sayin - 'An that mi might capture your money - pay tax toward 'Isra'iel fe mi' ~ him told them - 'But if unu don't pay tax - mi came that mi might punish unu an might capture your livestocks an tek your mares an capture your childran.'

[3] 'Mi will capture an tek unu toward the country unu don't know - an there mi will mek unu Water pourers an wood pickers' him told them.

[4] 'Don't boast while unu said - "InI are JAH kindreds an there are nothing able fe InI" - aren't JAH Who sent mi that mi might downstroy unu an plunder your money? an aren't mi whom JAH sent that mi might gather all your kindreds?

[5] Are there really a savin that them different idols saved the other kins that mi downstroyed? Mi captured them mares an them horses an mi killed them an captured them childran.

[6] An unless unu introduced the tax that mi commanded unu - mi will downstroy unu like unto them' him said - an him crossed Yordanos that him might plunder them livestocks an them money an capture them wives.

[7] An after this 'Isra'iel childran wept a firm mournin toward JAH - an them totally cried - however them lacked one who help them.

[8] An becaudis thing JAH gave firmness fe the three bredren - an them names are like unto this: - an them are Yihuda an Mebikyas an Meqabees - whose features were handsome an who were warriors ina them Power.

[9] An 'Isra'iel childran totally wept there ~ pon the time them heard - it saddened them ina them heart arisin from all 'Isra'iel childran shout ~ the child whose mother an faada dead pon him - an widows - an them officials an them priests - all 'Isra'iel kindred - both dawtaz an males - an all childran - would weep sprinklin ash pon them heads - an them nobles had worn sackcloth.

[10] But those bredren - who were attractive an comely - went an agreed that them might save them ~ them counseled sayin - 'Mek InI go an give InI bodies fe death becau these persons.'

[11] Tellin one another - 'Tek heart - tek heart' - them went girdin them swords pon them waists an seizin them spears ina them hands - an them went prepared that them might incriminate the warrior.

[12] An them arrived toward them camp ~ Mebikyus attacked the warrior (the king) when him had sat at a dinnertable ~ him cut him neck ina one blow when food were ina him mouth; an Meqabyus an Yihuda struck him armies pon the king left an right by sword an killed them.

[13] An pon the time them king were defeated - them entered toward them spears ina them companions hearts - an them all totally fled an them bows were broken an them were defeated.

[14] But those bredren who are attractive an comely were saved from death ~ there are no evil thing that found them - but as JAH have returned chastisemant toward them - them sliced up one another an were depleted.

[15] Them were defeated an dead an them crossed Yordanos - an up til them crossed them cast way all them money - an all them money remained - an pom the time 'Isra'iel childran sight up that them enemies fled - them went toward them camp an took both what them plundered an them money fe them ras selves.

[16] JAH saved 'Isra'iel doin thus by the bredren an Mebikyu hand.

[17] 'Isra'iel sat a few days while them made JAH Irie.

[18] But after that them again returned toward them sin ~ 'Isra'iel childran neglected worshippin JAH by what are due.

[19] An Him shall again sadden them by kins who don't know them an who will gather them field crops an downstroy them grape places an plunder them flocks an slaughter an feed them them livestocks before them...

[20] an who will capture them wives an them dawta childran an them male childran ~ becau it were that them sadden JAH everytime; as themare kindreds who demolished the LAW - them will hammer them childran before them pon each of them heads ~ them won't save them.

Chapter 16

[1] Them who do this are Theeros an Seedona an them who live beyond Yordanos river an pon the sea edge - Keran an Gele`ad - 'Iyabuseewon an Kenaniewon - 'Edom an Giegiesiewon an 'Amalieq persons.

[2] All peoples do thus - who live firmed up ina each of them tribes an countries an regions an ina each of them Works an country languages - an all live firmed up like unto JAH worked them.

[3] An there are persons from them who know JAH - an whose Work were beautiful.

[4] An there are persons from them whose Work were evil an who don't know JAH Who Irated them - an like unto them worked sin - Him ruled them ina Sorya king Silminasor hand.

[5] As him plunder an tek Demasqo money - an as him share Semarya loot that are before Gibts king - Him ruled them ina Silminasor hand.

[6] Gielabuhie region an also persons ina Fars an Miedon - Qephedoqya an Sewseegya - who live ina the West mountains - ina Gele`ad fortress an Phasthos that are part of Yihuda land...

[7] an these are who live in them region - an them are kindreds who don't know JAH nor keep Him Command - an whose collar of reasonin were firm.

[8] An Him shall pay them them hardship like unto them Work evil an them hands Work.

[9] Fe Gele`ad kindreds an Qeesarya region an 'Amalieq have become one there - that them might downstroy JAH country that were filled of a Truth thing - an within which 'Isra'iel Irator are praised - Him Who are Most Glorified an Conquerin - an Whom Angels who are many many ina Keerubiel chariots - them who stand before Him - serve fearin an tremblin - an Him shall pay them them hardship like unto them Work evil an them hands Work.

Chapter 17

[1] 'Amalieq an 'Edomyas persons don't worship JAH by Whose Itority Earth an Heaven rulership were seized ~ as them are criminals who don't live firmed up ina Truth Work - them don't fear fe demolish Him Lodgin - the Temple.

[2] An there are no fearin JAH before them - apart from sheddin blood an adultery an eatin what were beaten an sacrificed fe a idol an all that resemble what lodged dead - an these are scorned sinners.

[3] Them have no virtue nor religion ~ as them are who hated goodly Work - an as them don't know JAH - an as them don't know Love Work - apart from robbin a person money an from sin - an apart from downsturbin a person an all hated Work - apart from games an song like unto them faada Deeyablos taught them - them have no virtue nor religion.

[4] As him have ruled them with him host - demons - him teach them all evil Work that were fe each of them ras selves - all robbery an sin - theft an falsehood - robbin money an eatin what were beaten an what lodged dead - an adultery Work.

[5] An him teach them all that resemble this - an goin toward a youtmon wife - an sheddin blood - eatin what were sacrificed fe idol an what lodged dead - an killin a person soul ina violence - an envy an winkin an greed an all evil Work that JAH don't love ~ Deeyablos who were them enemy teach them this teachin that him might distance them from JAH LAW Who rule all the world.

[6] But JAH Work are innocence an humility - not annoyin a bredren an lovin a companion - harmonisin an lovin with all persons.

[7] Don't be hypocrites fe favour fe a person face - an don't be wrongdoers nor totally robbers nor persons who go toward a youtmon wife - nor persons who work iniquity an evil Work pon them companion - nor who cajole that them might wrong them companion ina violence.

[8] Them wink an shake them heads an provoke fe evil ~ them discourage fe mislead that them might lower them toward Iternity Definite Judgemant.

Chapter 18

[1] Think that thou will go ina death toward JAH ina Whose Hand all are - an thou will stand before Him that Him might canvict thee before Him pon all the sin thou Worked.

[2] As them who are arrogant an evil - an powerful ones childran who aren't strengthenin more than them - were likewise formerly - becau them sight up them stature an them Power an them firm authority - them didn't mek JAH before them - an them didn't know that Him were them Irator Who Irated them bringin from not livin toward livin.

[3] An when them faadas bein like unto "Angels" praised pon Mount Hola with Angels - pon the time them accord misled them - them alit toward this world where Definite Judgemant shall be done foriva.

[4] As JAH ina the Antiquity have Irated human flesh fe them - that it might mislead them becau them reasonin arrogance an might test them as it were them kept Him LAW an Him Command - them married wives from Qayel childran.

[5] But them didn't keep Him LAW ~ Him lowered them toward *Gehannem* fiyah with them faada Deeyablos; fe JAH have vexed pon the offspring of Siet who wronged like unto persons - an persons era diminished becau them sin.

[6] An them took 'Adam childran toward sin with them ~ Him lowered them toward *See'ol* where them shall raceive a verdict.

[7] As persons era have been divided becau Siet childran erred by Qayel childran - when a person eras were nine hundred ina the Antiquity - them returned toward livin a hundred twenty eras.

[8] An as them are flesh an blood - JAH said - I Spirit of Support won't live firmed up pon them.

[9] An becaudis thing InI era were divided - fe becau InI sin an InI iniquity - InI era have been divided from InI faadas who preceded - an when them are ina them infancy again - them are dyin.

[10] But InI faadas era had abounded - becau them kept Him LAW an becau them didn't sadden JAH.

[11] But InI faadas era had abounded - becau them vexed pon them dawta childran that them might teach them - an becau them vexed pon them male childran lest them demolish JAH LAW.

[12] Becau them didn't demolish JAH LAW with them dawta childran an them male childran - becaudis thing them era had abounded fe true.

Chapter 19

[1] Pon the time Qayen childran abounded them worked drums an harps - *santee* an violins - an them made songs an all the games.

[2] Childran who are attractive an comely were birthed fe Qayen from the wife of the kind man 'Abiel - whom him killed becau she - fe she were attractive - an after him killed him bredda him took that an she who were him money.

[3] An separatin from him faada - him seized them an went toward Qiefaz region that are toward the West - an that attractive one childran were attractive like unto them mother.

[4] An becaudis thing Siet childran downscended toward Qayen childran - an after them sight them up them didn't wait one iwa - an them made the dawtaz whom them chose wives fe them ras selves.

[5] As them have taken InI toward error together with them becau them error - becaudis thing JAH vexed pon InI an vexed pon them.

[6] An Deeyablos havin cajoled sayin - 'Unu will become irators like unto your Irator JAH' - him took InI mother Hiewan an InI faada 'Adam toward him error.

[7] But it seemin Truth fe them ina them dullness - them demolished JAH LAW - Him Who Irated them bringin from not-livin toward livin that them might bow an praise Him glorified Name.

[8] But Him - them Irator - downbased those 'Adam an Hiewan who made godhood fe them ras selves - an Him downbased him who are arrogant.

[9] Like unto Daweet spoke sayin - ' 'Adam perish by the sinner Deeyablos arrogance' - Him abused them - fe InI faada 'Adam have been canvicted pon Deeyablos arrogance by Him true Judgemant.

[10] An Siet childran who erred by Qayel childran took InI toward them sin thus ~ becaudis thing InI era that JAH gave InI were less than InI faadas eras.

[11] But them had worked goodly Work - fe them had firmed up them reasonins ina JAH - fe them had taught them dawta childran an them male childran lest them depart from JAH LAW that them taught them - an there were no evil enemy who approach them.

[12] But if them worked goodly Work - there are nothing that benefit them if them didn't tell nor teach fe them childran.

[13] Like unto Daweet spoke sayin - 'Them didn't hide from them childran fe another child - an teach JAH praise - the wondrous miracles Him did - an Him Power' - there are nothing that benefit them if them didn't teach fe them childran that them might teach fe them childran fe mek heart like unto them knew - an that them might know an do Him Accord - an that them might tell them JAH LAW Trust - an that them might keep Him LAW like unto them faadas who made JAH Irie with them beautiful Work.

[14] An them who told them Trust from them faadas ina them infancy didn't demolish Him Command - like unto them faadas learned JAH Worship an the Nine Laws from them faadas.

[15] Them childran learned from them faadas that them might work goodly Work an might present praise fe them Irator - fe them have kept Him LAW - an fe them have loved Him.

[16] An Him shall hear them ina them priah - an Him won't ignore them plea - but Him are a Forgiver.

[17] Havin multiplied Him wrath - Him shall return it fe them - an Him wouldn't downstroy all ina Him chastisemant.

Chapter 20

[1] InI bredren - think - don't forget what them told unu formerly - that JAH keep the true Work of persons who work goodly Work.

[2] An Him multiply them childran ina this world - an them name invocation shall live firmed up fe a goodly thing up til the Iternity - an them childran won't be troubled fe grain ina this world.

[3] As Him shall dispute fe them becau them - an as Him won't cast them ina them enemy hand - Him shall save them from them enemies hand who hate them.

[4] An fe persons who love Him Name - Him shall be them Helper ina them tribulation time ~ Him shall guard them an pardon them all them sin.

Chapter 21

[1] Daweet believed ina JAH - fe Him have believed ina him - an Him saved him bein a Refuge from the king Sa'ol hand.

[2] An as him have believed ina Him an kept Him LAW pon the time when him child 'Abiesielom arose - an pon the time when the 'Iloflans arose - an pon the time when the 'Edomyans an the 'Amalieqans arose - pon the time when the one from the four Rafayn arose - JAH saved Daweet from all this tribulation that enemies who disputed him brought pon him.

[3] As prevailin are by JAH Accord - them were defeated by them enemies hand - yet but JAH didn't save the evil kings who didn't believe ina Him.

[4] An Hiziqyas believed ina JAH ~ Him saved him from Senakriem hand who were arrogant.

[5] But him child Minassie were defeated by him enemy hand - fe him didn't mek him trustin ina JAH ~ as him didn't mek him trustin ina JAH an as him didn't fear JAH Who totally honoured an famed him - them bound an took him toward them country - yet but those enemies who defeated Minassie weren't like unto him.

[6] At that time Him denied him the kingdom Him gave him - fe him didn't work goodly Work before him Irator JAH - that him era might abound an that Him might dispute him enemy fe him an that him might have Power an firmness behind an in front.

[7] Fe it are better fe believe ina JAH than ina many armies - than believin ina horses an bows an shields.

[8] Believin ina JAH surpass ~ a person who believed ina Him shall firm up an be honoured an totally lofty.

[9] Fe JAH don't favour fe a face - but persons who didn't believe ina JAH - who believed ina them money abundance - became them who departed from the grace an honour that Him gave them.

[10] Him shall guard the persons who believe ina Him - but Him shall mek the persons ignorant who call Him ignorant - an as them didn't discipline them reasonins fe follow JAH nor keep Him LAW - Him won't quickly help them ina them tribulation time nor ina the time them enemies disputed with them.

[11] But fe a person who were disciplined ina worshippin JAH an fe keep Him LAW - Him shall be a Refuge ina him tribulation time.

[12] By downstroyin him enemy - an by plunderin him enemy livestock - an by capturin him enemy country persons - an by rainin eras rain - an by growin sprouts - an by introducin the grain pile - ina the plant fruit...

[13] An by rainin the first an the spring rains - an by makin the grass verdant - an by givin the rain that rain at each time that thy kindreds beneath thy Itority might be Irie - Him shall mek him Irie.

[14] Him shall mek him Irie - that them might eat the other one money - that them might satta havin eaten the money them plundered from them enemy - that them might plunder animals an sheeps an cows - an that them might eat the other one dinnertable - an that them might tek them enemies childran captive.

[15] JAH shall do all this fe the person whom Him love - but Him will mek the person who hate Him fe him enemy ransackery.

[16] An Him shall bind him feet an him hands an shall cast him ina him enemy hand - an Him shall mek him fe him enemies derision - an as him have become a blood shedder who demolished JAH LAW - Him won't mek him Irie ina him house seed.

[17] An him won't firm up ina Judgemant time - an that Him might bring the hardship fe persons who work sin - Him will also give persons who work evil Work them sin hardship.

[18] But it were commanded from alongside JAH fe give persons who work goodly Work them reward - that Him might keep them ina Him Itority.

[19] Fe Him are empowered pon all the Iration Him Irated that Him might do goodly Work an might give them Iternal welfare an that them might praise JAH Who Irated them - an Him commanded that him might keep Him LAW ~ apart from only man there are none from all the Irations Him Irated that departed from Him Command.

[20] Like unto JAH commanded all who live firmed up ina each of them Works - them all know an are kept ina Him LAW.

[21] But man are emboldened pon JAH Who crowned all pon each of them inventions - pon animal an beasts an pon Heaven birds.

[22] Be it what are ina sea or all pon land - JAH gave all the Iration Him Irated fe them faada 'Adam ~ JAH gave them that him might do what him loved - an that them might eat them like unto grain that grew pon Earth - an that them might rule an tax them - an that be them beasts or animals them might be commanded fe man - an Him Ipointed them pon all Him Irated that persons who reigned might be commanded fe JAH Who gave them honour an that them might favour Him.

[23] But if them depart from Him LAW Him will separate them from the lordship Him gave them ~ as Him are Who rule Earth an Heaven - Him will give it fe him who do Him Accord.

[24] Him Ipoint whom Him loved fe Ipoint - but Him dismiss whom Him loved fe dismiss ~ Him kill ~ Him save ~ Him whip ina tribulation ~ Him forgive.

[25] There are no other Irator like unto Him ~ as Him are Ruler fe all the Iration Him Irated - as there are no other without Him - the Irator - ina Heaven above Earth nor pon Earth beneath Heaven - there are none who shall criticise Him.

[26] Him Ipoint ~ Him dismiss ~ Him kill ~ Him save ~ Him whip ina tribulation ~ Him forgive ~ Him impoverish ~ Him honour.

[27] Him hear persons who beg Him ina them plea ~ Him accept a person plea who do Him Accord with a clean reasonin; an Him hear them ina them priah - an Him do them accord fe them ina all that them begged Him.

[28] An Him mek the great an the small fe be commanded fe them ~ all this are them money pon hills an mountains an at trees roots an ina caves an Earth wells an all them kindreds pon both dry an sea.

[29] An fe persons who do them Irator Accord all this are them money - an Him won't trouble them from them plenty - an Him shall give them them praise reward.

[30] An Him shall give them the honour Him prepared ina Heaven fe them faadas Yis'haq an 'Abriham an Ya`iqob ~ Him shall give them what Him prepared fe Hiziqyas an Daweet an Samu'iel who didn't depart from Him LAW an Him Command.

[31] That them might be Irie ina Him Lordship - Him shall give them who served Him Iginnin from Antiquity the honour Him prepared fe them faadas Yis'haq an 'Abriham an Ya`iqob - fe whom Him swore fe give them a inheritance.

Chapter 22

[1] Please - think of persons name who work goodly Work - an don't forget them Work.

[2] Straighten up that thy name be called like unto them name - that thou might be Irie with them ina the Kingdom of Heaven - that were Light Lodgin that Him prepared fe nobles an kings who did JAH Accord an were kind persons.

[3] An again - know an be canvinced of evil nobles an kings names - that Him shall canvict them an revile them alongside man after them dead.

[4] Fe them didn't line up them Work while them sight up an heard - an know an be canvinced that unless them did JAH Accord - Him shall judge pon them ina the Kingdom of Heaven more than criminals an persons who forgot JAH LAW.

[5] Be kindly - innocent - honest - yet don't thou also go pon persons path who forgot JAH LAW - pon whom JAH vexed becau them evil Work.

[6] Judge Truth an save the child whose mother an faada dead pon him - an the widow from sinner persons hand who rob them.

[7] Be a guardian like unto him faada fe the child whose mother an faada dead pon him - that thou might save him from the wealthy one hand who rob him - an stand fe him - an be alarmed pon the time the child - whose mother an faada dead pon him - tears flowed before thee-I - lest thou be alarmed ina fiyah sea where sinner persons who didn't enter repentance are punished.

[8] An straighten up thy feet toward Love an Inity path ~ as JAH Eyes check up Him friends - an as Him Ears hear them plea - seek Love an follow she.

[9] But JAH Face of Him Wrath are toward persons who work evil Work - that Him might downstroy them name invocation from this world - an Him won't preserve a person who near pon ramparts nor mountains.

[10] As I-man am JAH Who am jealous pon I Godhood - as I-man am a Irator who revenge an downstroy persons who hate I an don't keep I Word - I-man won't return I Face of Support reachin up til I-man downstroy the person who don't keep I Word.

[11] An I-man shall honour persons who honour I an keep I Word.

Chapter 23

[1] Don't live firmed up ina Qayel order - who killed him bredda who followed him ina innocence - it seemin fe him that him bredda love him.

[2] An him killed him bredda envyin pon a dawta ~ persons who mek envy an iniquity an betrayal pon them companion are like unto him.

[3] But as 'Abiel are innocent like unto a sheep - an as him blood are like unto the clean sheep blood that them sacrificed fe JAH by a clean reasonin - them went pon Qayel path that aren't pon 'Abiel path.

[4] Fe becau all the persons who live ina innocence were persons whom JAH love - like unto a kind man 'Abiel - them have been innocent ones like unto 'Abiel - but those persons who live firmed up ina 'Abiel Work love JAH.

[5] But JAH neglect evil ones - an them Definite Judgemant mek application fe them pon them bodies - an it are written pon the record of them reasonins - an pon the time when Judgemant are judged - them shall read she before man an Angels an before all the Iration.

[6] At that time them shall shame ~ wrongdoers an refusers who didn't do JAH Accord shall shame.

[7] An a alarmin Word shall be given them that say - Place them ina *Gehannem* where are no exit up til Iternity.

Chapter 24

[1] But pon the time Giediewon trusted JAH - him defeated uncircumcise peoples armies who were many many ina army of a few tens of thousands an without number like unto locusts.

[2] As there are no Irator without I - o nobles an kings - don't believe ina the different idols.

[3] As I-man am your Irator JAH Who sent unu forth from your mothers wombs an raised unu an fed unu an clothed unu - why do unu pretext? How about why do unu worship other idols without I?

[4] I-man did all this fe unu ~ what did unu give I? It are that unu might live firmed up ina I LAW an I Order an I Command an that I-man might give unu your bodies welfare - yet what will I-man want from unu?

[5] JAH Who rule all said thus ~ Him said - Save your ras selves from worshippin idols an practisin sorcery an discouragin pessimism.

[6] As JAH chastisemant shall come pon these who do this - an pon them who hear them an do them accord an are them friends an who live firmed up ina them command - save your ras selves from worshippin idols.

[7] As peoples - who don't know unu an aren't nice fe unu - shall arise pon unu - unless unu who feared did JAH Accord - them will eat the money wherefor unu wearied ~ like unto Him servants the prophets spoke an like unto Hienok spoke an like unto 'Asaf spoke - unless unu did JAH Accord - them will eat the money wherefor unu wearied.

[8] Evil persons will come havin changed them clothes Him said ~ there are no other law alongside them apart from eatin an drinkin an adornin ina silver an gold - an livin havin firmed up ina sin all the Work JAH don't love.

[9] But them are prepared fe go toward drink an food ~ after them were aroused from them slumber Iginnin from mornin up til evenin them go toward evil Work; there are misery an tribulation ina them path - yet them feet have no Love path.

[10] An them don't know Love an Inity Work - an there are no fearin JAH ina them faces ~ them are crooked evil ones without religion nor virtue ~ them are greedy ones who eat an drink alone ~ them are drunkards - an them sin are without LAW an without measure ~ them are who go toward seducin - sheddin blood - theft an perfidy an violently robbin him money who don't have it.

[11] An them are who criticise without Love an without LAW - fe them don't fear JAH Who Irated them - an there are no fear ina them faces.

[12] Them don't shame ina the person face that them sight up - an them don't shame a grey-hair nor a elder face ~ pon the time them heard when them said - 'An there are money ina this world' - them mek it them ras self money before them sight it up with them eyes - fe there are no fearin JAH ina them faces - an pon the time them sight it up with them eyes it seem fe them that them ate it.

[13] An them nobles eat trust money ~ them are who eat ~ as them are negativists an as there are no straight thing ina them tongues - them don't repeat ina evenin what them spoke ina mornin.

[14] Fe them ignore sufferahs an poor ones cries - an them kings hasten fe evil - them who downsturb a person - him havin saved refugees from wealthy ones hands who rob them.

[15] Mek them save him who were wronged an the refugee - yet mek the kings not be them who begrudge justice becaudis thing.

[16] But them are who exact tribute ~ them are who rob a person money - an them are criminals - an as them Work are evil - them aren't nice when them eat the newborn calf with she mother an a bird with she egg ~ them mek all them sight up an heard them ras self money.

[17] Them love that them might gather fe them ras selves - yet them aren't nice fe sick an poor ones - an them violently rob the money of a person who don't have it - an them gather all them found that them might be fattened an be Irie ina it.

[18] Fe them shall perish quickly like unto a scarab that proceeded from it pit an whose track aren't found an that don't return toward it house - an becau them didn't work goodly Work when them are ina them Life - woe fe them bodies pon the time JAH vexed an seized them.

[19] Pon the time JAH neglected them - them will perish at one time like unto them are ina one chastisemant - fe Him indure them meanin as it were them returned toward repentance - yet Him don't quickly downstroy them - an them shall perish pon the time when them shall perish.

[20] But if them don't return toward repentance - Him will quickly downstroy them like unto former persons who were precedin them - who didn't keep JAH LAW by what are due.

[21] Them are who eat a person flesh an drink a person blood ~ as them gird an work violence fe go toward sin - there are no fearin JAH ina them faces everytime - an after them arose from them beddin them don't rest fe work sin.

[22] An them Work are drink an food - goin toward downstruction an sin - that them might downstroy many persons bodies ina this world.

Chapter 25

[1] As them Work are crooked - an as all are who live firmed up ina Seythan Work that mislead - JAH Who rule all said - Woe fe your body pon the time I-man vexed an seized she.

[2] But fe them don't know JAH Work - fe them have returned it toward them rear - an fe them have neglected I LAW.

[3] An later ina fulfillmant era I-man shall bring the hardship pon them like unto them evil measure ~ like unto them sin were written alongside I - I-man shall revenge an downstroy them pon the day when Judgemant are judged.

[4] As I-man JAH am full from horizon up til horizon - an as all the Iration have been seized ina I Itority - there are none who escape from I Itority ina Heaven nor Earth nor depth nor sea.

[5] I-man command a snake that are beneath Earth - an I-man command a fish that are within sea - an I-man command birds ina Heaven - an I-man command the desert donkey ina wilderness - fe it are I money Iginnin from horizon up til horizon.

[6] As I-man am Who work wondrous Work an do miracles before I - there are none who escape from I Itority pon Earth nor ina Heaven ~ there are none who tell I - 'Where do Thou go? How about what do thou Work?'

[7] An I-man command pon Angels chiefs an hosts ~ all Irations whose name are called are I money - an beasts ina wilderness an all birds ina Heaven an livestocks are I moneys.

[8] It arise from 'Azieb wind an firm up ina drought ina Mesi` - later ina fulfillmant era 'Eritra sea shall perish bein heard - arisin from JAH - Who shall come toward she - bein feared an famousness.

[9] Fe Him rule them who dead an persons who are there - an she shall perish bein heard with Saba an Noba an Hindekie an 'Ityopphya limits an all them regions.

[10] An Him watch all ina lofty Itority an innocence - fe Him Itority surpass all the itority - an Him keep cangregations ina Him Itority.

[11] An fe Him Itority firm up more than all the itority - an fe Him Kingdom surpass all the kingdoms - an fe Him Itority are what rule all the world - fe Him able fe all - an fe there are nothing that fail Him.

[12] Him rule all clouds ina Heaven ~ Him grow grass fe livestocks pon Earth - an Him give fruit pon the buds.

[13] Him feed fe all ina each of the kinds like unto Him loved ~ Him feed all that Him Irated by each of the fruits an each of the foods - an Him feed ants an locusts beneath Earth an livestocks pon Earth an beasts - an fe a person who prayed Him give him him priah - an Him don't ignore the plea of the child whose mother an faada dead pon him - nor widows.

[14] As evil persons rebellion are like unto a swirlin wind an wrongdoers council like unto misty urine - Him shall rather accept the plea of them who beg toward Him at each time an clean ones.

[15] An as them body are like unto a flyin bird - an as them features comeliness that are silver an gold are perishable ina this world - examination will benefit persons who forgot JAH LAW yet not them gold - an moths shall eat them clothes.

[16] An weevils shall totally eat the wheat an the barley fatness - an all shall pass like unto the day that passed yesterday - an like unto a word that proceeded from a mouth don't return - sinner persons money also are like unto it - an them 'beautiful lifestyle' are like unto a passin shadow ~ sinner persons money before JAH are like unto a lie clothes.

[17] But if kind persons are honoured JAH won't ignore them - fe them have been honoured while them were nice fe poor ones - an them hear justice of sufferahs an a child whose mother an faada dead pon him ~ JAH won't ignore them - fe without neglectin them house childran - them honour Him while them clothe the naked from the clothes JAH gave them that them might give fe the refugee sufferah.

[18] Them don't favour loyal persons judgemant - an them don't mek a hireling salary lodge ~ as JAH thing are Truth an honoured like unto a sword whose mouths were two - them won't do iniquity ina them seasons number an ina them balance measuremant.

Chapter 26

[1] But poor ones will think again pon them beddin - but if wealthy ones don't accept them - them will be like unto dry wood that have no verdure - an a root won't be fertile from alongside where no moisture are - an the leaf won't be fertile if there are no root.

[2] As a leaf serve a flower fe be a ornamant fe fruit - unless the leaf were fertile it won't bear fruit ~ as man fulfillmant are religion - a person without religion have no virtue.

[3] If him firmed up religion him worked virtue - an JAH are Irie by a person who work Truth an straight Work.

[4] An fe the person who begged Him - Him shall give him him plea an him tongue reward - an Him won't wrong the true person becau him true Work that him worked.

[5] As JAH are true - an as Him have loved a Truth thing - Him won't justify the sinner person without repentance becau the Work evil him worked - an as all persons souls have been seized ina Him Itority becau Him were Who ruled Earth an Heaven - as Him won't favour for the wealthy more than the poor ina Judgemant time - Him won't justify him without repentance.

Chapter 27

[1] Him Irated havin brought all the world from not livin toward livin - an Him totally prepared hills an mountains - an Him firmed up Earth pon Water - an lest sea be shaken Him delineated she by sand - fe ina Him first Word JAH have said Mek Light be Irated.

[2] Light were Irated when this world had been covered ina darkness ~ JAH Irated all the Iration - an Him prepared this world - an Him firmed up this world by what are due an by money that are straight ~ Him said - Mek evenin be dark.

[3] An again JAH said Mek Light be Irated ~ it dawned an there were Light - an Him Ilivated the upper Water toward Heaven.

[4] An Him streached it forth like unto a tent - an Him firmed it up by a wind - an Him placed the lower Water within a pit.

[5] An Him shut the sea lock ina sand - an Him firmed them up ina Him Itority lest them drown ina Water - an Him placed animals an beasts within she - an Him placed within she Liewatan an Biehiemot who were great beasts - an Him placed within she the beasts without number - sight up an not sight up.

[6] Pon the third day JAH Irated pon Earth plants - all the roots an woods an fruits that bear forth ina each of them kinds - an a welfare wood beautiful fe them fe sight it up..

[7] An Him Irated a welfare wood that were both beautiful fe them fe sight it up an sweet fe them fe eat it - an Him Irated grass - an all plants whose seeds are found from within them - fe be food fe birds an livestocks an beasts.

[8] It dusked ~ it dawned - an pon the fourth day Him said - Mek Light be Irated ina Heaven called cosmos ~ JAH havin Irated moon an Sun an stars - Him placed them ina Heaven called cosmos that them might shine ina this world an that them might feed them daylight an night.

[9] An after this moon an Sun an stars alternated ina night an daylight.

[10] An pon the fifth day JAH Irated all animals an beasts that live within Water an all birds that fly pon Heaven - all that are sight up an not sight up - all this.

[11] An pon the sixth day Him Irated livestocks an beasts an others - an havin Irated an prepared all - Him Irated 'Adam ina Him Example an Him Appearance.

[12] Him gave him all animals an beasts Him Irated that him might reign pon them - an again - all animals an beasts an all fishes - an Liewatan an Biehiemot that are ina sea.

[13] An Him gave him all cows that live ina this world an sheeps - the animals not sight up an them that are sight up.

[14] An Him placed ina Garden 'Adam whom Him Irated ina Him Example an Him Appearance - that him might eat an might cultivate plants an might praise JAH there.

[15] An fe lest him demolish Him Command - Him have said - Pon the time when unu ate from this Herb of Fig unu will dead death.

[16] An Him commanded him lest him eat from the Herb of Fig that bring death - that draw attention fe evil an good - that bring death.

[17] InI mother Hiewan were cajoled by a snake misleadin an she ate from that Herb of Fig an gave it fe InI faada 'Adam.

[18] An 'Adam havin eaten from that Herb of Fig brought death pon him childran an pon him ras self.

[19] As him have demolished Him Command - an as him have eaten from that Herb of Fig that JAH commanded sayin - Don't eat from she - JAH vexed pon InI faada 'Adam an expelled an sent him way from the Garden - an Him gave him that Earth that grow thistle an thorn - that Him cursed becau him pon the time him demolished Him Command - that him might eat him weariness reward havin toiled an laboured that him might plow she.

[20] An pon the time JAH sent him forth toward this land - 'Adam returned toward complete sadness - an havin toiled an laboured that him might plow Earth - him began fe eat ina weariness an also ina struggles.

Chapter 28

[1] An after him childran lived havin abounded - there were from them ones who praise an honour JAH an don't demolish Him Command.

[2] There were prophets who spoke what were done an what will be done henceforth - an from him childran there were sinners who speak lies an who wrong persons ~ 'Adam firstborn child Qayel became evil an killed him bredda 'Abiel.

[3] JAH judged Judgemant pon Qayel becau him killed him bredda 'Abiel - an JAH vexed pon Earth becau she drank him blood.

[4] An JAH told Qayel - Where are thy bredda 'Abiel? - an Qayel ina him heart arrogance said - 'Are mi mi bredda 'Abiel keeper?'

[5] 'Abiel became a clean man - but Qayel became a sinner man by killin a kind man - him bredda 'Abiel.

[6] Again a kind child Siet were birthed ~ 'Adam birthed sixty childran ~ there are kind persons an evil persons from them.

[7] An there are kind persons from them ~ an there are persons who were prophets an them who were traitors an sinners.

[8] There are blessed persons who were kind persons - who fulfill them faada 'Adam accord an all him told fe him child Siet - Iginnin from 'Adam up til Noh who are a kind man who kept JAH LAW.

[9] An him sanctioned JAH LAW fe him childran ~ him told them - 'Guard' - lest them demolish JAH LAW - an that them might tell fe them childran like unto them faada Noh told them - an that them might keep JAH LAW.

[10] An them lived while them taught them childran - persons birthed after them.

[11] But Seythan lived when him spoke fe them faadas - havin lodged ina idols that reached fe a grave an that have vows pon them - an havin defeated the persons who told him alright - an when them did all that Seythan - who are sin teacher - commanded them.

[12] An them lived when them worshipped the idols like unto them order - up til a kind man 'Abriham who fulfill JAH Accord.

[13] Fe him have lived firmed up ina the LAW beforehand separate from him cousins - an JAH swore a oath with him - havin lodged ina wind an fiyah.

[14] JAH swore fe him that Him might give him a land of inheritance an that Him might give fe him childran up til the Iternity.

[15] An Him swore fe Yis'haq like unto him that Him might give him him faada 'Abriham inheritance - an Him swore fe Ya`iqob that Him might give him him faada Yis'haq inheritance ~ Him swore fe him like into Yis'haq.

[16] An Him separated them childran - who were birthed after them from Ya`iqob - from the twelve tribes of 'Isra'iel - an made them priests an kings ~ Him blessed them sayin - Abound an totally be many many.

[17] An Him gave them them faada inheritance - however while Him fed them an loved them - them didn't quit saddenin JAH ina all.

[18] An pon the time Him downstroyed them - at that time them will seek Him ina worship - an them will return from sin an go toward JAH - fe Him love them - an JAH shall pardon them.

[19] Fe bein nice fe all Him Irated - Him shall pardon them - an it are becau them faadas Work that Him love them - yet it aren't becau them ras selves Work.

[20] An Him streach forth Him Right Hand ina plenty that Him might satta a hungry body - an Him reveal Him Eye fe pardonin that Him might multiply grain fe food.

[21] Him give food fe crows chicks an fe beasts that beg Him ~ pon the time them cried toward Him - Him will save 'Isra'iel childran from them enemies hands who delayed from the time.

[22] An them will return toward sin again that them might sadden Him - an Him will arouse them enemies peoples ina them area pon them ~ them will downstroy them an kill them an capture them.

[23] An again them will shout toward JAH ina mournin an sadness - an there are the time when Him sent help an saved them by prophets hands.

[24] An there are the time when Him saved them by princes hands - an pon the time them saddened JAH them enemies taxed them an captured them.

[25] An Daweet arose an saved them from the 'Iloflans hands; an again them saddened JAH - an JAH aroused pon them peoples who worry them.

[26] An there are the time when Him saved them by Yoftahie hand - an again them forgot JAH Who saved them ina them tribulation time. As JAH have brought the hardship pon them - Him will arouse pon them enemies who were evil who will firm up tribulation pon them an totally capture them.

[27] An pon the time them were worried by tribulation them were seized an again cried toward Him - an Him saved them by Giediewon hand - an again them saddened JAH by them hands Work.

[28] An again Him aroused pon them peoples who firm up tribulation pon them - an them returned an wept an cried toward JAH.

[29] An again Him saved them from peoples by Somson hand - an them rested a likkle from the tribulation. An them arose that them might sadden JAH by them former sin.

[30] An again Him aroused pon them other peoples who worry them - an again them cried an wept toward JAH that Him might send help fe them - an Him saved them from peoples by Bariq an Deebora hands.

[31] Again them lived a likkle season while them worshipped JAH - an again them forgot JAH ina them former sin an saddened Him.

[32] An Him aroused pon them other peoples who worry them - an again Him saved them by Yodeet hand; an havin sat again a likkle season them arose that them might sadden JAH by them sin like unto formerly.

[33] An Him aroused pon them peoples who rule them - an them cried an wept toward JAH; fe Him have struck pon him head 'Abiemieliek who were a warrior who came that him might fight Yihuda country.

[34] An Him saved them by the childran ina the area an by Matatyu hand - an pon the time that warrior dead him army fled an were scattared - an 'Isra'iel childran followed an fought them up til 'Iyabboq - an them didn't preserve even one person from them.

[35] After this them waited a likkle an arose that them might sadden JAH - an Him aroused pon them peoples who rule them - an again them totally cried toward JAH; an JAH ignored them cryin an them mournin - fe them have saddened JAH everytime - an fe them have demolished Him LAW.

[36] An them captured an took them with them priests toward Babilon persons country.

[37] An then 'Isra'iel childran who were traitors didn't quit saddenin JAH while them worked sin an worshipped idols.

[38] JAH vexed that Him might downstroy them one time ina them sin ~ Hama havin introduced ten thousand gold ina the king box - pon the day when it were known - him lodged anger ina the king 'Arthieksis reasonin - lest him preserve them childran ina Fars country Iginnin from Hindekie an up til 'Ityopphya pon the time him told him that him might downstroy them.

[39] Him did thus - an him wrote a letter where a message were written by the king authority - an him gave him a seal ina him hand that him might deliver toward Fars country.

[40] Him gave him a seal that him might downstroy them pon one day when him loved them fe downstroy them like unto the king commanded - but him commanded that him might introduce them money - the gold an the silver - toward the king box.

[41] An pon the time 'Isra'iel childran heard this thing them totally cried an wept toward JAH - an them told it fe Merdokyos - an Merdokyos told fe 'Astier.

[42] An 'Astier said - 'Fast - beg - an all 'Isra'iel childran kindreds - cry toward JAH ina the place where unu are.'

[43] An Merdokyos wore sackcloth an sprinkled dust pon him ras self - an 'Isra'iel childran fasted - begged - an entered repentance ina the country where them were.

[44] An 'Astier were totally sad - an bein a queen she wore sackcloth ~ she sprinkled dust an shaved she head - an she didn't anoint perfume like unto Fars queens anoint perfume - an ina she deep reasonin she cried an wept toward she faadas Irator JAH.

[45] An becaudis thing Him gave she bein loved alongside Fars king 'Arthieksis - an she made a kind lunch fe she faadas Irator.

[46] An Hama an the king entered toward the lunch that 'Astier prepared - an like unto him loved that him might do pon Merdokyos - JAH paid the hardship pon that Hama - an them hanged him pon a tall wood.

[47] The king letter were commanded that them might quit 'Isra'iel like unto them were ina all them accord - an lest them tax them nor rob them nor wrong them nor tek them money pon them.

[48] As JAH shall pardon 'Isra'iel doin thus pon the time them cried enterin repentance - it are that them might love them an honour them ina Fars country where them lived - yet a king letter were commanded lest them downstroy them country nor plunder them livestocks.

[49] An pon them time them saddened Him - Him will arouse pon them peoples who worry them ~ at that time them will totally weep an cry that Him might send them help fe them an that Him might save them from peoples hand who firm up tribulation pon them.

Chapter 29

[1] An pon the time Gibts persons also made 'Isra'iel childran work by makin them work bricks ina difficulty - an pon the time them worried them all the Work by kickin mud without straw an heatin bricks...

[2] An pon the time them made them work havin appointed chiefs pon them who rush workers - them cried toward JAH that Him might save them from workin all Gibts bricks.

[3] At that time Him sent fe them 'Aron an Mussie who help them - fe JAH have sent them that them might send forth Him kindreds from Fer`on rulership house - an Him saved them from brick Work ~ becau ina him arrogance him refused fe adjourn 'Isra'iel lest them be ruled an sacrifice sacrifice fe JAH ina wilderness - JAH have sent them that them might send forth Him kindreds 'Isra'iel from Gibts king Fer`on rulership house - an them saved them.

[4] Fe JAH neglect arrogant ones - an Him drowned Fer`on ina 'Eritra sea with him army becau him arrogance.

[5] An like unto him - Him shall downstroy them who didn't work goodly Work ina all the kingdoms that Him I-pointed an crowned them - that them who ignore JAH Word when them are nobles an kings might fulfill Him Accord fe Him - an that them might give persons who serve ina goodly thing them wage - an that them might honour Him famous Name.

[6] JAH Who rule all said - But if them will straighten up I Kingdom - I-man will straighten up them kingdom fe them.

[7] Work goodly Work fe I - an I-man shall work goodly Work fe unu ~ keep I LAW - an I-man shall keep unu your bodies ~ live firmed up ina I LAW - an I-man shall live lodgin honesty ina unu like unto your reasonin.

[8] Love I - an I-man shall love your welfare ~ near toward I - an I-man shall heal unu.

[9] JAH Who rule all said - Believe ina I - an I-man shall save unu from the tribulation.

[10] Don't live side by side ~ as JAH Who rule all love straight Work - Him said - Unu - approach toward I - an I-man shall approach toward unu ~ unu persons who are sinners an traitors - cleanse your hands from sin - an distance your reasonins from evil.

[11] An I-man shall distance I anger from unu - an I-man shall return fe unu ina Charity an Forgiveness.

[12] I-man shall distance criminals an enemies who work iniquity from unu - like unto I-man saved I slave Daweet from him enemies who met him - from them much malice - an from Gwolyad hand who were a warrior - an also from Sa'ol hand who sought that him might kill him - an from him child 'Abiesielom hand who loved that him might tek him kingdom.

[13] I-man shall save persons who keep I LAW an fulfill I Accord like unto him ~ I-man shall bequeath them honour - an them shall be Irie ina the present world an yonder ina the world that shall come ~ I-man shall crown them pon all that them might be Irie.

[14] Them shall be one with kings who served JAH an were honoured ina them beautiful way of Life - like unto the prophet Samu'iel served Him ina him beautiful way of Life Iginnin from him infancy - whom JAH - Him bein LAW - chose.

[15] Him told him that him might tell 'Elee who were a servant elder - an when him served ina JAH Lodgin the Temple - Samu'iel Work also were merciful an I-loved.

[16] An pon the time him grew when him served ina JAH Lodgin the Temple - Him made him fe be Ipointed an Inointed - that him might Ipoint him people an that kings might be Inointed by JAH Accord. As JAH have loved him that the kindred him chose from 'Isra'iel childran might be Ipointed - pon the time him fulfilled JAH Accord Who Irated him - Him gave him the Inointin of the Kingdom ina him hand.

[17] An when Sa'ol were ina him kingdom JAH told Him prophet Samu'iel - Go - an as I-man have loved `Issiey child Daweet who were birthed from Yihuda kin - Inoint him.

Chapter 30

[1] I-man have hated Sa'ol kin - fe him have saddened I becau him violated I Word.

[2] An I-man neglected him - fe him didn't keep I LAW - an I-man won't crown from him kin again.

[3] An persons who didn't keep I LAW an I Word an I Order like unto him - I-man shall downstroy I Kingdom an I gift from them childran up til the Iternity.

[4] An as them didn't mek I famous pon the time I-man made them famous - I-man shall downstroy them - yet I-man won't again return fe lift them up ~ though I-man honour them - as them didn't honour I - I-man won't mek them famous.

[5] Fe them didn't do a goodly thing fe I pon the time I-man did a goodly thing fe them - an fe them didn't forgive I pon the time I-man forgave them.

[6] An as them didn't mek I a Ruler pon the time I-man made them rulers pon all - as them didn't honour I pon the time I-man honoured them more than all - I-man won't mek them famous again nor honour them - an fe them didn't keep I LAW.

[7] An I-man withheld the gift I-man gave them - an I-man won't return the money I-man withheld from them like unto the measure I-man vexed an swore ~ JAH Who rule all said thus ~ Him said - I-man shall honour them who honoured I - an love them who loved I.

[8] I-man shall separate them who didn't honour I nor keep I LAW from the gift I-man gave them.

[9] JAH Who rule all said; I-man love them who loved I - an mek famous him who made I famous - Him said..

[10] As I-man JAH am Who rule all - there are none who escape I Itority ina Earth nor Heaven - fe I-man am JAH Who kill an Who save an Who sadden an Who forgive.

[11] As famousness an honour are I money - I-man honour him whom I-man loved - fe I-man am Who judge an Who revenge an downstroy - an I-man mek wretched him whom I-man hated.

[12] Fe I-man am Who forgive them who love I an call I Name everytime - fe I-man am Who feed food fe the wealthy an fe the poor.

[13] An I-man feed birds an animals - fishes ina sea an beasts an flowers - yet I-man aren't Who feed only man.

[14] I-man feed crocodiles an whales - gophers an hippos - an badgers...

[15] an all that live within Water - all that fly pon wind - yet I-man aren't Who feed only man ~ all this are I money.

[16] I-man am Who feed all that seek I by all that are due an I-loved.

Chapter 31

[1] An the kings don't reign without I Accord - an sufferahs are by I Command - yet them aren't poor without I Command - an powerful ones are by I Accord - yet them aren't strong without I Accord.

[2] I-man gave bein I-loved fe Daweet an Wisdom fe Selomon - an I-man added eras fe Hiziqyas.

[3] I-man diminished Gwolyad era - an I-man gave Power fe Somson - an again I-man weakened him Power.

[4] An I-man saved I slave Daweet from Gwolyad hand who were a warrior.

[5] An again I-man saved him from the king Sa'ol hand an from the secand warrior who disputed him - an fe him have kept I Command - an I-man saved him from the persons hand who dispute him an fight him.

[6] An I-man loved him - an I-man love all the nobles an the kings who keep I LAW ~ as them have made I Irie - I-man shall give them prevailin an Power pon them enemies.

[7] An again that them might inherit them faadas land - I-man shall give them the cleansed an shinin land of inheritance that I-man swore fe them faadas.

Chapter 32

[1] JAH Who rule all said - An unu the nobles an also the kings - hear I ina I Word - an keep I Command ~ lest unu sadden I an worship like unto 'Isra'iel childran saddened I an worshipped different idols - them whom I-man kept an saved when I-man JAH am them Irator - JAH Who rule all said - Hear I ina I Word; an all whom I-man raised an loved an fed Iginnin that them were birthed from them mother an faada.

[2] An whom I-man sent forth toward Earth crops - an whom I-man fed the fatness found from Earth makin like unto are due - an whom I-man gave the grape vine an the oil-tree fruit that them didn't plant an the clear Water well that them didn't dig.

[3] Hear I ina I Word lest unu sadden I like unto 'Isra'iel childran saddened I worshippin other idols when I-man JAH am them Irator - Him told them - Who fed them the sheep milk an the honey comb with the hulled wheat - an Who clothed them clothes where ornamant are - an Who gave them all them love.

[4] An without it livin that I-man deprived them all them begged I.

Chapter 33

[1] Like unto Daweet spoke sayin - "Isra'iel childran were fed the menna that Angels lowered' - an again hear I ina I Word lest unu sadden I like unto 'Isra'iel childran saddened I worshippin the idols when I-man am them Irator JAH Who fed them sweet *menna* ina wilderness - Him said ~ I-man did all this fe them that them might worship I by what are due an fe true.

[2] JAH Who rule all said - But them didn't worship I - an I-man neglected them ~ them saddened I an lived firmed up ina law of idols that weren't I LAW.

[3] An I-man shall bring the hardship pon them like unto them sin ~ as them have neglected I Worship an as them didn't firm up ina I counsel an I Order - I-man neglected them ina the sin measure that them worked by them hands - an I-man shall lower them toward *Gehannem* ina Definite Judgemant that are done ina Heaven.

[4] Fe them didn't keep I LAW - an fe I-man vex pon them - an I-man shall diminish them era ina this world.

[5] If thou be a king - aren't thou a man who shall dead an be demolished an tomorrow who shall be worms an dust?

[6] But today thou boast an are proud like unto a man who won't dead foriva.

[7] JAH Who rule all said - But thou who are sight up bein well today are a man who will dead tomorrow.

[8] But if unu keep I Command an I Word - I-man shall bequeath thee-I a honoured country with honoured kings who did I Accord - whose lodgin were Light an whose crowns were beautiful - an whose thrones were silver an gold an whom persons who sit pon them adorned - Him said.

[9] An them shall be Irie within Him country that are a place that approached fe persons who worked goodly Work.

[10] But fe persons who work sin - as them didn't keep I LAW - said JAH Who rule all...

[11] it aren't due them that them might enter toward that country where honoured kings shall enter.

Chapter 34

[1] Miedon kingdom shall perish - but Rom kingdom shall totally firm up pon Meqiedonya kingdom - an Nenewie kingdom shall firm up pon Fars kingdom.

[2] An 'Ityopphya kingdom shall firm up pon 'Iskindriya kingdom ~ as peoples shall arise - Mo`ab kingdom shall firm up pon 'Amalieq kingdom.

[3] An bredda shall arise pon him bredda - an JAH shall revenge an downstroy like unto Him spoke that it might perish.

[4] Kingdom shall arise pon kingdom - an the people pon the people an country pon country - Him said.

[5] An argumants shall be done an there shall be formations - famine - plague - earthquake - drought ~ as Love have perished from this world - JAH chastisemant downscended pon she.

[6] Fe the day have arrived suddenly when JAH shall come - Who frighten like unto lightnin that are sight up from East up til West.

[7] Pon the day when HIM JAH judge Judgemant - at that time everyone shall raceive him hardship like unto him hand weakness an him sin firmness - fe Him have said I-man shall revenge them pon the day when HIM JAH judge Judgemant an pon the day when them feet are hindered - fe the day when them are counted fe downstruction have arrived.

[8] At that time JAH shall downstroy ina *Gehannem* foriva persons who won't live firmed up ina Him LAW - who work sin.

[9] An them who live ina the West ilands an Noba an Hindekie - Saba an 'Ityopphya an Gibts persons - all persons who live ina them...

[10] at that time shall know I that I-man were JAH Who rule Earth an Heaven - an Who give bein I-loved an honour - an Who save an Who kill.

[11] I-man am Who send forth Sun - Who send it toward it settin - Who bring the evil an the good.

[12] I-man am Who bring peoples whom unu don't know - who slaughter an eat the money whereby unu wearied - your sheeps an your cows flocks.

[13] An them shall capture your childran while them hammer them before unu - an unu cyaan save them. Becau JAH Spirit of Support didn't lodge ina unu - as unu didn't fear JAH Command that unu heard - Him shall downstroy your lavishmants an your assignmants.

[14] But a person ina whom JAH Spirit of Support lodged will know all - like unto Nabukedenetsor told Dan'iel sayin - 'Mi sight up JAH Spirit of Support that lodged ina thee-I.'

[15] An a person ina whom JAH Spirit of Support lodged will know all - an what were hidden will be revealed fe him - an him will know all that were revealed an that were hidden - yet there are nothing hidden from a person ina whom JAH Spirit of Support lodged.

[16] But as InI are persons who will dead tomorrow - InI sins that InI hid an worked shall be revealed.

[17] An like unto them test silver an gold ina fiyah - like unto there are sinners - later pon the Day of Advent them shall be examined - fe them didn't keep JAH Command.

[18] At that time all peoples an all 'Isra'iel childran Works shall be examined.

Chapter 35

[1] As JAH vex pon unu becau unu didn't judge a Truth Judgemant fe the child whose mother an faada dead pon him - woe fe unu 'Isra'iel nobles.

[2] Woe fe unu persons who go toward a drinkin house mornin an evenin an get drunk - who are partial ina judgemant - an who don't hear the widow justice nor the child whose mother an faada dead pon him - who live ina sin an seducin.

[3] JAH told 'Isra'iel nobles sayin thus: - Unless unu lived firmed up ina I Command an kept I LAW an loved what I-man love - woe fe unu - Him told them.

[4] An I-man shall bring downstruction an chastisemant an tribulation pon unu - an unu will perish like unto what weevils an moths ate - an your tracks an your region won't be found - Him told them.

[5] An your country will be a wilderness - an all persons who sight she up formerly shall clap them hands ~ them shall marvel pon she while them said - 'Weren't this country filled of she plenty an all who love it?; JAH made she thus by persons sin who live ina she.'

[6] Them shall say - 'As she have made she heart proud - an as she have ilivated she ras self - an as she have firmed up she collar of reasonin up til JAH mek she wretched pon Earth - an as she shall be a desert by persons arrogance who live ina she - an as thorns have grown pon she with thistles - woe fe she.'

[7] An she grow weeds an nettles - an she became a wilderness an a desert - an beasts shall live within she.

[8] Fe JAH Judgemant have firmed up pon she - an fe she shall raceive JAH Judgemant Chalice becau she reasonin arrogance by persons sin who live ina she - an she became frightenin fe persons who go toward she.

Chapter 36

[1] Meqiedon persons - don't boast ~ as JAH are there Who shall downstroy unu - 'Amalieqans - don't firm up your collar of reasonin.

[2] Fe unu will be lofty up til Heaven an unu will downscend up til *Gehannem*.

[3] Pon the time 'Isra'iel formerly entered toward Gibts country ina Mo`ab an Miedon kingdom Him said - Don't boast - fe it aren't due fe pretend pon JAH that unu might pretend pon Him.

[4] Thou Yisma'iel kindred - slave child - why do thou firm up thy collar of reasonin by what weren't thy money? How about don't thou think that JAH shall judge pon thee pon the time Him arose that it might be judged pon Earth - pon the day when it are judged pon thee?

[5] JAH Who rule all said - At that time thou will raceive thy hardship like unto thy hand Work - how about why do thou ilivate thy reasonin? How about why do thou firm up thy collar of reasonin?

[6] An I-man shall pretend pon thee like unto thou pretended pon persons who weren't thy kindreds - fe thou do what thou love that thou might work sin - an I-man shall neglect thee ina the place where them sent thee.

[7] JAH Who rule all said - An I-man shall do thus pon thee ~ Him said - But if thou worked goodly Work an if thou love what I-man loved - I-man also shall hear thee-I ina all that thou begged.

[8] An if thou fulfill I Accord fe I - I-man shall fulfill thy accord fe thee-I - an I-man shall dispute thy enemies fe thee-I - an I-man shall bless thy childran an thy seed fe thee-I.

[9] An I-man shall multiply thy sheeps an thy cows flocks fe thee-I - an if thou lived firmed up ina I Command an also if thou did what I-man love - JAH Who rule all said - I-man shall bless fe thee-I all thou seized ina thy hand.

[10] But if thou don't do I Accord - if thou don't live firmed up ina I LAW an I Command - all this tribulation that were told formerly shall find thee - fe thou didn't indure tribulation firmed up ina I Command - an fe thou didn't live firmed up ina I LAW - an thou cyaan escape from I anger that will come pon thee everytime.

[11] An as thou didn't love what I-man loved - when I-man am Who Irated thee bringin from not livin toward livin...

[12] all this were thy money - that thou might kill an heal fe do all that thou loved - that thou might work an demolish - that thou might honour an abuse - that thou might ilivate an downbase - an as thou have neglected I Worship an I praise when I-man am Who gave thee lordship an also honour alongside persons who are beneath thy authority - thou cyaan escape from I anger that will come pon thee.

[13] An if thou did JAH Accord an if thou lived frmed up ina Him Command - Him will love thee-I that thou might be Irie with Him ina Him Lordship - an that thou might be a partaker with persons who inherited a honoured country.

[14] Fe Him have said - If them indure I - I-man will bequeath them bein I-loved an honour - fe I-man shall mek them Irie ina the Temple where priah are prayed - fe JAH Who rule all have said - An them shall be I-loved an chosen like unto a sacrifice.

[15] Don't neglect fe do Work whereby welfare are done an a goodly thing that unu might cross from death toward Life.

[16] But persons who work goodly Work - JAH shall keep them ina all Him goodly Work - that them might be Him slaves like unto 'Iyob whom JAH kept from all the tribulation

[17] JAH shall keep them ina all goodly Work - that them might be Him slaves fe Him like unto 'Abriham whom Him saved pon the time him killed the kings - an like unto Mussie whom Him saved from Kenaniewon hand an Fer`on hand - ina whom 'Abriham lived - an who were also downsturbin him body evenin an mornin night an day that them might mek him worship idols.

[18] But when them took him toward the idols that were them money - him would indure the tribulation while him refused.

[19] Fe 'Abriham who believed Him Iginnin from him childhood were fe JAH Him trusted friend - an while him refused him would worship JAH Who Irated him.

[20] As him totally love JAH - him didn't quit worshippin JAH up til him dead - an him didn't depart from Him LAW up til when him dead - an him taught him childran that them might keep JAH LAW.

[21] An like unto them faada 'Abriham kept Him LAW - them didn't depart from JAH LAW ~ like unto Him told fe Angels sayin - I-man have a friend ina this world called 'Abriham - 'Abriham childran Ya`iqob an Yis'haq - who are Him slaves becau whom JAH spoke - didn't depart from JAH LAW.

[22] JAH Who were praised alongside them an Who rule all said - 'Abriham are I friend ~ Yis'haq are I canfidante - an Ya`iqob are I friend whom I Reasonin loved.

[23] But when Him totally loved 'Isra'iel childran - them lived when them Itinually saddened Him - an Him lived when Him indured them an when Him fed them *menna* ina wilderness.

[24] Them clothes didn't age - fe them have been fed *menna* that are knowledge *'injera* - an them feet didn't awaken.

[25] But them reasonins would distance from JAH everytime ~ as them were who work sin Iginnin from Antiquity - them had no hope fe be saved.

[26] Them became like unto a crooked bow - yet them didn't become like unto them faadas Yis'haq an 'Abriham an Ya`iqob who served JAH ina them beautiful way of Life ~ them would sadden Him everytime by them idols pon the mountains an the hills ~ them would eat pon the mountain an at the caves an the trees roots.

[27] Them would slaughter a steer ~ them would sacrifice a sacrifice - an them would be Irie ina them hands Work ~ them would eat the rest of the sacrifice ~ them would drink

of them sacrifice - an them would play with demons while them sang.

[28] An demons would admire all them games an them songs fe them - an them would work them drunkenness an adultery without measure - an them would do the robbery an greed that JAH don't love.

[29] Fe Kene`an idols - an fe Midyam idols an fe Be`al - an fe 'Aphlon an Dagon an Seraphyon an 'Arthiemadies who are 'Eloflee idols...

[30] an fe all peoples idols ina them area - them would sacrifice sacrifice; an all 'Isra'iel would worship idols like unto peoples worship idols by money that them sight up an heard ~ them would mek them games an them songs an them bluster that peoples mek.

[31] All 'Isra'iel kindreds do likewise - who say 'Wi will worship JAH' - without keepin Him Command an Him LAW that Mussie told them ina 'Oreet that them might keep JAH LAW an might distance from worshippin idols.

[32] Lest them worship separated idols - apart from them faadas Irator Who fed them the honey found from Maga who fed them the plantation grain an sent them forth toward the Earth crops - an Who fed them the *menna*...

[33] Mussie commanded them sayin 'Don't worship' - fe Him are them Irator - an fe Him feed them who loved Him - an Him won't deprive them who loved Him an desired Him.

[34] But them didn't quit saddenin JAH - an them would sadden JAH pon the time Him made them Irie.

[35] An pon the time Him saddened them - them would cry toward Him - an Him would save them from the tribulation that found them - an them would again be totally Irie an would live many eras.

[36] An at that time them would totally return them heart toward sin that them might sadden JAH like unto formerly - an Him would arouse pon them peoples ina them area that them might downstroy them - an them would worry an tax them.

[37] An again them would totally return an cry toward them Irator JAH.

[38] An Him would forgive them ~ it are becau them faadas - Noh - Yis'haq an 'Abriham an Ya`iqob - who served JAH ina them beautiful way of Life Iginnnin from Antiquity - fe whom Him firmed up Him Oath - yet it aren't becau them ras selves Work that Him forgive them.

[39] An Him loved persons who kept Him LAW lovin that them might multiply them childran like unto Heaven stars an sea sand.

[40] But pon the time dead ones arose that them have like unto sea sand - them are sinner persons souls that will separate from 'Isra'iel childran an enter toward Gehannem.

[41] As JAH have told 'Abriham - Sight up toward Heaven at night an count Heaven stars as it were thou could count - likewise as Him have told him - Thy childran an righteous ones shall shine ina Heaven like unto Heaven stars - them are like unto stars that shine ina Heaven - but what them have are kind persons souls birthed from 'Isra'iel.

[42] An again as Him have told him - Overstand toward the river edge an the sea - an sight up what are amidst the sand ~ count as it were thou could count - an thy sinner childran are likewise - who will downscend toward *Gehannem* pon the time dead ones arose - them are sinner persons souls.

[43] An 'Abriham believed ina JAH ~ becaudis thing it were counted fe him bein Truth ~ him found him morale ina this world - an after him wife Sora aged she birthed a child called Yis'haq.

[44] Fe him have believed that persons who worked goodly Work shall arise an go toward the Kingdom of Heaven that live firmed up foriva - an again him shall find a Kingdom ina Heaven.

[45] But fe him have believed that persons who worked sin shall go toward *Gehannem* that live firmed up foriva pon the time dead ones arose - but that righteous ones who worked goodly Work shall reign with Him foriva.

[46] But fe him have believed that it shall be judged foriva fe true without falsehood pon persons who worked sin - fe him shall find Life Kingdom ina Heaven."

Mek glory an praise enter fe JAH fe true without falsehood - an the first book that speak the Meqabyans thing were filled an fulfilled.

II MEQABYAN

Chapter 1

[1] This are a book that speak that Meqabees found 'Isra'iel ina Mesphiethomya that are Sorya part an killed them ina them region iginnin from 'Iyabboq up til 'Iyerusaliem square - an that him downstroyed the country.

[2] Becau Sorya an 'Edomyas persons an the 'Amalieqans were one with the Mo`ab man Meqabees who downstroyed 'Iyerusaliem country - as them have camped iginnin from Semarya up til 'Iyerusaliem square an up til all she region - them killed ina war without preservin persons who fled apart from a few persons.

[3] An pon the time 'Isra'iel childran wronged - Him aroused Mo`ab man Meqabees pon them - an him killed them by a sword.

[4] An becaudis thing JAH enemies the peoples bragged pon Him honoured country - an them swore ina them crime.

[5] An 'Iloflee an 'Idomyas persons camped - as Him have sent them becau them pretended JAH Word - them began fe revenge an downstroy JAH country.

[6] An that Meqabees country are Riemat that are Mo`ab part - an him arose from him country ina Power an them swore also with persons with him.

[7] An them camped ina Gielabuhie region that are Mesphiethomya lot up til Sorya that them might downstroy JAH country - an there him begged the 'Amalieqans an 'Iloflans ~ him gave them much silver an gold an chariots an horses that them might be one with him ina crime.

[8] Them came together an crushed the fortress ~ persons who lived ina she shed blood like unto Water.

[9] An them made 'Iyerusaliem like unto a plant keepin hut - an him made a voice heard within she ~ him worked all the sin Work that JAH don't love - an them also defouled JAH country that were filled of praise an honour.

[10] Them made thy friends flesh an thy slaves corpses food fe wilderness beasts an Heaven birds.

[11] An them robbed childran whose mother an faada dead pon them an widows - fe without fearin JAH them have done like unto Seythan taught them - an up til JAH Who examine kidneys an reasonins vexed - them took out the fetus ina pregnant dawtaz belly.

[12] Them returned toward them country while them were Irie becau them worked evil Work pon JAH kindreds - an them took the plunder that them captured from a honoured country.

[13] Pon the time them returned an entered toward them houses them made Ites an song an clappin.

Chapter 2

[1] The prophet whom them call Re`ay told him thus: - "Today be Irie a likkle pon the time when Irie Ites were made ~ JAH Whom 'Isra'iel glorified have that Him might revenge an downstroy thee ina the chastisemant thou didn't doubt.

[2] Will thou say - 'Mi horses are swift ~ becaudis mi will escape by runnin'?

[3] As fe I - I-man tell thee - Persons who will follow thee are swifter than vultures ~ thou won't escape from JAH Judgemant an downstruction that shall come pon thee.

[4] Will thou say - 'Mi wear iron clothes - an spear flingin an bow stingin aren't able fe mi'?; JAH Who honour 'Isra'iel said - It aren't by spear flingin that I-man will revenge an downstroy thee" Him told him ~ "I-man shall bring pon thee heart sickness an itch an rheumatism sickness that were worse an firmer than spear flingin an bow stingin - yet it aren't by this that I-man shall revenge an downstroy thee.

[5] Thou have aroused I anger ~ I-man shall bring heart sickness pon thee - an thou will lack one who help thee - an thou won't escape from I Itority up til I-man downstroy thy name invocation from this world.

[6] As thou have firmed up thy collar of reasonin - an as thou have ilivated thy ras self pon I country - pon the time I-man quickly did this thing like unto a eye wink - thou will know I that I-man were thy Irator ~ as thou are before I like unto grass before the wind that fiyah eat - an as thou are like unto the dust that winds spill an scattar from Earth - thou are like unto them alongside I.

[7] Fe thou have aroused I anger - an fe thou didn't know thy Irator - an I-man shall neglect all thy kindred - an

neither will I-man preserve him who neared pon thy fortress.

[8] An now return from all thy sin that thou worked ~ if thou return from thy sin an totally appease ina mournin an sadness before JAH - an if thou beg toward him ina clean reasonin - JAH will forgive thee all thy sin that thou worked before Him" - him told him.

[9] At that time Meqabees wore dust an mourned before JAH becau him sin - fe JAH have vexed pon him.

[10] Fe Him eyes are revealed - fe Him don't withhold - an fe Him ears are opened - fe Him don't neglect - an fe Him don't mek the word Him spoke false - an fe Him quickly do she at one time - fe JAH knew lest Him preserve the chastisemant Him spoke by the prophet Word.

[11] Him cast him clothes an wore sackcloth an sprinkled dust pon him head an cried an wept before him Irator JAH becau him sin that him worked.

Chapter 3

[1] An the prophet came from Riemat an told him - fe Riemat that are Mo`ab part are near fe Sorya.

[2] Him dug a pit an entered up til him neck an wept firm tears - an him entered repentance becau him sin that him worked before JAH.

[3] An JAH told the prophet thus: - Return from Yihuda country Riemat toward the Mo`ab official Meqabees Him told him. Tell him - "JAH told thee thus" - Tell him - "Him told thee - I-man JAH Who am thy Irator sent thee by I Accord that thou might downstroy I country - lest thou say - 'Mi destroyed the honoured country 'Iyerusaliem by mi Power firmness an mi army abundance' - yet it aren't thou who did this thing.

[4] Fe she have saddened I by all she greed an she perfidy an she lustfulness.

[5] An I-man neglected an cast she by thy hand - an now JAH forgave thee thy sin becau thy childran whom thou birthed ~ it aren't becau thou who firmed up thy collar of reasonin an say 'Mi incircled the country 'Iyerusaliem by mi authority firmness.'

[6] As persons who doubt aren't disciplined fe enter repentance - don't be a doubter - an now enter repentance bein disciplined ina thy complete reasonin."

[7] However persons are admired who enter repentance ina them complete reasonins an who don't again return toward thirst an sin by all that entered toward repentance becau them sin.

[8] Persons are admired who return toward them Irator JAH bein disciplined ina mournin an sadness - ina bowin an many pleas. Persons are admired who are disciplined an

enter repentance - fe Him have told them - Unu are I moneys who entered repentance after unu misled persons who entered repentance.

[9] Him told arrogant Meqabees pon the time him returned toward Him ina repentance after him misled - I-man forgive thee thy sin becau thy fright an thy alarm; fe I-man am JAH thy Irator Who bring hardship pon childran by a faada sin up til seven generations if the child work the sin that the faada worked - an Who do Charity up til ten thousand generations fe persons who love I an keep I LAW.

[10] An now I-man will firm up I Oath with thee becau these thy childran whom thou birthed - an JAH Who rule all an Who honoured 'Isra'iel said - I-man will accept the repentance thou made becau thy sin that thou worked.

[11] At that time him proceeded from the pit an bowed fe the prophet ~ him swore sayin - "As mi have saddened JAH - mek mi what thou loved - yet mek JAH do mi thus thus lest mi separate from thee-I ~ as wi have no Law - mi didn't live firmed up ina Him Command like unto mi faadas ~ thou know that wi faadas taught wi an that wi worship idols.

[12] Fe mi are a sinner who lived firmed up ina mi sin - who firmed up ina mi collar of reasonin firmness an mi reasonin arrogance whereby mi saddened JAH Command - but up til now mi hadn't heard JAH servants the prophets Word - an mi didn't live firmed up ina Him LAW an Him Command that Him commanded mi."

[13] Him told him sayin - "As there are none from your kindred precedin unu who trusted him sin - mi knew that the prophet raceived repentance today."

[14] "But now quit thy worshippin idols an return toward knowin JAH that thou might have true repentance" him told him ~ him fell an bowed at the prophet feet - an the prophet lifted up an commanded him all the goodly Work that are due him.

[15] An him returned toward him house doin also like unto JAH commanded him.

[16] An that Meqabees returned him body toward worshippin JAH - an him downstroyed from him house the idols an also the sorcery - persons who worship idols an pessimists an magicians.

[17] An mornin an evenin like unto them faadas do - him would examine the childran him captured an brought from 'Iyerusaliem ina all JAH Commands an Him Order an Him LAW.

[18] An from the childran him captured - him appointed knowin ones pon him house.

[19] An again from the infants him appointed knowin childran who keep levelled childran who were small - who enter toward the beddin that them might teach them JAH LAW that 'Isra'iel childran do ~ him would hear from captured 'Isra'iel childran the Order an the LAW an the Nine Laws - that Mo`ab persons order an them mosques that them mek were vain.

[20] Him downstroyed them mosques - them idols an them sorcery - an the sacrifice an the grapes sacrificed fe the idols mornin an evenin from the goat kids an fattened sheeps flocks.

[21] An him downstroyed him idols whom him worship an beg an believe ina all him Work while him sacrificed sacrifice afternoon an at noon - an fe all priests told him - an him idols fe whom him do them accord.

[22] As it would seem fe him that them save him ina all that them told - him wouldn't scorn all the thing them told him.

[23] But that Meqabees quit them Work.

[24] After him heard the Ra`ay thing - whom them call a prophet - him accomplished him Work ina repentance ~ as 'Isra'iel childran would sadden Him at one time - an pon the time Him chastised them ina the tribulation - as them know an also cry toward JAH - all Him kindreds worked goodly Work more than 'Isra'iel childran ina that season.

[25] Pon the time Him heard that them were seized an abused by peoples hand who firm up tribulation pon them an that them cried toward Him - Him thought of them faadas oath an at that time Him would forgive them becau them faadas Yis'haq - 'Abriham - an Ya`iqob.

[26] An pon the time Him saved them - them would forget JAH Who saved them from tribulation - an them would return toward worshippin the idols.

[27] An at that time Him would arouse pon them peoples who firm up tribulation pon them - an pon the time them firmed up tribulation pon them an saddened them - them would cry toward JAH ~ as Him love them becau them were Him Itority Iration - at that time Him would be nice an forgive them.

[28] An pon the time Him kept them - them again returned toward sin that them might sadden Him by them hands Work that were firm an by worshippin idols ina them councils.

[29] But Him would arouse pon them Mo`ab an 'Iloflee - Sorya - Midyam an Gibts persons; an pon the time them enemies defeated them - them would cry an weep ~ pon the time them firmed up pon them an taxed them an ruled them - JAH would arouse princes fe them that Him might save them pon the time Him loved.

Chapter 4

[1] An ina 'Iyasu time are a day when Him saved them.

[2] An ina Giediewon time are a day when Him saved them.

[3] An ina Somson time an ina Deebora an Bariq an Yodeet time are a day when Him saved them - an lodgin whether pon male or pon dawta - Him would arouse princes fe them that them might save them from them enemies hands who firm up tribulation pon them.

[4] An like unto JAH loved - Him would save them from persons who firm up tribulation pon them.

[5] An them would be totally Irie ina all the Work that Him accomplished fe them ~ them would be Irie ina them land seed an ina multiplyin all them flocks ina wilderness an them livestock.

[6] An Him would bless them plants an them livestock fe them - fe Him sight them up ina Eye of Mercy - an fe Him wouldn't diminish them livestock pon them - fe them are kind persons childran an Him would totally love them.

[7] But pon the time them were evil ina them Work - Him would cast them ina them enemies hands.

[8] An pon the time Him downstroyed them - them would seek Him ina worship - an them would return from sin an march toward JAH ina repentance.

[9] An pon the time them returned ina them complete reasonin - Him would atone them sin fe them ~ Him wouldn't think of them former sin pon them - fe Him know them that them were flesh an blood - fe them have this world misleadin thoughts pon them - an fe them have demons ina them.

[10] But pon the time that Meqabees heard this Order that JAH worked ina Him worshippin place the Temple - him were slain ina repentance.

[11] After him sight up an heard this - him didn't scorn workin goodly Work; him didn't scorn workin all the goodly Work that 'Isra'iel childran work pon the time JAH forgave them - an after them trespassed from Him LAW - them weep an would cry pon the time JAH whipped them - an again Him would forgive them - an them would keep Him LAW.

[12] An Meqabees likewise would straighten up him Work - an him would keep Him LAW - an him would live firmed up ina 'Isra'iel Irator JAH Command.

[13] At that time after him heard all the Work whereby 'Isra'iel childran boast - Him would boast like unto them ina keepin JAH LAW.

[14] Him would urge him kindred an childran that them might live firmed up ina JAH Command an all Him LAW.

[15] An him would forbid the order that 'Isra'iel forbid - an him would hear an keep the Law that 'Isra'iel keep - an when him kindred are another Mo`ab man - him would forbid the food that 'Isra'iel forbid.

[16] An him would send forth tithes ~ him would give all that were first birthed an that him owned from him cows

an him sheeps an him donkeys - an returnin him face toward 'Iyerusaliem him would sacrifice the sacrifice that 'Isra'iel sacrifice.

[17] Him would sacrifice sin an vow sacrifices - a sacrifice whereby welfare are done an a accord sacrifice - an the Itinual sacrifice.

[18] An him would give him first crops - an him would gush an pour the grapes that 'Isra'iel pour - an him would give this fe him priest whom him I-pointed - an likewise him would do all that 'Isra'iel do - an him would sweeten him ishence.

[19] Him built a candlestick an a bowl an a seat an a tent an the four links of rings - an diluted oil fe the Hola of Holas lamps - an the curtain that 'Isra'iel mek ina the Hola of Holas pon the time them served JAH.

[20] An like unto them worked goodly Work pon the time them lived firmed up ina Him Order an Him LAW an pon the time JAH didn't neglect an cast them ina them enemies hands - Meqabees also would work goodly Work like unto them.

[21] Him would beg toward 'Isra'iel Irator JAH everytime that Him might be him Teacher an lest Him separate him from 'Isra'iel childran whom Him chose an who did Him Accord.

[22] An again him would beg Him that Him might give him childran ina Tsiyon an a house ina 'Iyerusaliem - that Him might give them Heavenly Seed of Virtue ina Tsiyon an a Heavenly House of Soul ina 'Iyerusaliem - an that Him might save him from the downstruction spoken by the prophet tongue - that Him might accept him repentance ina all the mournin him wept before JAH bein sad an enterin repentance...

[23] an lest Him downstroy childran ina this world pon him - an that Him might keep him ina him proceedin an enterin.

[24] Kindreds from Mo`ab peoples beneath Meqabees Itority were Irie that them might believe - fe them chief live firmed up ina straight Work - an them would check up him judgemant an fulfill him accord - an them would scorn them country language an them country justice ~ them would overstand that Meqabees Work surpassed an were straight.

[25] An them would come an hear Meqabees charity an Truth judgemants.

[26] Him had much money ~ him had dawta slaves an male slaves an camels an donkeys - an him had five hundred horses that wear breastplates ~ him would totally defeat the 'Amalieqans an 'Iloflans an Sorya persons - but formerly when him worshipped idols him lived when them defeated him.

[27] Him prevailed - yet but from him worshippin JAH onward - when him went toward battle there are none who defeated him.

[28] But them would come ina them idols Power that them might fight him - an them would call them idols names an curse him - however there were none who defeat him - fe him have made him faith pon him Irator JAH.

[29] An when him did thus an when him defeated him enemies - him lived when him ruled peoples ina him Itority.

[30] Him would revenge an downstroy wronged persons enemy fe them ~ him would judge Truth fe a child whose mother an faada dead pon him.

[31] An him would raceive widows ina them trouble time - an him would give from him food an satta them who hungered - an him would clothe the naked from him clothes.

[32] An him would be Irie ina him hands Work - an him would give from the money him had without begrudgin - an him would give tithes fe the Temple ~ Meqabees dead havin lived ina Irie Ites when him did this.

Chapter 5

[1] An him dead quittin him childran who were small - an them grew up like unto them faada taught them ~ them kept them house Order - an them would keep all them kindred - an them wouldn't mek poor ones cry - nor widows nor a child whose mother an faada dead pon him.

[2] Them would fear JAH - an them would give them money alms fe poor ones - an them would keep all the trust them faada told them - an them would calm the child whose mother an faada dead pon them an widows ina them trouble time - an them would be them mother an faada ~ them would mek them cast from persons hand who wrong them - an calm them from all the downsturbance an sadness that found them.

[3] Them lived five years while them did thus.

[4] After this the Keledans king Tseerutsaydan came ~ him downstroyed all them country - an him captured Meqabees childran an downstroyed all them villages.

[5] An him plundered all them money ~ them lived firmed up ina all evil Work an sin - ina adultery - insult an greed an not thinkin of them Irator - yet persons who don't live firmed up ina JAH LAW an Him Command an who worship idols seized them also an took them toward them country.

[6] Them eat what a beast bit an the blood an the carcass - an what a scavenger beat an cast - all that JAH don't love - yet them have no order from all the true Commands written ina 'Oreet.

[7] Them don't know JAH them Irator - Who sent them forth from them mothers wombs an fed them by what are due - were them Medicine.

[8] Them marry from them aunt an them faada wife - them step mother - an them go toward robbery an evil thing an sin an adultery - yet them have no order ina Judgemant time - an them work all evil Work an them marry them aunts an them sistren an them have no LAW.

[9] An all them roads are dark an slippery - an them Work are sin an adultery.

[10] But those Meqabees childran would keep ina all them Order ~ them wouldn't eat what a scavenger beat nor what dead an lodged ~ them wouldn't work all the Work that the Keledans childran work - fe them many Works are evil that weren't written ina this book - that sinners work - an doubters an criminals - betrayers totally filled of robbery an sin an pagans childran.

[11] All the Work them Irator JAH love aren't there alongside them.

[12] An again them would worship a idol called Bi'iel Fiegor ~ them would trust it like unto them Irator JAH when it were deaf an dumb. Fe it are the idol that a person hand worked - fe it are the person hand Work that a smith worked who work silver an gold - that have no breath nor knowledge - an it had nothing that it sight up nor hear.

[13] It don't eat nor drink.

[14] It don't kill nor save.

[15] It don't plant nor uproot.

[16] It don't harm it enemy nor benefit it friend.

[17] It don't impoverish nor honour.

[18]It will be a hindrance fe mislead the Keledans persons who were lazy - yet it don't chastise nor forgive.

Chapter 6

[1] JAH enemy Tseerutsaydan who were arrogant appointed them who veil an falsehood priests fe him idols.

[2] Him would sacrifice sacrifice fe them an pour the grapes fe them.

[3] An it would seem fe him that them eat an drink.

[4] An while it dawned him would give them cows an donkeys an heifers - an him would sacrifice sacrifice mornin an evenin - an him would eat from that defouled sacrifice.

[5] An again him would downsturb an obligate other persons that them might sacrifice fe him idols - yet it weren't that only them do it.

[6] Pon the time them sight up Meqabees childran that them were handsome an that them worship them Irator JAH - the idols priests loved that them might mislead them

fe sacrifice sacrifice an fe eat from that hated sacrifice - but these honoured Meqabees childran refused them.

[7] As them keep them faada command - an as them have firmed up ina workin goodly Work - an as them totally fear JAH - it failed them fe agree...

[8] pon the time them bound them an insulted them an robbed them.

[9] Them told fe the king Tseerutsaydan that them refused sacrifice an bowin fe him idols.

[10] An becaudis thing the king vexed ~ him were sad an commanded that them might bring them - an them brought an stood them before him - an the king told them fe him idols - "Sacrifice a sacrifice fe mi idols."

[11] An them spoke an told him - "An InI won't answer thee ina this thing - an InI won't sacrifice sacrifice fe thy defouled idols."

[12] Him frightened them by Works that abounded - yet him couldn't able fe them - fe them have disciplined them reasonins believin ina JAH.

[13] Him flamed a fiyah an cast them ina fiyah - an them gave them bodies fe JAH.

[14] After them dead them arose an were sight up fe him at night drawin them swords when him had reclined pon him lordship throne - an him totally feared.

[15] "Mi sirs - tell mi alright - what should mi do fe unu? Don't tek mi body ina death - that mi might do all thou commanded mi."

[16] Them told him all that are due fe him while them said - "Think that JAH were thy Irator - an JAH are there Who shall dismiss from this thy kingdom where thou are arrogant - an Who shall lower thee toward *Gehannem* of Fiyah with thy faada Deeyablos ~ when InI worshipped InI Irator JAH without a iniquity livin that InI wronged thee - an when InI bowed fe Him ina fearin Him JAH-ness - like unto thou burned InI ina fiyah - thou will finish all thy hardship by that also.

[17] Fe Him are Who Irated all - Earth an Heaven an sea an all that are within she.

[18] An fe Him are Who Irated moon an Sun an stars - an fe Him Who Irated all the Iration are JAH.

[19] Fe there are no other irator withou Him ina Earth nor Heaven - fe Him are Who able fe all - an fe there are nothing that fail Him. As Him are Who kill an Who save - Who whip ina tribulation an Who forgive - when InI bowed fe Him ina fearin JAH - like unto thou burned InI ina fiyah - thou will finish thy hardship by that" them told him.

[20] "As Him are Who rule Earth an Heaven - there are none who escape from Him Itority.

[21] There are none from the Iration Him Irated who departed from Him Command - apart from thou who are a

criminal - an criminals like unto thee whose reasonins thy faada Seythan hid - an thou an those thy priests an thy idols will downscend together toward *Gehannem* where are no exits up til Iternity.

[22] Thy teacher are Seythan who taught thee this evil Work that thou might do a evil thing pon InI - yet as it aren't only thou who do this - unu will downscend toward *Gehannem* together.

[23] Fe thou mek thy ras self like unto thy Irator JAH - yet thou didn't know JAH Who Irated thee.

[24] An thou are arrogant ina thy idols an thy hand Work up til JAH mek thee wretched ~ Him shall canvict thee pon all thy sin an iniquity that thou worked ina this world.

Chapter 7

[1] Woe fe unu who don't know JAH Who Irated unu - fe thy idols who are like unto thee - an fe thee - an fe unu have that unu might regret a regrets that won't profit pon the time unu were sad bein seized ina *See'ol* difficulty - an woe fe thee - fe unu who don't keep Him Word and Him LAW.

[2] Unu will have no exit from she up til Iternity - thy priests an thou who sacrifice fe them like unto your Irator JAH - fe thy idols who have no breath nor soul - who won't revenge an downstroy him who did a evil thing pon them - nor do a goodly thing fe him who did a goodly thing fe them.

[3] Woe fe unu who sacrifice fe them - fe them are a person hands Work where Seythan live - lodgin there fe mislead lazy ones reasonin like unto thee - that him might lower unu toward *Gehannem* of Fiyah - an the priests who serve demons commanded fe unu an your idols.

[4] As unu don't know that there are nothing that will profit unu - unu wrong an err.

[5] As fe the animals that JAH Irated fe be food fe unu - an dogs an beasts - them are better than unu - fe besides one death there are no more candemnation pon them.

[6] But as unu will dead an raceive hardship ina *Gehannem* Fiyah where are no exits up til Iternity - animals are better."

[7] Havin spoken this - them went an were hidden from him.

[8] But that Tseerutsaydan lodged when him trembled - seized by a firm fright - an fright didn't quit him up til it dawned.

Chapter 8

[1] An him lived firmed up ina reasonin malice an arrogance.

[2] An as iron have been called firm - like unto Dan'iel sight it up pon him kingdom - him turned ina peoples countries ina him area.

[3] Him lived firmed up ina evil an all him laziness an ina downsturbin persons.

[4] An him totally downstroy what InI spoke formerly - an him eat a person money.

[5] Fe him are diligent fe evil like unto him faada Deeyablos who firmed up him collar of reasonin - an him downstroy what remained with him army.

[6] Him say - "Mi era became like unto the Sun era" - yet him don't know JAH that Him were him Irator.

[7] An ina him reasonin him think that the Sun are found from him.

[8] Him arise in Power - him camp ina Tribe of Zablon lot an begin a formation ina Meqiedonya - an him receive him food from Semarya - an them give him presents from Semarya.

[9] Him camp ina nomads region - an him reach up til Seedona - an him cast a tax pon 'Akayya - an him elevate him collar of reasonin up til the flowin sea - an him return an send messengers up til Hindekie sea.

[10] An likewise him elevate him collar of reasonin up til Heaven.

[11] Him live firmed up ina bein arrogant an ina evil - yet him don't have humblin him ras self.

[12] An him path are toward darkness an slipperiness - an toward crime an bein arrogant - an toward sheddin blood an tribulation.

[13] An all him Work are what JAH hate ~ him do like unto robbery an evil an sin teacher Deeyablos taught him ~ him mek a child cry whose mother an faada dead pon him - an him aren't nice fe a poor one.

[14] An him defeated an downstroyed peoples kings by him authority.

[15] An him ruled enemies chiefs - an him ruled many peoples - an him taxed them like unto him loved.

[16] Even if him downstroyed - him didn't quit ~ there are no person whom him didn't snatch Iginnin from Tersies sea up til 'Iyareeko sea.

[17] Him would bow fe idols ~ him would eat what dead an lodged - the blood - what a sword bloated an cut - an what were sacrificed fe idols ~ all him Work are without justice - yet him have no justice ~ as him have been who alarm peoples beneath him authority - him would tax them tax like unto him loved.

[18] As him do all that him loved before him - there are no fearin JAH before him - an him live ina malice before JAH Who Irated him.

[19] Him didn't do it like unto him Irator - an like unto him did a evil thing pon him companion pon the time him vexed an seized him - JAH shall also pay him him hardship.

[20] As JAH have said - I-man shall revenge an downstroy sinner persons who don't live by I Command - that I-man might downstroy them name invocation from this world - like unto Him downstroyed peoples who were precedin him - Him shall revenge an downstroy him pon the time when Him downstroy.

[21] An like unto evil persons did evil things - them shall raceive them hardship.

[22] But bein commanded from JAH - goodly Work shall follow persons who work goodly Work.

[23] Fe like unto 'Iyasu downstroyed the five Kene`an kings ina cave ina one day - an like unto him made Sun stand ina Geba`on by him priah that him might downstroy them armies - Sun have stood amidst Heaven up til him downstroyed 'Ewiewon an Kenaniewon - Fierziewon an Kiethiewon an 'Iyabusiewon armies - an like unto him killed around twenty thousand persons at one time - an like unto him killed them - an like unto him bound them makin foot from neck - an like unto him killed them ina cave by spear - an like unto him fitted a stone pon them...

[24] Tribulation like unto this shall find all persons who sadden JAH ina them evil Work.

Chapter 9

[1] "O thou weak man who aren't JAH - why are thou proud? thou who are sight up today bein a man are Earth ashes tomorrow - an thou will totally be worms ina thy grave.

[2] Fe thy teacher are Deeyablos who return all persons sin hardship toward him ras self becau him misled InI faada 'Adam - an *See'ol* will find thee again - an she will find persons who work thy sin.

[3] Fe ina firmin up him collar of reasonin an makin him ras self proud - like unto him refused fe bow fe 'Adam whom the Irator Irated...

[4] thou also have refused fe bow fe thy Irator JAH like unto thy teacher Deeyablos did.

[5] Like unto thy precedin faadas - who don't know them Irator JAH ina worship - will go toward *Gehannem* - thou also will go toward *Gehannem*.

[6] Like unto Him revenged an downstroyed them becau them evil Work that them worked ina this world - an like unto them downscended toward *Gehannem*...

[7] thou also will downscend toward *Gehannem* like unto them.

[8] As thou have aroused Him anger - an as thou have neglected fe worship JAH Who gave thee Itority pon the five

kingdoms - do it seem fe thee that thou will escape from JAH Itority?

[9] Thou don't do thus that thou do Him Accord - thus Him examined thee - but if thou work goodly Work ina this world - JAH will accomplish all thy Work fe thee-I - an Him will accomplish an bless all the Work thou seized ina thy hand fe thee-I - an Him will subject thy Antiquity of enemies an thy day enemies fe thee-I

[10] Thou will be Irie ina thy enterins an thy proceedins an ina thy child birthed from thy nature - an ina thy flocks an thy fatnesses - an ina all Work where thou placed thy hand - an ina all that thou thought ina thy heart ~ as Itority have been given thee-I from alongside JAH that thou might do thus an might work an plant an demolish - all will be commanded fe thee-I.

[11] However if thou won't hear JAH Word nor live firmed up ina Him LAW - like unto criminals who were precedin thee - an who don't worship JAH by what are due - an who didn't believe firmed up ina HIM straight LAW - there are nothing whereby thou will escape from JAH Itority - fe JAH Judgemant are Truth.

[12] All are totally revealed before Him - yet there are nothing hidden from before Him.

[13] Him are Who seize the kings Itority an Who overturn powerful ones thrones.

[14] Him are Who Ilivate them who were downbased an Who lift up them who fell.

[15] Him are Who loose them who were bound an Who arouse them who dead ~ as pardon dew are found from alongside Him - pon the time Him loved Him shall arouse persons whose flesh were demolished an rotten an were like unto dust.

[16] An havin aroused an judged persons who worked evil Work - Him will tek them toward *Gehannem* - fe them have saddened Him.

[17] Fe them are who demolished JAH Order an Him LAW - an Him will downstroy them child from this world.

[18] As kind persons Work are more difficult than sinner persons Work - sinner persons don't love that them might live ina kind persons counsel.

[19] Like unto Heavens were distanced from Earth - likewise kind persons Work were distanced from evil persons Work.

[20] But sinner persons Work are robbery an sin - adultery an iniquity - greed an perfidy Work ~ it are bein drunk ina iniquity an robbin a person money.

[21] It are quickly goin toward sheddin a person blood - an it are goin toward downstruction that don't benefit - an it are makin a child weep whose mother an faada dead pon him ~ it are eatin blood an what dead an lodged - an it are

eatin camel an boar flesh - an it are goin toward a dawta ina she blood before she are cleansed - an toward a dawta ina childbirth.

[22] All this are sinner persons Work ~ she are Seythan trap that were a wide an prepared path - an that tek toward *Gehannem* that live firmed up foriva - an toward *See'ol*.

[23] But righteous ones path that were totally narrow are what tek toward welfare - an innocence an humbleness - an Inity an Love - an priah an fast - an flesh purity - toward keepin from what don't benefit - from eatin what a sword bloated an cut an what dead an lodged - an from goin toward a youtmon wife an from adultery.

[24] Them keep from what weren't commanded by LAW - from eatin disgustin food an from all hated Work - an from all the Work that JAH don't love - fe sinner persons do all this.

[25] As fe kind persons - them distance from all the Work that JAH don't love.

[26] Him love them an shall keep them from all them tribulation like unto Trust money.

[27] Fe them keep Him Order an Him LAW an all that Him love - but Seythan rule sinner persons.

Chapter 10

[1] Fear JAH Who Irated unu an kept unu up til today - yet unu the nobles an the kings - don't go pon Seythan path.

[2] Live ina the LAW an Command of JAH Who rule all - yet don't go pon Seythan path.

[3] As pon the time 'Isra'iel childran came toward 'Amalieq that them might inherit Kiethiewon an Kenaniewon an Fierziewon country - Siefor child Balaq an Bele`am...

[4] whom thou cursed are cursed - an him whom thou blessed blessed ~ don't go pon Seythan road - fe him have said - "An mi will give thee much silver an gold that honour thee - that thou might curse fe mi an - an havin cursed - that thou might downstroy fe mi."

[5] An fe Bele`am have come makin him sorcery reward a morale - an fe Siefor child Balaq have shown him the place where 'Isra'iel childran camped.

[6] Fe him have done him pessimism - an fe him have sacrificed him sacrifice - an fe him have slaughtered from him fattened cows an sheeps - an fe him have loved that him might curse an downstroy 'Isra'iel childran.

[7] Him returned a curse toward a bless - yet but as JAH didn't love that him might curse them by Him Word - don't go pon Seythan road.

[8] "As thou are the kindred that JAH chose - as thou are JAH Lodgin that shall come from Heaven - mek persons be cursed who curse thee-I - an mek persons who bless thee-I be blessed" him said.

[9] Pon the time him blessed them before him - after this Siefor child Balaq were sad - an him totally vexed an commanded that him might curse them.

[10] Fe the kindred that JAH blessed have come toward this country - an Bele`am told him - "Mi won't curse 'Isra'iel whom JAH blessed."

[11] An Siefor child Balaq told Bele`am - "As fe mi - mi had loved that thou might curse fe mi ~ thou blessed them before mi - yet but thou didn't curse them ~ if thou had cursed fe mi an told mi 'Give mi' - as fe mi - mi would have given thee a house full of silver an gold - but thou totally blessed them - an thou didn't do a goodly thing fe mi - an mi won't do a goodly thing fe thee."

[12] Bele`am said - "What JAH told mi Speak with mi tongue - mi will speak it - yet as fe mi - mi cyaan dare fe ignore JAH thing.

[13] Lest mi curse a blessed kindred - as JAH shall vex pon mi if mi love money - as fe mi - mi don't love money more than mi soul.

[14] As JAH have told them faada Ya`iqob - Mek persons who bless thee-I be blessed an mek persons who curse thee-I be cursed - lest mi curse blessed Ya`iqob - as fe mi - mi don't love money more than mi soul" him said - an as JAH have told him - Him who bless thee-I are blessed...

[15] an a person who curse thee-I unjustly are cursed - accomplish thy path an thy Work that JAH might love thee.

[16] An don't be like unto former persons who saddened JAH ina them sin an whom Him neglected - an there are them whom Him downstroyed ina Downstruction Water.

[17] An there are them whom Him downstroyed by them haters hands ~ there are them whom Him downstroyed by them enemies hands - bringin enemies who were evil persons who firmed up tribulation pon them - an them captured them lords with them priests an them prophets.

[18] An them delivered them toward the foreign country them don't know ~ them totally captured them - an them plundered them livestocks pon them an downstroyed them country.

[19] Fe them have demolished the honoured country 'Iyerusaliem fences an ramparts - an them made 'Iyerusaliem like unto a field.

[20] An the priests were capture - an the LAW were demolished - an warriors fought ina war an fell.

[21] An widows were capture ~ as them have been capture - them wept fe them ras selves - yet them didn't weep fe them husbands who dead.

[22] An the childran wept - an elders shamed - an them weren't nice fe neither a grey haired person nor a elder.

[23] Them downstroyed all them found ina the country - yet them weren't nice fe beauties nor fe them ina LAW ~ as JAH have vexed pon Him kindreds pon the time Him loved that Him might beforehand downstroy Him Lodgin the Temple - them captured an took them toward the country them don't know an toward peoples.

[24] As them sadden them Irator everytime - becaudis thing pon the time JAH neglected 'Isra'iel childran - JAH made 'Iyerusaliem fe be ploughed like unto a field.

[25] Fe Him are nice fe them becau them faadas - but Him didn't downstroy them at one time ~ as Him love them faadas Yis'haq an 'Abriham an Ya`iqob who reigned fe true an lived firmed up ina straight LAW before them Irator - it are becau them faadas kindness - yet it aren't becau them ras selves kindness that him forgive them.

[26] An Him I-pointed them pon honours that were twofold - an them found two Kingdoms - pon Earth an ina Heaven.

[27] An unu the kings an the nobles who live ina this passin world - like unto your faadas who lived firmed up ina Work that are due an who were precedin unu likewise inherited the Kingdom of Heaven - an like unto them names were beautiful fe a child childran - think of them.

[28] An thou - straighten up thy Work - that Him might straighten up thy Kingdom fe thee - an that thy name might be called ina goodly invocation like unto the kind kings who were precedin thee who served JAH ina them beautiful lifestyle.

Chapter 11

[1] Think of JAH slave Mussie who weren't annoyed when him kept around this kindred ina him humbleness an him priah an whom not even one person downstroyed - an him begged toward JAH ina him innocence fe him sista an bredda who backbit him an loved that JAH might downstroy them while him said - "As them have wronged Thee-I - Lord - pardon an don't neglect thy kindreds" - an him atoned them sin fe them - yet Him thought of JAH servant Mussie who weren't annoyed.

[2] "Fe I-man have wronged Thee-I - an forgive I Thy slave who am a sinner - fe Thou are Merciful - an fe Thou are a Pardoner - an forgive them them sin."

[3] An Mussie likewise atoned them sin fe him sista an bredda who backbit him.

[4] An becaudis thing him were called innocent.

[5] An JAH totally loved him more than all the priests childran who were him bredren - fe Him I-point the priests - an JAH made him like unto Him Ras Self alongside them.

[6] But Him also sank beneath Earth Qorie childran who challenged ~ Him lowered them toward See'ol with them

livestocks an them tents when them said "Wi are there - wi are there ina flesh an soul" ~ as him Irator JAH have loved him - an as him didn't depart from Him Command - all the word him spoke would be done fe him like unto JAH Word.

[7] An unless thou demolished JAH Command likewise - JAH will do thy accord fe thee-I an will love thy thing fe thee-I - an Him will keep thy Kingdom fe thee-I.

[8] An 'Asaf an Qorie childran who departed from Mussie command grumbled pon him becau him told them - "Straighten up your reasonins fe be ruled fe JAH."

[9] Them grumbled sayin - "How about aren't wi Liewee childran who work priesthood Work ina Tent that were special?"

[10] Them went an smoked up ishence seizin them censers that them might smoke up - but JAH didn't accept them plea - an them were burnt by the fiyah ina them censers - an them melted like unto the wax that fiyah melt - an not even one person remained from them ~ as Him have said - Them censers were honoured by them bodies bein burnt - apart from them censers that entered toward JAH Lodgin fe JAH Command - neither them clothes nor them bones remained.

[11] Becaudis thing JAH told 'Aron an Mussie - Gather them censers toward the Tent ~ mek it be a instrumant fe I Lodgin wherefor I-man prepared all I-ginnin from outside up til within.

[12] An him prepared the honoured Tent instrumants ~ him prepared the rings an the joiners - *Keerubiel* picture sea.

[13] Him worked the cups - the curtains - the Tent area grounds fe the mobilisation - the altar an the jugs whereby them sacrifice ina the Tent that were special.

[14] Them sacrificed the sacrifice that them sacrifice by them accord - the sacrifice whereby welfare are made - the sacrifice whereby Him atone sin - an the vow sacrifice an the mornin an the evenin sacrifice.

[15] All that Him commanded fe Mussie - him commanded them ina the Tent that were special - that them might work Work ina she.

[16] Them didn't scorn bein ruled fe them Irator JAH - that Him Name might be praised by them ina the LAW Lodgin Tent of them Irator JAH Who gave them a promise that Him might give them fe give them them faadas inheritance that produce honey an milk that Him swore fe 'Abriham.

[17] Them didn't scorn bein ruled fe them Irator JAH - Who swore fe Yis'haq an firmed up Him Worship fe Ya`iqob...

[18] an Who firmed up fe 'Aron an Mussie the Tent where Him Worship are kept...

[19] an Who firmed up Him Worship fe both 'Elyas an Samu'iel ina the Temple an Tent that Selomon worked up

til it became JAH Lodgin ina 'Iyerusaliem - an up til JAH Name Lodgin became JAH Lodgin that honoured 'Isra'iel.

[20] Fe she are a supplication - an fe she are a sin atonemant where it are overturned fe them who live ina innocence an fe the priests.

[21] An fe she are a place fe persons who do Him Accord where Him will hear them pleas...

[22] an JAH LAW Canstruction that honoured 'Isra'iel.

[23] Fe she are where sacrifice are sacrificed an where Ishence are smoked up that JAH Who honoured 'Isra'iel be ina goodly Fragrance.

[24] An Him would speak bein pon the joiner where Him forgive ina the Tent that were special ~ JAH Light would be revealed fe Ya`iqob childran whom Him chose an fe friends who live firmed up ina Him LAW an Him Command.

[25] But persons who ignored JAH LAW will be like unto Qorie childran whom Earth sank - an likewise sinner persons have that them might enter toward *Gehannem* that have no exits up til Iternity.

Chapter 12

[1] Unu who didn't keep the LAW Him commanded unu ina Tent - woe fe unu 'Isra'iel nobles who also didn't do Him Accord - yet unu did your ras selves accord - an this are bein arrogant an pride - greed an adultery - drink an bein drunk - an swearin ina lie.

[2] An becaudis thing I anger - like unto chaff are burnt before a fiyah - an like unto fiyah burn the mountain - an like unto a whirl wind spill the crushed chaff from Earth an scattar it toward Heaven - lest it trace be found ina it place - I anger will downstroy unu like unto that.

[3] JAH Who honoured 'Isra'iel said - I-man shall likewise downstroy all persons who work sin - an think of JAH Who rule all an fe Whom nothing fail.

[4] Him love persons who love Him - an fe persons who live firmed up ina Him Command - Him will atone them iniquity an them sin fe them ~ don't be dull an stingy of heart by not believin.

[5] An mek your reasonins straight fe be ruled fe JAH - an believe ina Him that unu might firm up your bodies - an I-man shall save unu from your enemy hand ina your tribulation day.

[6] An ina your plea time I-man tell unu - Check - I-man am there with unu ina Support ~ I-man shall save unu from your enemy hand ~ as unu have believed ina I - an as unu have done I Command - an as unu didn't depart from I LAW - an as unu have loved what I-man love - JAH Who rule all said - I-man won't neglect unu pon your tribulation day.

[7] Him love them who love Him - fe Him are a Pardoner - an fe Him are nice - an Him keep persons who keep Him LAW - like unto a trust money.

[8] Him return Him anger fe them many times ~ becau Him were who know them that them are flesh an blood - as Him are a Pardoner - Him didn't downstroy all ina Him chastisemant - an pon the time them souls were separated from them flesh - them will return toward them Earthliness.

[9] As Him have Irated them bringin from not livin toward livin - them won't know the place where them live up til JAH love that Him might bring them from not livin toward livin ~ again Him separated them souls from them flesh - an Earth nature returned toward it Earthliness.

[10] An again Him Accord shall bring them from not livin toward livin."

[11] But Tseerutsaydan who denied JAH multiplied bein arrogant before JAH ~ him made him ras self lofty up til the day that him loved pon the time him quit Him.

[12] "An mi era became like unto Heaven era - an mi are who send forth Sun - an mi won't dead up til Iternity" him said.

[13] An before him finished speakin this thing the Angel of Death whose name are called Thilimyakos alit an struck him heart ~ him dead ina that iwa ~ as him didn't praise him Irator - him were separated from him beautiful lifestyle an him perished arisin from him arrogance abundance an him Work evil.

[14] But when the Keledans king army had camped ina the city an the country squares lovin fe fight him - pon the time him dead - them proceeded an downstroyed him country ~ them plundered all him livestock - an them didn't preserve a elder who near an sight up ramparts.

[15] Them plundered all him money - an them took him tiny money - an them burned him country ina fiyah an returned toward them country.

Chapter 13

[1] But these five Meqabees childran who believed gave them bodies fe death refusin fe eat the sacrifice sacrificed fe idols.

[2] Fe them have known that pretendin with JAH surpass from pretendin with persons - an JAH anger from the king anger.

[3] Havin known that this world will totally pass an that the Irie Ites won't live firmed up foriva - them gave them bodies fe fiyah that them might be saved from fiyah ina Heaven.

[4] An as them have known that bein made Irie ina Garden one day are better than livin many eras ina this world - an

that findin Thy Pardon one iwa Lord - are better than many eras - them gave them bodies fe fiyah.

[5] What are InI era? Like unto a shadow - like unto passin wax melt an perish pon a fiyah edge - aren't it like unto that?

[6] But Thou Lord live foriva - an Thy Era aren't fulfilled - an Thy Name invocation are fe a child childran.

[7] An Meqabees childran thought that it seemed all this ~ refusin fe eat a disgustin sacrifice them chose believin ina JAH.

[8] Knowin that them will arise with persons who dead - an meanin becau JAH - knowin that Judgemant shall be judged after Resurrection of Council - becaudis thing them gave them bodies fe martyrdom.

[9] Unu persons who don't know nor believe persons who dead risin - knowin that the Life them find later will surpass from this them passin Earthly Life - arisin from these five Meqabees childran who gave them bodies together fe the death and whose appearance were handsome - after this them knew Resurrection.

[10] Becau them believed ina Him knowin that all shall pass - an becau them didn't bow fe idols - becau them didn't eat a disgustin sacrifice that don't give Support - them gave them bodies fe death that them might find thanks from JAH.

[11] Fe becaudis thing knowin that Him will mek them Irie ina flesh an soul ina later era - them didn't know this world flavour an death tribulation a serious thing fe them who have child an wife - an knowin that Resurrection be made ina flesh an soul pon the Day of Advent - them gave them bodies fe death.

[12] An knowin that persons who kept JAH LAW - with the nobles an the kings who believed JAH Word an were nice...

[13] shall live reignin fe a child childran many eras ina Kingdom of Heaven where are no sadness an tribulation nor death - an knowin ina them reasonins what will be done later - like unto wax melt amidst a fiyah - becaudis thing them gave them bodies fe death.

[14] Believin that them faces will shine seven hands more than the Sun - an that them will be Irie ina Him Love pon the time all arose ina flesh an soul - them gave them bodies fe death.

Chapter 14

[1] But the Samrans an 'Ayhuds thing - the Seduqans who don't believe persons who dead risin - an the Fereesans thing quite totally sadden I - an it help I fe I reasonin ~ "Wi will dead tomorrow" 'Ayhuds say - "Mek wi eat an drink ~ wi will dead tomorrow ~ there are no Irie Ites wi will sight up ina grave."

[2] But the Samrans say - "As wi flesh will be dust - it won't arise.

[3] Becau she were invisible like unto wind an like unto iyunder voice - check - she are here - an becau she were what them don't call an invisible - as soul won't arise if flesh dead - pon the time Resurrection are done wi will believe wi souls arisin.

[4] But as beasts will eat she an as worms will eat she ina the grave - wi flesh are sight up alongside all ~ she will become dust an ashes.

[5] An those beasts who ate she will become dust - fe them have been like unto grass - an fe them have become dust like unto them weren't irated - an fe them trace won't be found - but wi flesh won't arise."

[6] An the Fereesans say - "Wi believe as fe persons who dead arisin - however Him will bring an Inite souls with another flesh that are ina Heaven - that aren't pon Earth ~ where will demolished an rotten fleshes be found?"

[7] But the Seduqans say - "After wi soul proceeded from wi flesh - wi won't arise with persons who dead - an flesh an soul have no arisin after them dead - an after wi dead wi won't arise."

[8] An becaudis thing them totally err - an as them speak insult pon JAH Lordship - them thing sadden I.

[9] As them didn't believe JAH Who honour them - them have no hope fe be saved - however them have no hope fe dead an arise an be saved.

[10] O 'Ayhudan who are blind of reasonin - when thou are whom Him Irated bringin from not livin toward livin - an scorned like unto spit - will thou mek JAH ignorant - Who made thee a person? Will it fail JAH Who Irated thee ina Him Example an Him Appearance fe arouse Initin thy flesh an thy soul?

[11] As thou won't escape from JAH Itority - don't think a thing that are thus ~ thou will arise without thou lovin - fe there are the hardship thou will raceive ina See'ol where thou were seized pon the time thou dead - an it shall be judged pon thee without thou lovin.

[12] Fe the sin found from demons that demons place ina thy reasonin are worked alongside thee after thou were birthed from thy mother womb - an fe she are worked abundantly pon the time thou grew up.

[13] Them place she ina thy body pon the time thou dead - an she will bring hardship pon them pon the time them worked she.

[14] Like unto there are sin ina them collar of reasonin - as there are persons who work sin bein seized by she - she kindreds will present demons.

[15] All sinner persons souls shall come from Heaven edge where them are - an thy sin likewise shall introduce thee

toward *Gehannem* pullin an bringin thy soul from where thou are.

[16] An after thy flesh lived separate from thy soul - JAH Charity dew shall arouse thee bein seven fold like unto InI faada 'Adam flesh.

[17] Thou who live ina grave - thou also err ina thy error - yet mek it not seem fe thee that thou only mislead the others ~ thou say - "The arisin that persons who dead shall arise aren't there" - that them might depart from JAH Command an err.

[18] Him shall arouse thee that Him might give thee thy hardship like unto thy Work that thou worked - yet who shall quit thee that thou might remain bein dust?

[19] But at that time - whether wind ina wind be thy nature - or if Water ina Water be thy nature - or if Earth ina Earth be thy nature - or if fiyah ina fiyah be thy nature - it shall come.

[20] An if a soul that lodged ina thee be what lived ina *See'ol* - she shall come.

[21] An righteous ones souls that live ina Garden ina Ites shall come.

[22] But thou 'Ayhudan - Samran - Fereesan - Seduqan - will live ina *See'ol* up til it are judged pon thee.

[23] At that time thou will sight up that JAH shall pay thee the hardship like unto thy sin becau thou misled persons.

[24] "Persons who dead won't arise ~ as wi will dead - mek wi eat an drink" - an becau thou sat ina Mussie chair an misled by thy words while thou said - "Persons who dead won't arise" - thou will sight up that Him shall pay thee thy hardship.

[25] An without thy knowin *'Oreet* Book - an when thou teach the books word - becaudis thing thou erred ~ it would be better had thou remained without learnin from thy misleadin a person.

[26] It would have been better if thou didn't know the books word - when thou promulgate JAH kindreds ina thy evil teachin an thy worthless words.

[27] Fe JAH don't favour havin sight up a face - an fe Him shall give the grace an glory Him prepared fe Him friends - persons who teach goodly Work - but thou have that thou might raceive thy reward like unto thy Work an the things that thou spoke.

[28] But there are nothing whereby thou will escape from JAH Itority Who shall judge pon thee - an Him have that Him might pay thee like unto thy Work - fe them whom thou taught an thou together will receive a sentance.

[29] Know that persons who dead shall arise - an if them are persons who kept Him LAW them shall arise - an like unto Earth send forth grass pon the time rain rained - as Him Command shall send them forth from a grave - it aren't possible fe it fe remain demolished an rotten.

[30] Like unto moist wood drink dew an send forth leaves pon the time Him satta she rain fe Earth - like unto wheat bear forth fruit - an like unto grain produce buds - like unto it aren't possible fe she fe withhold that she might prevent she fruit if JAH loved...

[31] an like unto it aren't possible fe a dawta who canceived fe close an prevent she womb pon the time labour seized she - like unto it aren't possible fe she fe escape without birthin...

[32] as dew have alit toward she bein commanded from JAH - at that time she shall produce them at one time - yet after she heard JAH Word - a grave also likewise cyaan prevent the persons gathered alongside she from arisin.

[33] An fleshes shall be gathered ina the place where them corpses fell - an them places where souls live shall be opened - an souls shall return toward the flesh where them were formerly separated.

[34] An pon the time a drum were beaten - persons who dead shall quickly arise like unto a eye wink - an havin arisen them shall stand before JAH - an Him shall give them them reward like unto them hand Work.

[35] At that time thou will sight up that thou arise with dead ones - an thou will marvel at all the Work thou worked ina this world - an pon the time thou sight up all thy sins written before thee - at that time thou will regret a useless regret.

[36] Thou know that thou will arise with dead ones an that thou will raceive thy hardship like unto the Work that thou worked.

Chapter 15

[1] But persons who found them reward by them goodly Work shall be Irie at that time ~ persons who ignored while them said - "Persons who dead won't arise" shall be sad at that time pon the time them sight up that persons who dead arose with them evil Work that don't benefit.

[2] That - them Work that them worked shall canvict them - an them ras selves shall know that it canvict them without one livin who will dispute them.

[3] Pon the day when Judgemant an mournin are done - pon the day when JAH shall come - pon the day when Definite Judgemant are judged - persons who forgot JAH LAW shall stand ina the place where them stand.

[4] Pon the day when there shall be total darkness - an pon the day when mist are pulled - pon the day when flashes are sight up an when lightnin are heard...

[5] an pon the day when quakes an fright an heatwave an sleet frost are made...

[6] pon the day when a evil person who worked evil Work raceive hardship - an pon the day when a clean person raceive him reward like unto him worked clean Work - an pon the day when persons who forgot JAH LAW receive the hardship like unto a sinner person worked sin - them shall stand ina the place where them stand.

[7] Fe pon the day when a master aren't more honoured than him slave - an pon the time when a mistress aren't more honoured than she slave...

[8] an pon the time when the king aren't more honoured than a poor one - an pon the time when a elder aren't more honoured than a infant - pon the time when a faada aren't more honoured than him child - an pon the time when a mother aren't more honoured than she child...

[9] pon the time when a wealthy one aren't more honoured than a poor one - an pon the time when a arrogant one aren't more honoured than a downbased one - an pon the time when the great aren't more honoured than the small - she are the day when Judgemant are judged - fe she are the day when them receive sentance an hardship - an fe she are the day when all will raceive hardship like unto them worked sin.

[10] An fe she are the day when persons who worked goodly Work receive them reward - an fe she are the day when persons who worked sin raceive hardship.

[11] An as she are the day when persons who found them reward are made Irie - persons who forgot JAH LAW shall stand ina the place where them stand. Persons who mek liars - who digest books while them said - "Persons who dead won't arise" - them shall sight up Resurrection.

[12] At that time this world sinners - who didn't work goodly Work ina this world - shall weep pon them sin that them worked - becau sadness found them without calmin.

[13] An all likewise - kind persons who worked goodly Work - them Irie Ites won't be fulfilled up til Iternity - fe them have worked goodly Work when them were ina this world.

[14] Fe them have known that them will arise after them dead - an them didn't depart from them Irator LAW.

[15] Becau them didn't depart from Him LAW - them shall inherit two welfares ~ Him multiplied them seed ina this world - an Him honoured them childran.

[16] Him bequeathed them the Kingdom of Heaven where shall be found the welfare him swore fe them faadas pon the time when persons who dead arise - an pon the time when rich ones become poor.

[17] Persons shall weep who worked sin - who don't believe persons who dead arisin - who don't keep JAH LAW - an who don't think of Arisin Day.

[18] At that time them will sight up the tribulation that shall find them an shall have no endin - an where are no calmin nor welfare - an it have the sadness that have no rest nor calmin ina them reasonin.

[19] An a fiyah that don't perish an worms that don't sleep shall find them.

[20] An ina the place where are them flesh are fiyah - sulphur - whirl wind - frost - hail - sleet ~ all this shall rain over them.

[21] Fe persons who don't believe persons who dead arisin - there are fiyah of *Gehannem* pon them.

Chapter 16

[1] Thou - please think of what are pon thy flesh - an thy feet an thy hands nails - an thy head hair - fe them proceed quickly pon the time thou cut them ~ know Resurrection by this - that thou have a reasonin - an that thou have religion an knowledge.

[2] Thy feet an thy hands nails an thy head hair - thou say - "Where do these come from?" ~ aren't it JAH Who prepared it that them might proceed - that thou know arisin that shall be done pon thy flesh that aren't pon another flesh - that thou might know that thou will arise after thou dead?

[3] Becau thou misled persons while thou said - "There are no Resurrection of the dead ones" - pon the time when dead ones arise thou will raceive thy hardship like unto thou worked sin an iniquity.

[4] An as even what thou planted now won't remain refusin that it might grow - whether it be wheat or barley - thou will sight she up pon the time the day arrived when thou raceive thy hardship.

[5] An again - the plant thou planted won't say - "I-man won't grow" - an be it a fig wood or a grape vine - it fruit an it leaf won't be changed.

[6] If thou plant grapes - it won't be changed that it might be a fig - an if thou plant figs - it won't be changed that it might be grapes - an if thou sow wheat it won't be changed that it might be barley.

[7] All - ina each of the seeds - ina each of it kinds - each of the fruits - each of the woods - each of the leaves - each of the roots - send forth fruit havin raceived Pardon Dew blessin by what are found from JAH - yet if thou sow barley also it won't be changed that it might be wheat.

[8] An all likewise - that a grave might produce flesh an soul - she shall produce persons like unto JAH sowed pon she ~ the flesh an soul that JAH sowed shall arise bein Inited - yet persons who worked goodly Work won't be changed ina persons who worked evil Work - an persons who worked

evil Work also won't be changed ina persons who worked goodly Work.

[9] Pon pon the time the iwa arrived when a drum are beaten - persons who dead shall arise by the Pardon Dew found from JAH ~ persons who worked goodly Work shall arise ina Life Resurrection - an them reward are the Garden where are Irie Ites that JAH prepared fe kind persons - where are no tribulation nor disease - an that are clean ones lodgin where them won't again dead after this.

[10] But persons who worked evil Work shall arise a Definite Judgemant arisin - an with Deeyablos who misled them...

[11] an with him armies - demons who don't love that even one person might be saved from all 'Adam childran...

[12] them shall downscend toward *Gehannem* that were darkness edge - where are tooth grindin an mournin - where are no charity nor pardon - an where are no exits up til Iternity - that are beneath *See'ol* foriva. Fe them didn't work goodly Work ina them Life ina this world when them were ina them flesh.

[13] Becaudis thing it shall be judged pon them pon the time when flesh an soul arise bein Inited.

[14] Woe fe persons who don't believe the flesh an soul arisin whereby JAH show Him miracles abundance together.

[15] An all an each one shall raceive him reward like unto him Work and him hands weariness.

Chapter 17

[1] A wheat kernel won't grow nor bear fruit unless she were demolished. But if a wheat kernel are demolished she will send roots toward Earth ~ she will send forth leaves ~ there will be buds ~ it will bear fruit.

[2] Unu know that the one wheat kernel will become many kernels.

[3] An all likewise - this kernel grow risin up from Water an wind an Earth dew - fe wheat cyaan bear fruit without Sun - but Sun are becau fiyah stead.

[4] An wind are becau a soul stead - an wheat cyaan bear fruit without wind - an the Water give Earth fe drink an satta she.

[5] An after Earth that are ashes drank Water - she produce roots - an she tips are lofty upward ~ she bear fruit around what JAH blessed she.

[6] But a wheat kernel are 'Adam example - ina whom lodged a resonatin soul that JAH Irated - an likewise a grape wood drink Water an send forth roots - an the thin root kinds drink Water.

[7] Fe Pardon Dew found from JAH give fe drink vines tips that were long - an it send the Water upward toward the leaf tips ~ it bud up from the Sun heat - an by JAH Accord it bear fruit.

[8] It shall be a goodly fragrance that mek a reasonin Irie - an pon the time them ate it - it shall satta like unto Water that don't mek thirsty an grain that don't mek hungry - an pon the time them immersed it - it will be the cluster blood.

[9] An like unto it were told ina Psalm sayin - "Grapes mek a person reasonin Irie" - pon the time them drank it - it mek a person heart Irie - an pon the time a person who came loose opened him mouth an drank it - him are drunk ~ him drink an fill ina him lungs - an the blood flow toward him heart.

[10] As grapes drunkenness totally mislead - an as it deprive him him mind - it mek the pit an the cliff like unto a wide meadow - an him don't know obstacles an thorns pon him feet an hands.

[11] JAH did thus pon she fruit an grape wood that Him Name might be praised by persons who believe dead persons arisin an who do Him Accord.

[12] Ina the Kingdom of Heaven Him shall mek persons Irie who believe persons who dead arisin.

Chapter 18

[1] Unu persons who don't believe persons who dead arisin - around what error unu err! An pon the time them took unu toward the place unu don't know - unu will regret a useless regrets - an becau unu didn't believe the arisin that persons who dead shall arise Inited ina soul an flesh - an pon the time persons cast unu toward *Gehannem*...

[2] if unu work whether the good or the evil - unu will raceive your reward like unto your Work - fe unu have misled them companions reasonin while unu said - "Wi know that persons who dead - who were dust an ashes - won't arise."

[3] As them death have no exit - an as them have no Power fe them chastisemant that shall come pon them - an as them weren't firm ina them tribulation - becaudis thing them mislead them companions ~ fe them have that them might stand ina JAH Square.

[4] Pon the time Him vexed pon them ina Him wrath them will totally fear ~ becau them didn't know that them were Irated bringin from not livin toward livin - as them speak JAH LAW without knowin - it shall be judged pon them all becau them worked evil.

[5] Them don't know *Gehannem* where them will go - fe becau them were angry an becau them were crooked ina them Work - them teach fe them companions like unto them reasonin thirst measure - an fe them are evil ones who teach a crooked thing while them said - "There are no Resurrection of dead ones."

[6] At that time them shall know that persons who dead shall arise - an them shall know that it shall be judged pon them becau them didn't believe the persons who dead arisin that are fe all 'Adam childran.

[7] Fe all InI are 'Adam childran - an fe InI have dead becau 'Adam - an fe death judgemant have found InI all from alongside JAH becau InI faada 'Adam error.

[8] InI will again arise there with InI faada 'Adam that InI might raceive InI hardship by InI Work that InI worked - fe the world have been ruled fe death by InI faada 'Adam ignorance.

[9] By 'Adam infringin JAH Command - becaudis thing InI raceived hardship ~ InI flesh ina grave melted like unto wax - an InI bodies perished.

[10] An Earth drank InI marrow ~ InI perished an InI comeliness perished ina grave - an InI flesh were buried ina grave - an InI beautiful words were buried ina Earth.

[11] An worms proceeded from InI shinin eyes - an InI features perished ina grave an became dust.

[12] Where are youtmons features comeliness - who were attractive - whose stance were handsome an whose word thing succeeded? How about where are warriors firmness?

[13] Where are the kings armies - or how about the nobles lordship? Where are adornin ina horses an adornin ina silver an gold an adornin ina shinin weapons? Didn't it perish?

[14] Where are sweet grape drink - an how about food flavour?

Chapter 19

[1] O Earth who gathered the nobles an the kings an rich ones an elders an dawtaz who were attractive an beauties who were attractive - woe arisin from thee-I.

[2] O Earth who gathered persons who were warriors - them who have comeliness - an them who were fine of leg - an them who have reasonin an knowledge - an them whose words have words that were beautiful like unto a hummin harp an like unto a lyre an a violin beat...

[3] an them who have a tune that mek Irie like unto grape drink mek Irie - an them whose eyes shine like unto a mornin star...

[4] an them who sketch what were firm like unto them right hands lift up what are given an withheld an like unto them were - an them whose feet were beautiful fe sight up - an them who run like unto rushin wheels - woe arisin from thee-I.

[5] O death who separated attractive persons souls from them flesh - woe arisin from thee-I - fe thou have been sent by JAH Accord.

[6] As thou have gathered many persons whom JAH produced from thee-I an returned toward thee-I - thou Earth - woe arisin from thee-I ~ InI were found from thee-I ~ InI returned toward thee-I by Accord of JAH ~ InI were Irie over thee-I by JAH Accord.

[7] Thou became a carpet fe InI corpses ~ InI recurred over thee-I - an InI were buried within thee-I ~ InI ate thy fruit - an thou ate InI flesh.

[8] An InI drank the Water found from thy springs - an thou drank InI blood springs ~ InI ate the fruit found from thy Earthliness - an thou ate InI body flesh.

[9] Like unto JAH commanded thee-I fe be InI food - InI ate grain from thy Earthliness that have beautiful dew - an thou raceived InI fleh comeliness an made it dust fe thy food like unto JAH commanded thee-I.

[10] O death who gathered the nobles an the kings who were powerful - woe arisin from thee-I ~ thou didn't fear arisin from them famousness an them frightenin - like unto JAH Who Irated them commanded thee-I ~ o death - woe arisin from thee-I - an thou didn't scorn the sufferah.

[11] An thou weren't nice fe persons whose features are beautiful - an thou didn't quit powerful ones an warriors ~ thou didn't quit poor nor rich ones - neither kind nor evil ones - neither childran nor elders - neither dawtaz nor males.

[12] Thou didn't quit persons who think a goodly thing an who didn't depart from the LAW - an thou didn't quit them who were like unto animals ina them Work - who think a evil thing - who were totally beautiful ina them features comeliness - ina them thing flavour an ina them words ~ o death - woe arisin from thee-I.

[13] Thou didn't quit persons whose words were angry an whose mouths were full of curses ~ thou gathered persons who live in darkness an ina light an them souls ina thy places ~ o death - woe arisin from thee-I.

[14] An Earth gathered the persons flesh who live whether ina cave or ina Earth - up til a drum are beaten an persons who dead arise.

[15] As persons who dead shall arise quickly like unto a eye wink by JAH Command an pon a drum bein beaten - persons who worked evil Work shall raceive them hardship ina them sin abundance measure that them worked it - an persons who worked goodly Work shall be Irie.

Chapter 20

[1] An believe I that all InI Work that InI worked ina this world won't remain nor be hidden pon the time InI stood before Him fearin an tremblin.

[2] An pon the time InI didn't seize provisions fe InI path - an pon the time InI won't have clothes fe InI bodies...

[3] pon the time InI won't have a staff fe InI hands nor shoes fe InI feet...

[4] an pon the time InI won't know the paths where demons tek InI - whether it be slippery or smooth - or be it dark - an whether it be thorns or nettles - or whether it be a Water depth or a pit depth - believe I that InI Work that InI worked ina this world won't remain nor be hidden.

[5] InI won't know the demons who tek InI - an InI won't hear them thing.

[6] As them are black ones - an as them lead InI toward darkness - InI don't sight up them faces.

[7] An like unto the prophet spoke sayin - "Pon the time I soul were separated from I flesh - Lord I Lord - Thou know I path - an them hid a trap pon that path where I-man went - an I-man sight up returnin toward the right ~ I-man lacked one who know I - an I-man have nothing there whereby I-man will escape" - as them tek InI toward darkness - InI won't sight up them faces.

[8] As him know that demons ridicule pon him - an as them will lead him toward the path him don't know - him speakin this are becaudis - an if him return leftward an rightward - there are no person who know him.

[9] Him are alone amidst demons - an yet there are none who know him.

[10] Angels of Light who are subtle are who are sent toward kind persons that them might raceive righteous ones souls - an might tek toward a Light place - toward the Garden - where welfare are found.

[11] Demons an Angels of darkness are who are sent that them might raceive them an might tek them toward *Gehannem* that were prepared fe them that them might raceive them hardship by them sin that them worked.

[12] Woe fe sinner persons souls who tek them toward downstruction - who have no welfare nor rest - nor escapin from the tribulation that found them - nor proceedin from *Gehannem* up til Iternity.

[13] As them have lived firmed up ina Qayel Work - an as them have perished by Bele`am iniquity price - an as them have lacked what them will do - woe fe sinner persons - fe them pretext fe raceive interest an presents that ina downgression them might tek a foreigner money that weren't them money.

[14] Them shall raceive them hardship ina *Gehannem* by them sin that them worked.

Chapter 21

[1] Where are persons who gather a foreigner money that weren't them hands Work nor them money?

[2] Fe them tek a person money for free - an fe them shll be gathered without knowin the day when them dead that shall arrive pon them - however them quit them money for a foreigner.

[3] Fe like unto them faadas - them are sinners kindreds who worry an seize sinners like unto them whether it be by theft or by robbery - an them childran won't be Irie by them faadas money.

[4] As them have gathered fe them ina downgression - an as it are like unto misty urine an like unto the smoke that wind scattar an like unto wiltin grass - an like unto wax that melt arisin from before a fiyah - as sinners glory shall perish like unto that - there are none whom them faadas money will benefit ~ like unto Daweet spoke sayin - "I-man sight up a sinner man...

[5] bein honoured an famed like unto a cordia an like unto a cypress - but pon the time I-man returned I-man lacked him ~ I-man searched an didn't find him place" - there are none whom them faadas money will profit nor benefit.

[6] Becau them gathered a person money ina downgression - it seemin fe them that them won't dead - like unto persons who wrong them companions won't boast - sinner persons downstruction are likewise at one time.

[7] Unu lazy ones - think that unu will perish an that your money will perish with unu - an if your silver an your gold abound it shall be rusted.

[8] An if unu birth many childran them shall be fe many graves - an if unu work many houses them shall be demolished.

[9] Fe unu didn't fulfill your Irator JAH Accord - an if unu multiply livestock them shall be for your enemies capture - an all the money unu seized ina your hands won't be found - fe it have been what weren't blessed.

[10] Whether it be ina house or ina forest - an be it ina wilderness or a pasture place - an be it ina grape threshinfloor or ina grain threshinfloor - it won't be found.

[11] Becau unu didn't keep JAH Command - as JAH won't save unu with all your house hold from the tribulation - there shall be sadness pon unu arisin from all your enemies - yet unu won't be Irie ina your childran birthed from your nature.

[12] But from Him plenty - Him won't trouble persons who kept Him Order an Him LAW ~ Him give all who begged

Him - yet Him bless them childran birthed from them nature an also them land fruit fe them.

[13] An Him mek them rulers pon all peoples ina them area that them might rule lest them be who are ruled - an Him give them all Him plenty ina them pasture place.

[14] Him bless fe them all them seized ina them hand - all them field fruit - an all them livestocks places - an Him mek them Irie in them childran birthed from them nature.

[15] An Him don't diminish them livestocks pon them ~ Him save them from all them tribulation an from weariness an illness an downstruction - an from them enemy them don't know an from him them know.

[16] An Him will dispute fe them ina Judgemant time - an Him shall save them from a evil thing an from tribulation an from all who dispute them ~ ina the first era if a priest lived who work the Tent Work - who keep the LAW an keep the Tent Order an live firmed up ina JAH Accord - by the first Order an all the LAW as them would give him the tithe an what were birthed first Iginnin from man up til livestock - Him would save them from all the tribulation.

[17] Like unto Mussie commanded Newie child 'Iyasu - there was a country of sanctuary ina all them country ~ by not knowin an by knowin up til them judged judgemant pon whom them canvicted an fe whom them acquitted...

[18] if a person lived who killed a soul - him would be measured there that him might be saved.

[19] Him told them - "Examine ina your reasonins that him have a quarrel with him formerly - an be it by axe or be it by a stone or be it by wood - as it have fallen from him hand by not knowin - if him say "That person pon whom it fell dead pon mi" - examine an save him ~ if him did it ina not knowin mek him be saved.

[20] But if him do it knowin - him will raceive him hardship like unto him sin - an there are none who will pardon him; but if him kill him ina not knowin - as him have done it ina not knowin - examine an save him lest him dead.

[21] Him worked fe them that them might distance from all the sin - yet Mussie would work like unto this fe 'Isra'iel childran lest them depart from JAH LAW.

[22] Him commanded them that 'Adam childran - who live firmed up ina JAH Command from worshippin idols an eatin what dead an lodged an what a sword bloated an cut - an who distance from all evil work like unto him worked fe them - that them might work it an might totally distance from all that aren't due.

[23] Him commanded them lest them depart from the Command Him worked fe them ina the Tent example ina Heaven - that them might save them bodies an might find them lodgin with them faadas.

[24] As them have been birthed from Siet an 'Adam who did JAH Accord - persons who believed ina JAH Word an lived firmed up ina Him Command will be called kind persons childran.

[25] As InI are 'Adam childran - as Him have Irated InI ina Him Example an Him Appearance that InI might work all goodly Work that mek JAH Irie - Him won't scorn it.

[26] As Him totally won't separate Him friends - if InI work goodly Work - InI shall inherit the Kingdom of Heaven where are welfare with persons who work goodly Work.

[27] Him totally love persons who beg him cleanly - an Him hear them ina them priah - an Him accept the repentance of persons who are disciplined an enter repentance ~ Him give firmness an Power fe persons who keep Him Order an Him LAW an Him Command.

[28] Persons who did Him Accord shall be Irie with Him ina Him Kingdom foriva - an whether them be persons who preceded or who arose later - them will present praise fe Him Iginnin from today up til Iternity.

Mek glory due fe JAH foriva - an the secand Meqabyan arrived an were fulfilled.

III MEQABYAN

Chapter 1

[1] Kristos shall rejoice Gibts persons - becau Him shall come toward them ina later era that Him will revenge an downstroy Deeyablos - who wronged them who were kindly an innocent - an who misled persons - an who hate him Irator Work.

[2] Him shall revenge an downstroy him ~ Him shall return him lordship toward wretchedness an bein downbased - fe him have been arrogant ina him reasonin.

[3] Him shall return him lordship toward bein downbased - fe him have said - "As mi will enter toward the sea midst - an as mi will proceed toward Heaven - an as mi will sight up depths - an as mi will grasp an seize 'Adam childran like unto bird chicks - who are it who are loftier than mi?

[4] Becau mi became by them reason that mi might distance them from the straight LAW of JAH - as mi will strengthen pon persons who live ina this world unless them did JAH Accord - there are none who will depose mi from mi authority" him said.

[5] "Fe mi will be a reason fe return them toward a path that were smooth fe go toward *Gehannem* with mi.

[6] Persons who loved Him an kept Him LAW hate mi becaudis thing - but persons who departed from them Lord LAW an who erred will come toward mi an love mi an keep mi oath ~ as mi will mek them reasonin evil an change them thoughts lest them return toward them Irator JAH - them will do mi command like unto mi commanded them.

[7] An pon the time mi showed them this world money - mi will mislead them reasonin from straight LAW - an pon the time mi showed them beautiful an attractive dawtaz - mi will distance them by these from straight LAW.

[8] An pon the time mi showed them shinin Hindekie jewels an silver an gold - mi will distance them by this also from straight LAW that them might return toward mi Work.

[9] An pon the time mi showed them thin clothes an red silk an white silk - an linens an white silk - mi will distance them by this also from straight LAW - an mi will return them toward mi thoughts ~ pon the time mi multiplied money an livestocks like unto sand an showed them - by this also mi will return them toward mi Work.

[10] An pon the time mi showed them jealousy done in arrogance becau dawtaz an becau anger an quarrels - by all this mi will return them toward mi Work.

[11] An pon the time mi showed them signs - mi will lodge ina them companions reasonin - an mi will lodge a sign thing that were fe each of the ras selves ina them reasonin - an mi showed them words signs an misled them.

[12] An fe persons ina whom mi lodged mi lodgin - mi will show them signs - an be it ina stars gait - or be it ina cloud proceedin or ina fiyah flickerin - or be it ina beasts an birds cries - as them are mi lodgins - mi will lodge signs ina them reasonin pon them by all this.

[13] Them will speak an give signs fe them companions - an like unto those them naysayers told them - mi will precede an be a sign fe them.

[14] Mi will do them words signs fe them - that persons who examined them might be misled - an that them might give a wage fe magicians - an that them might tell fe them companions sayin - 'There are no savants like unto so-an-so an so-an-so fe whom it are done like unto them spoke - an who know prophecy - an who separate good an evil - an fe whom all are like unto them spoke - an fe whom it are done like unto them word.'

[15] Mi will be Irie pon the time them spoke this - that persons who perish an err by mi might totally abound an that 'Adam childran might perish - fe JAH have downbased mi from mi rank becau them faada 'Adam - pon mi sayin 'Mi won't bow fe 'Adam who are downbased fe mi.'

[16] An mi will tek toward downstruction all him childran who live firmed up ina mi command ~ mi have a Oath from JAH Who Irated mi - that all persons whom mi misled might downscend toward *Gehannem* with mi.

[17] An pon the time Him multiplied Him anger pon mi - an pon the time Him commanded that them might bind an cast mi toward *Gehannem* - pon the time mi Irator commanded sayin thus - mi interceded with mi Lord ~ mi interceded before Him while mi said - 'As Thou have vexed pon mi - an as Thou have admonished mi by Thy chastisemant - an as Thou have chastised mi by Thy wrath

- Lord mi Lord - adjourn mi that mi might speak one thing before Thee-I.'

[18] An mi Lord answered fe mi sayin - Speak - I-man will hear thee ~ at that time mi began mi plea toward Him sayin - 'After mi were downbased from mi rank - mek the persons whom mi misled be like unto mi ina *Gehannem* where mi will raceive tribulation.

[19] An mek them be fe Thy Lordship who refused mi - who didn't err by mi - who didn't keep mi command - that them might do Thy Command an might fulfill Thy Accord an might keep Thy Word - pon the time them didn't err by mi like unto mi misled them havin refused like unto mi taught them - an pon the time Thou loved mi - mek them tek the crown Thou gave fe mi.

[20] Give them the crown of the authorities called Seythans who were sent with mi ~ seat them pon mi throne pon Thy Right that were a wilderness from mi an mi hosts.

[21] An mek them praise Thee-I like unto Thou loved - an mek them be like unto mi hosts an like unto mi ~ becau Thou hated mi an loved them who were Irated from ashes an Earth - as mi authority have perished - an as them authority have been lofty - mek them praise Thee-I like unto Thou loved.'

[22] Mi Lord answered fe mi sayin - As thou have misled them while them sight up an while them heard - if thou misled them without them lovin I Order - mek them be fe thee like unto thy accord an like unto thy word.

[23] If them quit the Books Word an I Command an came toward thee - an if thou misled them while them downstruction also saddened mi - mek them raceive tribulation ina *Gehannem* like unto thee - Him told mi.

[24] Unu will raceive tribulation ina *Gehannem* up til the Iternity - yet unu will have no exits from *Gehannem* up til the Iternity - fe them whom thou misled nor fe thee.

Chapter 2

[1] But I-man shall bequeath thy throne ina lordship fe them whom it failed thee fe mislead - like unto I slave 'Iyob ~ JAH Who rule all said - I-man will give the Kingdom of Heaven fe persons whom it failed thee fe mislead.

[2] An mi provoke pon 'Adam childran ina all ~ if it were possible fe mi fe mislead them - mi won't quit them that them might firm up ina goodly Work ~ fe mi provoke pon all 'Adam childran - an mi sweeten this world Irie Ites fe them.

[3] Be it by lovin drink an food an clothes - or by lovin things - or by withholdin an givin...

[4] or be it by lovin fe hear an sight up - or be it by lovin fe caress an go - or be it by multiplyin arrogance an things - or be it by lovin dreams an slumber...

[5] or be it by multiplyin drunkenness an drink - or be it by multiplyin insults an anger - be it by speakin games an useless things...

[6] or be it by quarrels an by backbitin them companion - or be it by sightin up this world dawtaz who were attractive - be it by smellin perfumes fragrance that mislead them...

[7] mi hate them by all this lest them able fe be saved ~ mi distance them from JAH LAW that them might enter with mi toward the downstruction whereby mi were downbased from mi rank."

[8] An the prophet told him - "Thou who downstroy persons - perish ~ pon the time thou departed from JAH LAW an committed crime ina thy reasonin firmness an thy arrogance - an by saddenin thy Irator an not worshippin thy Irator ina thy reasonin firmness - will thou thus be arrogant pon JAH Iration?

[9] Pon the time thy Irator vexed pon thee - Him downbased thee from thy rank becau thy evil Work ~ why do thou tek 'Adam toward sin - him whom him Irator Irated from Earth - whom Him made like unto Him loved - an whom Him placed fe Him praise?" him told him.

[10] "Pon the time thou - who are subtle an were Irated from wind an fiyah - were arrogant ina sayin 'Mi are the Irator'...

[11] pon the time thou boasted - as JAH have sight up thy evil Work an thou have denied JAH with thy hosts - Him Irated 'Adam who will praise becau thy stead - that him might praise Him Name without diminishin.

[12] As thou have made thy ras self prouder than all Angels hosts who are like unto thee - becau thy arrogance JAH Irated 'Adam with him childran that them might praise JAH Name becau the praise that thou praise with thy hosts whom Him scorned.

[13] An becaudis thing JAH downstroyed thee separatin from all Angels chiefs like unto thee - an thy hosts Irated ina one counsel with thee - an thou - unu proceeded an erred from JAH praise becau your useless reasonin arrogance an becau your reasonin firmness - an unu were arrogant pon your Irator - that aren't pon another.

[14] Becaudis thing Him Irated 'Adam from Earth that Him might be praised by downbased persons - an Him gave him a Command an Law sayin Don't eat lest him eat from fig fruit.

[15] An Him I-pointed him pon all the Iration Him Irated ~ Him notified him sayin - Don't eat from one fig fruit that bring death - lest thou bring death pon thy ras self - yet eat fruit from all the woods amidst the Garden.

[16] An pon the time thou heard this Word - thou lodged perfidy ina him arisin from the thing thou spoke ina thy tongue fe Hiewan who were found from 'Adam side bone.

[17] Thou misled 'Adam who were clean - ina firm perfidy that thou might mek him a Law demolisher like unto thee.

[18] Pon the time thou misled Hiewan - who were Irated bein like unto a innocent dove an who don't know thy malice - thou made she betray by thy thing that succeeded an thy crooked word - an after thou misled that Hiewan who were Irated beforehand - she also went an misled JAH Iration 'Adam who were Irated from Earth beforehand.

[19] An thou made him betray a downsturbance that aren't by thy arrogance - an thou made him fe deny that him might deny him Irator Word - an thou downstroyed 'Adam ina thy arrogance.

[20] An ina thy malice thou distanced him from him Irator Love - an by thy reason thou sent him way from the Garden where Irie Ites are - an by thy hindrance thou made him quit the Garden food.

[21] Fe Iginnin from Antiquity thou have quarreled with the innocent Iration 'Adam that thou might lower him toward *See'ol* where thou will raceive hardship - an that thou might send him way from the Love that brought him an Irated him from not livin toward true livin - an by thy false thing thou made him thirst a drink from the Garden.

[22] An when him are Earthly - Him made him a subtle Angel who totally praise him Irator ina him flesh an him soul an him reasonin.

[23] An Him Irated many thoughts fe him - like unto harps praise ina each of them styles.

Chapter 3

[1] But Him Irated one thought fe thee - that thou might totally praise while thou were sent toward where thy Irator sent thee.

[2] But fe 'Adam were given five thoughts that were evil an five thoughts that were goodly - ten thoughts.

[3] An again him have many thoughts like unto sea waves - an like unto a whirl wind that scattar dust liftin up from Earth - an like unto the sea waves that shake - an arisin from him unnumbered thoughts abundance ina him heart like unto unnumbered rain drops - 'Adam thoughts are like unto that.

[4] But thy thought are one ~ as thou aren't fleshly - thou have no other thought.

[5] But thou lodged ina snake reasonin ~ ina evil perfidy thou downstroyed 'Adam who were one limb - an Hiewan heard the snake thing - an havin heard - she did like unto she commanded she.

[6] After she ate a fig fruit - she came an misled JAH first Iration 'Adam - an she brought death pon him an pon she childran becau she infringed she Irator Command.

[7] Them proceeded from the Garden fe JAH by Him true Judgemant ~ Him calmed them ina the land where them were sent by them childran birthed from them nature an by them crops found from Earth - yet Him didn't distance them from the Garden quarrelin.

[8] An pon the time thou expelled them straight from the Garden - that them might plant plants an childran fe be calmed an fe renew them reasonin ina the Earth fruit that Earth prepared from she Earthliness - an that them might be calmed by Earth fruit an the Garden fruit that JAH gave them...

[9] JAH gave them woods more verdant than the Garden woods - an Hiewan an 'Adam - whom thou sent way from the Garden pon them eatin it - were totally calmed from sadness.

[10] As JAH know fe calm Him Iration - them reasonins are calmed becau them childran an becau the crops found from Earth.

[11] As them have been sent toward this world that grow nettles an thorns - them firm up them reasonins ina Water an grain.

Chapter 4

[1] The Lord have that Him might ransom 'Adam - an Him shall shame thee ~ Him will save a sheep from a wolf mouth ('Adam from Deeyablos).

[2] However thou will go toward *Gehannem* seizin with thee the persons whom thou ruled.

[3] Persons who kept them Irator JAH LAW shall be Irie with them Irator JAH Who hid them from evil Work that Him might mek them Him fortune - an that them might praise Him with honoured Angels who didn't infringe them Irator JAH LAW like unto thee.

[4] But JAH - Who chose an gave thee more than all Angels like unto thee that thou might praise Him with Him servant Angels - withheld from thee a lofty throne ina thy arrogance.

[5] But thou became famous an were called one who love godhood - an thy hosts were called demons.

[6] But persons who loved JAH shall be Him kindreds like unto honoured Angels - an the *Surafiel* an *Keerubiel* who praise Him streach forth them wings an praise without slackness.

[7] But ina thy arrogance an thy laziness thou downstroyed thy praise that thou might praise Him everytime with thy host an thy kindreds Irated ina thy features.

[8] Lest the praise of JAH - Who Irated thee makin a tenth tribe - be diminished pon the time thou forgot the praise of JAH Who Irated thee - it havin seemed fe thee that it aren't posssible fe Him fe Irate a Iration like unto thee - an lest the praise of JAH - Who Irated thee - be diminished pon the time thou were separated from thy bredren Inity - Him Irated 'Adam becau thy stead.

[9] But ina thy reasonin arrogance thou neglected the praise of JAH Who Irated thee - an Him vexed pon thee ~ Him ridiculed thee - an Him bound an banished thee ina *Gehannem* with thy hosts also.

[10] Him brought Soil from Earth with Him glorified Hands - an addin fiyah an Water an wind - Him Irated 'Adam ina Him Example an Him Features.

[11] Him I-pointed him pon all the Iration Him Irated ina Him Itority - that Him praise might be filled by the praise thou would praise Him ~ 'Adam praise became one with Angels praise - an them praise were level.

[12] But ina thy collar of reasonin firmness an thy arrogance thou were downbased from thy rank - an havin departed from JAH Lordship - Who Irated thee - thou downstroyed thy ras self.

[13] Know that Him praise weren't diminished - fe JAH have Irated 'Adam who praised Him ina him reasonin counsel lest Him JAH-ness praise be diminished.

[14] Fe Him know all before it are done - an Him knew thee before Him Irated thee that thou will demolish Him Command ~ as there are a counsel hidden alongside Him before Him Irated the world - pon the time thou denied Him - Him Irated Him slave 'Adam ina Him Features an Him Example.

[15] Like unto Selomon spoke sayin - 'Before hills were Irated an before the world succeeded bein Irated - an before winds that are Earth grounations were Irated...

[16] an before Him firmed up hills an mountains grounations - an before this world Work firmed up - an before moon an Sun light shone - before eras an stars caretakin were known...

[17] an before daylight an night alternated - an before the sea were delineated by sand - before all the Irated Iration were Irated...

[18] an before all sight up today were sight up - before all the names called today were called - Him Irated I Selomon' - Angels like unto unu an thou an Him slave 'Adam were ina JAH Reasonin.

[19] Him Irated 'Adam that Him glorified Name might be praised pon the time thou mutinied - an that Him might be praised by Him downbased slave 'Adam who were Irated from Earth pon the time thou were arrogant.

[20] Fe bein ina Heaven JAH hear poor ones plea - an Him love downbased persons praise.

[21] Him love fe save havin lodged ina persons who fear Him - yet as Him don't love horse Power - an as Him don't step meanin fe the lap of a concubine - JAH shall ignore arrogant ones thing.

[22] An them shall weep while them cried becau them sin that them worked.

[23] It failed thee fe plead ina repentance.

[24] But 'Adam who were Irated from Earth returned ina repentance while him totally wept before JAH becau him sin.

[25] But ina thy collar of reasonin firmness an thy heart arrogance thou didn't know Love Work an thou didn't know repentance ~ it failed thee fe plead before thy Irator JAH ina repentance an mournin an sadness.

[26] But that 'Adam who are ashes an Earth returned toward repentance ina mournin an sadness - an him returned toward humbleness an Love Work.

[27] But thou didn't downbase thy reasonin an thy ras self fe JAH Who Irated thee.

[28] As fe 'Adam - him downbased him ras self an pleaded pon the iniquity him wronged ~ him weren't proud.

[29] As thou have totally produced crime - it were found from thee - yet it aren't him who produced that error ~ ina thy arrogance thou took him with thee toward thy downstruction.

[30] Before him Irated unu both - as Him have known unu that unu were sinners - an as Him have known your Works - Him know that this that were done were ina thy heart arrogance.

[31] But Him returned that 'Adam - who were without arrogance or malice - ina repentance mournin an sadness.

[32] Fe a person who wrong an don't plead ina repentance have multiplied him iniquity more than him earlier iniquity - but ina thy heart arrogance it failed thee fe plead ina repentance - but a person who plead an weep enterin repentance before Him Irator JAH...

[33] him entered repentance fe true - an him found Work whereby him will be saved that him might fear him Lord Heart - an him pleaded before him Irator - fe him have pleaded before Him ina bowin an much repentance - an arisin from the earlier tribulation the Lord shall lighten him sin fe him lest Him vex pon Him slave - an Him will forgive him him former sin.

[34] If him didn't return toward him former sin an if him did this - this are perfect repentance ~ 'Adam didn't forget fe think of him Irator nor fe implore him Irator JAH ina repentance.

[35] An thou - plea ina repentance toward thy Irator JAH - an don't wrong them becau them were flesh an blood - fe JAH Who Irated them know them weakness - an don't wrong the persons Him Irated by Him Itority.

[36] An after them soul were separated from them flesh - them flesh shall be dust up til the day that JAH love.

Chapter 5

[1] Know JAH WHo Irated thee-I ~ as JAH have Irated thee-I ina Him Features an Him Example when thou are Earth - don't forget JAH Who firmed thee-I up an saved thee-I an Whom 'Isra'iel glorified ~ Him placed thee-I ina Garden that thou might be Irie an might dig Earth.

[2] Pon the time thou demolished Him Command - Him sent thee way from the Garden toward this world that Him cursed becau thee - that grow nettles an thorns.

[3] *Fe thou are Earth - an fe she are Earth - fe thou are dust - an fe she are dust - fe thou are Soil - an fe she are Soil - fe thou are fed the grain found from she - an fe thou will return toward she* - fe thou will be Soil up til Him love that Him might raise thee - an fe Him shall examine thee the sin thou worked an all the iniquity.

[4] Know what thou will answer Him at that time ~ think of the good an evil thou worked ina this world ~ examine whether the evil would abound or whether the good would abound ~ try.

[5] If thou work a goodly thing - it are a goodly thing fe thee-I that thou might be Irie pon the day when persons who dead will arise.

[6] But if thou work evil Work - woe fe thee - fe thou will raceive thy hardship like unto thy hands Work an like unto thy reasonin evil ~ fe if thou work a evil thing pon thy companion an if thou didn't fear JAH - thou will receive thy hardship.

[7] An if thou betray thy companion an if thou call JAH Name an swear ina lie - as thou will receive thy hardship like unto thy Work - woe fe thee.

[8] An thou tell thy false thing fe thy companion simulatin Truth - but thou know that thou spoke a lie.

[9] An thou persuade the persons with thee thy false thing simulatin Truth - an thou multiply false things that weren't Truth - an thou will raceive thy hardship like unto thy sin ~ thou deny thy companion while thou tell thy companion 'mi will give thee' what thou won't give him.

[10] An pon the time thou said 'Mi will give' ina thy pure reasonin - demons mek application fe thee like unto dogs - an them mek thee forget all - an if thou withhold or if thou love that thou might give - them don't know the person fe whom them gather - yet as Him have said - Them shall

fatten - this world money appetise thee that thou might fatten the money that won't benefit thee an that thou won't eat.

[11] An again - as Him have said - 'Adam liar childran mek a balance false ~ as fe them - them go from robbery toward robbery - this world money appetise thee.

[12] O persons - don't mek hope ina distortin scales an balances - an ina stealin a person money - an ina makin a person money one ina downgression - an ina infringin your companions money - an ina stealin him field - ina all the lies unu do fe your ras selves profit that aren't fe your companions.

[13] If unu do this unu will raceive your hardship like unto your Work.

[14] O persons - be fed by your hands Work that were straight - yet don't desire robbery ~ don't love that unu might totally rob an eat a person money without justice by what aren't due.

[15] An if unu eat it - it won't satta unu ~ pon the time unu dead unu will quit it fe another - yet even if unu fatten - it won't benefit unu.

[16] An if your money abound - don't distort your reasonins ~ as sinner persons money are like unto the smoke that proceed from a griddle an the wind tek it - better than sinner persons money are the likkle money them accumulated ina Truth.

Chapter 6

[1] Think of the day when unu will dead ~ pon the time your souls were separated from your flesh - an pon the time unu quit your money fe another - an pon the time unu went pon the path unu don't know - think of the tribulation that shall come pon unu.

[2] An the demons that will raceive unu are evil - an them features are ugly - an them are frightenin ina them splendour - an them won't hear your words - an unu won't hear them words.

[3] An becau unu didn't do your Irator JAH Accord - them won't hear unu ina your plea pon the time unu begged them ~ becaudis thing them will totally frighten unu.

[4] But persons who fulfilled JAH Accord have no fear - fe demons fear them. But demons shall ridicule sinner persons souls pon them.

[5] But kind persons souls shall be Irie pon Angels ina Irie Ites - fe them shall totally mek them Irie becau them scorned this world - but angels who are evil shall raceive sinner persons souls.

[6] Pardon Angels shall raceive kind persons an righteous ones souls - fe them are sent from JAH that them might

calm righteous ones souls ~ as Angels that were evil are sent from Deeyablos that them might ridicule pon sinner persons souls - demons shall raceive sinner persons souls.

[7] Sinner persons - woe fe unu ~ weep fe your ras selves before the day when unu dead arrive pon unu ~ pon the time unu reach toward JAH...

[8] enter repentance ina your era that are there before your era pass - that unu might live ina Irieness an Ites without tribulation nor disease - yet as after unu dead your era won't return that passed - weep.

[9] Lest it be pon unu toward a vain accord that distance from JAH - ina your firm criticism mek lovin fe be lavished an food an Irie Ites not be found ina unu ~ as a body that are sated without measure won't think of JAH Name - Deeyablos wealth shall lodge pon it - yet as the Hola Spirit won't lodge ina it - mek lovin the Irie Ites not be found ina unu.

[10] Like unto Mussie spoke - Mussie havin said - "Ya`iqob ate an were sated an fattened an tall an wide - an JAH Who Irated him were separated from him.

[11] An him lifestyle distanced from JAH" - as a body that were sated without measure nor moderation won't think of JAH Name - mek lovin Irie Ites not be found alongside unu ~ as belly satiety without measure are bein like unto a boar an like unto a wanderin horse - mek drinkin an eatin without measure an adultery not be found ina unu.

[12] But a person who eat ina measure shall live firmed up ina JAH Support - an him shall live firmed up like unto the horizon an like unto a tower that have a stone fence; a person who forgot JAH LAW shall flee without one livin who chase him.

[13] A kind person shall live ina bein raspected like unto a lion.

[14] But persons who don't love JAH won't keep Him LAW - an them reasonins aren't straight.

[15] An JAH shall bring sadness an alarm pon them when them are ina this world - an bein seized ina tremblin an fright - an bein seized ina the tribulations without number by them money bein snatched - bein bound by them hands ina chains from them masters hands...

[16] lest them be who rested from the tribulation - an lest them lifestyle be ina Irie Ites - lest them rest when them are ina alarmin tribulations that are pon each of them ras selves - Him shall bring sadness an alarm pon them.

Chapter 7

[1] But like unto Daweet spoke sayin - "I-man believed ina JAH ~ I-man won't fear havin said - 'What would a person mek I?'" - there are no fright an alarm pon persons who believed ina JAH.

[2] An again like unto him spoke sayin - "If warriors surround I - I-man believed ina Him ~ I-man begged JAH one thing ~ I-man seek that" - persons who believed ina Him have no fright pon them ~ a person who believed ina Him shall live ina Life foriva - an him won't fear arisin from a evil thing.

[3] Who are a person who shamed believin in JAH? how about who ignored Him fe a desire?

[4] As Him have said - I-man love him who loved I - an I-man shall honour him who glorified I ~ I-man shall keep him who returned toward I ina repentance - who are a person who shamed believin ina Him?

[5] Judge Truth an save the widow body ~ save them that JAH might save unu from all that oppose unu ina evil thing ~ keep them ~ as kind persons childran are honoured - them are given makin a profit - an yet Him shall save your childran after unu - fe them won't be troubled fe grain.

Chapter 8

[1] 'Iyob believed ina JAH ~ as him didn't neglect fe praise him Irator JAH - JAH saved him from all the tribulation that 'Adam childran enemy Deeyablos brought pon him ~ him said - "JAH gave ~ JAH withheld ~ it happened like unto JAH loved pon I - an mek JAH Name be praised by all pon Earth an ina Heaven" - yet as him didn't sadden him reasonin - JAH saved him.

[2] An pon the time JAH sight up 'Iyob that him heart were cleansed from sin - Him raceived him ina much honour.

[3] An Him gave him money that abounded more than him money that preceded ~ fe him have totally indured him tribulation - an Him cured him from him wounds becau him indurin all the tribulation that arrived pon him.

[4] An if unu like unto him indure the tribulation arisin from demons sent toward unu - unu will be admired.

[5] Indure the tribulation ~ that JAH might be fe unu a fortress Refuge from persons who hate unu - an that Him might be a fortress Refuge fe your childran childran an fe your childran after unu - don't sadden your reasonins arisin from the tribulation that came pon unu ~ believe ina Him - an Him shall be a fortress Refuge fe unu.

[6] Beg Him ~ Him will hear unu ~ mek hope - an Him will forgive unu ~ beg Him - an Him will be a Faada fe unu;

[7] Think of Merdokyos an 'Astier - Yodeet an Giediewon an Deebora an Bariq an Yoftahie an Somson...

[8] an other persons like unto them who were disciplined fe believe ina JAH an whose enemies didn't defeat them.

[9] Fe JAH are True - an fe Him don't favour havin sight up a face - but persons raceived hardship who love that them might work sin pon them ras selves ~ all persons who fear Him an keep Him LAW shall keep bodies - an Him shall give them bein I-loved an honour.

[10] Him shall mek them Irie ina them proceedin an them enterin - ina them Life an them death - an ina them arisin an sittin ~ Fe Him save - an Him seclude.

[11] Fe Him sadden - an Him pardon.

[12] Fe Him mek poor - an Him honour ~ Him mek wretched - an as Him honour - Him mek them Irie.

Chapter 9

[1] An whether it be what are ina Heaven - or whether it be what are pon Earth - an be it either subtle or stout - everything n all Him money live bein firmed up ina Him Order.

[2] There are nothing that departed from JAH LAW an Him Order - Who Irated all the world ~ be it a vulture track that fly ina Heaven - Him command toward it destination where Him loved.

[3] An Him command a Earth snake path that live ina cave toward where Him loved - an a boat path that go pon sea - apart from only JAH there are none who know it path.

[4] An apart from only JAH - there are none who know the path where a soul go pon the time it were separated from it flesh - be it a righteous or a sinner soul.

[5] Who know where it will turn - that it would turn ina wilderness or pon a mountain? or that it would fly like unto a bird - that it would be like unto Heaven dew that alight pon a mountain...

[6] or that it would be like unto deep wind - or that it would be like unto lightnin that straighten up it path...

[7] or that it would be like unto stars that shine amidst the deep - or that it would be like unto sand pon a sea shore that are piled amidst the deep...

[8] or that it would be like unto a horizon stone that firmed up pon the sea deep edge - or like unto a wood that give she beautiful fruit that grew by a Water spout...

[9] or that it would be that I likened unto the reed that heat of the Sun burnt - an that wind lift an tek toward another place where it didn't grow - an whose trace aren't found...

[10] or that it would be like unto misty urine whose trace aren't found - who know JAH Work? who are Him counsellors? how about with whom did Him counsel?

[11] As JAH Thoughts are hidden from persons - who will examine an know Him Work?

[12] As Him have Irated Earth pon Water - an as Him have firmed she up without stakes - there are none who examine

an know JAH Counsel or Him Wisdom - an Him Irated Heaven ina Him perfect Wisdom an firmed it up ina winds - an Him streached forth a lofty cosmos like unto a tent.

[13] Him commanded clouds that them might rain rain pon Earth - an Him grow grass - an Him grow fruits without number fe be food fe persons - that InI might believe ina JAH an be Irie ina Inity.

[14] JAH are Who give 'Adam childran the Irie Ites an all the fatness an all the satiety ~ JAH are Who give that them might satta an praise JAH Who gave them fruit from Earth...

[15] an Who dressed them ina beautiful robes - Who gave them all the I-loved plenty - the Irieness an the Ites that are given fe persons who fulfill JAH Accord.

[16] Him give bein I-loved an honour ina the house Him prepared an ina the Kingdom of Heaven fe them faadas who keep JAH LAW.

[17] Him give bein I-loved an honour ina the place Him prepared an ina the Kingdom of Heaven fe them faadas who lived firmed up ina Him Worship an Him LAW - an who didn't depart from Him LAW - whom Him famed an raised that them might keep Him Order an Him LAW - an I-man sight up what JAH do fe Him friends ina this world by weakenin them enemies an by keepin them bodies.

[18] I-man sight up that Him give them all them begged Him an that Him fulfill them accord fe them ~ don't depart from JAH - an fulfill JAH Accord.

[19] Don't depart from Him Command an Him LAW - lest Him vex pon unu an lest Him downstroy unu at one time - an lest Him vex an whip unu ina the tribulation from where unu lived formerly - lest unu depart from your faadas Order where unu were formerly - an lest uour lodgin be ina Gehannem where are no exits up til the Iternity.

[20] Keep your Irator JAH LAW when your soul are separated from your flesh that Him might do goodly Work fe unu pon the time unu stood before JAH.

[21] Fe Earth an Heaven Kingdoms are fe Him - an fe Kingdom an capability are fe Him - an fe bein nice an pardonin are only fe Him.

[22] As Him mek rich an Him mek poor - as Him mek wretched an Him honour - keep JAH LAW.

[23] An Daweet spoke becau Him while him said - "Man seem vain - an him era pass like unto a shadow."

[24] Him spoke becau Him sayin - "But Lord - Thou live foriva - an Thy Name Invocation are fe a child childran."

[25] An again him said - "Thy Kingdom are all the world Kingdom - an Thy Rulership are fe a child childran" ~ Thou returned a kingdom fe Daweet bringin from Sa'ol.

[26] But there are none who will I-point Thee-I ~ there are none who can dismiss ~ Thou sight up all - yet there are none who can sight up Thee-I.

[27] An Thy kingdom won't perish foriva fe a child childran ~ there are none who will rule Him - but Him rule all ~ Him sight up all - but there are none who sight Him up.

[28] As Him have Irated man ina Him Features an ina Him example that them might praise Him an might know Him Worship ina straight reasonin without doubt - Him examine an know what kidneys smoked up an what a reasonin transported.

[29] Yet them bow fe stone - fe wood - an fe silver an gold that a person hand worked.

[30] An them sacrifice sacrifice fe them up til them sacrifice smoke proceed toward Heaven - that them sin might live firmed up before JAH - but yet them refused fe worship JAH Who Irated them ~ Him shall downcuse them becau all them sin that them worked ina worshippin them idols.

[31] Them learned bowin fe idols an all stained Work that aren't due - naysayin by stars - sorcery - worshippin idols - evil accord - an all the Work that JAH don't love - yet them didn't keep JAH Command that them learned.

[32] As them didn't love fe worship JAH that them might save them bodies from sin an iniquity by Him servants the Angels an by money that them praise before JAH - them work all this ina lackin goodly Work.

[33] An pon the time them all arose together from the graves where them were buried an where them bodies perished - them souls shall stand empty before JAH - an them souls lived ina the Kingdom of Heaven prepared fe kind persons.

[34] But sinner persons souls shall live ina *Gehannem* - an pon the time graves were opened - persons who dead shall arise - an souls shall return toward the flesh that them were separated formerly.

[35] Like unto them were bithed ina them nakedness from them mother belly - them shall stand ina them nakedness before JAH - an them sins that them worked Iginnin from them infancy up til that time shall be revealed.

[36] Them shall raceive them sin hardship pon them bodies - an whether them likkle or much sin - them shall raceive them hardship like unto them sin.

Chapter 10

[1] Fe the blood of soul found from JAH shall lodge ina them like unto it lodged ina them formerly - an if unu didn't believe persons who dead arisin - hear that Irations shall arise ina rainy season without bein birthed from them mother nor faada.

[2] An Him command them formerly by Him Word that them dead.

[3] An them flesh bein demolished an rotten an again renewed - them shall arise like unto Him loved.

[4] An again pon the time rain alit an pon the time it sated Earth - them shall live havin arisin like unto them were Irated formerly.

[5] As them who are everlivin ina bloodly soul an who live ina this world an them whom Water produce have been Irated - Him havin said Mek them be Irated - an as JAH Itority lodge pon the Water - she give them a bloodly soul by Him Itority an by Him Word.

[6] As them are Irated by Him Itority an by Him Word without a faada nor mother - thou blind of reasonin who say "Persons who dead won't arise" - if thou have knowledge or Wisdom - how will thou say persons who dead won't arise by them Irator JAH Word?

[7] As persons who dead - who were ashes an dust ina grave - shall arise by JAH Word - as fe thou - enter repentance an return toward thy religion.

[8] Like unto Him Word spoke formerly - them shall arise by the Pardon Dew found from JAH - an that Word shall turn all the world an arouse the persons who dead like unto Him loved.

[9] An know that thou will arise an stand before Him - an mek it not seem fe thee ina thy reasonin dullness that thou will remain ina grave.

[10] It aren't thus ~ thou will arise an raceive thy hardship like unto the Work measure that thou worked - whether it be goodly or evil - yet mek it not seem fe thee that thou will remain - fe this Day are the day when them will raceive hardship.

[11] An ina Resurrection time thou will raceive thy hardship by all thy sin that thou worked ~ thou will finish thy sin hardship that were written Iginnin from thy infancy up til that time - an thou have no reason that thou will pretext pon thy sin like unto this world Work that thou might deny thy sin.

[12] Like unto thou mek thy false word truth before thee - an like unto thou mek the lie thing that thou spoke truth - thou have no reason that thou will pretext like unto this world Work.

[13] Becau it were that she know pon thee all thy evil Work thou worked - an becau it were that she will reveal pon thee before she Irator JAH - as JAH Word shall lodge pon thee an speak pon thee - thou have no reason pon what thou pretext.

[14] Thou will shame there becau thy sin that thou worked ~ it are that thou might be thanked with persons who are thanke pon them beautiful Work - yet lest thou shame before man an Angels pon the day when Judgemant are judged - quickly enter repentance ina this world before thou arrive toward there.

[15] Persons who praise JAH with Angels shall raceive them reward from them Irator without shamin - an them shall be Irie ina the Kingdom of Heaven - however unless thou worked goodly Work when thou are ina thy flesh ina Life - thou have no fortune with righteous ones.

[16] As thou weren't prepared when thou have knowledge an when thou have this world where thou enter repentance - there shall be a useless regret pon thee - an fe thou didn't give a morsel fe the hungry when thou have money.

[17] An fe thou didn't clothe the naked when thou have clothes - an fe thou didn't save the wronged when thou have Itority.

[18] Fe thou didn't teach the sinner person when thou have knowledge - that him might return an enter repentance - an that JAH might forgive him him sin that him formerly worked ina ignorance - an fe thou didn't fight with demons who quarrel with thee when thou have Power that thou able fe prevail.

[19] An fe thou didn't fast nor pray when thou have firmness that thou might weaken thy infancy Power that are pon flesh - an that thou might subject thy ras self fe Rightness that aren't favorin pon flesh...

[20] that aren't favorin Irie Ites when it are ina this world ina beautiful drink an sweet food - an that aren't adornin ina thin clothes an silver an gold...

[21] an as thou didn't fast nor pray when thou have firmness that thou might subject thy ras self fe Rightness that aren't adornin ina honoured Hindekie jewels called emerald an phazyon - there shall be a useless regret pon thee ~ this aren't a person ornamant that are due.

[22] As fe a person ornamant - it are purity - Wisdom - knowledge - lovin one another by what are due without envyin nor jealousy nor doubtin nor quarrels ~ while thou loved thy companion like unto thy ras self...

[23] an without thy doin a evil thing pon a person who did a evil thing pon thee-I - it are lovin one another by what are due - that thou might enter toward the Kingdom of Heaven that are given fe person who indured the tribulation - that Him might give thee the honoured Kingdom of Heaven an thy reward pon makin hope ina the Kingdom of Heaven ina Resurrection time with honoured persons ina knowledge an Wisdom.

[24] An don't say "After wi dead wi won't arise" - fe Deeyablos cut off hope of persons who speak an think this lest them be saved in Resurrection time ~ them will know that them have hardship pon them pon the time Advent arrived pon them ~ ina Resurrection time persons will be totally sad who worked sin ina not knowin that Him might think of them sin pon them - fe them didn't believe ina Him that them will arise pon that Day.

[25] Becaudis thing them shall be reproached like unto them Work evil measure that them worked ina this world - an them shall sight up the Resurrection that them denied whereby them will arise together ina flesh.

[26] Them shall weep at that time becau them didn't work goodly Work ~ it would have been better fe them if them wept ina this world if it are possible fe them lest them be who weep ina *Gehannem*.

[27] If InI didn't weep ina this world by InI accord - demons will mek InI weep without InI accord ina *Gehannem* ~ if InI didn't enter repentance ina this world - InI prepare worthless an useless cries an mournin ina *Gehannem*.

[28] Prepare goodly Work - that unu might cross from death toward Life - an that unu might go from this passin world toward the Kingdom of Heaven - an that unu might sight up the Kingdom of Heaven Light that surpass light ina this world.

[29] Refuse Irie Ites that are ina this world - that thou might be Irie without measure ina the Kingdom of Heaven ina Irie Ites that aren't fulfilled Iginnin from today up til the Iternity with persons who believe persons who dead arisin. Mek Glory an praise due JAH foriva - an the third book that speak the Meqabyans thing were fulfilled.

The Book Of Enoch

The Book Of Watchers – Enoch's Ethiopic Book 1

Chapter 1

[1] Who will be living in the day of tribulation, when all the wicked and godless are to be removed.

[2] And he took up his parable and said -Enoch a righteous man, whose eyes were opened by God, saw the vision of the Holy One in the heavens, which the angels showed me, and from them I heard everything, and from them I understood as I saw, but not for this generation, but for a remote one which is for to come.

[3] Concerning the elect I said, and took up my parable concerning them: The Holy Great One will come forth from His dwelling,

[4] And the eternal God will tread upon the earth, even on Mount Sinai, and appear from His camp. And appear in the strength of His might from the heaven of heavens.

[5] And all shall be smitten with fear and the watchers shall quake, and great fear and trembling shall seize them unto the ends of the earth.

[6] And the high mountains shall be shaken, and the high hills shall be made low, and shall melt like wax before the flame,

[7] And the earth shall be wholly rent in sunder, and all that is upon the earth shall perish, and there shall be a judgement upon all men.

[8] But with the righteous He will make peace, and will protect the elect, and mercy shall be upon them. And they shall all belong to God, and they shall be prospered, and they shall all be blessed. And He will help them all, and light shall appear unto them, and He will make peace with them'.

[9] And behold! He cometh with ten thousands of His holy ones to execute judgement upon all, and to destroy all the ungodly: and to convict all flesh of all the works of their ungodliness which they have ungodly committed, and of all the hard things which ungodly sinners have spoken against Him.

Chapter 2

[1] Observe ye everything that takes place in the heaven, how they do not change their orbits, and the luminaries which are in the heaven, how they all rise and set in order each in its season,

[2] And transgress not against their appointed order. Behold ye the earth, and give heed to the things which take place upon it from first to last, how steadfast they are, how none of the things upon earth change,

[3] But all the works of God appear to you. Behold the summer and the winter, how the whole earth is filled with water, and clouds and dew and rain lie upon it.

Chapter 3

[1] Observe and see how, in the winter, all the trees seem as though they had withered and shed all their leaves, except fourteen trees, which do not lose their foliage but retain the old foliage from two to three years till the new comes.

Chapter 4

[1] And again, observe ye the days of summer how the sun is above the earth over against it.

[2] And you seek shade and shelter by reason of the heat of the sun, and the earth also burns with growing heat, and so you cannot tread on the earth, or on a rock by reason of its heat.

Chapter 5

[1] Observe ye how the trees cover themselves with green leaves and bear fruit: wherefore give ye heed and know with regard to all His works, and recognize how He that liveth for ever hath made them so.

[2] And all His works go on thus from year to year for ever, and all the tasks which they accomplish for Him, and their tasks change not, but according as God hath ordained so is it done.

[3] And behold how the sea and the rivers in like manner accomplish and change not their tasks from His commandments'.

[4] But ye - ye have not been steadfast, nor done the commandments of the Lord, but ye have turned away and spoken proud and hard words with your impure mouths against His greatness. Oh, ye hard-hearted, ye shall find no peace.

[5] Therefore shall ye execrate your days, and the years of your life shall perish, and the years of your destruction shall be multiplied in eternal execration, and ye shall find no mercy.

[6] In those days ye shall make your names an eternal execration unto all the righteous, and by you shall all who curse, curse, and all the sinners and godless shall imprecate by you, and for you the godless there shall be a curse. And all shall rejoice, and there shall be forgiveness of sins, and every mercy and peace and forbearance: There shall be salvation unto them, a goodly light. And for all of you sinners there shall be no salvation, but on you all shall abide a curse.

[7] But for the elect there shall be light and joy and peace, and they shall inherit the earth.

[8] And then there shall be bestowed upon the elect wisdom, and they shall all live and never again sin, either through ungodliness or through pride: but they who are wise shall be humble.

[9] And they shall not again transgress, nor shall they sin all the days of their life, nor shall they die of the divine anger or wrath, but they shall complete the number of the days of their life. And their lives shall be increased in peace, and the years of their joy shall be multiplied, in eternal gladness and peace, all the days of their life.

Chapter 6

[1] And it came to pass when the children of men had multiplied that in those days were born unto them beautiful and comely daughters.

[2] And the angels, the children of the heaven, saw and lusted after them, and said to one another: 'Come, let us choose us wives from among the children of men,

[3] And beget us children.' And Semjaza, who was their leader, said unto them: 'I fear ye will not,

[4] Indeed agree to do this deed, and I alone shall have to pay the penalty of a great sin.' And they all answered him and said: 'Let us all swear an oath, and all bind ourselves by mutual imprecations,

[5] Not to abandon this plan but to do this thing.' Then sware they all together and bound themselves by mutual imprecations upon it.

[6] And they were in all two hundred; who descended in the days of Jared on the summit of Mount Hermon, and they called it Mount Hermon, because they had sworn,

[7] And bound themselves by mutual imprecations upon it. And these are the names of their leaders: Samlazaz, their leader, Araklba, Rameel, Kokablel, Tamlel, Ramlel, Danel, Ezeqeel, Baraqijal,

[8] Asael, Armaros, Batarel, Ananel, Zaqiel, Samsapeel, Satarel, Turel, Jomjael, Sariel. These are their chiefs of tens.

Chapter 7

[1] And all the others together with them took unto themselves wives, and each chose for himself one, and they began to go in unto them and to defile themselves with them, and they taught them charms,

[2] And enchantments, and the cutting of roots, and made them acquainted with plants.

[3] And they became pregnant, and they bare great giants, whose height was three thousand ells:

[4] Who consumed all the acquisitions of men. And when men could no longer sustain the m, the giants turned against them,

[5] And devoured mankind. And they began to sin against birds, and beasts, and reptiles,

[6] And fish, and to devour one another's flesh, and drink the blood. Then the earth laid accusation against the lawless ones.

Chapter 8

[1] And Azazel taught men to make swords, and knives, and shields, and breastplates, and made known to them the metals of the earth and the art of working them, and bracelets, and ornaments, and the use of antimony, and the beautifying of the eyelids, and all kinds of costly stones,

[2] And all colouring tinctures. And there arose much godlessness, and they committed fornication,

[3] And theywere led astray, and became corrupt in all their ways. Semjaza taught enchantments, and root-cuttings, 'Armaros the resolving of enchantments, Baraqijal (taught) astrology, Kokabel the constellations, Ezeqeel the knowledge of the clouds, Araqiel the signs of the earth, Shamsiel the signs of the sun, and Sariel the course of the moon. And as men perished, they cried, and their cry went up to heaven.

Chapter 9

[1] And then Michael, Uriel, Raphael, and Gabriel looked down from heaven,

[2] And saw much blood being shed upon the earth, and all lawlessness being wrought upon the earth. And they said one to another: 'The earth made without inhabitant cries the voice of their cryingst up to the gates of heaven.

[3] And now to you, the holy ones of heaven, the souls of men make their suit, saying, "Bring our cause,

[4] Before the Most High."' And they said to the Lord of the ages: 'Lord of lords, God of gods, king of kings, and God of the ages, the throne of Thy glory standeth unto all the generations of the ages,

[5] And Thy name holy and glorious and blessed unto all the ages! Thou hast made all things, and power over all things hast Thou: and all things are naked and open in Thy sight, and Thou seest all things,

[6] And nothing can hide itself from Thee. Thou seest what Azazel hath done, who hath taught all unrighteousness on earth and revealed the eternal secrets which were preserved in heaven,

[7] Which men were striving to learn: And Semjaza, to whom Thou hast given authority to bear rule over his associates. And they have gone to the daughters of men upon the earth, and have slept with the women,

[8] And have defiled themselves, and revealed to them all kinds of sins. And the women have borne giants,

[9] And the whole earth has thereby been filled with blood and unrighteousness.

[10] And now, behold, the souls of those who have died are crying and making their suit to the gates of heaven, and the ir lamentations have ascended: and cannot cease because of the lawless deeds which are wrought on the earth.

[11] And Thou knowest all things before they come to pass, and Thou seest these things and Thou dost suffer them, and Thou dost not say to us what we are to do to them in regard to these.'

Chapter 10

[1] Then said the Most High, the Holy and Great One spake, and sent Uriel to the son of Lamech,

[2] And said to him: Go to Noah and tell him in my name "Hide thyself!" and reveal to him the end that is approaching: that the whole earth will be destroyed, and a deluge is about to come upon the whole earth,

[3] And will destroy all that is on it. And now instruct him that he may escape,

[4] And his seed may be preserved for all the generations of the world. And again the Lord said to Raphael: Bind Azazel hand and foot, and cast him into the darkness: and make an opening in the desert,

[5] Which is in Dudael, and cast him therein. And place upon him rough and jagged rocks, and cover him with darkness, and let him abide there for ever, and cover his face that he may not see light.

[6] And on the day of the great judgement he shall be cast into the fire.

[7] And heal the earth which the angels have corrupted, and proclaim the healing of the earth, that they may heal the plague, and that all the children of men may not perish through all the secret things that the Watchers have disclosed and have taught their sons.

[8] And the whole earth has been corrupted through the works that were taught by Azazel: to him ascribe all sin.

[9] And to Gabriel said the Lord: Proceed against the bastards and the reprobates, and against the children of fornication: and destroy the children of fornication and the children of the Watchers from amongst men and cause them to go forth: send them one against the other that they may destroy each other in

[10] battle: for length of days shall they not have. And no request that they make of thee shall be granted unto their fathers on their behalf; for they hope to live an eternal life,

[11] And that each one of them will live five hundred years. And the Lord said unto Michael: Go, bind Semjaza and his associates who have united themselves with women so as to have defiled themselves,

[12] with them in all their uncleanness. And when their sons have slain one another, and they have seen the destruction of their beloved ones, bind them fast for seventy generations in the valleys of the earth, till the day of their judgement and of their consummation,

[13] Till the judgement that is forever and ever is consummated. In those days they shall be led off to the abyss of fire:

[14] And to the torment and the prison in which they shall be confined for ever. And whosoever shall be condemned and destroyed will from thenceforth be bound together with them to the end of all generations.

[15] And destroy all the spirits of the reprobate and the children of the Watchers,

[16] Because they have wronged mankind. Destroy all wrong from the face of the earth and let every evil work come to an end: and let the plant of righteousness and truth appear: and it shall prove a blessing; the works of righteousness and truth shall be planted in truth and joy for evermore.

[17] And then shall all the righteous escape, and shall live till they beget thousands of children, and all the days of their youth and their old age shall they complete in peace.

[18] And then shall the whole earth be tilled in righteousness, and shall all be planted with trees and be full of blessing.

[19] And all desirable trees shall be planted on it, and they sha ll plant vines on it: and the vine which they plant thereon shall yield wine in abundance, and as for all the seed which is sown thereon each measure of it shall bear a thousand, and each measure of olives shall yield ten presses of oil.

[20] And cleanse thou the earth from all oppression, and from all unrighteousness, and from all sin, and from all godlessness: and all the uncleanness that is wrought upon the earth destroy from off the earth. And all the children of men shall become righteous,

[21] And all nations shall offer adoration and shall praise Me, and all shall worship Me. And the earth shall be cleansed from all defilement, and from all sin, and from all punishment, and from all torment, and I will never again send them upon it from generation to generation and for ever.

Chapter 11

[1] And in those days I will open the store chambers of blessing which are in the heaven,

[2] So as to send 2 them down upon the earth over the work and labour of the children of men. And truth and peace shall be associated together throughout all the days of the world and throughout all the generations of men.

Chapter 12

[3] Before these things Enoch was hidden, and no one of the children of men knew where he was hidden,

[4] And where he abode, and what had become of him. And his activities had to do with the Watchers, and his days were with the holy ones.

[5] And I Enoch was blessing the Lord of majesty and the King of the ages, and lo!

[6] The Watchers called me - Enoch the scribe- and said to me: 'Enoch, thou scribe of righteousness, go, declare to the Watchers of the heaven who have left the high heaven, the holy eternal place, and have defiled themselves with women, and have done as the children of earth do,

[7] And have taken unto themselves wives: "Ye have wrought great destruction on the earth: And ye shall have no peace nor forgiveness of sin:

[8] And inasmuch as they delight themselves in their children, The murder of their beloved ones shall they see, and over the destruction of their children shall they lament, and shall make supplication unto eternity, but mercy and peace shall ye not attain."

Chapter 13

[1] And Enoch went and said: Azazel, thou shalt have no peace: a severe sentence has gone forth,

[2] Against thee to put thee in bonds: And thou shalt not have toleration nor request granted to thee, because of the unrighteousness which thou hast taught, and because of all the works of godlessness,

[3] And unrighteousness and sin which thou hast shown to men. Then I went and spoke to them all together,

[4] And they were all afraid, and fear and trembling seized them. And they besought me to draw up a petition for them that they might find forgiveness, and to read their petition in the presence of the Lord of heaven.

[5] For from thenceforward they could not speak with Him nor lift up their eyes to heaven for shame of their sins for which they had been condemned. Then I wrote out their petition, and the prayer in regard to their spirits and their deeds individually and in regard to their requests that they should have forgiveness and length.

[6] And I went off and sat down at the waters of Dan, in the land of Dan, to the south of the west of Hermon: I read their petition till I fell asleep.

[7] And behold a dream came to me, and visions fell down upon me, and I saw visions of chastisement, and a voice came bidding me I to tell it to the sons of heaven, and reprimand them.

[8] And when I awaked, I came unto them, and they were all sitting gathered together, weeping in Abelsjail,

[9] Which is between Lebanon and Seneser, with their faces covered. And I recounted before them all the visions which I had seen in sleep, and I began to speak the words of righteousness, and to reprimand the heavenly Watchers.

Chapter 14

[1] The book of the words of righteousness, and of the reprimand of the eternal Watchers,

[2] In accordance with the command of the Holy Great One in that vision. I saw in my sleep what I will now say with a tongue of flesh and with the breath of my mouth: which the Great One has given to men to converse therewith and understand with the heart.

[3] As He has created and given to man the power of understanding the word of wisdom, so hath He created me also and given me the power of reprimanding the Watchers,

[4] The children of heaven. I wrote out your petition, and in my vision it appeared thus, that your petition will not be granted unto you throughout all the days of eternity,

[5] And that judgement has been finally passed upon you: yea (your petition) will not be granted unto you. And from henceforth you shall not ascend into heaven unto all eternity, and in bonds of the earth the decree has gone forth to bind you for all the days of the world.

[6] And (that) previously you shall have seen the destruction of your beloved sons and ye shall have no pleasure in them, but they shall fall before you by the sword.

[7] And your petition on their behalf shall not be granted, nor yet on your own: even though you weep and pray and speak all the words contained in the writing which I have written.

[8] And the vision was shown to me thus: Behold, in the vision clouds invited me and a mist summoned me, and the course of the stars and the lightnings sped and hastened me,

[9] And the winds in the vision caused me to fly and lifted me upward, and bore me into heaven. And I went in till I drew nigh to a wall which is built of crystals and surrounded by tongues of fire: and it began to affright me.

[10] And I went into the tongues of fire and drew nigh to a large house which was built of crystals: and the walls of the house were like a tesselated floor made of crystals, and its groundwork was of crystal.

[11] Its ceiling was like the path of the stars and the lightnings, and between them were fiery cherubim, and their heaven was (clear as) water. A flaming fire surrounded the walls, and its portals blazed with fire.

[12] And I entered into that house, and it was hot as fire and cold as ice:

[13] There were no delights of life therein: fear covered me, and trembling got hold upon me.

[14] And as I quaked and trembled, I fell upon my face.

[15] And I beheld a vision, And lo! There was a second house, greater than the former,

[16] And the entire portal stood open before me, and it was built of flames of fire. And in every respect it so excelled in splendour and magnificence and extent that I cannot describe to you its splendour and its extent.

[17] And its floor was of fire, and above it were lightnings and the path of the stars,

[18] And its ceiling also was flaming fire. And I looked and saw therein a lofty throne: its appearance was as crystal, and the wheels thereof as the shining sun, and there was the vision of cherubim.

[19] And from underneath the throne came streams of flaming fire so that I could not look thereon.

[20] And the Great Glory sat thereon, and His raiment shone more brightly than the sun and was whiter than any snow.

[21] None of the angels could enter and could behold His face by reason of the magnificence and glory and no flesh could behold Him.

[22] The flaming fire was round about Him, and a great fire stood before Him, and none around could draw nigh Him: ten thousand times ten thousand stood before Him,

[23] Yet He needed no counselor. And the most holy ones who were nigh to Him did not leave by night nor depart from Him.

[24] And until then I had been prostrate on my face, trembling: and the Lord called me with His own mouth, and said to me: 'Come hither,

[25] Enoch, and hear my word.' And one of the holy ones came to me and waked me, and He made me rise up and approach the door: and I bowed my face downwards.

Chapter 15

[1] And He answered and said to me, and I heard His voice: 'Fear not, Enoch, thou righteous man and scribe of righteousness:

[2] Approach hither and hear my voice. And go, say to the Watchers of heaven, who have sent thee to intercede for them: "You should intercede" for men, and not men for you:

[3] Wherefore have ye left the high, holy, and eternal heaven, and lain with women, and defiled yourselves with the daughters of men and taken to yourselves wives, and done like the children of earth,

[4] And begotten giants as your sons? And though ye were holy, spiritual, living the eternal life, you have defiled yourselves with the blood of women, and have begotten children with the blood of flesh, and, as the children of men, have lusted after flesh and blood as those also do who die and perish.

[5] Therefore have I given them wives also that they might impregnate them, and beget children by them,

[6] That thus nothing might be wanting to them on earth. But you were formerly spiritual,

[7] Living the eternal life, and immortal for all generations of the world. And therefore I have not appointed wives for you; for as for the spiritual ones of the heaven, in heaven is their dwelling.

[8] And now, the giants, who are produced from the spirits and flesh, shall be called evil spirits upon the earth,

[9] And on the earth shall be their dwelling. Evil spirits have proceeded from their bodies; because they are born from men and from the holy Watchers is their beginning and primal origin;

[10] They shall be evil spirits on earth, and evil spirits shall they be called. As for the spirits of heaven, in heaven shall be their dwelling, but as for the spirits of the earth which were born upon the earth, on the earth shall be their dwelling.

[11] And the spirits of the giants afflict, oppress, destroy, attack, do battle, and work destruction on the earth, and cause trouble: they take no food, but nevertheless hunger and thirst,

[12] And cause offences. And these spirits shall rise up against the children of men and against the women, because they have proceeded from them.

Chapter 16

[1] From the days of the slaughter and destruction and death of the giants, from the souls of whose flesh the spirits, having gone forth, shall destroy without incurring judgement –thus shall they destroy until the day of the consummation, the great judgement in which the age shall be consummated,

[2] Over the Watchers and the godless, yea, shall be wholly consummated." And now as to the Watchers who have sent thee to intercede for them, who had been aforetime in heaven, say to them:

[3] "You have been in heaven, but all the mysteries had not yet been revealed to you, and you knew worthless ones, and these in the hardness of your hearts you have made known to the women, and through these mysteries women and men work much evil on earth."

[4] Say to them therefore: " You have no peace."'

Chapter 17

[1] And they took and brought me to a place in which those who were there were like flaming fire,

[2] And, when they wished, they appeared as men. And they brought me to the place of darkness, and to a mountain the point of whose summit reached to heaven.

[3] And I saw the places of the luminaries and the treasuries of the stars and of the thunder and in the uttermost depths,

[4] Where were a fiery bow and arrows and their quiver, and a fiery sword and all the lightnings. And they took me to the living waters,

[5] And to the fire of the west, which receives every setting of the sun.

[6] And I came to a river of fire in which the fire flows like water and discharges itself into the great sea towards the west. I saw the great rivers and came to the great river and to the great darkness,

[7] And went to the place where no flesh walks. I saw the mountains of the darkness of winter and the place,

[8] Whence all the waters of the deep flow. I saw the mouths of all the rivers of the earth and the mouth of the deep.

Chapter 18

[1] I saw the treasuries of all the winds: I saw how He had furnished with them the whole creation,

[2] And the firm foundations of the earth. And I saw the corner-stone of the earth: I saw the four winds,

[3] Which bear the earth and the firmament of the heaven. And I saw how the winds stretch out the vaults of heaven, and have their station between heaven and earth: these are the pillars of the heaven.

[4] I saw the winds of heaven which turn and bring the circumference of the sun,

[5] And all the stars to their setting. I saw the winds on the earth carrying the clouds: I saw the paths of the angels.

[6] I saw at the end of the earth the firmament of the heaven above. And I proceeded and saw a place which burns day and night, where there are seven mountains of magnificent stones,

[7] Three towards the east, and three towards the south. And as for those towards the east, was of coloured stone, and one of pearl, and one of jacinth, and those towards the south of red stone.

[8] But the middle one reached to heaven like the throne of God, of alabaster, and the summit of the throne was of sapphire.

[9] And I saw a flaming fire.

[10] And beyond these mountains Is a region the end of the great earth: there the heavens were completed.

[11] And I saw a deep abyss, with columns of heavenly fire, and among them I saw columns of fire fall, which were beyond measure alike towards

[12] the height and towards the depth. And beyond that abyss I saw a place which had no firmament of the heaven above, and no firmly founded earth beneath it: there was no water upon it,

[13] And no birds, but it was a waste and horrible place. I saw there seven stars like great burning mountains,

[14] And to me, when I inquired regarding them, The angel said: 'This place is the end of heaven and earth: this has become a prison for the stars and the host of heaven.

[15] And the stars which roll over the fire are they which have transgressed the commandment of the Lord in the beginning of their rising,

[16] Because they did not come forth at their appointed times. And He was wroth with them, and bound them till the time when their guilt should be consummated even for ten thousand years.'

Chapter 19

[1] And Uriel said to me: 'Here shall stand the angels who have connected themselves with women, and their spirits assuming many different forms are defiling mankind and shall lead them astray into sacrificing to demons as gods, here shall they stand, till the day of the great judgement in

[2] Which they shall be judged till they are made an end of. And the women also of the angels,

[3] who went astray shall become sirens.' And I, Enoch, alone saw the vision, the ends of all things: and no man shall see as I have seen.

Chapter 20

[1] And these are the names of the holy angels who watch.

[2] Uriel, one of the holy angels,

[3] Who is over the world and over Tartarus. Raphael, one of the holy angels, who is over the spirits of men.

[4] Raguel, one of the holy angels who takes vengeance on the world of the luminaries.

[5] Michael, one of the holy angels, to wit, he that is set over the best part of ma nkind and over chaos.

[6] Saraqael, one of the holy angels, who is set over the spirits, who sin in the spirit.

[7] Gabriel, one of the holy angels, who is over Paradise and the serpents and the Cherubim.

[8] Remiel, one of the holy angels, whom God set over those who rise.

Chapter 21

[1] And I proceeded to where things were chaotic.

[2] And I saw there something horrible: I saw neither

[3] Heaven above nor a firmly founded earth, but a place chaotic and horrible.

[4] And there I saw seven stars of the heaven bound together in it, like great mountains and burning with fire.

[5] Then I said: 'For what sin are they bound, and on what account have they been cast in hither?' Then said Uriel, one of the holy angels, who was with me, and was chief over them, and said: 'Enoch, why dost thou ask,

[6] And why art thou eager for the truth? These are of the number of the stars of heaven, which have transgressed the commandment of the Lord, and are bound here till ten thousand years,

[7] The time entailed by their sins, are consummated.' And from thence I went to another place, which was still more horrible than the former, and I saw a horrible thing: a great fire there which burnt and blazed, and the place was cleft as far as the abyss, being full of great descending columns of fire:

[8] Neither its extent or magnitude could I see, nor could I conjecture.

[9] Then I said: 'How fearful is the place and how terrible to look upon!' Then Uriel answered me, one of the holy angels who was with me, and said unto me: 'Enoch, why hast thou such fear and affright?'

[10] And I answered: 'Because of this fearful place, and because of the spectacle of the pain.' And he said unto me: 'This place is the prison of the angels, and here they will be imprisoned for ever.'

Chapter 22

[1] And thence I went to another place, and he mountain and of hard rock.

[2] And there was in it four hollow places, deep and wide and very smooth. How smooth are the hollow places and deep and dark to look at.

[3] Then Raphael answered, one of the holy angels who was with me, and said unto me: 'These hollow places have been created for this very purpose, that the spirits of the souls of the dead should assemble therein,

[4] Yea that all the souls of the children of men should assemble here. And these places have been made to receive them till the day of their judgement and till their appointed period [till the period appointed], till the great judgement (comes) upon them.' I saw (the spirit of) a dead man making suit,

[5] And his voice went forth to heaven and made suit. And I asked Raphael the angel who was with me,

[6] And I said unto him: 'This spirit which maketh suit, whose is it, whose voice goeth forth and maketh suit to heaven ?'

[7] And he answered me saying: 'This is the spirit which went forth from Abel, whom his brother Cain slew, and he makes his suit against him till his seed is destroyed from the face of the earth, and his seed is annihilated from amongst the seed of men.'

[8] The I asked regarding it, and regarding all the hollow places: 'Why is one separated from the other?'

[9] And he answered me and said unto me: 'These three have been made that the spirits of the dead might be separated. And such a division has been make for the spirits of the righteous, in which there is the bright spring of water.

[10] And such has been made for sinners when they die and are buried in the earth and judgement has not been executed on them in their lifetime.

[11] Here their spirits shall be set apart in this great pain till the great day of judgement and punishment and torment of those who curse for ever and retribution for their spirits.

[12] There He shall bind them for ever. And such a division has been made for the spirits of those who make their suit, who make disclosures concerning their destruction, when they were slain in the days of the sinners.

[13] Such has been made for the spirits of men who were not righteous but sinners, who were complete in transgression, and of the transgressors they shall be companions: but their spirits shall not be slain in the day of judgement nor shall they be raised from thence.'

[14] The I blessed the Lord of glory and said: 'Blessed be my Lord, the Lord of righteousness, who ruleth for ever.'

Chapter 23

[1] From thence I went to another place to the west of the ends of the earth.

[2] And I saw a burning fire which ran without resting,

[3] And paused not from its course day or night but ran regularly.

[4] And I asked saying: 'What is this which rests not?' Then Raguel, one of the holy angels who was with me, answered me and said unto me: 'This course of fire which thou hast seen is the fire in the west which persecutes all the luminaries of heaven.'

Chapter 24

[1] And from thence I went to another place of the earth, and he showed me a mountain range of fire,

[2] Which burnt day and night. And I went beyond it and saw seven magnificent mountains all differing each from the other, and the stones thereof were magnificent and beautiful, magnificent as a whole, of glorious appearance and fair exterior: three towards the east, one founded on the other, and three towards the south, one upon the other,

and deep rough ravines, no one of which joined with any other.

[3] And the seventh mountain was in the midst of these, and it excelled them in height,

[4] Resembling the seat of a throne: and fragrant trees encircled the throne. And amongst them was a tree such as I had never yet smelt, neither was any amongst them nor were others like it: it had a fragrance beyond all fragrance, and its leaves and blooms and wood wither not for ever:

[5] And its fruit is beautiful, and its fruit n resembles the dates of a palm. Then I said: 'How beautiful is this tree, and fragrant, and its leaves are fair, and its blooms very delightful in appearance.'

[6] Then answered Michael, one of the holy and honoured angels who was with me, and was their leader.

Chapter 25

[1] And he said unto me: 'Enoch, why dost thou ask me regarding the fragrance of the tree,

[2] And why dost thou wish to learn the truth?' Then I answered him saying: 'I wish to know about everything,

[3] But especially about this tree.' And he answered saying: 'This high mountain which thou hast seen, whose summit is like the throne of God, is His throne, where the Holy Great One, the Lord of Glory, the Eternal King, will sit, when He shall come down to visit the earth with goodness.

[4] And as for this fragrant tree no mortal is permitted to touch it till the great judgement, when He shall take vengeance on all and bring everything to its consummation for ever.

[5] It shall then be given to the righteous and holy. Its fruit shall be for food to the elect: it shall be transplanted to the holy place, to the temple of the Lord, the Eternal King.

[6] Then shall they rejoice with joy and be glad, and into the holy place shall they enter; And its fragrance shall be in their bones, and they shall live a long life on earth, Such as thy fathers lived: And in their days shall no sorrow or plague or torment or calamity touch them.'

[7] Then blessed I the God of Glory, the Eternal King, who hath prepared such things for the righteous, and hath created them and promised to give to them.

Chapter 26

[1] And I went from thence to the middle of the earth, and I saw a blessed place,

[2] In which there were trees with branches abiding and blooming of a dismembered tree. And there I saw a holy mountain,

[3] And underneath the mountain to the east there was a stream and it flowed towards the south. And I saw towards the east another mountain higher than this, and between them a deep and narrow ravine:

[4] In it also ran a stream underneath the mountain. And to the west thereof there was another mountain, lower than the former and of small elevation, and a ravine deep and dry between them: and another deep and dry ravine was at the extremities of the three mountains.

[5] And all the ravines were deep rand narrow, being formed of hard rock, and trees were not planted upon them. And I marveled at the rocks, and I marveled at the ravine, yea, I marveled very much.

Chapter 27

[1] Then said I: 'For what object is this blessed land, which is entirely filled with trees,

[2] And this accursed valley between?' Then Uriel, one of the holy angels who was with me, answered and said: 'This accursed valley is for those who are accursed for ever: Here shall all the accursed be gathered together who utter with their lips against the Lord unseemly words and of His glory speak hard things. Here shall they be gathered together,

[3] And here shall be their place of judgement. In the last days there shall be upon them the spectacle of righteous judgement in the presence of the righteous for ever: here shall the merciful bless the Lord of glory, the Eternal King.

[4] In the days of judgement over the former, they shall bless Him for the mercy in accordance with

[5] Which He has assigned them (their lot).' Then I blessed the Lord of Glory and set forth His glory and lauded Him gloriously.

Chapter 28

[1] And thence I went towards the east, into the midst of the mountain range of the desert,

[2] And I saw a wilderness and it was solitary, full of trees and plants. And water gushed forth from above.

[3] Rushing like a copious watercourse which flowed towards the north-west it caused clouds and dew to ascend on every side.

Chapter 29

[1] And thence I went to another place in the desert, and approached to the east of this mountain range.

[2] And there I saw aromatic trees exhaling the fragrance of frankincense and myrrh, and the trees also were similar to the almond tree.

Chapter 30

[1] And beyond these, I went afar to the east,

[2] And I saw another place, a valley full of water.

[3] And therein there was a tree, the colour of fragrant trees such as the mastic. And on the sides of those valleys I saw fragrant cinnamon. And beyond these I proceeded to the east.

Chapter 31

[1] And I saw other mountains, and amongst them were groves of trees, and there flowed forth from them nectar,

[2] Which is named sarara and galbanum. And beyond these mountains I saw another mountain to the east of the ends of the earth, whereon were aloe-trees, and all the trees were full of stacte, being like almond-trees.

[3] And when one burnt it, it smelt sweeter than any fragrant odour.

Chapter 32

[1] And after these fragrant odours, as I looked towards the north over the mountains I saw seven mountains full of choice nard and fragrant trees and cinnamon and pepper.

[2] And thence I went over the summits of all these mountains, far towards the east of the earth, and passed above the Erythraean sea and went far from it, and passed over the angel Zotiel. And I came to the Garden of Righteousness,

[3] I and from afar off trees more numerous than I these trees and great-two trees there, very great, beautiful, and glorious, and magnificent, and the tree of knowledge, whose holy fruit they eat and know great wisdom.

[4] That tree is in height like the fir, and its leaves are like (those of) the Carob tree:

[5] And its fruit is like the clusters of the vine, very beautiful: and the fragrance of the tree penetrates afar.

[6] Then I said: 'How beautiful is the tree, and how attractive is its look!' Then Raphael the holy angel, who was with me, answered me and said: 'This is the tree of wisdom, of which thy father old (in years) and thy aged mother, who were before thee, have eaten, and they learnt wisdom and their eyes were opened, and they knew that they were naked and they were driven out of the garden.'

Chapter 33

[1] And from thence I went to the ends of the earth and saw there great beasts, and each differed from the other; and I saw birds also differing in appearance and beauty and voice, the one differing from the other. And to the east of those beasts I saw the ends of the earth whereon the heaven rests,

[2] And the portals of the heaven open. And I saw how the stars of heaven come forth,

[3] And I counted the portals out of which they proceed, and wrote down all their outlets, of each individual star by itself, according to their number and their names, their courses and their positions, and their times and their months,

[4] As Uriel the holy angel who was with me showed me. He showed all things to me and wrote them down for me: also their names he wrote for me, and their laws and their companies.

Chapter 34

[1] And from thence I went towards the north to the ends of the earth, and there I saw a great and glorious device at the ends of the whole earth. And here I saw three portals of heaven open in the heaven: through each of them proceed north winds: when they blow there is cold, hail, frost, snow, dew, and rain.

[2] And out of one portal they blow for good: but when they blow through the other two portals, it is with violence and affliction on the earth, and they blow with violence.

Chapter 35

[1] And from thence I went towards the west to the ends of the earth, and saw there three portals of the heaven open such as I had seen in the east, the same number of portals, and the same number of outlets.

Chapter 36

[1] And from thence I went to the south to the ends of the earth, and saw there three open portals of the heaven:

[2] And thence there come dew, rain, and wind. And from thence I went to the east to the ends of the heaven, and saw here the three eastern portals of heaven open and small portals above them.

[3] Through each of these small portals pass the stars of heaven and run their course to the west on the path which is shown to them. And as often as I saw I blessed always the Lord of Glory, and I continued to bless the Lord of Glory who has wrought great and glorious wonders, to show the greatness of His work to the angels and to spirits and to men, that they might praise His work and all His creation: that they might see the work of His might and praise the great work of His hands and bless Him for ever.

The Book Of Parables – Enoch's Ethiopic Book 2

Chapter 37

[1] The second vision which he saw, the vision of wisdom - which Enoch the son of Jared,

[2] The son of Mahalalel, the son of Cainan, the son of Enos, the son of Seth, the son of Adam, saw. And this is the beginning of the words of wisdom which I lifted up my voice to speak and say to those which dwell on earth: Hear, ye men of old time, and see, ye that come after,

[3] The words of the Holy one which I will speak before the Lord of Spirits. It were better to declare, them only, to the men of old time, but even from those that come after we will not withhold the beginning of wisdom.

[4] Till the present day such wisdom has never been given by the Lord of Spirits as I have received according to my insight, according to the good pleasure of the Lord of Spirits by whom the lot of eternal life has been given to me.

[5] Now three Parables were imparted to me, and I lifted up my voice and recounted them to those that dwell on the earth.

Chapter 38

[1] The first Parable. When the congregation of the righteous shall appear, and sinners shall be judged for their sins, and shall be driven from the face of the earth:

[2] And when the Righteous One shall appear before the eyes of the righteous, whose elect works hang upon the Lord of Spirits, and light shall appear to the righteous and the elect who dwell on the earth, where then will be the dwelling of the sinners, and where the resting-place of those who have denied the Lord of Spirits? It had been good for them if they had not been born.

[3] When the secrets of the righteous shall be revealed and the sinners judged, and the godless driven from the presence of the righteous and elect,

[4] From that time those that possess the earth shall no longer be powerful and exalted: And they shall not be able to behold the face of the holy, For the Lord of Spirits has caused His light to appear on the face of the holy, righteous, and elect.

[5] Then shall the kings and the mighty perish and be given into the hands of the righteous and holy.

[6] And thenceforward none shall seek for themselves mercy from the Lord of Spirits for their life is at an end.

Chapter 39

[1] And it shall come to pass in those days that elect and holy children will descend from the high heaven,

[2] And their seed will become one with the children of men. And in those days Enoch received books of zeal and wrath, and books of disquiet and expulsion. And mercy shall not be accorded to them, saith the Lord of Spirits.

[3] And in those days a whirlwind carried me off from the earth, and set me down at the end of the heavens.

[4] And there I saw another vision, the dwelling-places of the holy, and the resting-places of the righteous.

[5] Here mine eyes saw their dwellings with His righteous angels, and their resting-places with the holy. And they petitioned and interceded and prayed for the children of men, and righteousness flowed before them as water, and mercy like dew upon the earth: Thus it is amongst them for ever and ever.

[6] And in that place mine eyes saw the Elect One of righteousness and of faith, and I saw his dwelling-place under the wings of the Lord of Spirits. And righteousness shall prevail in his days, and the righteous and elect shall be without number before Him for ever and ever.

[7] And all the righteous and elect before Him shall be strong as fiery lights, and their mouth shall be full of blessing, and their lips extol the name of the Lord of Spirits, and righteousness before Him shall never fail, and uprightness shall never fail before Him.

[8] There I wished to dwell, and my spirit longed for that dwelling-place: And there heretofore hath been my portion, For so has it been established concerning me before the Lord of Spirits.

[9] In those days I praised and extolled the name of the Lord of Spirits with blessings and praises, because He hath

destined me for blessing and glory according to the good pleasure of the Lord of Spirits.

[10] For a long time my eyes regarded that place, and I blessed Him and praised Him, saying: Blessed is He, and may He be blessed from the beginning and for evermo re. And before Him there is no ceasing. He knows before the world was created what is for ever and what will be from generation unto generation.

[11] Those who sleep not bless Thee: they stand before Thy glory and bless, praise, and extol, saying: "Holy, holy, holy, is the Lord of Spirits:

[12] He filleth the earth with 12 spirits." And here my eyes saw all those who sleep not: they stand before Him and bless and say: Blessed be Thou, and blessed be the name of the Lord for ever and ever. And my face was changed; for I could no longer behold.

Chapter 40

[1] And after that I saw thousands of thousands and ten thousand times ten thousand, I saw a multitude beyond number and reckoning,

[2] Who stood before the Lord of Spirits. And on the four sides of the Lord of Spirits I saw four presences, different from those that sleep not, and I learnt their names: for the angel that went with me made known to me their names, and showed me all the hidden things.

[3] And I heard the voices of those four presences as they uttered praises before the Lord of glory.

[4] The first voice blesses the Lord of Spirits for ever and ever.

[5] And the second voice I heard blessing the Elect One,

[6] And the elect ones who hang upon the Lord of Spirits. And the third voice I heard pray and intercede for those who dwell on the earth and supplicate in the name of the Lord of Spirits.

[7] And I heard the fourth voice fending off the Satans and forbidding them to come before the Lord of Spirits to accuse them who dwell on the earth.

[8] After that I asked the angel of peace who went with me, who showed me everything that is hidden: Who are these four presences which I have seen and whose words I have heard and written down?

[9] And he said to me: This first is Michael, the merciful and long-suffering: and the second, who is set over all the diseases and all the wounds of the children of men, is Raphael: and the third, who is set over all the powers, is Gabriel: and the fourth, who is set over the repentance unto hope of those who inherit eternal life, is named Phanuel.

[10] And these are the four angels of the Lord of Spirits and the four voices I heard in those days.

Chapter 41

[1] And after that I saw all the secrets of the heavens, and how the kingdom is divided,

[2] And how the actions of men are weighed in the balance. And there I saw the mansions of the elect and the mansions of the holy, and mine eyes saw there all the sinners being driven from thence which deny the name of the Lord of Spirits, and being dragged off: and they could not abide because of the punishment which proceeds from the Lord of Spirits.

[3] And there mine eyes saw the secrets of the lightning and of the thunder, and the secrets of the winds, how they are divided to blow over the earth, and the secrets of the clouds and dew,

[4] And these I saw from whence they proceed in that place and from whence they saturate the dusty earth. And there I saw closed chambers out of which the winds are divided, the chamber of the hail and winds, the chamber of the mist, and of the clouds, and the cloud thereof hovers over the earth from the beginning of the world.

[5] And I saw the chambers of the sun and moon, whence they proceed, and whither they come again, and their glorious return, and how one is superior to the other, and their stately orbit, and how they do not leave their orbit, and they add nothing to their orbit, and they take nothing from it, and they keep faith with each other, in accordance with the oath by which they are bound together.

[6] And first the sun goes forth and traverses his path according to the commandment of the Lord of Spirits,

[7] And mighty is His name for ever and ever. And after that I saw the hidden and the visible path of the moon, and she accomplishes the course of her path in that place by day and by night-the one holding a position opposite to the other before the Lord of Spirits. And they give thanks and praise and rest not; For unto them is their thanksgiving rest.

[8] For the sun changes oft for a blessing or a curse, and the course of the path of the moon is light to the righteous. And darkness to the sinners in the name of the Lord, who made a separation between the light and the darkness, and divided the spirits of men, and strengthened the spirits of the righteous, in the name of His righteousness.

[9] For no angel hinders and no power is able to hinder; for He appoints a judge for them all and He judges them all before Him.

Chapter 42

[1] Wisdom found no place where she might dwell; Then a dwelling-place was assigned her in the heavens.

[2] Wisdom went forth to make her dwelling among the children of men, and found no dwelling-place: Wisdom returned to her place, and took her seat among the angels.

[3] And unrighteousness went forth from her chambers: Whom she sought not she found, and dwelt with them, as rain in a desert, and dew on a thirsty land.

Chapter 43

[1] And I saw other lightnings and the stars of heaven, and I saw how He called them all by their names and they hearkened unto Him.

[2] And I saw how they are weighed in a righteous balance according to their proportions of light: I saw the width of their spaces and the day of their appearing, and how their revolution produces lightning: and I saw their revolution according to the number of the angels,

[3] And how they keep faith with each other. And I asked the angel who went with me who showed me what was hidden: What are these? And he said to me: The Lord of Spirits hath showed thee their parabolic meaning: these are the names of the holy who dwell on the earth and believe in the name of the Lord of Spirits for ever and ever.

Chapter 44

[1] Also another phenomenon I saw in regard to the lightnings: how some of the stars arise and become lightnings and cannot part with their new form.

Chapter 45

[1] And this is the second Parable concerning those who deny the name of the dwelling of the holy ones and the Lord of Spirits.

[2] And into the heaven they shall not ascend, and on the earth they shall not come: Such shall be the lot of the sinners who have denied the name of the Lord of Spirits, who are thus preserved for the day of suffering and tribulation.

[3] On that day Mine Elect One shall sit on the throne of glory, and shall try their works, and their places of rest shall be innumerable. And their souls shall grow strong within them when they see Mine Elect Ones, and those who have called upon My glorious name:

[4] Then will I cause Mine Elect One to dwell among them. And I will transform the heaven and make it an eternal blessing and light,

[5] And I will transform the earth and make it a blessing: And I will cause Mine elect ones to dwell upon it: But the sinners and evil-doers shall not set foot thereon.

[6] For I have provided and satisfied with peace My righteous ones, and have caused them to dwell before Me: But for the sinners there is judgement impending with Me, so that I shall destroy them from the face of the earth.

Chapter 46

[1] And there I saw one who had a head of days, and His head was white like wool, and with Him was another being whose countenance had the appearance of a man, and his face was full of graciousness, like one of the holy angels.

[2] And I asked the angel who went with me and showed me all the hidden things, concerning that Son of Man,

[3] who he was, and whence he was, and why he went with the Head of Days? And he answered and said unto me: This is the son of Man who hath righteousness, with whom dwelleth righteousness, and who revealeth all the treasures of that which is hidden, because the Lord of Spirits hath chosen him, and whose lot hath the pre-eminence before the Lord of Spirits in uprightness for ever.

[4] And this Son of Man whom thou hast seen shall raise up the kings and the mighty from their seats, and the strong from their thrones, and shall loosen the reins of the strong, and break the teeth of the sinners.

[5] And he shall put down the kings from their thrones and kingdoms because they do not extol and praise Him, nor humbly acknowledge whence the kingdom was bestowed upon them.

[6] And he shall put down the countenance of the strong, and shall fill them with shame. And darkness shall be their dwelling, and worms shall be their bed, and they shall have no hope of rising from their beds, because they do not extol the name of the Lord of Spirits.

[7] And these are they who judge the stars of heaven, and raise their hands against the Most High, and tread upon the earth and dwell upon it. And all their deeds manifest unrighteousness, and their power rests upon their riches, and their faith is in the gods which they have made with their hands, and they deny the name of the Lord of Spirits,

[8] And they persecute the houses of His congregations, and the faithful who hang upon the name of the Lord of Spirits.

Chapter 47

[1] And in those days shall have ascended the prayer of the righteous, and the blood of the righteous from the earth before the Lord of Spirits.

[2] In those days the holy ones who dwell above in the heavens shall unite with one voice and supplicate and pray and praise, and give thanks and bless the name of the Lord of Spirits on behalf of the blood of the righteous which has been shed, and that the prayer of the righteous may not be in vain before the Lord of Spirits, that judgement may be done unto them, and that they may not have to suffer for ever.

[3] In those days I saw the Head of Days when He seated himself upon the throne of His glory, and the books of the living were opened before Him: And all His host which is in heaven above and His counselors stood before Him,

[4] And the hearts of the holy were filled with joy; Because the number of the righteous had been offered, and the prayer of the righteous had been heard, and the blood of the righteous been required before the Lord of Spirits.

Chapter 48

[1] And in that place I saw the fountain of righteousness which was inexhaustible: And around it were many fountains of wisdom: And all the thirsty drank of them, and were filled with wisdom, and their dwellings were with the righteous and holy and elect.

[2] And at that hour that Son of Man was named In the presence of the Lord of Spirits, and his name before the Head of Days.

[3] Yea, before the sun and the signs were created, before the stars of the heaven were made, his name was named before the Lord of Spirits.

[4] He shall be a staff to the righteous whereon to stay themselves and not fall, and he shall be the light of the Gentiles, and the hope of those who are troubled of heart.

[5] All who dwell on earth shall fall down and worship before him, and will praise and bless and celebrate with song the Lord of Spirits.

[6] And for this reason hath he been chosen and hidden before Him, before the creation of the world and for evermore.

[7] And the wisdom of the Lord of Spirits hath revealed him to the holy and righteous; For he hath preserved the lot of the righteous, because they have hated and despised this world of unrighteousness, and have hated all its works and ways in the name of the Lord of Spirits: For in his name they are saved, and according to his good pleasure hath it been in regard to their life.

[8] In these days downcast in countenance shall the kings of the earth have become, and the strong who possess the land because of the works of their hands, for on the day of their anguish and affliction they shall not (be able to) save themselves. And I will give them over into the hands of Mine elect:

[9] As straw in the fire so shall they bur n before the face of the holy: As lead in the water shall they sink before the face of the righteous, and no trace of them shall any more be found.

[10] And on the day of their affliction there shall be rest on the earth, and before them they shall fall and not rise again: And there shall be no one to take them with his hands and raise them: For they have denied the Lord of Spirits and His Anointed. The name of the Lord of Spirits be blessed.

Chapter 49

[1] For wisdom is poured out like water, and glory faileth not before him for evermore.

[2] For he is mighty in all the secrets of righteousness, and unrighteousness shall disappear as a shadow, and have no continuance; Because the Elect One standeth before the Lord of Spirits, and his glory is for ever and ever, and his might unto all generations.

[3] And in him dwells the spirit of wisdom, and the spirit which gives insight, and the spirit of understanding and of might, and the spirit of those who have fallen asleep in righteousness.

[4] And he shall judge the secret things, and none shall be able to utter a lying word before him; For he is the Elect One before the Lord of Spirits according to His good pleasure.

Chapter 50

[1] And in those days a change shall take place for the holy and elect, and the light of days shall abide upon them, and glory and honour shall turn to the holy,

[2] On the day of affliction on which evil shall have been treasured up against the sinners. And the righteous shall be victorious in the name of the Lord of Spirits: And He will cause the others to witness this that they may repent, and forgot the works of their hands.

[3] They shall have no honour through the name of the Lord of Spirits, yet through His name shall they be saved, and the Lord of Spirits will have compassion on them, for His compassion is great.

[4] And He is righteous also in His judgement, and in the presence of His glory unrighteousness also shall not maintain itself: At His judgement the unrepentant shall perish before Him.

[5] And from henceforth I will have no mercy on them, saith the Lord of Spirits.

Chapter 51

[1] And in those days shall the earth also give back that which has been entrusted to it, and Sheol also shall give back that which it has received, and hell shall give back that which it owes. For in those days the Elect One shall arise,

[2] And he shall choose the righteous and holy from among them: For the day has drawn nigh that they should be saved.

[3] And the Elect One shall in those days sit on My throne, and his mouth shall pour forth all the secrets of wisdom and counsel: For the Lord of Spirits hath given (them) to him and hath glorified him.

[4] And in those days shall the mountains leap like rams, and the hills also shall skip like lambs satisfied with milk,

[5] And the faces of all the angels in heaven shall be lighted up with joy. And the earth shall rejoice, and the righteous shall dwell upon it, and the elect shall walk thereon.

Chapter 52

[1] And after those days in that place where I had seen all the visions of that which is hidden,

[2] For I had been carried off in a whirlwind and they had borne me towards the west-there mine eyes saw all the secret things of heaven that shall be, a mountain of iron, and a mountain of copper, and a mountain of silver, and a mountain of gold, and a mountain of soft metal, and a mountain of lead.

[3] And I asked the angel who went with me, saying, What things are these which I have seen in secret?

[4] And he said unto me: All these things which thou hast seen shall serve the dominion of His Anointed that he may be potent and mighty on the earth.

[5] And that angel of peace answered, saying unto me: Wait a little, and there shall be revealed unto thee all the secret things which surround the Lord of Spirits.

[6] And these mountains which thine eyes have seen, the mountain of iron, and the mountain of copper, and the mountain of silver, and the mountain of gold, and the mountain of soft metal, and the mountain of lead, all these shall be in the presence of the Elect One as wax: before the fire, and like the water which streams down from above upon those mountains, and they shall become powerless before his feet.

[7] And it shall come to pass in those days that none shall be saved, either by gold or by silver, and none be able to escape.

[8] And there shall be no iron for war, nor shall one clothe oneself with a breastplate. Bronze shall be of no service, and tin [shall be of no service and] shall not be esteemed, and lead shall not be desired.

[9] And all these things shall be [denied and] destroyed from the surface of the earth, when the Elect One shall appear before the face of the Lord of Spirits.

Chapter 53

[1] There mine eyes saw a deep valley with open mouths, and all who dwell on the earth and sea and islands shall bring to him gifts and presents and tokens of homage, but that deep valley shall not become full.

[2] And their hands commit lawless deeds, and the sinners devour all whom they lawlessly oppress: Yet the sinners shall be destroyed before the face of the Lord of Spirits, and they shall be banished from off the face of His earth, and they shall perish for ever and ever.

[3] For I saw all the angels of punishment abiding there and preparing all the instruments of Satan.

[4] And I asked the angel of peace who went with me: For whom are they preparing these instruments?

[5] And he said unto me: They prepare these for the kings and the mighty of this earth, that they may thereby be destroyed.

[6] And after this the Righteous and Elect One shall cause the house of his congregation to appear: henceforth they shall be no more hindered in the name of the Lord of Spirits.

[7] And these mountains shall not stand as the earth before his righteousness, but the hills shall be as a fountain of water, and the righteous shall have rest from the oppression of sinners.

Chapter 54

[1] And I looked and turned to another part of the earth, and saw there a deep valley with burning fire.

[2] And they brought the kings and the mighty, and began to cast them into this deep valley.

[3] And there mine eyes saw how they made these their instruments, iron chains of immeasurable weight.

[4] And I asked the angel of peace who went with me, saying: For whom are these chains being prepared?

[5] And he said unto me: These are being prepared for the hosts of Azazel, so that they may take them and cast them into the abyss of complete condemnation, and they shall cover their jaws with rough stones as the Lord of Spirits commanded.

[6] And Michael, and Gabriel, and Raphael, and Phanuel shall take hold of them on that great day, and cast them on that day into the burning furnace, that the Lord of Spirits may take vengeance on them for their unrighteousness in becoming subject to Satan and leading astray those who dwell on the earth.

[7] And in those days shall punishment come from the Lord of Spirits, and he will open all the chambers of waters which are above the heavens, and of the fountains which are beneath the earth.

[8] And all the waters shall be joined with the waters: that which is above the heavens is the masculine,

[9] And the water which is beneath the earth is the feminine. And they shall destroy all who dwell on the earth,

[10] And those who dwell under the ends of the heaven. And when they have recognized their unrighteousness which they have wrought on the earth, then by these shall they perish.

Chapter 55

[1] And after that the Head of Days repented and said: In vain have I destroyed all who dwell on the earth.

[2] And He sware by His great name: Henceforth I will not do so to all who dwell on the earth, and I will set a sign in the heaven: and this shall be a pledge of good faith between Me and them for ever, so long as heaven is above the earth. And this is in accordance with My command.

[3] When I have desired to take hold of them by the hand of the angels on the day of tribulation and pain because of this, I will cause My chastisement and My wrath to abide upon them, saith God, the Lord of Spirits.

[4] Ye mighty kings who dwell on the earth, ye shall have to behold Mine Elect One, how he sits on the throne of glory and judges Azazel, and all his associates, and all his hosts in the name of the Lord of Spirits.

Chapter 56

[1] And I saw there the hosts of the angels of punishment going, and they held scourges and chains of iron and bronze. And I asked the angel of peace who went with me, saying:

[2] To whom are these who hold the scourges going? And he said unto me:

[3] To their elect and beloved ones, that they may be cast into the chasm of the abyss of the valley.

[4] And then that valley shall be filled with their elect and beloved, And the days of their lives shall be at an end, And the days of their leading astray shall not thenceforward be reckoned.

[5] And in those days the angels shall return, and hurl themselves to the east upon the Parthians and Medes: They shall stir up the kings, so that a spirit of unrest shall come upon them, and they shall rouse them from their thrones, that they may break forth as lions from their lairs, and as hungry wolves among their flocks.

[6] And they shall go up and tread under foot the land of His elect ones, and the land of His elect ones shall be before them a threshing-floor and a highway :

[7] But the city of my righteous shall be a hindrance to their horses. And they shall begin to fight among themselves, and their right hand shall be strong against themselves, and a man shall not know his brother, nor a son his father or his mother, till there be no number of the corpses through their slaughter, and their punishment be not in vain.

[8] In those days Sheol shall open its jaws, and they shall be swallowed up therein, and their destruction shall be at an end; Sheol shall devour the sinners in the presence of the elect.

Chapter 57

[1] And it came to pass after this that I saw another host of wagons, and men riding thereon,

[2] And coming on the winds from the east, and from the west to the south. And the noise of their wagons was heard, and when this turmoil took place the holy ones from heaven remarked it, and the pillars of the earth were moved from their place, and the sound thereof was heard from the one end of heaven to the other, in one day.

[3] And they shall all fall down and worship the Lord of Spirits. And this is the end of the second Parable.

Chapter 58

[1] And I began to speak the third Parable concerning the righteous and elect.

[2] Blessed are ye, ye righteous and elect, for glorious shall be your lot.

[3] And the righteous shall be in the light of the sun. And the elect in the light of eternal life: The days of their life shall be unending, and the days of the holy without number.

[4] And they shall seek the light and find righteousness with the Lord of Spirits: There shall be peace to the righteous in the name of the Eternal Lord.

[5] And after this it shall be said to the holy in heaven that they should seek out the secrets of righteousness, the heritage of faith: For it has become bright as the sun upon earth, and the darkness is past.

[6] And there shall be a light that never endeth, and to a limit of days they shall not come, for the darkness shall first have been destroyed, and the light established before the Lord of Spirits, and the light of uprightness established for ever before the Lord of Spirits.

Chapter 59

[1] In those days mine eyes saw the secrets of the lightnings, and of the lights, and the judgements they execute and they lighten for a blessing or a curse as the Lord of Spirits willeth.

[2] And there I saw the secrets of the thunder, and how when it resounds above in the heaven, the sound thereof is heard, and he caused me to see the judgements executed on the earth, whether they be for well-being and blessing, or for a curse according to the word of the Lord of Spirits.

[3] And after that all the secrets of the lights and lightnings were shown to me, and they lighten for blessing and for satisfying.

The Book Of Noah – Apocryphal Part Of Noah's Book Excluded From Canonical Bible

Chapter 60

[1] In the year 500, in the seventh month, on the fourteenth day of the month in the life of Enoch. In that Parable I saw how a mighty quaking made the heaven of heavens to quake, and the host of the Most High, and the angels, a thousand thousands and ten thousand times ten thousand,

[2] Were disquieted with a great disquiet. And the Head of Days sat on the throne of His glory, and the angels and the righteous stood around Him.

[3] And a great trembling seized me, and fear took hold of me, and my loins gave way, and dissolved were my reins, and I fell upon my face.

[4] And Michael sent another angel from among the holy ones and he raised me up, and when he had raised me up my spirit returned; for I had not been able to endure the look of this host,

[5] And the commotion and the quaking of the heaven. And Michael said unto me: Why art thou disquieted with such a vision ? Until this day lasted the day of His mercy; and He hath been merciful,

[6] And long-suffering towards those who dwell on the earth. And when the day, and the power, and the punishment, and the judgement come, which the Lord of Spirits hath prepared for those who worship not the righteous law, and for those who deny the righteous judgement, and for those who take His name in vain- that day is prepared, for the elect a covenant, but for sinners an inquisition.

[7] When the punishment of the Lord of Spirits shall rest upon them, it shall rest in order that the punishment of the Lord of Spirits may not come, in vain, and it shall slay the children with their mothers and the children with their fathers. Afterwards the judgement shall take place according to His mercy and His patience. And on that day were two monsters parted, a female monster named Leviathan,

[8] To dwell in the abysses of the ocean over the fountains of the waters. But the male is named Behemoth, who occupied with his breast a waste wilderness named Duidain, on the east of the garden where the elect and righteous dwell, where my grandfather was taken up, the seventh from Adam,

[9] The first man whom the Lord of Spirits created. And I besought the other angel that he should show me the might of those monsters, how they were parted on one day and cast, the one into the abysses of the sea,

[10] And the other unto the dry land of the wilderness. And he said to me: Thou son of man, herein thou dost seek to know what is hidden.

[11] And the other angel who went with me and showed me what was hidden told me what is first and last in the heaven in the height, and beneath the earth in the depth, and at the ends of the heaven,

[12] And on the foundation of the heaven. And the chambers of the winds, and how the winds are divided, and how they are weighed, and how the portals of the winds are reckoned, each according to the power of the wind, and the power of the lights of the moon, and according to the power that is fitting: and the divisions of the stars according to their names, and how all the divisions are divided.

[13] And the thunders according to the places where they fall, and all the divisions that are made among the lightnings that it may lighten, and their host that they may at once obey.

[14] For the thunder has places of rest (which) are assigned (to it) while it is waiting for its peal; And the thunder and lightning are inseparable, and although not one and undivided, they both go together through the spirit and separate not.

[15] For when the lightning lightens, the thunder utters its voice, and the spirit enforces a pause during the peal, and divides equally between them; for the treasury of their peals is like the sand, and each one of them as it peals is held in with a bridle, and turned back by the power of the spirit, and pushed forward according to the many quarters of the earth.

[16] And the spirit of the sea is masculine and strong, and according to the might of his strength he draws it back with

a rein, and in like manner it is driven forward and disperses amid all the mountains of the earth.

[17] And the spirit of the hoar-frost is his own angel, and the spirit of the hail is a good angel.

[18] And the spirit of the snow has forsaken his chambers on account of his strength - There is a special spirit therein, and that which ascends from it is like smoke, and its name is frost.

[19] And the spirit of the mist is not united with them in their chambers, but it has a special chamber; for its course is glorious both in light and in darkness, and in winter and in summer, and in its chamber is an angel.

[20] And the spirit of the dew has its dwelling at the ends of the heaven, and is connected with the chambers of the rain, and its course is in winter and summer: and its clouds and the clouds of the mist are connected,

[21] And the one gives to the other. And when the spirit of the rain goes forth from its chamber, the angels come and open the chamber and lead it out, and when it is diffused over the whole earth it unites with the water on the earth. And whensoever it unites with the water on the earth.

[22] For the waters are for those who dwell on the earth; for they are nourishment for the earth from the Most High who is in heaven: therefore there is a measure for the rain, and the angels take it in charge. And these things I saw towards the Garden of the Righteous.

[23] And the angel of peace who was with me said to me: These two monsters, prepared conformably to the greatness of God, shall feed.

Chapter 61

[1] And I saw in those days how long cords were given to those angels, and they took to themselves wings and flew, and they went towards the north.

[2] And I asked the angel, saying unto him: Why have those (angels) taken these cords and gone off? And he said unto me: They have gone to measure.

[3] And the angel who went with me said unto me: These shall bring the measures of the righteous, and the ropes of the righteous to the righteous, that they may stay themselves on the name of the Lord of Spirits for ever and ever.

[4] The elect shall begin to dwell with the elect, and those are the measures which shall be given to faith, and which shall strengthen righteousness.

[5] And these measures shall reveal all the secrets of the depths of the earth, and those who have been destroyed by the desert, and those who have been devoured by the beasts, and those who have been devoured by the fish of the sea, that they may return and stay themselves on the day of the Elect One; For none shall be destroyed before the Lord of Spirits, and none can be destroyed.

[6] And all who dwell above in the heaven received a command and power and one voice and one light like unto fire.

[7] And that One with their first words they blessed, and extolled and lauded with wisdom, and they were wise in utterance and in the spirit of life.

[8] And the Lord of Spirits placed the Elect one on the throne of glory. And he shall judge all the works of the holy above in the heaven, and in the balance shall their deeds be weighed.

Chapter 62

[1] And thus the Lord commanded the kings and the mighty and the exalted, and those who dwell on the earth, and said: Open your eyes and lift up your horns if ye are able to recognize the Elect One.

[2] And the Lord of Spirits seated him on the throne of His glory, and the spirit of righteousness was poured out upon him, and the word of his mouth slays all the sinners, and all the unrighteous are destroyed from before his face.

[3] And there shall stand up in that day all the kings and the mighty, and the exalted and those who hold the earth, and they shall see and recognize How he sits on the throne of his glory, and righteousness is judged before him, and no lying word is spoken before him.

[4] Then shall pain come upon them as on a woman in travail, and she has pain in bringing forth, when her child enters the mouth of the womb, and she has pain in bringing forth.

[5] And one portion of them shall look on the other, and they shall be terrified, and they shall be downcast of countenance, and pain shall seize them, when they see that Son of Man Sitting on the throne of his glory.

[6] And the kings and the mighty and all who possess the earth shall bless and glorify and extol him who rules over all, who was hidden.

[7] For from the beginning the Son of Man was hidden, and the most High preserved him in the presence of His might, and revealed him to the elect.

[8] And the congregation of the elect and holy shall be sown, and all the elect shall stand before him on that day.

[9] And all the kings and the mighty and the exalted and those who rule the eart. Shall fall down before him on their faces, and worship and set their hope upon that Son of Man, and petition him and supplicate for mercy at his hands.

[10] Nevertheless that Lord of Spirits will so press them that they shall hastily go forth from His presence, and their faces shall be filled with shame, and the darkness grow deeper on their faces.

[11] And He will deliver them to the angels for punishment, to execute vengeance on them because they have oppressed His children and His elect,

[12] And they shall be a spectacle for the righteous and for His elect: They shall rejoice over them, because the wrath of the Lord of Spirits resteth upon them, and His sword is drunk with their blood.

[13] And the righteous and elect shall be saved on that day, and they shall never thenceforward see the face of the sinners and unrighteous.

[14] And the Lord of Spirits will abide over them, and with that Son of Man shall they eat and lie down and rise up for ever and ever.

[15] And the righteous and elect shall have risen from the earth, and ceased to be of downcast countenance. And they shall have been clothed with garments of glory,

[16] And these shall be the garments of life from the Lord of Spirits: And your garments shall not grow old, nor your glory pass away before the Lord of Spirits.

Chapter 63

[1] In those days shall the mighty and the kings who possess the earth implore Him to grant them a little respite from His angels of punishment to whom they were delivered,

[2] That they might fall down and worship before the Lord of Spirits, and confess their sins before Him. And they shall bless and glorify the Lord of Spirits, and say: Blessed is the Lord of Spirits and the Lord of kings, And the Lord of the mighty and the Lord of the rich, And the Lord of glory and the Lord of wisdom,

[3] And splendid in every secret thing is Thy power from generation to generation, and Thy glory for ever and ever: Deep are all Thy secrets and innumerable, and Thy righteousness is beyond reckoning.

[4] We have now learnt that we should glorify and bless the Lord of kings and Him who is king over all kings.

[5] And they shall say: Would that we had rest to glorify and give thanks and confess our faith before His glory !

[6] And now we long for a little rest but find it not: We follow hard upon and obtain (it) not: And light has vanished from before us, and darkness is our dwelling-place for ever and ever:

[7] For we have not believed before Him nor glorified the name of the Lord of Spirits, nor glorified our Lord but our hope was in the sceptre of our kingdom, and in our glory.

[8] And in the day of our suffering and tribulation He saves us not, and we find no respite for confession that our Lord is true in all His works, and in His judgements and His justice, and His judgements have no respect of persons.

[9] And we pass away from before His face on account of our works, and all our sins are reckoned up in righteousness.

[10] Now they shall say unto themselves: Our souls are full of unrighteous gain, but it does not prevent us from descending from the midst thereof into the burden of Sheol.

[11] And after that their faces shall be filled with darkness, and shame before that Son of Man, and they shall be driven from his presence, and the sword shall abide before his face in their midst.

[12] Thus spake the Lord of Spirits: This is the ordinance and judgement with respect to the mighty and the kings and the exalted and those who possess the earth before the Lord of Spirits.

Chapter 64

[1] And other forms I saw hidden in that place. I heard the voice of the angel saying: These are the angels who descended to the earth,

[2] And revealed what was hidden to the children of men and seduced the children of men into committing sin.

Chapter 65

[1] And in those days Noah saw the earth that it had sunk down and its destruction was nigh.

[2] And he arose from thence and went to the ends of the earth, and cried aloud to his grandfather Enoch:

[3] And Noah said three times with an embittered voice: Hear me, hear me, hear me. And I said unto him: Tell me

what it is that is falling out on the earth that the earth is in such evil plight,

[4] And shaken, lest perchance I shall perish with it? And thereupon there was a great commotion , on the earth, and a voice was heard from heaven, and I fell on my face.

[5] And Enoch my grandfather came and stood by me, and said unto me: Why hast thou cried unto me with a bitter cry and weeping,

[6] And a command has gone forth from the presence of the Lord concerning those who dwell on the earth that their ruin is accomplished because they have learnt all the secrets of the angels, and all the violence of the Satans, and all their powers -the most secret ones- and all the power of those who practice sorcery, and the power of witchcraft, and the power of those who make molten images for the whole earth:

[7] And how silver is produced from the dust of the earth, and how soft metal originates in the earth.

[8] For lead and tin are not produced from the earth like the first: it is a fountain that produces them,

[9] And an angel stands therein, and that angel is pre-eminent. And after that my grandfather Enoch took hold of me by my hand and raised me up, and said unto me:

[10] Go, for I have asked the Lord of Spirits as touching this commotion on the earth. And He said unto me: "Because of their unrighteousness their judgement has been determined upon and shall not be withheld by Me for ever. Because of the sorceries which they have searched out and learnt, the earth,

[11] and those who dwell upon it shall be destroyed." And these-they have no place of repentance forever, because they have shown them what was hidden, and they are the damned: but as for thee, my son, the Lord of Spirits knows that thou art pure, and guiltless of this reproach concerning the secrets.

[12] And He has destined thy name to be among the holy, And will preserve thee amongst those who dwell on the earth, and has destined thy righteous seed both for kingship and for great honours, and from thy seed shall proceed a fountain of the righteous and holy witho ut number forever.

Chapter 66

[1] And after that he showed me the angels of punishment who are prepared to come and let loose all the powers of the waters which are beneath in the earth in order to bring judgement and destruction on all who abide and dwell on the earth.

[2] And the Lord of Spirits gave commandment to the angels who were going forth, that they should not cause the waters to rise but should hold them in check;

[3] For those angels were over the powers of the waters. And I went away from the presence of Enoch.

Chapter 67

[1] And in those days the word of God came unto me, and He said unto me: Noah, thy lot has come up before Me,

[2] A lot without blame, a lot of love and uprightness. And now the angels are making a wooden building, and when they have completed that task I will place My hand upon it and preserve it, and there shall come forth from it the seed of life, and a change shall set in so that the earth will not remain without inhabitant.

[3] And I will make fast thy seed before me for ever and ever, and I will spread abroad those who dwell with thee: it shall not be unfruitful on the face of the earth, but it shall be blessed and multiply on the earth in the name of the Lord.

[4] And He will imprison those angels, who have shown unrighteousness, in that burning valley which my grandfather Enoch had formerly shown to me in the west among the mountains of gold and silver and iron and soft metal and tin.

[5] And I saw that valley in which there was a great convulsion and a convulsion of the waters.

[6] And when all this took place, from that fiery molten metal and from the convulsion thereof in that place, there was produced a smell of sulphur, and it was connected with those waters, and that valley of the angels who had led astray mankind burned beneath that land.

[7] And through its valleys proceed streams of fire, where these angels are punished who had led astray those who dwell upon the earth.

[8] But those waters shall in those days serve for the kings and the mighty and the exalted, and those who dwell on the earth, for the healing of the body, but for the punishment of the spirit; Now their spirit is full of lust, that they may be punished in their body, for they have denied the Lord of Spirits and see their punishment daily,

[9] And yet believe not in His name. And in proportion as the burning of their bodies becomes severe, a corresponding change shall take place in their spirit for ever and ever;

[10] For before the Lord of Spirits none shall utter an idle word. For the judgement shall come upon them,

[11] Because they believe in the lust of their body and deny the Spirit of the Lord. And those same waters will undergo a change in those days; for when those angels are punished in these waters, these water-springs shall change their temperature, and when the angels ascend, this water of the springs shall change and become cold.

[12] And I heard Michael answering and saying: This judgement wherewith the angels are judged is a testimony for the kings and the mighty who possess the earth.

[13] Because these waters of judgement minister to the healing of the body of the kings and the lust of their body; therefore they will not see and will not believe that those waters will change and become a fire which burns for ever.

Chapter 68

[1] And after that my grandfather Enoch gave me the teaching of all the secrets in the book in the Parables which had been given to him, and he put them together for me in the words of the book of the Parables.

[2] And on that day Michael answered Raphael and said: The power of the spirit transports and makes me to tremble because of the severity of the judgement of the secrets, the judgement of the angels: who can endure the severe judgement which has been executed,

[3] And before which they melt away ? And Michael answered again, and said to Raphael: Who is he whose heart is not softened concerning it, and whose reins are not troubled by this word of judgement that has gone forth upon them because of those who have thus led them out ?

[4] And it came to pass when he stood before the Lord of Spirits, Michael said thus to Raphael: I will not take their part under the eye of the Lord; for the Lord of Spirits has been angry with them because they do as if they were the Lord.

[5] Therefore all that is hidden shall come upon them forever and ever; for neither angel nor man shall have his portion in it, but alone they have received their judgement for ever and ever.

Chapter 69

[1] And after this judgement they shall terrify and make them to tremble because they have shown this to those who dwell on the earth.

[2] And behold the names of those angels [and these are their names: the first of them is Samjaza, the second Artaqifa, and the third Armen, the fourth Kokabel, the fifth Turael, the sixth Rumjal, the seventh Danjal, the eighth Neqael, the ninth Baraqel, the tenth Azazel, the eleventh Armaros, the twelfth Batarjal, the thirteenth Busasejal, the fourteenth Hananel, the fifteenth Turel, and the sixteenth Simapesiel, the seventeenth Jetrel, the eighteenth Tumael, the nineteenth Turel, the twentieth Rumael, the twenty-first Azazel.

[3] And these are the chiefs of their angels and their names, and their chief ones over hundreds and over fifties and over tens.

[4] The name of the first Jeqon: that is, the one who led astray [all] the sons of God, and brought them down to the earth, and led them astray through the daughters of men.

[5] And the second was named Asbeel: he imparted to the holy sons of God evil counsel, and led them astray so that they defiled their bodies with the daughters of men. And the third was named Gadreel: he it is who showed the children of men all the blows of death, and he led astray Eve,

[6] And showed the weapons of death to the sons of men the shield and the coat of mail, and the sword for battle, and all the weapons of death to the children of men.

[7] And from his hand they have proceeded against those who dwell on the earth from that day and for evermore.

[8] And the fourth was named Penemue: he taught the children of men the bitter and the sweet,

[9] And he taught them all the secrets of their wisdom. And he instructed mankind in writing with ink and paper, and thereby many sinned from eternity to eternity and until this day.

[10] For men were not created for such a purpose, to give confirmation to their good faith with pen and ink.

[11] For me n were created exactly like the angels, to the intent that they should continue pure and righteous, and death, which destroys everything, could not have taken hold of them, but through this their knowledge they are perishing, and through this power it is consuming me.

[12] And the fifth was named Kasdeja: this is he who showed the children of men all the wicked smitings of spirits and demons, and the smitings of the embryo in the womb, that it may pass away, and the smitings of the soul the bites of the serpent, and the smitings,

[13] Which befall through the noontide heat, the son of the serpent named Tabaet. And this is the task of Kasbeel, the

chief of the oath which he showed to the holy ones when he dwelt high above in glory, and its name is Biqa.

[14] This angel requested Michael to show him the hidden name, that he might enunciate it in the oath, so that those might quake before that name and oath who revealed all that was in secret to the children of men.

[15] And this is the power of this oath, for it is powerful and strong, and he placed this oath Akae in the hand of Michael.

[16] And these are the secrets of this oath , And they are strong through his oath: And the heaven was suspended before the world was created, and forever.

[17] And through it the earth was founded upon the water, and from the secret recesses of the mountains come beautiful waters, from the creation of the world and unto eternity.

[18] And through that oath the sea was created, and as its foundation He set for it the sand against the time of its anger, and it dare not pass beyond it from the creation of the world unto eternity.

[19] And through that oath are the depths made fast, and abide and stir not from their place from eternity to eternity.

[20] And through that oath the sun and moon complete their course, and deviate not from their ordinance from eternity to eternity.

[21] And through that oath the stars complete their course, and He calls them by their names, and they answer Him from eternity to eternity.

[22] And in like manner the spirits of the water, and of the winds, and of all zephyrs, andtheir paths from all the quarters of the winds.

[23] And there are preserved the voices of the thunder and the light of the lightnings: and there are preserved the chambers of the hail and the chambers of the hoarfrost,

[24] And the chambers of the mist, and the chambers of the rain and the dew. And all these believe and give thanks before the Lord of Spirits, and glorify Him with all their power, and their food is in every act of thanksgiving: they thank and glorify and extol the name of the Lord of Spirits for ever and ever.

[25] And this oath is mighty over them and through it they are preserved and their paths are preserved, And their course is not destroyed.

[26] And there was great joy amongst them, and they blessed and glorified and extolled because the name of that Son of Man had been revealed unto them.

[27] And he sat on the throne of his glory, and the sum of judgement was given unto the Son of Man, and he caused the sinners to pass away and be destroyed from off the face of the earth, and those who have led the world astray.

[28] With chains shall they be bound, and in their assemblage-place of destruction shall they be imprisoned, and all their works vanish from the face of the earth.

[29] And from henceforth there shall be nothing corruptible; For that Son of Man has appeared, and has seated himself on the throne of his glory, and all evil shall pass away before his face, and the word of that Son of Man shall go forth and be strong before the Lord of Spirits.

Chapter 70

[1] And it came to pass after this that his name during his lifetime was raised aloft to that Son of Man,

[2] And to the Lord of Spirits from amongst those who dwell on the earth.

[3] And he was raised aloft on the chariots of the spirit and his name vanished among them. And from that day I was no longer numbered amongst them: and he set me between the two winds, between the North and the West,

[4] Where the angels took the cords to measure for me the place for the elect and righteous. And there I saw the first fathers and the righteous who from the beginning dwell in that place.

Chapter 71

[1] And it came to pass after this that my spirit was translated and it ascended into the heavens: And I saw the holy sons of God. They were stepping on flames of fire: Their garments were white and their raiment, and their faces shone like snow.

[2] And I saw two streams of fire, and the light of that fire shone like hyacinth, and I fell on my face before the Lord of Spirits.

[3] And the angel Michael[one of the archangels] seized me by my right hand, and lifted me up and led me forth into all the secrets, and he showed me all the secrets of righteousness.

[4] And he showed me all the secrets of the ends of the heaven, and all the chambers of all the stars, and all the luminaries, whence they proceed before the face of the holy ones.

[5] And he translated my spirit into the heaven of heavens, and I saw there as it were a structure built of crystals, and between those crystals tongues of living fire.

[6] And my spirit saw the girdle which girt that house of fire, and on its four sides were streams full of living fire, and they girt that house.

[7] And round about were Seraphin, Cherubic, and Ophannin: And these are they who sleep not and guard the throne of His glory.

[8] And I saw angels who could not be counted, a thousand thousands, and ten thousand times ten thousand, encircling that house. And Michael, and Raphael, and Gabriel, and Phanuel, and the holy angels who are above the heavens, go in and out of that house.

[9] And they came forth from that house, and Michael and Gabriel, Raphael and Phanuel, and many holy angels without number.

[10] And with them the Head of Days, His head white and pure as wool, and His raiment indescribable.

[11] And I fell on my face, and my whole body became relaxed, and my spirit was transfigured; and I cried with a loud voice, with the spirit of power, and blessed and glorified and extolled.

[12] And these blessings which went forth out of my mouth were well pleasing before that Head of Days. And that Head of Days came with Michael and Gabriel, Raphael and Phanuel, thousands and ten thousands of angels without number.

[13] Lost passage where in the Son of Man was described as accompanying the Head of Days, and Enoch asked one of the angels concerning the Son of Man as to who he was.

[14] And he, the angel, came to me and greeted me with His voice, and said unto me this is the Son of Man who is born unto righteousness, and righteousness abides over him, and the righteousness of the Head of Days forsakes him not.

[15] And he said unto me: He proclaims unto thee peace in the name of the world to come; For from hence has proceeded peace since the creation of the world, and so shall it be unto thee for ever and for ever and ever.

[16] And all shall walk in his ways since righteousness never forsaketh him: With him will be their dwelling-places, and with him their heritage, and they shall not be separated from him for ever and ever and ever. And so there shall be length of days with that Son of Man, and the righteous shall have peace and an upright way in the name of the Lord of Spirits for ever and ever.

Chapter 72

[1] The book of the courses of the luminaries of the heaven, the relations of each, according to their classes, their dominion and their seasons, according to their names and places of origin, and according to their months, which Uriel, the holy angel, who was with me, who is their guide, showed me; and he showed me all their laws exactly as they are, and how it is with regard to all the years of the world and unto eternity,

[2] Till the new creation is accomplished which dureth till eternity. And this is the first law of the luminaries: the luminary the Sun has its rising in the eastern portals of the heaven,

[3] And its setting in the western portals of the heaven. And I saw six portals in which the sun rises, and six portals in which the sun sets and the moon rises and sets in these portals, and the leaders of the stars and those whom they lead: six in the east and six in the west, and all following each other in accurately corresponding order:

[4] also many windows to the right and left of these portals. And first there goes forth the great luminary, named the Sun, and his circumference is like the circumference of the heaven,

[5] And he is quite filled with illuminating and heating fire. The chariot on which he ascends, the wind drives, and the sun goes down from the heaven and returns through the north in order to reach the east, and is so guided that he comes to the appropriate portal and shines in the face of the heaven.

[6] In this way he rises in the first month in the great portal,

[7] Which is the fourth [those six portals in the cast]. And in that fourth portal from which the sun rises in the first month are twelve window-openings, from which proceed a flame when they are opened in their season.

[8] When the sun rises in the heaven, he comes forth through that fourth portal thirty,

[9] Mornings in succession, and sets accurately in the fourth portal in the west of the heaven. And during this period the day becomes daily longer and the night nightly shorter to the thirtieth morning.

[10] On that day the day is longer than the night by a ninth part, and the day amounts exactly to ten parts and the night to eight parts. And the sun rises from that fourth portal, and sets in the fourth and returns to the fifth portal of the east thirty mornings, and rises from it and sets in the fifth portal.

[11] And then the day becomes longer by two parts and amounts to eleven parts, and the night becomes shorter and amounts to seven parts.

[12] And it returns to the east and enters into the sixth portal,

[13] And rises and sets in the sixth portal one-and-thirty mornings on account of its sign.

[14] On that day the day becomes longer than the night, and the day becomes double the night, and the day becomes twelve parts,

[15] And the night is shortened and becomes six parts. And the sun mounts up to make the day shorter and the night longer, and the sun returns to the east and enters into the sixth portal,

[16] And rises from it and sets thirty mornings. And when thirty mornings are accomplished,

[17] The day decreases by exactly one part, and becomes eleven parts, and the night seven. And the sun goes forth from that sixth portal in the west, and goes to the east and rises in the fifth portal for thirty mornings,

[18] And sets in the west again in the fifth western portal. On that day the day decreases by two parts, and amounts to ten parts and the night to eight parts.

[19] And the sun goes forth from that fifth portal and sets in the fifth portal of the west, and rises in the fourth portal for one-and-thirty mornings on account of its sign, and sets in the west.

[20] On that day the day is equalized with the night, and becomes of equal length, and the night amounts to nine parts and the day to nine parts.

[21] And the sun rises from that portal and sets in the west, and returns to the east and rises thirty mornings in the third portal and sets in the west in the third portal.

[22] And on that day the night becomes longer than the day, and night becomes longer than night, and day shorter than day till thhe thirtieth morning, and the night amounts exactly to ten parts and the day to eight parts.

[23] And the sun rises from that third portal and sets in the third portal in the west and returns to the east, and for thirty mornings rises in the second portal in the east,

[24] And in like manner sets in the second portal in the west of the heaven. And on that day the night amounts to eleven parts and the day to seven parts.

[25] And the sun rises on that day from that second portal and sets in the west in the second portal, and returns to the east into the first portal for one and thirty mornings,

[26] And sets in the first portal in the west of the heaven. And on that day the night becomes longer and amounts to the double of the day: and the night amounts exactly to twelve parts and the day to six.

[27] And the sun has therewith traversed the divisions of his orbit and turns again on those divisions of his orbit, and enters that portal thirty mornings and sets also in the west opposite to it.

[28] And on that night has the night decreased in length by a ninth part, and the night has become eleven parts and the day seven parts. And the sun has returned and entered into the second portal in the east, and returns on those his divisions of his orbit for thirty mornings, rising and setting.

[29] And on that day the night decreases in length, and the night amounts to ten parts and the day to eight.

[30] And on that day the sun rises from that portal, and sets in the west,

[31] And returns to the east, and rises in the third portal for one-and-thirty mornings, and sets in the west of the heaven.

[32] On that day the night decreases and amounts to nine parts, and the day to nine parts, and the night is equal to the day and the year is exactly as to its days three hundred and sixty-four. And the length of the day and of the night,

[33] And the shortness of the day and of the night arisethrough the course of the sun these distinctions are made.

[34] So it comes that its course becomes daily longer, and its course nightly shorter.

[35] And this is the law and the course of the sun, and his return as often as he returns sixty times and rises, i.e. the great luminary which is named the sun, forever and ever.

[36] And that which, thus, rises is the great luminary, and is so named according to its appearance, according as the Lord commanded. As he rises, so he sets and decreases not, and rests not, but runs day and night, and his light is sevenfold brighter than that of the moon; but as regards size they are both equal.

Chapter 73

[1] And after this law I saw another law dealing with the smaller luminary, which is named the Moon.

[2] And her circumference is like the circumference of the heaven, and her chariot in which she rides is driven by the wind, and light is given to her in definite measure. And her rising and setting change every month:

[3] And her days are like the days of the sun, and when her light is uniform it amounts to the seventh part of the light of the sun.

[4] And thus she rises. And her first phase in the east comes forth on the thirtieth morning: and on that day she becomes visible, and constitutes for you the first phase of the moon on the thirtieth day together with the sun in the portal where the sun rises.

[5] And the one half of her goes forth by a seventh part, and her whole circumference is empty, without light, with the exception of one-seventh part of it, and the fourteenth part of her light.

[6] And when she receives one-seventh part of the half of her light, her light amounts to one-seventh part and the half thereof.

[7] And she sets with the sun, and when the sun rises the moon rises with him and receives the half of one part of light, and in that night in the beginning of her morning in the commencement of the lunar day the moon sets with the sun,

[8] And is invisible that night with the fourteen parts and the half of one of them. And she rises on that day with exactly a seventh part, and comes forth and recedes from the rising of the sun,

[9] And in her remaining days she becomes bright in the remaining thirteen parts.

Chapter 74

[1] And I saw another course, a law for her, (and) how according to that law she performs her monthly revolution.

[2] And all these Uriel, the holy angel who is the leader of them all, showed to me, and their positions, and I wrote down their positions as he showed them to me, and I wrote down their months as they were,

[3] And the appearance of their lights till fifteen days were accomplished. In single seventh parts she accomplishes all her light in the east, and in single seventh parts accomplishes all her darkness in the west.

[4] And in certain months she alters her settings, and in certain months she pursues her own peculiar course.

[5] In two months the moon sets with the sun: in those two middle portals the third and the fourth.

[6] She goes forth for seven days, and turns about and returns again through the portal where the sun rises, and accomplishes all her light: and she recedes from the sun, and in eight days enters the sixth portal from which the sun goes forth.

[7] And when the sun goes forth from the fourth portal she goes forth seven days, until she goes forth from the fifth and turns back again in seven days into the fourth portal and accomplishes all her light: and she recedes and enters into the first portal in eight days.

[8] And she returns again in seven days into the fourth portal from which the sun goes forth.

[9] Thus I saw their position how the moons rose and the sun set in those days.

[10] And if five years are added together the sun has an overplus of thirty days, and all the days which accrue to it for one of those five years,

[11] When they are full, amount to 364 days. And the overplus of the sun and of the stars amounts to six days: in 5 years 6 days every year come to 30 days: and the moon falls behind the sun and stars to the number of 30 days.

[12] And the sun and the stars bring in all the years exactly, so that they do not advance or delay their position by a single day unto eternity; but complete the years with perfect justice in 364 days.

[13] In 3 years there are 1,092 days, and in 5 years 1,820 days, so that in 8 years there are 2,912 days.

[14] For the moon alone the days amount in 3 years to 1,062 days, and in 5 years she falls 50 days behind:i.e. to the sum (of 1,770) there is 5 to be added (1,000 and) 62 days.

[15] And in 5 years there are 1,770 days, so that for the moon the days 6 in 8 years amount to 21,832 days.

[16] For in 8 years she falls behind to the amount of 80 days, all the 17 days she falls behind in 8 years are 80. And the year

is accurately completed in conformity with their world stations and the stations of the sun, which rise from the portals through which it the sun rises and sets 30 days.

Chapter 75

[1] And the leaders of the heads of the thousands, who are placed over the whole creation and over all the stars, have also to do with the four intercalary days, being inseparable from their office, according to the reckoning of the year, and these render service on the four days which are not reckoned in the reckoning of the year.

[2] And owing to them men go wrong therein, for those luminaries truly render service on the world-stations, one in the first portal, one in the third portal of the heaven, one in the fourth portal, and one in the sixth portal, and the exactness of the year is accomplished through its separate three hundred and sixty- four stations.

[3] For the signs and the times and the years and the days the angel Uriel showed to me, whom the Lord of glory hath set for ever over all the luminaries of the heaven, in the heaven and in the world, that they should rule on the face of the heaven and be seen on the earth, and be leaders for the day and the night, i.e. the sun, moon, and stars, and all the ministering creatures which make their revolution in all the chariots of the heaven.

[4] In like manner twelve doors Uriel showed me, open in the circumference of the suns chariot in the heaven, through which the rays of the sun break forth: and from them is warmth diffused over the earth, when they are opened at their appointed seasons. And for the winds and the spirit of the dew when they are opened,

[5] Standing open in the heavens at the ends. As for the twelve portals in the heaven, at the ends of the earth, out of which go forth the sun, moon, and stars, and all the works of heaven in the east and in the west,

[6] There are many windows open to the left and right of them, and one window at its appointed season produces warmth, corresponding as these do to those doors from which the stars come forth according as He has commanded them, and where in they set corresponding to their number. And I saw chariots in the heaven, running in the world, above those portals in which revolve the stars that never set. And one is larger than all the rest, and it is that that makes its course through the entire world.

Chapter 76

[1] And at the ends of the earth I saw twelve portals open to all the quarters of the heaven,

[2] From which the winds go forth and blow over the earth. Three of them are open on the face of the heavens, and three in the west, and three on the right of the heaven, and three on the left.

[3] And the three first are those of the east, and three are of the north,

[4] And three after those on the left of the south, and three of the west. Through four of these come winds of blessing and prosperity, and from those eight come hurtful winds: when they are sent, the y bring destruction on all the earth and on the water upon it, and on all who dwell thereon, and on everything which is in the water and on the land.

[5] And the first wind from those portals, called the east wind, comes forth through the first portal which is in the east, inclining towards the south: from it come forth desolation, drought, heat, and destruction.

[6] And through the second portal in the middle comes what is fitting, and from it there come rain and fruitfulness and prosperity and dew; and through the third portal which lies toward the north come cold and drought.

[7] And after these come forth the south winds through three portals: through the first portal of them inclining to the east comes forth a hot wind.

[8] And through the middle portal next to it there come forth fragrant smells,

[9] And dew and rain, and prosperity and health. And through the third portal lying to the west come forth dew and rain, locusts and desolation.

[10] And after these the north winds: from the seventh portal in the east come dew and rain, locusts and desolation.

[11] And from the middle portal come in a direct direction health and rain and dew and prosperity; and through the third portal in the west come cloud and hoar-frost, and snow and rain, and dew and locusts.

[12] And after thesefour are the west winds: through the first portal adjoining the north come forth dew and hoar-frost, and cold and snow and frost. And from the middle portal come forth dew and rain, and prosperity and blessing; and through the last portal which adjoins the south come forth drought and desolation, and burning and destruction. And the twelve portals of the four quarters of the heaven are therewith completed, and all their laws and all their plagues and all their benefactions have I shown to thee, my son Methuselah.

Chapter 77

[1] And the first quarter is called the east, because it is the first: and the second, the south, because the Most High will descend there, yea, there in quite a special sense will He who is blessed for ever descend.

[2] And the west quarter is named the diminished, because there all the luminaries of the heaven wane and go down.

[3] And the fourth quarter, named the north, is divided into three parts: the first of them is for the dwelling of men: and the second contains seas of water, and the abysses and forests and rivers, and darkness and clouds; and the third part contains the garden of righteousness.

[4] I saw seven high mountains, higher than all the mountains which are on the earth: and thence comes forth hoar frost,

[5] And days, seasons, and years pass away. I saw seven rivers on the earth larger than all the rivers: one of them coming from the west pours its waters into the Great Sea.

[6] And these two come from the north to the sea and pour their waters into the Erythraean Sea in the east.

[7] And the remaining, four come forth on the side of the north to their own sea, two of them to the Erythraean Sea, and two into the Great Sea and discharge themselves thereand some say: into the desert.

[8] Seven great islands I saw in the sea and in the mainland: two in the mainland and five in the Great Sea.

Chapter 78

[1] And the names of the sun are the following: the first Orjares, and the second Tomas.

[2] And the moon has four names: the first name is Asonja, the second Ebla, the third Benase, and the fourth Erae.

[3] These are the two great luminaries: their circumference is like the circumference of the heaven, and the size of the circumference of both is alike.

[4] In the circumference of the sun there are seven portions of light which are added to it more than to the moon, and in definite measures it is s transferred till the seventh portion of the sun is exhausted.

[5] And they set and enter the portals of the west, and make their revolution by the north, and come forth through the eastern portals on the face of the heaven.

[6] And when the moon rises one- fourteenth part appears in the heaven:

[7] The light becomes full in her: on the fourteenth day she accomplishes her light. And fifteen parts of light are transferred to her till the fifteenth day when her light is accomplished, according to the sign of the year, and she becomes fifteen parts, and the moon grows by (the addition of) fourteenth parts.

[8] And in her waning (the moon) decreases on the first day to fourteen parts of her light, on the second to thirteen parts of light, on the third to twelve, on the fourth to eleven, on the fifth to ten, on the sixth to nine, on the seventh to eight, on the eighth to seven, on the ninth to six, on the tenth to five, on the eleventh to four, on the twelfth to three, on the thirteenth to two, on the fourteenth to the half of a seventh,

[9] And all her remaining light disappears wholly on the fifteenth.

[10] And in certain months the month has twenty-nine days and once twenty-eight. And Uriel showed me another law: when light is transferred to the moon, and on which side it is transferred to her by the sun.

[11] During all the period during which the moon is growing in her light, she is transferring it to herself when opposite to the sun during fourteen daysher light is accomplished in the heaven,

[12] And when she is illumined throughout, her light is accomplished full in the heaven. And on the first day she is called the new moon,

[13] For on that day the light rises upon her. She becomes full moon exactly on the day when the sun sets in the west, and from the east she rises at night, and the moon shines the whole night through till the sun rises over against her and the moon is seen over against the sun.

[14] On the side whence the light of the moon comes forth, there again she wanes till all the light vanishes and all the days of the month are at an end, and her circumference is empty, void of light.

[15] And three months she makes of thirty days, and at her time she makes three months of twenty nine days each, in which she accomplishes her waning in the first period of time,

[16] And in the first portal for one hundred and seventy-seven days. And in the time of her going out she appears for three months of thirty days each, and for three months she appears of twentynine each. At night she appears like a man for twenty days each time, and by day she appears like the heaven, and there is nothing else in her save her light.

Chapter 79

[1] And now, my son, I have shown thee everything, and the law of all the stars of the heaven is completed.

[2] And he showed me all the laws of these for every day, and for every season of bearing rule, and for every year, and for its going forth, and for the order prescribed to it every month and every week:

[3] And the waning of the moon which takes place in the sixth portal: for in this sixth portal her light is accomplished,

[4] And after that there is the beginning of the waning: And the waning which takes place in the first portal in its season, till one hundred and seventy seven days are accomplished:

[5] Reckoned according to weeks, twenty five weeks and two days. She falls behind the sun and the order of the stars exactly five days in the course of one period,

[6] And when this place which thou seest has been traversed. Such is the picture and sketch of every luminary which Uriel the archangel, who is their leader, showed unto me.

Chapter 80

[1] And in those days the angel Uriel answered and said to me: Behold, I have shown thee everything, Enoch, and I have revealed everything to thee that thou shouldst see this sun and this moon, and the leaders of the stars of the heaven and all those who turn them, their tasks and times and departures.

[2] And in the days of the sinners the years shall be shortened, and their seed shall be tardy on their lands and fields, and all things on the earth shall alter, and shall not appear in their time: And the rain shall be kept back and the heaven shall withhold it.

[3] And in those times the fruits of the earth shall be backward, and shall not grow in their time, and the fruits of the trees shall be withheld in their time.

[4] And the moon shall alter her order, and not appear at her time.

[5] And in those days the sun shall be seen and he shall journey in the evening on the extremity of the great chariot in the west and shall shine more brightly than accords with the order of light.

[6] And many chiefs of the stars shall transgress the order prescribed. And these shall alter their orbits and tasks, and not appear at the seasons prescribed to them.

[7] And the whole order of the stars shall be concealed from the sinners, and the thoughts of those on the earth shall err concerning them, and they shall be altered from all their ways, Yea, they shall err and take them to be gods.

[8] And evil shall be multiplied upon them, and punishment shall come upon them So as to destroy all.

Chapter 81

[1] And he said unto me: Observe, Enoch, these heavenly tablets, and read what is written thereon, and mark every individual fact.

[2] And I observed the heavenly tablets, and read everything whic h was written thereon and understood everything, and read the book of all the deeds of mankind, and of all the children of flesh that shall be upon the earth to the remotest generations.

[3] And forthwith I blessed the great Lord the King of glory for ever, in that He has made all the works of the world, and I extolled the Lord because of His patience, and blessed Him because of the children of men.

[4] And after that I said: Blessed is the man who dies in righteousness and goodness, Concerning whom there is no book of unrighteousness written, And against whom no day of judgement shall be found.

[5] And those seven holy ones brought me and placed me on the earth before the door of my house, and said to me: Declare everything to thy son Methuselah, and show to all thy children that no flesh is righteous in the sight of the Lord,

[6] For He is their Creator. One year we will leave thee with thy son, till thou givest thy last commands, that thou mayest teach thy children and record it for them, and testify to all thy children; and in the second year they shall take thee from their midst.

[7] Let thy heart be strong, for the good shall announce righteousness to the good; The righteous with the righteous shall rejoice, And shall offer congratulation to one another.

[8] But the sinners shall die with the sinners, And the apostate go down with the apostate.

[9] And those who practice righteousness shall die on account of the deeds of men, And be taken away on account of the doings of the godless.

[10] And in those days they ceased to speak to me, and I came to my people, blessing the Lord of the world.

Chapter 82

[1] And now, my son Methuselah, all these things I am recounting to thee and writing down for thee! and I have revealed to thee everything, and given thee books concerning all these: so preserve, my son Methuselah, the books from thy fathers hand, and see that thou deliver them to the generations of the world.

[2] I have given Wisdom to thee and to thy children, And thy children that shall be to thee, That they may give it to their children for generations, This wisdom (namely) that passeth their thought.

[3] And those who understand it shall not sleep, but shall listen with the ear that they may learn this wisdom, And it shall please those that eat thereof better than good food.

[4] Blessed are all the righteous, blessed are all those who walk In the way of righteousness and sin not as the sinners, in the reckoning of all their days in which the sun traverses the heaven, entering into and departing from the portals for thirty days with the heads of thousands of the order of the stars, together with the four which are intercalated which divide the four portions of the year,

[5] Which lead them and enter with them four days. Owing to them men shall be at fault and not reckon them in the whole reckoning of the year: yea, men shall be at fault, and not recognize them accurately.

[6] For they belong to the reckoning of the year and are truly recorded thereon for ever, one in the first portal and one in the third, and one in the fourth and one in the sixth, and the year is completed in three hundred and sixty-four days.

[7] And the account thereof is accurate and the recorded reckoning thereof exact; for the luminaries, and months and festivals, and years and days, has Uriel shown and revealed to me, to whom the Lord of the whole creation of the world hath subjected the host of heaven.

[8] And he has power over night and day in the heaven to cause the light to give light to men -sun, moon, and stars,

[9] And all the powers of the heaven which revolve in their circular chariots. And these are the orders of the stars, which set in their places, and in their seasons and festivals and months.

[10] And these are the names of those who lead them, who watch that they enter at their times, in their orders, in their seasons, in their months, in their periods of dominion, and in their positions. Their four leaders who divide the four parts of the year enter first; and after them the twelve leaders of the orders who divide the months;

[11] And for the three hundred and sixty (days) there are heads over thousands who divide the days; and for the four intercalary days there are the leaders which sunder the four parts of the year.

[12] And these heads over thousands are intercalated between leader and leader, each behind a station, but their leaders make the division.

[13] And these are the names of the leaders who divide the four parts of the year which are ordained: Milkiel, Helemmelek, and Melejal, and Narel.

[14] And the names of those who lead them: Ad narel, and Ijasusael, and Elomeelthese three follow the leaders of the orders,

[15] And there is one that follows the three leaders of the orders which follow those leaders of stations that divide the four parts of the year. In the beginning of the year Melkejal rises first and rules, who is named Tamaini and sun,

[16] And all the days of his dominion whilst he bears rule are ninety-one days. And these are the signs of the days which are to be seen on earth in the days of his dominion: sweat, and heat, and calms; and all the trees bear fruit, and leaves are produced on all the trees, and the harvest of wheat, and the rose- flowers, and all the flowers which come forth in the field,

[17] But the trees of the winter season become withered. And these are the names of the leaders which are under them: Berkael, Zelebsel, and another who is added a head of a thousand, called Hilujaseph: and the days of the dominion of this leader are at an end.

[18] The next leader after him is Helemmelek, whom one names the shining sun, and all the days of his light are ninety-one days.

[19] And these are the signs of (his) days on the earth: glowing heat and dryness, and the trees ripen their fruits and produce all their fruits ripe and ready, and the sheep pair and become pregnant, and all the fruits of the earth are gathered in, and everything that is in the fields,

[20] And the winepress: these things take place in the days of his dominion. These are the names, and the orders, and the leaders of those heads of thousands: Gidaljal, Keel, and Heel, and the name of the head of a thousand which is added to them, Asfael: and the days of his dominion are at an end.

The Book Of Dream And Vision – Enoch's Ethiopic Book 4

Chapter 83

[1] And now, my son Methuselah, I will show thee all my visions which I have seen, recounting them before thee.

[2] Two visions I saw before I took a wife, and the one was quite unlike the other: the first when I was learning to write: the second before I took thy mother, when I saw a terrible vision.

[3] And regarding them I prayed to the Lord. I had laid me down in the house of my grandfather Mahalalel, when I saw in a vision how the heaven collapsed and was borne off and fell to the earth.

[4] And when it fell to the earth I saw how the earth was swallowed up in a great abyss, and mountains were suspended on mountains, and hills sank down on hills, and high trees were rent from their stems,

[5] And hurled down and sunk in the abyss. And thereupon a word fell into my mouth,

[6] And I lifted up my voice to cry aloud, and said: The earth is destroyed. And my grandfather Mahalalel waked me as I lay near him, and said unto me: Why dost thou cry so, my son,

[7] And why dost thou make such lamentation? And I recounted to him the whole vision which I had seen, and he said unto me: A terrible thing hast thou seen, my son, and of grave moment is thy dream- vision as to the secrets if all the sin of the earth: it must sink into the abyss and be destroyed with a great destruction.

[8] And now, my son, arise and make petition to the Lord of glory, since thou art a believer, that a remnant may remain on the earth, and that He may not destroy the whole earth.

[9] My son, from heaven all this will come upon the earth, and upon the earth there will be great destruction.

[10] After that I arose and prayed and implored and besought, and wrote down my prayer for the generations of the world, and I will show everything to thee, my son Methuselah. And when I had gone forth below and seen the heaven, and the sun rising in the east, and the moon setting in the west, and a few stars, and the whole earth, and everything as He had known it in the beginning, then I blessed the Lord of judgement and extolled Him because He had made the sun to go forth from the windows of the east, and he ascended and rose on the face of the heaven, and set out and kept traversing the path shown unto him.

Chapter 84

[1] And I lifted up my hands in righteousness and blessed the Holy and Great One, and spake with the breath of my mouth, and with the tongue of flesh, which God has made for the children of the flesh of men, that they should speak therewith, and He gave them breath and a tongue and a mouth that they should speak therewith:

[2] Blessed be Thou, O Lord, King, Great and mighty in Thy greatness, Lord of the whole creation of the heaven, King of kings and God of the whole world. And Thy power and kingship and greatness abide for ever and ever, And throughout all generations Thy dominion; And all the heavens are Thy throne for ever, And the whole earth Thy footstool for ever and ever.

[3] For Thou hast made and Thou rule st all things, And nothing is too hard for Thee, Wisdom departs not from the place of Thy throne, Nor turns away from Thy presence. And Thou knowest and seest and hearest everything, And there is nothing hidden from Theefor Thou seest everything.

[4] And now the angels of Thy heavens are guilty of trespass, And upon the flesh of men abideth Thy wrath until the great day of judgement.

[5] And now, O God and Lord and Great King, I implore and beseech Thee to fulfil my prayer, To leave me a posterity on earth, And not destroy all the flesh of man, And make the earth without inhabitant, So that there should be an eternal destruction.

[6] And now, my Lord, destroy from the earth the flesh which has aroused Thy wrath, But the flesh of righteousness and uprightness establish as a plant of the eternal seed, And hide not Thy face from the prayer of Thy servant, O Lord.

Chapter 85

[1] And after this I saw another dream, and I will show the whole dream to thee, my son.

[2] And Enoch lifted up his voice and spake to his son Methuselah: To thee, my son, will I speak: hear my words-incline thine ear to the dream- vision of thy father.

[3] Before I took thy mother Edna, I saw in a vision on my bed, and behold a bull came forth from the earth, and that bull was white; and after it came forth a heifer, and along with this latter came forth two bulls, one of them black and the other red.

[4] And that black bull gored the red one and pursued him over the earth, and thereupon I could no longer see that red bull.

[5] But that black bull grew and that heifer went with him, and I saw that many oxen proceeded from him which resembled and followed him.

[6] And that cow, that first one, went from the presence of that first bull in order to seek that red one, but found him not,

[7] And lamented with a great lamentation over him and sought him. And I looked till that first bull came to her and quieted her,

[8] And from that time onward she cried no more. And after that she bore another white bull, and after him she bore many bulls and black cows.

[9] And I saw in my sleep that white bull likewise grow and become a great white bull, and from Him proceeded many white bulls, and they resembled him. And they began to beget many white bulls, which resembled them, one following the other, even many.

Chapter 86

[1] And again I saw with mine eyes as I slept, and I saw the heaven above, and behold a star fell from heaven, and it arose and eat and pastured amongst those oxen.

[2] And after that I saw the large and the black oxen, and behold they all changed their stalls and pastures and their cattle, and began to live with each other.

[3] And again I saw in the vision, and looked towards the heaven, and behold I saw many stars descend and cast themselves down from heaven to that first star, and they became bulls amongst those cattle and pastured with themamongst them.

[4] And I looked at them and saw, and behold they all let out their privy members, like horses, and began to cover the cows of the oxen, and they all became pregnant and bare elephants, camels, and asses.

[5] And all the oxen feared them and were affrighted at them, and began to bite with their teeth and to devour, and to gore with their horns.

[6] And they began, moreover, to devour those oxen; and behold all the children of the earth began to tremble and quake before them and to flee from them.

Chapter 87

[1] And again I saw how they began to gore each other and to devour each other, and the earth began to cry aloud.

[2] And I raised mine eyes again to heaven, and I saw in the vision, and behold there came forth from heaven beings who were like white men: and four went forth from that place and three with them.

[3] And those three that had last come forth grasped me by my hand and took me up, away from the generations of the earth, and raised me up to a lofty place, and showed me a tower raised high above the earth, and all the hills were lower.

[4] And one said unto me: Remain here till thou seest everything that befalls those elephants, camels, and asses, and the stars and the oxen, and all of them.

Chapter 88

[1] And I saw one of those four who had come forth first, and he seized that first star which had fallen from the heaven, and bound it hand and foot and cast it into an abyss: now that abyss was narrow and deep,

[2] And horrible and dark. And one of them drew a sword, and gave it to those elephants and camels and asses: then they began to smite each other, and the whole earth quaked because of them.

[3] And as I was beholding in the vision, lo, one of those four who had come forth stoned (them) from heaven, and gathered and took all the great stars whose privy members were like those of horses, and bound them all hand and foot, and cast them in an abyss of the earth.

Chapter 89

[1] And one of those four went to that white bull and instructed him in a secret, without his being terrified: he

was born a bull and became a man, and built for himself a great vessel and dwelt thereon;

[2] And three bulls dwelt with him in that vessel and they were covered in. And again I raised mine eyes towards heaven and saw a lofty roof, with seven water torrents thereon, and those torrents flowed with much water into an enclosure.

[3] And I saw again, and behold fountains were opened on the surface of that great enclosure, and that water began to swell and rise upon the surface,

[4] And I saw that enclosure till all its surface was covered with water. And the water, the darkness, and mist increased upon it; and as I looked at the height of that water, that water had risen above the height of that enclosure, and was streaming over that enclosure, and it stood upon the earth.

[5] And all the cattle of that enclosure were gathered together until I saw how they sank and were swallowed up and perished in that water.

[6] But that vessel floated on the water, while all the oxen and elephants and camels and asses sank to the bottom with all the animals, so that I could no longer see them,

[7] And they were not able to escape, but perished and sank into the depths. And again I saw in the vision till those water torrents were removed from that high roof, and the chasms of the earth were leveled up and other abysses were opened.

[8] Then the water began to run down into these, till the earth became visible; but that vessel settled on the earth, and the darkness retired and light appeared.

[9] But that white bull which had become a man came out of that vessel, and the three bulls with him, and one of those three was white like that bull, and one of them was red as blood, and one black: and that white bull departed from them.

[10] And they began to bring forth beasts of the field and birds, so that there arose different genera: lions, tigers, wolves, dogs, hyenas, wild boars, foxes, squirrels, swine, falcons, vultures, kites, eagles, and ravens;

[11] And among them was born a white bull. And they began to bite one another; but that white bull which was born amongst them begat a wild ass and a white bull with it,

[12] And the wild asses multiplied. But that bull which was born from him begat a black wild boar and a white sheep;

[13] And the former begat many boars, but that sheep begat twelve sheep. And when those twelve sheep had grown,

they gave up one of them to the asses, and those asses again gave up that sheep to the wolves,

[14] And that sheep grew up among the wolves. And the Lord brought the eleven sheep to live with it and to pasture with it among the wolves: and they multiplied and became many flocks of sheep.

[15] And the wolves began to fear them, and they oppressed them until they destroyed cry aloud on account of their little ones,

[16] And to complain unto their Lord. And a sheep which had been saved from the wolves fled and escaped to the wild asses; and I saw the sheep how they lamented and cried, and besought their Lord with all their might, till that Lord of the sheep descended at the voice of the sheep from a lofty abode, and came to them and pastured them.

[17] And He called that sheep which had escaped the wolves, and spake with it concerning the wolves that it should admonish them not to touch the sheep.

[18] And the sheep went to the wolves according to the word of the Lord, and another sheep met it and went with it, and the two went and entered together into the assembly of those wolves, and spake with them and admonished them not to touch the sheep from henceforth.

[19] And thereupon I saw the wolves, and how they oppressed the sheep exceedingly with all their power; and the sheep cried aloud. And the Lord came to the sheep and they began to smite those wolves:

[20] And the wolves began to make lamentation; but the sheep became quiet and forthwith ceased to cry out.

[21] And I saw the sheep till they departed from amongst the wolves; but the eyes of the wolves were blinded, and those wolves departed in pursuit of the sheep with all their power.

[22] And the Lord of the sheep went with them, as their leader, and all His sheep followed Him:

[23] And his face was dazzling and glorious and terrible to behold. But the wolves began to pursue those sheep till they reached a sea of water.

[24] And that sea was divided, and the water stood on this side and on that before their face, and their Lord led them and placed Himself between them and the wolves.

[25] And as those wolves did not yet see the sheep, they proceeded into the midst of that sea, and the wolves followed the sheep, and those wolves ran after them into that sea.

[26] And when they saw the Lord of the sheep, they turned to flee before His face, but that sea gathered itself together, and became as it had been created, and the water swelled and rose till it covered those wolves.

[27] And I saw till all the wolves who pursued those sheep perished and were drowned.

[28] But the sheep escaped from that water and went forth into a wilderness, where there was no water and no grass; and they began to open their eyes and to see; and I saw the Lord of the sheep pasturing them and giving them water and grass,

[28] And that sheep going and leading them. And that sheep ascended to the summit of that lofty rock, and the Lord of the sheep sent it to them.

[29] And after that I saw the Lord of the sheep who stood before them, and His appearance was great and terrible and majestic,

[30] And all those sheep saw Him and were afraid before His face. And they all feared and trembled because of Him, and they cried to that sheep with them which was amongst them:

[31] We are not able to stand before our Lord or to behold Him. And that sheep which led them again ascended to the summit of that rock, but the sheep began to be blinded and to wander from the way which he had showed them, but that sheep wot not thereof.

[32] And the Lord of the sheep was wrathful exceedingly against them, and that sheep discovered it, and went down from the summit of the rock, and came to the sheep, and found the greatest part of them blinded and fallen away.

[33] And when they saw it they feared and trembled at its presence, and desired to return to their folds.

[34] And that sheep took other sheep with it, and came to those sheep which had fallen away, and began to slay them; and the sheep feared its presence, and thus that sheep brought back those sheep that had fallen away, and they returned to their folds.

[35] And I saw in this vision till that sheep became a man and built a house for the Lord of the sheep, and placed all the sheep in that house. And I saw till this sheep which had met that sheep which led them fell asleep: and I saw till all the great sheep perished and little ones arose in their place, and they came to a pasture, and approached a stream of water.

[36] Then that sheep, their leader which had become a man, withdrew from them and fell asleep,

[37] And all the sheep sought it and cried over it with a great crying.

[38] And I saw till they left off crying for that sheep and crossed that stream of water, and there arose the two sheep as leaders in the place of those which had led them and fallen asleep.

[39] And I saw till the sheep came to a goodly place, and a pleasant and glorious land, and I saw till those sheep were satisfied; and that house stood amongst them in the pleasant land.

[40] And sometimes their eyes were opened, and sometimes blinded, till another sheep arose and led them and brought them all back, and their eyes were opened.

[41] And the dogs and the foxes and the wild boars began to devour those sheep till the Lord of the sheep raised up another sheep a ram from their midst, which led them. And that ram began to butt on either side those dogs, foxes, and wild boars till he had destroyed them all. And that sheep whose eyes were opened saw that ram, which was amongst the sheep, till it forsook its glory and began to butt those sheep, and trampled upon the m, and behaved itself unseemly.

[42] And the Lord of the sheep sent the lamb to another lamb and raised it to being a ram and leader of the sheep instead of that ram which had forsaken its glory.

[43] And it went to it and spake to it alone, and raised it to being a ram,

[44] And made it the prince and leader of the sheep; but during all these things those dogs oppressed the sheep.

[45] And the first ram pursued that second ram, and that second ram arose and fled before it; and I saw till those dogs pulled down the first ram.

[46] And that second ram arose and led the little sheep.

[47] And those sheep grew and multiplied; but all the dogs, and foxes, and wild boars feared and fled before it, and that ram butted and killed the wild beasts, and those wild beasts had no longer any power among the sheep and robbed them no more of ought.

[48] And that ram begat many sheep and fell asleep; and a little sheep became ram in its stead, and became prince and leader of those sheep,

[49] And that house became great and broad, and it was built for those sheep: and a tower lofty and great was built on the house for the Lord of the sheep, and that house was low, but the tower was elevated and lofty, and the Lord of the sheep stood on that tower and they offered a full table before Him.

[50] And again I saw those sheep that they again erred and went many ways, and forsook that their house, and the Lord of the sheep called some from amongst the sheep and sent them to the sheep,

[51] But the sheep began to slay them. And one of them was saved and was not slain, and it sped away and cried aloud over the sheep; and they sought to slay it, but the Lord of the sheep saved it from the sheep, and brought it up to me, and caused it to dwell there.

[52] And many other sheep He sent to those sheep to testify unto them and lament over them.

[53] And after that I saw that when they forsook the house of the Lord and His tower they fell away entirely, and their eyes were blinded; and I saw the Lord of the sheep how He wrought much slaughter amongst them in their herds until those sheep invited that slaughter and betrayed His place.

[54] And He gave them over into the hands of the lions and tigers, and wolves and hyenas, and into the hand of the foxes, and to all the wild beasts,

[55] And those wild beasts began to tear in pieces those sheep. And I saw that He forsook that their house and their tower and gave them all into the hand of the lions, to tear and devour them,

[56] Into the hand of all the wild beasts. And I began to cry aloud with all my power, and to appeal to the Lord of the sheep, and to represent to Him in regard to the sheep that they were devoured by all the wild beasts.

[57] But He remained unmoved, though He saw it, and rejoiced that they were devoured and swallowed and robbed, and left them to be devoured in the hand of all the beasts.

[58] And He called seventy shepherds, and cast those sheep to them that they might pasture them, and He spake to the shepherds and their companions: Let each individual of you pasture the sheep henceforward,

[59] And everything that I shall command you that do ye. And I will deliver them over unto you duly numbered, and tell you which of them are to be destroyed-and them destroy ye.

[60] And He gave over unto them those sheep. And He called another and spake unto him: Observe and mark everything that the shepherds will do to those sheep; for they will destroy more of them than I have commanded them.

[61] And every excess and the destruction which will be wrought through the shepherds, record namely how many they destroy according to my command, and how many according to their own caprice: record against every individual shepherd all the destruction he effects.

[62] And read out before me by number how many they destroy, and how many they deliver over for destruction, that I may have this as a testimony against them, and know every deed of the shepherds, that I may comprehend and see what they do, whether or not they abide by my command which I have commanded them.

[63] But they shall not know it, and thou shalt not declare it to them,

[64] Nor admonish them, but only record against each individual all the destruction which the shepherds effect each in his time and lay it all before me. And I saw till those shepherds pastured in their season, and they began to slay and to destroy more than they were bidden, and they delivered those sheep into the hand of the lions.

[65] And the lions and tigers eat and devoured the greater part of those sheep, and the wild boars eat along with them; and they burnt that tower and demolished that house.

[66] And I became exceedingly sorrowful over that tower because that house of the sheep was demolished, and afterwards I was unable to see if those sheep entered that house.

[67] And the shepherds and their associates delivered over those sheep to all the wild beasts, to devour them, and each one of them received in his time a definite number: it was written by the other in a book how many each one of them destroyed of them.

[68] And each one slew and destroyed many more than was prescribed;

[69] And I began to weep and lament on account of those sheep. And thus in the vision I saw that one who wrote, how he wrote down every one that was destroyed by those shepherds, day by day, and carried up and laid down and showed actually the whole book to the Lord of the sheep- (even) everything that they had done, and all that each one of them had made away with,

[70] And all that they had given over to destruction. And the book was read before the Lord of the sheep, and He took the book from his hand and read it and sealed it and laid it down.

[71] And forthwith I saw how the shepherds pastured for twelve hours, and behold three of those sheep turned back

and came and entered and began to build up all that had fallen down of that house;

[72] But the wild boars tried to hinder them, but they were not able. And they began again to build as before, and they reared up that tower, and it was named the high tower; and they began again to place a table before the tower, but all the bread on it was polluted and not pure.

[73] And as touching all this the eyes of those sheep were blinded so that they saw not, and the eyes of their shepherds likewise; and they delivered them in large numbers to their shepherds for destruction,

[74] And they trampled the sheep with their feet and devoured them. And the Lord of the sheep remained unmoved till all the sheep were dispersed over the field and mingled with them the beasts,

[75] And they the shepherds did not save them out of the hand of the beasts. And this one who wrote the book carried it up, and showed it and read it before the Lord of the sheep, and implored Him on their account, and besought Him on their account as he showed Him all the doings of the shepherds,

[76] And gave testimony before Him against all the shepherds. And he took the actual book and laid it down beside Him and departed.

Chapter 90

[1] And I saw till that in this manner thirty- five shepherds undertook the pasturing of the sheep, and they severally completed their periods as did the first; and others receive them into their hands,

[2] To pasture them for their period, each shepherd in his own period. And after that I saw in my vision all the birds of heaven coming, the eagles, the vultures, the kites, the ravens; but the eagles led all the birds; and they began to devour those sheep, and to pick out their eyes and to devour their flesh.

[3] And the sheep cried out because their flesh was being devoured by the birds,

[4] And as for me I looked and lamented in my sleep over that shepherd who pastured the sheep. And I saw until those sheep were devo ured by the dogs and eagles and kites, and they left neither flesh nor skin nor sinew remaining on them till only their bones stood there: and their bones too fell to the earth and the sheep became few.

[5] And I saw until that twenty-three had undertaken the pasturing and completed in their several periods fifty-eight times.

[6] But behold lambs were borne by those white sheep, and they began to open their eyes and to see,

[7] And to cry to the sheep. Yea, they cried to them, but they did not hearken to what the y said to them,

[8] But were exceedingly deaf, and their eyes were very exceedingly blinded. And I saw in the vision how the ravens flew upon those lambs and took one of those lambs, and dashed the sheep in pieces and devoured them.

[9] And I saw till horns grew upon those lambs, and the ravens cast down their horns; and I saw till there sprouted a great horn of one of those sheep, and their eyes were opened.

[10] And it looked at themand their eyes opened, and it cried to the sheep,

[11] And the rams saw it and all ran to it.

[12] And notwithstanding all this those eagles and vultures and ravens,

[13] And kites still kept tearing the sheep and swooping down upon them and devouring them:

[14] Still the sheep remained silent, but the rams lamented and cried out.

[15] And those ravens fought and battled with it and sought to lay low its horn, but they had no power over it.

[16] All the eagles and vultures and ravens and kites were gathered together,

[17] And there came with them all the sheep of the field,

[18] Yea, they all came together, and helped each other to break that horn of the ram.

[19] And I saw till a great sword was given to the sheep, and the sheep proceeded against all the beasts of the field to slay them, and all the beasts and the birds of the heaven fled before their face. And I saw that man, who wrote the book according to the command of the Lord, till he opened that book concerning the destruction which those twelve last shepherds had wrought, and showed that they had destroyed much more than their predecessors, before the Lord of the sheep. And I saw till the Lord of the sheep came unto them and took in His hand the staff of His wrath, and smote the earth, and the earth clave asunder, and all the beasts and all the birds of the heaven fell from among those sheep, and were swallowed up in the earth and it covered them.

[20] And I saw till a throne was erected in the pleasant land, and the Lord of the sheep sat Himself thereon, and the other took the sealed books and opened those books before the Lord of the sheep.

[21] And the Lord called those men the seven first white ones, and commanded that they should bring before Him, beginning with the first star which led the way, all the stars whose privy members were like those of horses,

[22] And they brought them all before Him. And He said to that man who wrote before Him, being one of those seven white ones, and said unto him: Take those seventy shepherds to whom I delivered the sheep, and who taking them on their own authority slew more than I commanded them.

[23] And behold they were all bound, I saw, and they all stood before Him.

[24] And the judgement was held first over the stars, and they were judged and found guilty, and went to the place of condemnation, and they were cast into an abyss, full of fire and flaming, and full of pillars of fire.

[25] And those seventy shepherds were judged and found guilty, and they were cast into that fiery abyss.

[26] And I saw at that time how a like abyss was opened in the midst of the earth, full of fire, and they brought those blinded sheep, and they were all judged and found guilty,

[27] And cast into this fiery abyss, and they burned; now this abyss was to the right of that house. And I saw those sheep burning and their bones burning.

[28] And I stood up to see till they folded up that old house; and carried off all the pillars, and all the beams and ornaments of the house were at the same time folded up with it, and they carried it off and laid it in a place in the south of the land.

[29] And I saw till the Lord of the sheep brought a new house greater and loftier than that first, and set it up in the place of the first which had beer folded up: all its pillars were new, and its ornaments were new and larger than those of the first, the old one which He had taken away, and all the sheep were within it.

[30] And I saw all the sheep which had been left, and all the beasts on the earth, and all the birds of the heaven, falling down and doing homage to those sheep and making petition to and obeying them in every thing.

[31] And thereafter those three who were clothed in white and had seized me by my handwho had taken me up before, and the hand of that ram also seizing hold of me,

[32] They took me up and set me down in the midst of those sheep before the judgement took place. And those sheep were all white,

[33] And their wool was abundant and clean. And all that had been destroyed and dispersed, and all the beasts of the field, and all the birds of the heaven, assembled in that house, and the Lord of the sheep rejoiced with great joy because they were all good and had returned to His house.

[34] And I saw till they laid down that sword, which had been given to the sheep, and they brought it back into the house, and it was sealed before the presence of the Lord, and all the sheep were invited into that house,

[35] But it held them not. And the eyes of them all were opened, and they saw the good,

[36] And there was not one among them that did not see. And I saw that that house was large and broad and very full.

[37] And I saw that a white bull was born, with large horns and all the beasts of the field and all the birds of the air feared him and made petition to him all the time of and I saw till all their generations were transformed,

[38] And they all became white bulls; and the first among them became a lamb, and that lamb became a great animal and had great black horns on its head; and the Lord of the sheep rejoiced over it and over all the oxen.

[39] And I slept in their midst: and I awoke and saw everything.

[40] This is the vision which I saw while I slept, and I awoke and blessed the Lord of righteousness and gave Him glory.

[41] Then I wept with a great weeping and my tears stayed not till I could no longer endure it: when I saw, they flowed on account of what I had seen; for everything shall come and be fulfilled,

[42] And all the deeds of men in their order were shown to me. On that night I remembered the first dream, and because of it I wept and was troubled-because I had seen that vision.

The Epistle Of Enoch – Enoch's Ethiopic Book 5

Chapter 91

[1] And now, my son Methuselah, call to me all thy brothers and gather together to me all the sons of thy mother; For the word calls me, And the spirit is poured out upon me, That I may show you everything that shall befall you for ever.

[2] And there upon Methuselah went and summoned to him all his brothers and assembled his relatives.

[3] And he spake unto all the children of righteousness and said: Hear, ye sons of Enoch, all the words of your father, And hearken aright to the voice of my mouth; For I exhort you and say unto you, beloved:

[4] Love uprightness and walk therein. And draw not nigh to uprightness with a double heart, And associate not with those of a double heart, But walk in righteousness, my sons. And it shall guide you on good paths, And righteousness shall be your companion.

[5] For I know that violence must increase on the earth, And a great chastisement be executed on the earth, And all unrighteousness come to an end: Yea, it shall be cut off from its roots, And its whole structure be destroyed.

[6] And unrighteousness shall again be consummated on the earth, And all the deeds of unrighteousness and of violence and transgression shall prevail in a twofold degree.

[7] And when sin and unrighteousness and blasphemy and violence in all kinds of deeds increase, and apostasy and transgression and uncleanness increase, a great chastisement shall come from heaven upon all these, and the holy Lord will come forth with wrath and chastisement to execute judgement on earth.

[8] In those days violence shall be cut off from its roots, and the roots of unrighteousness together with deceit, and they shall be destroyed from under heaven.

[9] And all the idols of the heathen shall be abandoned, and the temples burned with fire, And they shall remove them from the whole earth, And they the heathen shall be cast into the judgement of fire, And shall perish in wrath and in grievous judgement for ever.

[10] And the righteous shall arise from their sleep, and wisdom shall arise and be given unto them.

[11] And after that the roots of unrighteousness shall be cut off, and the sinners shall bedestroyed by the sword and the blasphemers destroyed in every place,

[12] And those who plan violence and those who commit blasphemy shall perish by the sword.

[13] And now I tell you, my sons, and show you the paths of righteousness and the paths of violence. Yea, I will show them to you again that ye may know what will come to pass.

[14] And now, hearken unto me, my sons, and walk in the paths of righteousness, and walk not in the paths of violence; For all who walk in the paths of unrighteousness shall perish for ever.

Chapter 92

[1] The book written by Enoch indeed wrote this complete doctrine of wisdom, which is praised of all men and a judge of all the earth for all my children who shall dwell on the earth. And for the future generations who shall observe uprightness and peace.

[2] Let not your spirit be troubled on account of the times; For the Holy and Great One has appointed days for all things.

[3] And the righteous one shall arise from sleep, shall arise and walk in the paths of righteousness, And all his path and conversation shall be in eternal goodness and grace.

[4] He will be gracious to the righteous and give him eternal uprightness, And He will give him power so that he shall be endowed with goodness and righteousness. And he shall walk in eternal light.

[5] And sin shall perish in darkness for ever, And shall no more be seen from that day for evermore.

Chapter 93

[1] And after that Enoch both gave and began to recount from the books. And Enoch said: Concerning the children of righteousness and concerning the elect of the world, And concerning the plant of uprightness, I will speak these things, Yea, I Enoch will declare (them) unto you, my sons: According to that which appeared to me in the heavenly vision,

[2] And which I have known through the word of the holy angels, And have learnt from the heavenly tablets.

[3] And Enoch began to recount from the books and said: I was born the seventh in the first week, while judgement and righteousness still endured.

[4] And after me there shall arise in the second week great wickedness, And deceit shall have sprung up; And in it there shall be the first end. And in it a man shall be saved; And after it is ended unrighteousness shall grow up,

[5] And a law shall be made for the sinners. And after that in the third week at its close a man shall be elected as the plant of righteous judgement, And his posterity shall become the plant of righteousness for evermore.

[6] And after that in the fourth week, at its close, Visions of the holy and righteous shall be seen, And a law for all generations and an enclosure shall be made for them. And after that in the fifth week, at its close, The house of glory and dominion shall be built for ever.

[7] And after that in the sixth week all who live in it shall be blinded, And the hearts of all of them shall godlessly forsake wisdom. And in it a man shall ascend;

[8] And at its close the house of dominion shall be burnt with fire, And the whole race of the chosen root shall be dispersed.

[9] And after that in the seventh week shall an apostate generation arise, And many shall be its deeds, And all its deeds shall be apostate.

[10] And at its close shall be elected the elect righteous of the eternal plant of righteousness, to receive sevenfold instruction concerning all His creation.

[11] For who is there of all the children of men that is able to hear the voice of the Holy One without being troubled? And who can think His thoughts? and who is there that can behold all the works of heaven?

[12] And how should there be one who could behold the heaven, and who is there that could understand the things of heaven and see a soul or a spirit and could tell thereof, or ascend and see all their ends and think them or do like them?

[13] And who is there of all men that could know what is the breadth and the length of the earth, and to whom has been shown the measure of all of them? Or is there any one who could discern the length of the heaven and how great is its height,

[14] and upon what it is founded, and how great is the number of the stars, and where all the luminaries rest?

Chapter 94

[1] And now I say unto you, my sons, love righteousness and walk therein; For the paths of righteousness are worthy of acceptation, but the paths of unrighteousness shall suddenly be destroyed and vanish.

[2] And to certain men of a generation shall the paths of violence and of death be revealed, And they shall hold themselves afar from them, And shall not follow them.

[3] And now I say unto you the righteous: Walk not in the paths of wickedness, nor in the paths of death, And draw not nigh to them, lest ye be destroyed.

[4] But seek and choose for yourselves righteousness and an elect life, And walk in the paths of peace, And ye shall live and prosper.

[5] And hold fast my words in the thoughts of your hearts, And suffer them not to be effaced from your hearts; For I know that sinners will tempt men to evilly-entreat wisdom, So that no place may be found for her, And no manner of temptation may minish.

[6] Woe to those who build unrighteousness and oppression and lay deceit as a foundation; For they shall be suddenly overthrown, And they shall have no peace.

[7] Woe to those who build their houses with sin; For from all their foundations shall they be overthrown, And by the sword shall they fall. And those who acquire gold and silver in judgement suddenly shall perish.

[8] Woe to you, ye rich, for ye have trusted in your riches, And from your riches shall ye depart, Because ye have not remembered the Most High in the days of your riches.

[9] Ye have committed blasphemy and unrighteousness, And have become ready for the day of slaughter, And the day of darkness and the day of the great judgement.

[10] Thus I speak and declare unto you: He who hath created you will overthrow you, And for your fall there shall be no compassion, And your Creator will rejoice at your destruction.

[11] And your righteous ones in those days shall be a reproach to the sinners and the godless.

Chapter 95

[1] Oh that mine eyes were a cloud of waters that I might weep over you, And pour down my tears as a cloud of waters: That so I might rest from my trouble of heart!

[2] Who has permitted you to practice reproaches and wickedness? And so judgement shall overtake you, sinners.

[3] Fear not the sinners, ye righteous; For again will the Lord deliver them into your hands, that ye may execute judgement upon them according to your desires.

[4] Woe to you who fulminate anathemas which cannot be reversed: Healing shall therefore be far from you because of your sins.

[5] Woe to you who requite your neighbour with evil; For ye shall be requited according to your works.

[6] Woe to you, lying witnesses, And to those who weigh out injustice, For suddenly shall ye perish.

[7] Woe to you, sinners, for ye persecute the righteous; For ye shall be delivered up and persecuted because of injustice, And heavy shall its yoke be upon you.

Chapter 96

[1] Be hopeful, ye righteous; for suddenly shall the sinners perish before you, And ye shall have lordship over them according to your desires.

[2] And in the day of the tribulation of the sinners, Your children shall mount and rise as eagles, And higher than the vultures will be your nest, And ye shall ascend and enter the crevices of the earth, And the clefts of the rock for ever as coneys before the unrighteous, And the sirens shall sigh because of you-and weep wherefore fear not, ye that have suffered;

[3] For healing shall be your portion, And a bright light shall enlighten you, And the voice of rest ye shall hear from heaven.

[4] Woe unto you, ye sinners, for your riches make you appear like the righteous, But your hearts convict you of being sinners, And this fact shall be a testimony against you for a memorial of (your) evil deeds.

[5] Woe to you who devour the finest of the wheat, And drink wine in large bowls, And tread under foot the lowly with your might.

[6] Woe to you who drink water from every fountain, For suddenly shall ye be consumed and wither away, Because ye have forsaken the fountain of life.

[7] Woe to you who work unrighteousness and deceit and blasphemy: It shall be a memorial against you for evil.

[8] Woe to you, ye mighty, Who with might oppress the righteous; For the day of your destruction is coming. In those days many and good days shall come to the righteous-in the day of your judgement.

Chapter 97

[1] Believe, ye righteous, that the sinners will become a shame and perish in the day of unrighteousness.

[2] Be it known unto you (ye sinners) that the Most High is mindful of your destruction, And the angels of heaven rejoice over your destruction.

[3] What will ye do, ye sinners, And whither will ye flee on that day of judgement, when ye hear the voice of the prayer of the righteous?

[4] Yea, ye shall fare like unto them, against whom this word shall be a testimony: " Ye have been companions of sinners."

[5] And in those days the prayer of the righteous shall reach unto the Lord, And for you the days of your judgement shall come.

[6] And all the words of your unrighteousness shall be read out before the Great Holy One, And your faces shall be covered with shame, And He will reject every work which is grounded on unrighteousness.

[7] Woe to you, ye sinners, who live on the mid ocean and on the dry land, Whose remembrance is evil against you.

[8] Woe to you who acquire silver and gold in unrighteousness and say: " We have become rich with riches and have possessions; And have acquired everything we have desired.

[9] And now let us do what we purposed: For we have gathered silver, And many are the husbandmen in our houses." And our granaries are (brim) full as with water, Yea and like water your lies shall flow away; For your riches shall not abide but speedily ascend from you; For ye have acquired it all in unrighteousness, And ye shall be given over to a great curse.

Chapter 98

[1] And now I swear unto you, to the wise and to the foolish, For ye shall have manifold experiences on the earth.

[2] For ye men shall put on more adornments than a woman, And coloured garments more than a virgin: In royalty and in grandeur and in power, And in silver and in gold and in purple, And in splendour and in food they shall be poured out as water.

[3] Therefore they shall be wanting in doctrine and wisdom, And they shall perish thereby together with their possessions; And with all their glory and their splendour, And in shame and in slaughter and in great destitution, Their spirits shall be cast into the furnace of fire.

[4] I have sworn unto you, ye sinners, as a mountain has not become a slave, And a hill does not become the handmaid of a woman, Even so sin has not been sent upon the earth, But man of himself has created it, And under a great curse shall they fall who commit it.

[5] And barrenness has not been given to the woman, but on account of the deeds of her own hands she dies without children.

[6] I have sworn unto you, ye sinners, by the Holy Great One, that all your evil deeds are revealed in the heavens, And that none of your deeds of oppression are covered and hidden.

[7] And do not think in your spirit nor say in your heart that ye do not know and that ye do not see that every sin is every day recorded in heaven in the presence of the Most High.

[8] From henceforth ye know that all your oppression wherewith ye oppress is written down every day till the day of your judgement woe to you, ye fools, for through your folly shall ye perish:

[9] And ye transgress against the wise,

[10] And so good hap shall not be your portion. And now, know ye that ye are prepared for the day of destruction: wherefore do not hope to live, ye sinners, but ye shall depart and die; for ye know no ransom; for ye are prepared for the day of the great judgement, for the day of tribulation and great shame for your spirits.

[11] Woe to you, ye obstinate of heart, who work wickedness and eat blood: Whence have ye good things to eat and to drink and to be filled? From all the good things which the Lord the Most High has placed in abundance on the earth; therefore ye shall have no peace.

[12] Woe to you who love the deeds of unrighteousness: wherefore do ye hope for good hap unto yourselves? know that ye shall be delivered into the hands of the righteous, and they shall cut off your necks and slay you,

[13] And have no mercy upon you. Woe to you who rejoice in the tribulation of the righteous; for no grave shall be dug for you. Woe to you who set at nought the words of the righteous;

[14] For ye shall have no hope of life. Woe to you who write down lying and godless words; for they write down their lies that men may hear them and act godlessly towards their neighbour.

[15] Therefore they shall have no peace but die a sudden death.

Chapter 99

[16] Woe to you who work godlessness, And glory in lying and extol them: Ye shall perish, and no happy life shall be yours.

[17] Woe to them who pervert the words of uprightness, And transgress the eternal law, And transform themselves into what they were notinto sinners: They shall be trodden under foot upon the earth.

[18] In those days make ready, ye righteous, to raise your prayers as a memorial, And place them as a testimony before the angels, that they may place the sin of the sinners for a memorial before the Most High.

[19] In those days the nations shall be stirred up, And the families of the nations shall arise on the day of destruction.

[20] And in those days the destitute shall go forth and carry off their children, And they shall abandon them, so that their children shall perish through them: Yea, they shall abandon their children (that are still) sucklings, and not return to them, And shall have no pity on their beloved ones.

[21] And again I swear to you, ye sinners, that sin is prepared for a day of unceasing bloodshed.

[22] And they who worship stones, and grave images of gold and silver and wood and stone and clay, and those who worship impure spirits and demons, and all kinds of idols not according to knowledge, shall get no manner of help from them.

[23] And they shall become godless by reason of the folly of their hearts, And their eyes shall be blinded through the fear of their hearts and through visions in their dreams.

[24] Through these they shall become godless and fearful; For they sha ll have wrought all their work in a lie, And shall have worshiped a stone: Therefore in an instant shall they perish.

[25] But in those days blessed are all they who accept the words of wisdom, and understand them, And observe the paths of the Most High, and walk in the path of His righteousness, And become not godless with the godless; For they shall be saved.

[26] Woe to you who spread evil to your neighbours; For you shall be slain in Sheol.

[27] Woe to you who make deceitful and false measures, And who cause bitterness on the earth; For they shall thereby be utterly consumed.

[28] Woe to you who build your houses through the grievous toil of others, And all their building materials are the bricks and stones of sin; I tell you ye shall have no peace.

[29] Woe to them who reject the measure and eternal heritage of their fathers and whose souls follow after idols; For they shall have no rest.

[30] Woe to them who work unrighteousness and help oppression, And slay their neighbours until the day of the great judgement.

[31] For He shall cast down your glory, And bring affliction on your hearts, And shall arouse His fierce indignation and destroy you all with the sword; And all the holy and righteous shall remember your sins.

Chapter 100

[1] And in those days in one place the fathers together with their sons shall be smitten and brothers one with another shall fall in death till the streams flow with their blood.

[2] For a man shall not withhold his hand from slaying his sons and his sons sons, And the sinner shall not withhold his hand from his honoured brother: From dawn till sunset they shall slay one another.

[3] And the horse shall walk up to the breast in the blood of sinners, And the chariot shall be submerged to its height.

[4] In those days the angels shall descend into the secret places and gather together into one place all those who brought down sin and the Most High will arise on that day of judgement to execute great judgement amongst sinners.

[5] And over all the righteous and holy He will appoint guardians from amongst the holy angels to guard them as the apple of an eye, until He makes an end of all wickedness and all sin, And though the righteous sleep a long sleep, they have nought to fear.

[6] And then the children of the earth shall see the wise in security, And shall understand all the words of this book, And recognize that their riches shall not be able to save them in the overthrow of their sins.

[7] Woe to you, Sinners, on the day of strong anguish, Ye who afflict the righteous and burn them with fire: Ye shall be requited according to your works.

[8] Woe to you, ye obstinate of heart, who watch in order to devise wickedness: Therefore shall fear come upon you and there shall be none to help you.

[9] Woe to you, ye sinners, on account of the words of your mouth, And on account of the deeds of your hands which

your godlessness as wrought, in blazing flames burning worse than fire shall ye burn.

[10] And now, know ye that from the angels He will inquire as to your deeds in heaven, from the sun and from the moon and from the stars in reference to your sins because upon the earth ye execute judgement on the righteous. And He will summon to testify against you every cloud and mist and dew and rain; for they shall all be withheld because of you from descending upon you, and they shall be mindful of your sins. And now give presents to the rain that it be not with held from descending upon you, nor yet the dew, when it has received gold and silver from you that it may descend. When the hoar-frost and snow with their chilliness, and all the snowstorms with all their plagues fall upon you, in those days ye shall not be able to stand before them.

Chapter 101

[1] Observe the heaven, ye children of heaven, and every work of the Most High, and fear ye Him and work no evil in His presence.

[2] If He closes the windows of heaven, and withholds the rain and the dew from descending on the earth on your account, what will ye do then?

[3] And if He sends His anger upon you because of yoour deeds, ye cannot petition Him; for ye spake proud and insolent words against His righteousness: therefore ye shall have no peace.

[4] And see ye not the sailors of the ships, how their ships are tossed to and fro by the waves, and are shaken by the winds, and are in sore trouble?

[5] And therefore do they fear because all their goodly possessions go upon the sea with them, and they have evil forebodings of heart that the sea will swallow them and they will perish therein.

[6] Are not the entire sea and all its waters, and all its movements, the work of the Most High, and has He not set limits to its doings, and confined it throughout by the sand?

[7] And at His reproof it is afraid and dries up, and all its fish die and all that is in it; But ye sinners that are on the earth fear Him not.

[8] Has He not made the heaven and the earth, and all that is therein? Who has given understanding and wisdom to everything that moves on the earth and in the sea.

[9] Do not the sailors of the ships fear the sea ? Yet sinners fear not the Most High.

Chapter 102

[1] In those days when He hath brought a grievous fire upon you, Whither will ye flee, and where will ye find deliverance? And when He launches forth His Word against you Will you not be affrighted and fear?

[2] And all the luminaries shall be affrighted with great fear, And all the earth shall be affrighted and tremble and be alarmed.

[3] And all the angels shall execute their commandst and shall seek to hide themselves from the presence of the Great Glory, And the children of earth shall tremble and quake; And ye sinners shall be cursed for ever, And ye shall have no peace.

[4] Fear ye not, ye souls of the righteous, And be hopeful ye that have died in righteousness.

[5] And grieve not if your soul into Sheol has descended in grief, And that in your life your body fared not according to your goodness, but wait for the day of the judgement of sinners and for the day of cursing and chastisement.

[6] And yet when ye die the sinners speak over you:" As we die, so die the righteous, And what benefit do they reap for their deeds? Behold, even as we, so do they die in grief and darkness, And what have they more than we?

[7] From henceforth we are equal. And what will they receive and what will they see for ever?

[8] Behold, they too have died, And henceforth for ever shall they see no light."

[9] I tell you, ye sinners, ye are content to eat and drink, and rob and sin, and strip men naked, and acquire wealth and see good days.

[10] Have ye seen the righteous how their end falls out, that no manner of violence is found in them till their death? "Nevertheless they perished and became as though they had not been, and their spirits descended into Sheol in tribulation."

Chapter 103

[1] Now, therefore, I swear to you, the righteous, by the glory of the Great and Honoured and Mighty One in dominion, and by His greatness I swear to you.

[2] I know a mystery and have read the heavenly tablets, And have seen the holy books, And have found written therein and inscribed regarding them:

[3] That all goodness and joy and glory are prepared for them, And written down for the spirits of those who have died in righteousness, And that manifold good shall be given to you in recompense for your labours, And that your lot is abundantly beyond the lot of the living.

[4] And the spirits of you who have died in righteousness shall live and rejoice, And their spirits shall not perish, nor their memorial from before the face of the Great One unto all the generations of the world: wherefore no longer fear their contumely.

[5] Woe to you, ye sinners, whe n ye have died, If ye die in the wealth of your sins, And those who are like you say regarding you: Blessed are the sinners: they have seen all their days.

[6] And how they have died in prosperity and in wealth, And have not seen tribulation or murder in their life; And they have died in honour, And judgement has not been executed on them during their life.

[7] "Know ye, that their souls will be made to descend into Sheol and they shall be wretched in their great tribulation.

[8] And into darkness and chains and a burning flame where there is grievous judgement shall your spirits enter; And the great judgement shall be for all the generations of the world. Woe to you, for ye shall have no peace.

[9] Say not in regard to the righteous and good who are in life: "In our troubled days we have toiled laboriously and experienced every trouble, And met with much evil and been consumed, And have become few and our spirit small.

[10] And we have been destroyed and have not found any to help us even with a word: We have been torturedand destroyed, and not hoped to see life from day to day.

[11] We hoped to be the head and have become the tail: We have toiled laboriously and had no satisfaction in our toil; And we have become the food of the sinners and the unrighteous, And they have laid their yoke heavily upon us.

[12] They have had dominion over us that hated us and smote us; And to those that hated us we have bowed our necks But they pitied us not.

[13] We desired to get away from them that we might escape and be at rest, but found no place whereunto we should flee and be safe from them.

[14] And are complained to the rulers in our tribulation, And cried out against those who devoured us, but they did not attend to our cries and would not hearken to our voice.

[15] And they helped those who robbed us and devoured us and those who made us few; and they concealed their oppression, and they did not remove from us the yoke of those that devoured us and dispersed us and murdered us,

and they concealed their murder, and remembered not that they had lifted up their hands against us.

Chapter 104

[1] I swear unto you, that in heaven the angels remember you for good before the glory of the Great One: and your names are written before the glory of the Great One.

[2] Be hopeful; for aforetime ye were put to shame through ill and affliction; but now ye shall shine as the lights of heaven, ye shall shine and ye shalll be seen, and the portals of heaven shall be opened to you.

[3] And in your cry, cry for judgement, and it shall appear to you; for all your tribulation shall be visited on the rulers, and on all who helped those who plundered you.

[4] Be hopeful, and cast not away your hopes for ye shall have great joy as the angels of heaven. What shall ye be obliged to do?

[5] Ye shall not have to hide on the day of the great judgement and ye shall not be found as sinners, and the eternal judgement shall be far from you for all the generations of the world.

[6] And now fear not, ye righteous, when ye see the sinners growing strong and prospering in their ways: be not companions with them,

[7] But keep afar from their violence; for ye shall become companions of the hosts of heaven. And, although ye sinners say: "All our sins shall not be searched out and be written down", nevertheless they shall write down all your sins every day.

[8] And now I show unto you that light and darkness, day and night, see all your sins.

[9] Be not godless in your hearts, and lie not and alter not the words of uprightness, nor charge with lying the words of the Holy Great One, nor take account of your idols;

[10] For all your lying and all your godlessness issue not in righteousness but in great sin. And now I know this mystery, that sinners will alter and pervert the words of righteousness in many ways, and will speak wicked words, and lie, and practice great deceits, and write books concerning their words.

[11] But when they write down truthfully all my words in their languages, and do not change or minish ought from my words but write them all down truthfully all that I first testified concerning them.

[12] Then, I know another mystery, that books will be given to the righteous and the wise to become a cause of joy and uprightness and much wisdom. And to them shall the books be given, and they shall believe in them and rejoice over them, and then shall all the righteous who have learnt therefrom all the paths of uprightness be recompensed.

Chapter 105

[1] In those days the Lord bade them to summon and testify to the children of earth concerning their wisdom: Show it unto them; for ye are their guides, and a recompense over the whole earth.

[2] For I and My son will be united with them for ever in the paths of uprightness in their lives; and ye shall have peace: rejoice, ye children of uprightness. Amen.

Chapter 106

[1] And after some days my son Methuselah took a wife for his son Lamech, and she became pregnant by him and bore a son.

[2] And his body was white as snow and red as the blooming of a rose, and the hair of his head and his long locks were white as wool, and his eyes beautiful. And when he opened his eyes, he lighted up the whole house like the sun, and the whole house was very bright.

[3] And thereupon he arose in the hands of the midwife, opened his mouth, and conversed with the Lord of righteousness.

[4] And his father Lamech was afraid of him and fled, and came to his father Methuselah.

[5] And he said unto him: I have begotten a strange son, diverse from and unlike man, and resembling the sons of the God of heaven; and his nature is different and he is not like us, and his eyes are as the rays of the sun, and his countenance is glorious.

[6] And it seems to me that he is not sprung from me but from the angels, and I fear that in his days a wonder may be wrought on the earth.

[7] And now, my father, I am here to petition thee and implore thee that thou mayest go to Enoch, our father, and learn from him the truth, for his dwelling place is amongst the angels.

[8] And when Methuselah heard the words of his son, he came to me to the ends of the earth; for he had heard that I was there,

[9] And he cried aloud, and I heard his voice and I came to him. And I said unto him: Behold, here am I, my son, wherefore hast thou come to me? And he answered and said: Because of a great cause of anxiety have I come to thee, and because of a disturbing vision have I approached.

[10] And now, my father, hear me: unto Lamech my son there hath been born a son, the like of whom there is none, and his nature is not like mans nature, and the colour of his body is whiter than snow and redder than the bloom of a rose, and the hair of his head is whiter than white wool, and his eyes are like the rays of the sun, and he opened his eyes and thereupon lighted up the whole house.

[11] And he arose in the hands of the midwife, and opened his mouth and blessed the Lord of heaven.

[12] And his father Lamech became afraid and fled to me, and did not believe that he was sprung from him, but that he was in the likeness of the angels of heaven; and behold I have come to thee that thou mayest make known to me the truth.

[13] And I, Enoch, answered and said unto him: The Lord will do a new thing on the earth, and this I have already seen in a vision, and make known to thee that in the generation of my father Jared some of the angels of heaven transgressed the word of the Lord.

[14] And behold they commit sin and transgress the law, and have united themselves with women and commit sin with them, and have married some of them, and have begot children by them.

[15] And they shall produce on the earth giants not according to the spirit, but according to the flesh, and there shall be a great punishment on the earth, and the earth shall be cleansed from all impurity. Yea, there shall come a great destruction over the whole earth, and there shall be a deluge and a great destruction for one year.

[16] And this son who has been born unto you shall be left on the earth, and his three children shall be saved with him: when all mankind that are on the earth shall diehe and his sons shall be saved.

[17] And now make known to thy son Lamech that he who has been born is in truth his son, and call his name Noah; for he shall be left to you, and he and his sons shall be saved from the destruction, which shall come upon the earth on account of all the sin and all the unrighteousness, which shall be consummated on the earth in his days. And after that there shall be still more unrighteousness than that which was first consummated on the earth; for I know the mysteries of the holy ones; for He, the Lord, has showed me and informed me, and I have read them in the heavenly tablets.

Chapter 107

[1] And I saw written on them that generation upon generation shall transgress, till a generation of righteousness arises, and transgression is destroyed and sin passes away from the earth, and all manner of good comes upon it.

[2] And now, my son, go and make known to thy son Lamech that this son, which has been born, is in truth his son, and that this is no lie.

[3] And when Methuselah had heard the words of his father Enoch for he had shown to him everything in secret he returned and showed them to him and called the name of that son Noah; for he will comfort the earth after all the destruction.

Chapter 108

[1] Another book which Enoch wrote for his son Methuselah and for those who will come after him, and keep the law in the last days.

[2] Ye who have done good shall wait for those days till an end is made of those who work evil; and an end of the might of the transgressors. And wait ye indeed till sin has passed away,

[3] For their names shall be blotted out of the book of life and out of the holy books, and their seed shall be destroyed for ever,

[4] And their spirits shall be slain, and they shall cry and make lamentation in a place that is a chaotic wilderness, and in the fire shall they burn; for there is no earth there. And I saw there something like an invisible cloud; for by reason of its depth I could not look over, and I saw a flame of fire blazing brightly, and things like shining mountains circling and sweeping to and fro.

[5] And I asked one of the holy angels who was with me and said unto him: What is this shining thing? for it is not a heaven but only the flame of a blazing fire,

[6] And the voice of weeping and crying and lamentation and strong pain. And he said unto me: This place which thou seest here are cast the spirits of sinners and blasphemers, and of those who work wickedness, and of those who pervert everything that the Lord hath spoken through the mouth of the prophets even the things that shall be.

[7] For some of them are written and inscribed above in the heaven, in order tha t the angels may read them and know that which shall befall the sinners, and the spirits of the

humble, and of those who have afflicted their bodies, and been recompensed by God;

[8] And of those who have been put to shame by wicked men: Who love God and loved neither gold nor silver nor any of the good things which are in the world, but gave over their bodies to torture.

[9] Who, since they came into being, longed not after earthly food, but regarded everything as a passing breath, and lived accordingly, and the Lord tried them much, and their spirits were found pure so that they should bless His name.

[10] And all the blessings destined for them I have recounted in the books. And he hath assigned them their recompense, because they have been found to be such as loved heaven more than their life in the world, and though they were trodden under foot of wicked men, and experienced abuse and reviling from them and were put to shame,

[11] Yet they blessed Me. And now I will summon the spirits of the good who belong to the generation of light, and I will transform those who were born in darkness, who in the flesh were not recompensed with such honour as their faithfulness deserved.

[12] And I will bring forth in shining light those who have loved My holy name, and I will seat each on the throne of his honour.

[13] And they shall be resplendent for times without number; for righteousness is the judgement of God; for to the faithful He will give faithfulness in the habitation of upright paths. And they shall see those who were, born in darkness led into darkness, while the righteous shall be resplendent.

[14] And the sinners shall cry aloud and see them resplendent, and they indeed will go where days and seasons are prescribed for them.

Esdras

1Esdr.1

[1] And Josias held the feast of the passover in Jerusalem unto his Lord, and offered the passover the fourteenth day of the first month;

[2] Having set the priests according to their daily courses, being arrayed in long garments, in the temple of the Lord.

[3] And he spake unto the Levites, the holy ministers of Israel, that they should hallow themselves unto the Lord, to set the holy ark of the Lord in the house that king Solomon the son of David had built:

[4] And said, Ye shall no more bear the ark upon your shoulders: now therefore serve the Lord your God, and minister unto his people Israel, and prepare you after your families and kindreds,

[5] According as David the king of Israel prescribed, and according to the magnificence of Solomon his son: and standing in the temple according to the several dignity of the families of you the Levites, who minister in the presence of your brethren the children of Israel,

[6] Offer the passover in order, and make ready the sacrifices for your brethren, and keep the passover according to the commandment of the Lord, which was given unto Moses.

[7] And unto the people that was found there Josias gave thirty thousand lambs and kids, and three thousand calves:

these things were given of the king's allowance, according as he promised, to the people, to the priests, and to the Levites.

[8] And Helkias, Zacharias, and Syelus, the governors of the temple, gave to the priests for the passover two thousand and six hundred sheep, and three hundred calves.

[9] And Jeconias, and Samaias, and Nathanael his brother, and Assabias, and Ochiel, and Joram, captains over thousands, gave to the Levites for the passover five thousand sheep, and seven hundred calves.

[10] And when these things were done, the priests and Levites, having the unleavened bread, stood in very comely order according to the kindreds,

[11] And according to the several dignities of the fathers, before the people, to offer to the Lord, as it is written in the book of Moses: and thus did they in the morning.

[12] And they roasted the passover with fire, as appertaineth: as for the sacrifices, they sod them in brass pots and pans with a good savour,

[13] And set them before all the people: and afterward they prepared for themselves, and for the priests their brethren, the sons of Aaron.

[14] For the priests offered the fat until night: and the Levites prepared for themselves, and the priests their brethren, the sons of Aaron.

[15] The holy singers also, the sons of Asaph, were in their order, according to the appointment of David, to wit, Asaph, Zacharias, and Jeduthun, who was of the king's retinue.

[16] Moreover the porters were at every gate; it was not lawful for any to go from his ordinary service: for their brethren the Levites prepared for them.

[17] Thus were the things that belonged to the sacrifices of the Lord accomplished in that day, that they might hold the passover,

[18] And offer sacrifices upon the altar of the Lord, according to the commandment of king Josias.

[19] So the children of Israel which were present held the passover at that time, and the feast of sweet bread seven days.

[20] And such a passover was not kept in Israel since the time of the prophet Samuel.

[21] Yea, all the kings of Israel held not such a passover as Josias, and the priests, and the Levites, and the Jews, held with all Israel that were found dwelling at Jerusalem.

[22] In the eighteenth year of the reign of Josias was this passover kept.

[23] And the works or Josias were upright before his Lord with an heart full of godliness.

[24] As for the things that came to pass in his time, they were written in former times, concerning those that sinned, and did wickedly against the Lord above all people and kingdoms, and how they grieved him exceedingly, so that the words of the Lord rose up against Israel.

[25] Now after all these acts of Josias it came to pass, that Pharaoh the king of Egypt came to raise war at Carchamis upon Euphrates: and Josias went out against him.

[26] But the king of Egypt sent to him, saying, What have I to do with thee, O king of Judea?

[27] I am not sent out from the Lord God against thee; for my war is upon Euphrates: and now the Lord is with me, yea, the Lord is with me hasting me forward: depart from me, and be not against the Lord.

[28] Howbeit Josias did not turn back his chariot from him, but undertook to fight with him, not regarding the words of the prophet Jeremy spoken by the mouth of the Lord:

[29] But joined battle with him in the plain of Magiddo, and the princes came against king Josias.

[30] Then said the king unto his servants, Carry me away out of the battle; for I am very weak. And immediately his servants took him away out of the battle.

[31] Then gat he up upon his second chariot; and being brought back to Jerusalem died, and was buried in his father's sepulchre.

[32] And in all Jewry they mourned for Josias, yea, Jeremy the prophet lamented for Josias, and the chief men with the women made lamentation for him unto this day: and this was given out for an ordinance to be done continually in all the nation of Israel.

[33] These things are written in the book of the stories of the kings of Judah, and every one of the acts that Josias did, and his glory, and his understanding in the law of the Lord, and the things that he had done before, and the things now recited, are reported in the book of the kings of Israel and Judea.

[34] And the people took Joachaz the son of Josias, and made him king instead of Josias his father, when he was twenty and three years old.

[35] And he reigned in Judea and in Jerusalem three months: and then the king of Egypt deposed him from reigning in Jerusalem.

[36] And he set a tax upon the land of an hundred talents of silver and one talent of gold.

[37] The king of Egypt also made king Joacim his brother king of Judea and Jerusalem.

[38] And he bound Joacim and the nobles: but Zaraces his brother he apprehended, and brought him out of Egypt.

[39] Five and twenty years old was Joacim when he was made king in the land of Judea and Jerusalem; and he did evil before the Lord.

[40] Wherefore against him Nabuchodonosor the king of Babylon came up, and bound him with a chain of brass, and carried him into Babylon.

[41] Nabuchodonosor also took of the holy vessels of the Lord, and carried them away, and set them in his own temple at Babylon.

[42] But those things that are recorded of him, and of his uncleaness and impiety, are written in the chronicles of the kings.

[43] And Joacim his son reigned in his stead: he was made king being eighteen years old;

[44] And reigned but three months and ten days in Jerusalem; and did evil before the Lord.

[45] So after a year Nabuchodonosor sent and caused him to be brought into Babylon with the holy vessels of the Lord;

[46] And made Zedechias king of Judea and Jerusalem, when he was one and twenty years old; and he reigned eleven years:

[47] And he did evil also in the sight of the Lord, and cared not for the words that were spoken unto him by the prophet Jeremy from the mouth of the Lord.

[48] And after that king Nabuchodonosor had made him to swear by the name of the Lord, he forswore himself, and rebelled; and hardening his neck, his heart, he transgressed the laws of the Lord God of Israel.

[49] The governors also of the people and of the priests did many things against the laws, and passed all the pollutions of all nations, and defiled the temple of the Lord, which was sanctified in Jerusalem.

[50] Nevertheless the God of their fathers sent by his messenger to call them back, because he spared them and his tabernacle also.

[51] But they had his messengers in derision; and, look, when the Lord spake unto them, they made a sport of his prophets:

[52] So far forth, that he, being wroth with his people for their great ungodliness, commanded the kings of the Chaldees to come up against them;

[53] Who slew their young men with the sword, yea, even within the compass of their holy temple, and spared neither young man nor maid, old man nor child, among them; for he delivered all into their hands.

[54] And they took all the holy vessels of the Lord, both great and small, with the vessels of the ark of God, and the king's treasures, and carried them away into Babylon.

[55] As for the house of the Lord, they burnt it, and brake down the walls of Jerusalem, and set fire upon her towers:

[56] And as for her glorious things, they never ceased till they had consumed and brought them all to nought: and the people that were not slain with the sword he carried unto Babylon:

[57] Who became servants to him and his children, till the Persians reigned, to fulfil the word of the Lord spoken by the mouth of Jeremy:

[58] Until the land had enjoyed her sabbaths, the whole time of her desolation shall she rest, until the full term of seventy years.

1Esdr.2

[1] In the first year of Cyrus king of the Persians, that the word of the Lord might be accomplished, that he had promised by the mouth of Jeremy;

[2] The Lord raised up the spirit of Cyrus the king of the Persians, and he made proclamation through all his kingdom, and also by writing,

[3] Saying, Thus saith Cyrus king of the Persians; The Lord of Israel, the most high Lord, hath made me king of the whole world,

[4] And commanded me to build him an house at Jerusalem in Jewry.

[5] If therefore there be any of you that are of his people, let the Lord, even his Lord, be with him, and let him go up to Jerusalem that is in Judea, and build the house of the Lord of Israel: for he is the Lord that dwelleth in Jerusalem.

[6] Whosoever then dwell in the places about, let them help him, those, I say, that are his neighbours, with gold, and with silver,

[7] With gifts, with horses, and with cattle, and other things, which have been set forth by vow, for the temple of the Lord at Jerusalem.

[8] Then the chief of the families of Judea and of the tribe of Benjamin stood up; the priests also, and the Levites, and all they whose mind the Lord had moved to go up, and to build an house for the Lord at Jerusalem,

[9] And they that dwelt round about them, and helped them in all things with silver and gold, with horses and cattle, and with very many free gifts of a great number whose minds were stirred up thereto.

[10] King Cyrus also brought forth the holy vessels, which Nabuchodonosor had carried away from Jerusalem, and had set up in his temple of idols.

[11] Now when Cyrus king of the Persians had brought them forth, he delivered them to Mithridates his treasurer:

[12] And by him they were delivered to Sanabassar the governor of Judea.

[13] And this was the number of them; A thousand golden cups, and a thousand of silver, censers of silver twenty nine, vials of gold thirty, and of silver two thousand four hundred and ten, and a thousand other vessels.

[14] So all the vessels of gold and of silver, which were carried away, were five thousand four hundred threescore and nine.

[15] These were brought back by Sanabassar, together with them of the captivity, from Babylon to Jerusalem.

[16] But in the time of Artexerxes king of the Persians Belemus, and Mithridates, and Tabellius, and Rathumus, and Beeltethmus, and Semellius the secretary, with others that were in commission with them, dwelling in Samaria and other places, wrote unto him against them that dwelt in Judea and Jerusalem these letters following;

[17] To king Artexerxes our lord, Thy servants, Rathumus the storywriter, and Semellius the scribe, and the rest of their council, and the judges that are in Celosyria and Phenice.

[18] Be it now known to the lord king, that the Jews that are up from you to us, being come into Jerusalem, that rebellious and wicked city, do build the marketplaces, and repair the walls of it and do lay the foundation of the temple.

[19] Now if this city and the walls thereof be made up again, they will not only refuse to give tribute, but also rebel against kings.

[20] And forasmuch as the things pertaining to the temple are now in hand, we think it meet not to neglect such a

matter,

[21] But to speak unto our lord the king, to the intent that, if it be thy pleasure it may be sought out in the books of thy fathers:

[22] And thou shalt find in the chronicles what is written concerning these things, and shalt understand that that city was rebellious, troubling both kings and cities:

[23] And that the Jews were rebellious, and raised always wars therein; for the which cause even this city was made desolate.

[24] Wherefore now we do declare unto thee, O lord the king, that if this city be built again, and the walls thereof set up anew, thou shalt from henceforth have no passage into Celosyria and Phenice.

[25] Then the king wrote back again to Rathumus the storywriter, to Beeltethmus, to Semellius the scribe, and to the rest that were in commission, and dwellers in Samaria and Syria and Phenice, after this manner;

[26] I have read the epistle which ye have sent unto me: therefore I commanded to make diligent search, and it hath been found that that city was from the beginning practising against kings;

[27] And the men therein were given to rebellion and war: and that mighty kings and fierce were in Jerusalem, who reigned and exacted tributes in Celosyria and Phenice.

[28] Now therefore I have commanded to hinder those men from building the city, and heed to be taken that there be no more done in it;

[29] And that those wicked workers proceed no further to the annoyance of kings,

[30] Then king Artexerxes his letters being read, Rathumus, and Semellius the scribe, and the rest that were in commission with them, removing in haste toward Jerusalem with a troop of horsemen and a multitude of people in battle array, began to hinder the builders; and the building of the temple in Jerusalem ceased until the second year of the reign of Darius king of the Persians.

1Esdr.3

[1] Now when Darius reigned, he made a great feast unto all his subjects, and unto all his household, and unto all the princes of Media and Persia,

[2] And to all the governors and captains and lieutenants that were under him, from India unto Ethiopia, of an hundred twenty and seven provinces.

[3] And when they had eaten and drunken, and being satisfied were gone home, then Darius the king went into his bedchamber, and slept, and soon after awaked.

[4] Then three young men, that were of the guard that kept the king's body, spake one to another;

[5] Let every one of us speak a sentence: he that shall overcome, and whose sentence shall seem wiser than the others, unto him shall the king Darius give great gifts, and great things in token of victory:

[6] As, to be clothed in purple, to drink in gold, and to sleep upon gold, and a chariot with bridles of gold, and an headtire of fine linen, and a chain about his neck:

[7] And he shall sit next to Darius because of his wisdom, and shall be called Darius his cousin.

[8] And then every one wrote his sentence, sealed it, and laid it under king Darius his pillow;

[9] And said that, when the king is risen, some will give him the writings; and of whose side the king and the three princes of Persia shall judge that his sentence is the wisest, to him shall the victory be given, as was appointed.

[10] The first wrote, Wine is the strongest.

[11] The second wrote, The king is strongest.

[12] The third wrote, Women are strongest: but above all things Truth beareth away the victory.

[13] Now when the king was risen up, they took their writings, and delivered them unto him, and so he read them:

[14] And sending forth he called all the princes of Persia and Media, and the governors, and the captains, and the lieutenants, and the chief officers;

[15] And sat him down in the royal seat of judgment; and the writings were read before them.

[16] And he said, Call the young men, and they shall declare their own sentences. So they were called, and came in.

[17] And he said unto them, Declare unto us your mind concerning the writings. Then began the first, who had spoken of the strength of wine;

[18] And he said thus, O ye men, how exceeding strong is wine! it causeth all men to err that drink it:

[19] It maketh the mind of the king and of the fatherless child to be all one; of the bondman and of the freeman, of the poor man and of the rich:

[20] It turneth also every thought into jollity and mirth, so that a man remembereth neither sorrow nor debt:

[21] And it maketh every heart rich, so that a man remembereth neither king nor governor; and it maketh to speak all things by talents:

[22] And when they are in their cups, they forget their love both to friends and brethren, and a little after draw out swords:

[23] But when they are from the wine, they remember not what they have done.

[24] O ye men, is not wine the strongest, that enforceth to do thus? And when he had so spoken, he held his peace.

1Esdr.4

[1] Then the second, that had spoken of the strength of the king, began to say,

[2] O ye men, do not men excel in strength that bear rule over sea and land and all things in them?

[3] But yet the king is more mighty: for he is lord of all these things, and hath dominion over them; and whatsoever he commandeth them they do.

[4] If he bid them make war the one against the other, they do it: if he send them out against the enemies, they go, and break down mountains walls and towers.

[5] They slay and are slain, and transgress not the king's commandment: if they get the victory, they bring all to the king, as well the spoil, as all things else.

[6] Likewise for those that are no soldiers, and have not to do with wars, but use husbundry, when they have reaped again that which they had sown, they bring it to the king, and compel one another to pay tribute unto the king.

[7] And yet he is but one man: if he command to kill, they kill; if he command to spare, they spare;

[8] If he command to smite, they smite; if he command to make desolate, they make desolate; if he command to build, they build;

[9] If he command to cut down, they cut down; if he command to plant, they plant.

[10] So all his people and his armies obey him: furthermore he lieth down, he eateth and drinketh, and taketh his rest:

[11] And these keep watch round about him, neither may any one depart, and do his own business, neither disobey they him in any thing.

[12] O ye men, how should not the king be mightiest, when in such sort he is obeyed? And he held his tongue.

[13] Then the third, who had spoken of women, and of the truth, (this was Zorobabel) began to speak.

[14] O ye men, it is not the great king, nor the multitude of men, neither is it wine, that excelleth; who is it then that ruleth them, or hath the lordship over them? are they not women?

[15] Women have borne the king and all the people that bear rule by sea and land.

[16] Even of them came they: and they nourished them up that planted the vineyards, from whence the wine cometh.

[17] These also make garments for men; these bring glory unto men; and without women cannot men be.

[18] Yea, and if men have gathered together gold and silver, or any other goodly thing, do they not love a woman which is comely in favour and beauty?

[19] And letting all those things go, do they not gape, and even with open mouth fix their eyes fast on her; and have not all men more desire unto her than unto silver or gold, or any goodly thing whatsoever?

[20] A man leaveth his own father that brought him up, and his own country, and cleaveth unto his wife.

[21] He sticketh not to spend his life with his wife. and remembereth neither father, nor mother, nor country.

[22] By this also ye must know that women have dominion over you: do ye not labour and toil, and give and bring all to the woman?

[23] Yea, a man taketh his sword, and goeth his way to rob and to steal, to sail upon the sea and upon rivers;

[24] And looketh upon a lion, and goeth in the darkness; and when he hath stolen, spoiled, and robbed, he bringeth it to his love.

[25] Wherefore a man loveth his wife better than father or mother.

[26] Yea, many there be that have run out of their wits for women, and become servants for their sakes.

[27] Many also have perished, have erred, and sinned, for women.

[28] And now do ye not believe me? is not the king great in his power? do not all regions fear to touch him?

[29] Yet did I see him and Apame the king's concubine, the daughter of the admirable Bartacus, sitting at the right hand of the king,

[30] And taking the crown from the king's head, and setting it upon her own head; she also struck the king with her left hand.

[31] And yet for all this the king gaped and gazed upon her with open mouth: if she laughed upon him, he laughed also: but if she took any displeasure at him, the king was fain to flatter, that she might be reconciled to him again.

[32] O ye men, how can it be but women should be strong, seeing they do thus?

[33] Then the king and the princes looked one upon another: so he began to speak of the truth.

[34] O ye men, are not women strong? great is the earth, high is the heaven, swift is the sun in his course, for he compasseth the heavens round about, and fetcheth his course again to his own place in one day.

[35] Is he not great that maketh these things? therefore great is the truth, and stronger than all things.

[36] All the earth crieth upon the truth, and the heaven blesseth it: all works shake and tremble at it, and with it is no unrighteous thing.

[37] Wine is wicked, the king is wicked, women are wicked, all the children of men are wicked, and such are all their

wicked works; and there is no truth in them; in their unrighteousness also they shall perish.

[38] As for the truth, it endureth, and is alwaYs strong; it liveth and conquereth for evermore.

[39] With her there is no accepting of persons or rewards; but she doeth the things that are just, and refraineth from all unjust and wicked things; and all men do well like of her works.

[40] Neither in her judgment is any unrighteousness; and she is the strength, kingdom, power, and majesty, of all ages. Blessed be the God of truth.

[41] And with that he held his peace. And all the people then shouted, and said, Great is Truth, and mighty above all things.

[42] Then said the king unto him, Ask what thou wilt more than is appointed in the writing, and we will give it thee, because thou art found wisest; and thou shalt sit next me, and shalt be called my cousin.

[43] Then said he unto the king, Remember thy vow, which thou hast vowed to build Jerusalem, in the day when thou camest to thy kingdom,

[44] And to send away all the vessels that were taken away out of Jerusalem, which Cyrus set apart, when he vowed to destroy Babylon, and to send them again thither.

[45] Thou also hast vowed to build up the temple, which the Edomites burned when Judea was made desolate by the Chaldees.

[46] And now, O lord the king, this is that which I require, and which I desire of thee, and this is the princely liberality proceeding from thyself: I desire therefore that thou make good the vow, the performance whereof with thine own mouth thou hast vowed to the King of heaven.

[47] Then Darius the king stood up, and kissed him, and wrote letters for him unto all the treasurers and lieutenants and captains and governors, that they should safely convey on their way both him, and all those that go up with him to build Jerusalem.

[48] He wrote letters also unto the lieutenants that were in Celosyria and Phenice, and unto them in Libanus, that they should bring cedar wood from Libanus unto Jerusalem, and that they should build the city with him.

[49] Moreover he wrote for all the Jews that went out of his realm up into Jewry, concerning their freedom, that no officer, no ruler, no lieutenant, nor treasurer, should forcibly enter into their doors;

[50] And that all the country which they hold should be free without tribute; and that the Edomites should give over the villages of the Jews which then they held:

[51] Yea, that there should be yearly given twenty talents to the building of the temple, until the time that it were built;

[52] And other ten talents yearly, to maintain the burnt offerings upon the altar every day, as they had a commandment to offer seventeen:

[53] And that all they that went from Babylon to build the city should have free liberty, as well they as their posterity, and all the priests that went away.

[54] He wrote also concerning. the charges, and the priests' vestments wherein they minister;

[55] And likewise for the charges of the Levites, to be given them until the day that the house were finished, and Jerusalem builded up.

[56] And he commanded to give to all that kept the city pensions and wages.

[57] He sent away also all the vessels from Babylon, that Cyrus had set apart; and all that Cyrus had given in commandment, the same charged he also to be done, and sent unto Jerusalem.

[58] Now when this young man was gone forth, he lifted up his face to heaven toward Jerusalem, and praised the King of heaven,

[59] And said, From thee cometh victory, from thee cometh wisdom, and thine is the glory, and I am thy servant.

[60] Blessed art thou, who hast given me wisdom: for to thee I give thanks, O Lord of our fathers.

[61] And so he took the letters, and went out, and came unto Babylon, and told it all his brethren.

[62] And they praised the God of their fathers, because he had given them freedom and liberty

[63] To go up, and to build Jerusalem, and the temple which is called by his name: and they feasted with instruments of musick and gladness seven days.

1Esdr.5

[1] After this were the principal men of the families chosen according to their tribes, to go up with their wives and sons and daughters, with their menservants and maidservants, and their cattle.

[2] And Darius sent with them a thousand horsemen, till they had brought them back to Jerusalem safely, and with musical [instruments] tabrets and flutes.

[3] And all their brethren played, and he made them go up together with them.

[4] And these are the names of the men which went up, according to their families among their tribes, after their several heads.

[5] The priests, the sons of Phinees the son of Aaron: Jesus the son of Josedec, the son of Saraias, and Joacim the son of Zorobabel, the son of Salathiel, of the house of David, out of the kindred of Phares, of the tribe of Judah;

[6] Who spake wise sentences before Darius the king of Persia in the second year of his reign, in the month Nisan, which is the first month.

[7] And these are they of Jewry that came up from the captivity, where they dwelt as strangers, whom Nabuchodonosor the king of Babylon had carried away unto Babylon.

[8] And they returned unto Jerusalem, and to the other parts of Jewry, every man to his own city, who came with Zorobabel, with Jesus, Nehemias, and Zacharias, and Reesaias, Enenius, Mardocheus. Beelsarus, Aspharasus, Reelius, Roimus, and Baana, their guides.

[9] The number of them of the nation, and their governors, sons of Phoros, two thousand an hundred seventy and two; the sons of Saphat, four hundred seventy and two:

[10] The sons of Ares, seven hundred fifty and six:

[11] The sons of Phaath Moab, two thousand eight hundred and twelve:

[12] The sons of Elam, a thousand two hundred fifty and four: the sons of Zathul, nine hundred forty and five: the sons of Corbe, seven hundred and five: the sons of Bani, six hundred forty and eight:

[13] The sons of Bebai, six hundred twenty and three: the sons of Sadas, three thousand two hundred twenty and two:

[14] The sons of Adonikam, six hundred sixty and seven: the sons of Bagoi, two thousand sixty and six: the sons of Adin, four hundred fifty and four:

[15] The sons of Aterezias, ninety and two: the sons of Ceilan and Azetas threescore and seven: the sons of Azuran, four hundred thirty and two:

[16] The sons of Ananias, an hundred and one: the sons of Arom, thirty two: and the sons of Bassa, three hundred twenty and three: the sons of Azephurith, an hundred and two:

[17] The sons of Meterus, three thousand and five: the sons of Bethlomon, an hundred twenty and three:

[18] They of Netophah, fifty and five: they of Anathoth, an hundred fifty and eight: they of Bethsamos, forty and two:

[19] They of Kiriathiarius, twenty and five: they of Caphira and Beroth, seven hundred forty and three: they of Pira, seven hundred:

[20] They of Chadias and Ammidoi, four hundred twenty and two: they of Cirama and Gabdes, six hundred twenty and one:

[21] They of Macalon, an hundred twenty and two: they of Betolius, fifty and two: the sons of Nephis, an hundred fifty and six:

[22] The sons of Calamolalus and Onus, seven hundred twenty and five: the sons of Jerechus, two hundred forty and five:

[23] The sons of Annas, three thousand three hundred and thirty.

[24] The priests: the sons of Jeddu, the son of Jesus among the sons of Sanasib, nine hundred seventy and two: the sons of Meruth, a thousand fifty and two:

[25] The sons of Phassaron, a thousand forty and seven: the sons of Carme, a thousand and seventeen.

[26] The Levites: the sons of Jessue, and Cadmiel, and Banuas, and Sudias, seventy and four.

[27] The holy singers: the sons of Asaph, an hundred twenty and eight.

[28] The porters: the sons of Salum, the sons of Jatal, the sons of Talmon, the sons of Dacobi, the sons of Teta, the sons of Sami, in all an hundred thirty and nine.

[29] The servants of the temple: the sons of Esau, the sons of Asipha, the sons of Tabaoth, the sons of Ceras, the sons of Sud, the sons of Phaleas, the sons of Labana, the sons of Graba,

[30] The sons of Acua, the sons of Uta, the sons of Cetab, the sons of Agaba, the sons of Subai, the sons of Anan, the sons of Cathua, the sons of Geddur,

[31] The sons of Airus, the sons of Daisan, the sons of Noeba, the sons of Chaseba, the sons of Gazera, the sons of Azia, the sons of Phinees, the sons of Azare, the sons of Bastai, the sons of Asana, the sons of Meani, the sons of Naphisi, the sons of Acub, the sons of Acipha, the sons of Assur, the sons of Pharacim, the sons of Basaloth,

[32] The sons of Meeda, the sons of Coutha, the sons of Charea, the sons of Charcus, the sons of Aserer, the sons of Thomoi, the sons of Nasith, the sons of Atipha.

[33] The sons of the servants of Solomon: the sons of Azaphion, the sons of Pharira, the sons of Jeeli, the sons of Lozon, the sons of Israel, the sons of Sapheth,

[34] The sons of Hagia, the sons of Pharacareth, the sons of Sabi, the sons of Sarothie, the sons of Masias, the sons of Gar, the sons of Addus, the sons of Suba, the sons of Apherra, the sons of Barodis, the sons of Sabat, the sons of Allom.

[35] All the ministers of the temple, and the sons of the servants of Solomon, were three hundred seventy and two.

[36] These came up from Thermeleth and Thelersas, Charaathalar leading them, and Aalar;

[37] Neither could they shew their families, nor their stock, how they were of Israel: the sons of Ladan, the son of Ban, the sons of Necodan, six hundred fifty and two.

[38] And of the priests that usurped the office of the priesthood, and were not found: the sons of Obdia, the sons of Accoz, the sons of Addus, who married Augia one of the daughters of Barzelus, and was named after his name.

[39] And when the description of the kindred of these men was sought in the register, and was not found, they were removed from executing the office of the priesthood:

[40] For unto them said Nehemias and Atharias, that they should not be partakers of the holy things, till there arose up an high priest clothed with doctrine and truth.

[41] So of Israel, from them of twelve years old and upward, they were all in number forty thousand, beside menservants and womenservants two thousand three hundred and sixty.

[42] Their menservants and handmaids were seven thousand three hundred forty and seven: the singing men and singing women, two hundred forty and five:

[43] Four hundred thirty and five camels, seven thousand thirty and six horses, two hundred forty and five mules, five thousand five hundred twenty and five beasts used to the yoke.

[44] And certain of the chief of their families, when they came to the temple of God that is in Jerusalem, vowed to set up the house again in his own place according to their ability,

[45] And to give into the holy treasury of the works a thousand pounds of gold, five thousand of silver, and an hundred priestly vestments.

[46] And so dwelt the priests and the Levites and the people in Jerusalem, and in the country, the singers also and the porters; and all Israel in their villages.

[47] But when the seventh month was at hand, and when the children of Israel were every man in his own place, they came all together with one consent into the open place of the first gate which is toward the east.

[48] Then stood up Jesus the son of Josedec, and his brethren the priests and Zorobabel the son of Salathiel, and his brethren, and made ready the altar of the God of Israel,

[49] To offer burnt sacrifices upon it, according as it is expressly commanded in the book of Moses the man of God.

[50] And there were gathered unto them out of the other nations of the land, and they erected the altar upon his own place, because all the nations of the land were at enmity with them, and oppressed them; and they offered sacrifices according to the time, and burnt offerings to the Lord both morning and evening.

[51] Also they held the feast of tabernacles, as it is commanded in the law, and offered sacrifices daily, as was meet:

[52] And after that, the continual oblations, and the sacrifice of the sabbaths, and of the new moons, and of all holy feasts.

[53] And all they that had made any vow to God began to offer sacrifices to God from the first day of the seventh month, although the temple of the Lord was not yet built.

[54] And they gave unto the masons and carpenters money, meat, and drink, with cheerfulness.

[55] Unto them of Zidon also and Tyre they gave carrs, that they should bring cedar trees from Libanus, which should be brought by floats to the haven of Joppa, according as it was commanded them by Cyrus king of the Persians.

[56] And in the second year and second month after his coming to the temple of God at Jerusalem began Zorobabel the son of Salathiel, and Jesus the son of Josedec, and their brethren, and the priests, and the Levites, and all they that were come unto Jerusalem out of the captivity:

[57] And they laid the foundation of the house of God in the first day of the second month, in the second year after they were come to Jewry and Jerusalem.

[58] And they appointed the Levites from twenty years old over the works of the Lord. Then stood up Jesus, and his sons and brethren, and Cadmiel his brother, and the sons of Madiabun, with the sons of Joda the son of Eliadun, with their sons and brethren, all Levites, with one accord setters forward of the business, labouring to advance the works in the house of God. So the workmen built the temple of the Lord.

[59] And the priests stood arrayed in their vestments with musical instruments and trumpets; and the Levites the sons of Asaph had cymbals,

[60] Singing songs of thanksgiving, and praising the Lord, according as David the king of Israel had ordained.

[61] And they sung with loud voices songs to the praise of the Lord, because his mercy and glory is for ever in all Israel.

[62] And all the people sounded trumpets, and shouted with a loud voice, singing songs of thanksgiving unto the Lord for the rearing up of the house of the Lord.

[63] Also of the priests and Levites, and of the chief of their families, the ancients who had seen the former house came to the building of this with weeping and great crying.

[64] But many with trumpets and joy shouted with loud voice,

[65] Insomuch that the trumpets might not be heard for the weeping of the people: yet the multitude sounded marvellously, so that it was heard afar off.

[66] Wherefore when the enemies of the tribe of Judah and Benjamin heard it, they came to know what that noise of trumpets should mean.

[67] And they perceived that they that were of the captivity did build the temple unto the Lord God of Israel.

[68] So they went to Zorobabel and Jesus, and to the chief of the families, and said unto them, We will build together

with you.

[69] For we likewise, as ye, do obey your Lord, and do sacrifice unto him from the days of Azbazareth the king of the Assyrians, who brought us hither.

[70] Then Zorobabel and Jesus and the chief of the families of Israel said unto them, It is not for us and you to build together an house unto the Lord our God.

[71] We ourselves alone will build unto the Lord of Israel, according as Cyrus the king of the Persians hath commanded us.

[72] But the heathen of the land lying heavy upon the inhabitants of Judea, and holding them strait, hindered their building;

[73] And by their secret plots, and popular persuasions and commotions, they hindered the finishing of the building all the time that king Cyrus lived: so they were hindered from building for the space of two years, until the reign of Darius.

1Esdr.6

[1] Now in the second year of the reign of Darius Aggeus and Zacharias the son of Addo, the prophets, prophesied unto the Jews in Jewry and Jerusalem in the name of the Lord God of Israel, which was upon them.

[2] Then stood up Zorobabel the son of Salatiel, and Jesus the son of Josedec, and began to build the house of the Lord at Jerusalem, the prophets of the Lord being with them, and helping them.

[3] At the same time came unto them Sisinnes the governor of Syria and Phenice, with Sathrabuzanes and his companions, and said unto them,

[4] By whose appointment do ye build this house and this roof, and perform all the other things? and who are the workmen that perform these things?

[5] Nevertheless the elders of the Jews obtained favour, because the Lord had visited the captivity;

[6] And they were not hindered from building, until such time as signification was given unto Darius concerning them, and an answer received.

[7] The copy of the letters which Sisinnes, governor of Syria and Phenice, and Sathrabuzanes, with their companions, rulers in Syria and Phenice, wrote and sent unto Darius; To king Darius, greeting:

[8] Let all things be known unto our lord the king, that being come into the country of Judea, and entered into the city of Jerusalem we found in the city of Jerusalem the ancients of the Jews that were of the captivity

[9] Building an house unto the Lord, great and new, of hewn and costly stones, and the timber already laid upon the walls.

[10] And those works are done with great speed, and the work goeth on prosperously in their hands, and with all glory and diligence is it made.

[11] Then asked we these elders, saying, By whose commandment build ye this house, and lay the foundations of these works?

[12] Therefore to the intent that we might give knowledge unto thee by writing, we demanded of them who were the chief doers, and we required of them the names in writing of their principal men.

[13] So they gave us this answer, We are the servants of the Lord which made heaven and earth.

[14] And as for this house, it was builded many years ago by a king of Israel great and strong, and was finished.

[15] But when our fathers provoked God unto wrath, and sinned against the Lord of Israel which is in heaven, he gave them over into the power of Nabuchodonosor king of Babylon, of the Chaldees;

[16] Who pulled down the house, and burned it, and carried away the people captives unto Babylon.

[17] But in the first year that king Cyrus reigned over the country of Babylon Cyrus the king wrote to build up this house.

[18] And the holy vessels of gold and of silver, that Nabuchodonosor had carried away out of the house at Jerusalem, and had set them in his own temple those Cyrus the king brought forth again out of the temple at Babylon, and they were delivered to Zorobabel and to Sanabassarus the ruler,

[19] With commandment that he should carry away the same vessels, and put them in the temple at Jerusalem; and that the temple of the Lord should be built in his place.

[20] Then the same Sanabassarus, being come hither, laid the foundations of the house of the Lord at Jerusalem; and from that time to this being still a building, it is not yet fully ended.

[21] Now therefore, if it seem good unto the king, let search be made among the records of king Cyrus:

[22] And if it be found that the building of the house of the Lord at Jerusalem hath been done with the consent of king Cyrus, and if our lord the king be so minded, let him signify unto us thereof.

[23] Then commanded king Darius to seek among the records at Babylon: and so at Ecbatane the palace, which is in the country of Media, there was found a roll wherein these things were recorded.

[24] In the first year of the reign of Cyrus king Cyrus commanded that the house of the Lord at Jerusalem should be built again, where they do sacrifice with continual fire:

[25] Whose height shall be sixty cubits and the breadth sixty cubits, with three rows of hewn stones, and one row of new wood of that country; and the expences thereof to be given out of the house of king Cyrus:

[26] And that the holy vessels of the house of the Lord, both of gold and silver, that Nabuchodonosor took out of the house at Jerusalem, and brought to Babylon, should be restored to the house at Jerusalem, and be set in the place where they were before.

[27] And also he commanded that Sisinnes the governor of Syria and Phenice, and Sathrabuzanes, and their companions, and those which were appointed rulers in Syria and Phenice, should be careful not to meddle with the place, but suffer Zorobabel, the servant of the Lord, and governor of Judea, and the elders of the Jews, to build the house of the Lord in that place.

[28] I have commanded also to have it built up whole again; and that they look diligently to help those that be of the captivity of the Jews, till the house of the Lord be finished:

[29] And out of the tribute of Celosyria and Phenice a portion carefully to be given these men for the sacrifices of the Lord, that is, to Zorobabel the governor, for bullocks, and rams, and lambs;

[30] And also corn, salt, wine, and oil, and that continually every year without further question, according as the priests that be in Jerusalem shall signify to be daily spent:

[31] That offerings may be made to the most high God for the king and for his children, and that they may pray for their lives.

[32] And he commanded that whosoever should transgress, yea, or make light of any thing afore spoken or written, out of his own house should a tree be taken, and he thereon be hanged, and all his goods seized for the king.

[33] The Lord therefore, whose name is there called upon, utterly destroy every king and nation, that stretcheth out his hand to hinder or endamage that house of the Lord in Jerusalem.

[34] I Darius the king have ordained that according unto these things it be done with diligence.

1Esdr.7

[1] Then Sisinnes the governor of Celosyria and Phenice, and Sathrabuzanes, with their companions following the commandments of king Darius,

[2] Did very carefully oversee the holy works, assisting the ancients of the Jews and governors of the temple.

[3] And so the holy works prospered, when Aggeus and Zacharias the prophets prophesied.

[4] And they finished these things by the commandment of the Lord God of Israel, and with the consent of Cyrus, Darius, and Artexerxes, kings of Persia.

[5] And thus was the holy house finished in the three and twentieth day of the month Adar, in the sixth year of Darius king of the Persians

[6] And the children of Israel, the priests, and the Levites, and others that were of the captivity, that were added unto them, did according to the things written in the book of Moses.

[7] And to the dedication of the temple of the Lord they offered an hundred bullocks two hundred rams, four hundred lambs;

[8] And twelve goats for the sin of all Israel, according to the number of the chief of the tribes of Israel.

[9] The priests also and the Levites stood arrayed in their vestments, according to their kindreds, in the service of the Lord God of Israel, according to the book of Moses: and the porters at every gate.

[10] And the children of Israel that were of the captivity held the passover the fourteenth day of the first month, after that the priests and the Levites were sanctified.

[11] They that were of the captivity were not all sanctified together: but the Levites were all sanctified together.

[12] And so they offered the passover for all them of the captivity, and for their brethren the priests, and for themselves.

[13] And the children of Israel that came out of the captivity did eat, even all they that had separated themselves from the abominations of the people of the land, and sought the Lord.

[14] And they kept the feast of unleavened bread seven days, making merry before the Lord,

[15] For that he had turned the counsel of the king of Assyria toward them, to strengthen their hands in the works of the Lord God of Israel.

1Esdr.8

[1] And after these things, when Artexerxes the king of the Persians reigned came Esdras the son of Saraias, the son of Ezerias, the son of Helchiah, the son of Salum,

[2] The son of Sadduc, the son of Achitob, the son of Amarias, the son of Ezias, the son of Meremoth, the son of Zaraias, the son of Savias, the son of Boccas, the son of Abisum, the son of Phinees, the son of Eleazar, the son of Aaron the chief priest.

[3] This Esdras went up from Babylon, as a scribe, being very ready in the law of Moses, that was given by the God of Israel.

[4] And the king did him honour: for he found grace in his

sight in all his requests.

[5] There went up with him also certain of the children of Israel, of the priest of the Levites, of the holy singers, porters, and ministers of the temple, unto Jerusalem,

[6] In the seventh year of the reign of Artexerxes, in the fifth month, this was the king's seventh year; for they went from Babylon in the first day of the first month, and came to Jerusalem, according to the prosperous journey which the Lord gave them.

[7] For Esdras had very great skill, so that he omitted nothing of the law and commandments of the Lord, but taught all Israel the ordinances and judgments.

[8] Now the copy of the commission, which was written from Artexerxes the king, and came to Esdras the priest and reader of the law of the Lord, is this that followeth;

[9] King Artexerxes unto Esdras the priest and reader of the law of the Lord sendeth greeting:

[10] Having determined to deal graciously, I have given order, that such of the nation of the Jews, and of the priests and Levites being within our realm, as are willing and desirous should go with thee unto Jerusalem.

[11] As many therefore as have a mind thereunto, let them depart with thee, as it hath seemed good both to me and my seven friends the counsellors;

[12] That they may look unto the affairs of Judea and Jerusalem, agreeably to that which is in the law of the Lord;

[13] And carry the gifts unto the Lord of Israel to Jerusalem, which I and my friends have vowed, and all the gold and silver that in the country of Babylon can be found, to the Lord in Jerusalem,

[14] With that also which is given of the people for the temple of the Lord their God at Jerusalem: and that silver and gold may be collected for bullocks, rams, and lambs, and things thereunto appertaining;

[15] To the end that they may offer sacrifices unto the Lord upon the altar of the Lord their God, which is in Jerusalem.

[16] And whatsoever thou and thy brethren will do with the silver and gold, that do, according to the will of thy God.

[17] And the holy vessels of the Lord, which are given thee for the use of the temple of thy God, which is in Jerusalem, thou shalt set before thy God in Jerusalem.

[18] And whatsoever thing else thou shalt remember for the use of the temple of thy God, thou shalt give it out of the king's treasury.

[19] And I king Artexerxes have also commanded the keepers of the treasures in Syria and Phenice, that whatsoever Esdras the priest and the reader of the law of the most high God shall send for, they should give it him with speed,

[20] To the sum of an hundred talents of silver, likewise also of wheat even to an hundred cors, and an hundred pieces of wine, and other things in abundance.

[21] Let all things be performed after the law of God diligently unto the most high God, that wrath come not upon the kingdom of the king and his sons.

[22] I command you also, that ye require no tax, nor any other imposition, of any of the priests, or Levites, or holy singers, or porters, or ministers of the temple, or of any that have doings in this temple, and that no man have authority to impose any thing upon them.

[23] And thou, Esdras, according to the wisdom of God ordain judges and justices, that they may judge in all Syria and Phenice all those that know the law of thy God; and those that know it not thou shalt teach.

[24] And whosoever shall transgress the law of thy God, and of the king, shall be punished diligently, whether it be by death, or other punishment, by penalty of money, or by imprisonment.

[25] Then said Esdras the scribe, Blessed be the only Lord God of my fathers, who hath put these things into the heart of the king, to glorify his house that is in Jerusalem:

[26] And hath honoured me in the sight of the king, and his counsellors, and all his friends and nobles.

[27] Therefore was I encouraged by the help of the Lord my God, and gathered together men of Israel to go up with me.

[28] And these are the chief according to their families and several dignities, that went up with me from Babylon in the reign of king Artexerxes:

[29] Of the sons of Phinees, Gerson: of the sons of Ithamar, Gamael: of the sons of David, Lettus the son of Sechenias:

[30] Of the sons of Pharez, Zacharias; and with him were counted an hundred and fifty men:

[31] Of the sons of Pahath Moab, Eliaonias, the son of Zaraias, and with him two hundred men:

[32] Of the sons of Zathoe, Sechenias the son of Jezelus, and with him three hundred men: of the sons of Adin, Obeth the son of Jonathan, and with him two hundred and fifty men:

[33] Of the sons of Elam, Josias son of Gotholias, and with him seventy men:

[34] Of the sons of Saphatias, Zaraias son of Michael, and with him threescore and ten men:

[35] Of the sons of Joab, Abadias son of Jezelus, and with him two hundred and twelve men:

[36] Of the sons of Banid, Assalimoth son of Josaphias, and with him an hundred and threescore men:

[37] Of the sons of Babi, Zacharias son of Bebai, and with him twenty and eight men:

[38] Of the sons of Astath, Johannes son of Acatan, and with him an hundred and ten men:

[39] Of the sons of Adonikam the last, and these are the names of them, Eliphalet, Jewel, and Samaias, and with them seventy men:

[40] Of the sons of Bago, Uthi the son of Istalcurus, and with him seventy men.

[41] And these I gathered together to the river called Theras, where we pitched our tents three days: and then I surveyed them.

[42] But when I had found there none of the priests and Levites,

[43] Then sent I unto Eleazar, and Iduel, and Masman,

[44] And Alnathan, and Mamaias, and Joribas, and Nathan, Eunatan, Zacharias, and Mosollamon, principal men and learned.

[45] And I bade them that they should go unto Saddeus the captain, who was in the place of the treasury:

[46] And commanded them that they should speak unto Daddeus, and to his brethren, and to the treasurers in that place, to send us such men as might execute the priests' office in the house of the Lord.

[47] And by the mighty hand of our Lord they brought unto us skilful men of the sons of Moli the son of Levi, the son of Israel, Asebebia, and his sons, and his brethren, who were eighteen.

[48] And Asebia, and Annus, and Osaias his brother, of the sons of Channuneus, and their sons, were twenty men.

[49] And of the servants of the temple whom David had ordained, and the principal men for the service of the Levites to wit, the servants of the temple two hundred and twenty, the catalogue of whose names were shewed.

[50] And there I vowed a fast unto the young men before our Lord, to desire of him a prosperous journey both for us and them that were with us, for our children, and for the cattle:

[51] For I was ashamed to ask the king footmen, and horsemen, and conduct for safeguard against our adversaries.

[52] For we had said unto the king, that the power of the Lord our God should be with them that seek him, to support them in all ways.

[53] And again we besought our Lord as touching these things, and found him favourable unto us.

[54] Then I separated twelve of the chief of the priests, Esebrias, and Assanias, and ten men of their brethren with them:

[55] And I weighed them the gold, and the silver, and the holy vessels of the house of our Lord, which the king, and his council, and the princes, and all Israel, had given.

[56] And when I had weighed it, I delivered unto them six hundred and fifty talents of silver, and silver vessels of an hundred talents, and an hundred talents of gold,

[57] And twenty golden vessels, and twelve vessels of brass, even of fine brass, glittering like gold.

[58] And I said unto them, Both ye are holy unto the Lord, and the vessels are holy, and the gold and the silver is a vow unto the Lord, the Lord of our fathers.

[59] Watch ye, and keep them till ye deliver them to the chief of the priests and Levites, and to the principal men of the families of Israel, in Jerusalem, into the chambers of the house of our God.

[60] So the priests and the Levites, who had received the silver and the gold and the vessels, brought them unto Jerusalem, into the temple of the Lord.

[61] And from the river Theras we departed the twelfth day of the first month, and came to Jerusalem by the mighty hand of our Lord, which was with us: and from the beginning of our journey the Lord delivered us from every enemy, and so we came to Jerusalem.

[62] And when we had been there three days, the gold and silver that was weighed was delivered in the house of our Lord on the fourth day unto Marmoth the priest the son of Iri.

[63] And with him was Eleazar the son of Phinees, and with them were Josabad the son of Jesu and Moeth the son of Sabban, Levites: all was delivered them by number and weight.

[64] And all the weight of them was written up the same hour.

[65] Moreover they that were come out of the captivity offered sacrifice unto the Lord God of Israel, even twelve bullocks for all Israel, fourscore and sixteen rams,

[66] Threescore and twelve lambs, goats for a peace offering, twelve; all of them a sacrifice to the Lord.

[67] And they delivered the king's commandments unto the king's stewards' and to the governors of Celosyria and Phenice; and they honoured the people and the temple of God.

[68] Now when these things were done, the rulers came unto me, and said,

[69] The nation of Israel, the princes, the priests and Levites, have not put away from them the strange people of the land, nor the pollutions of the Gentiles to wit, of the Canaanites, Hittites, Pheresites, Jebusites, and the Moabites, Egyptians, and Edomites.

[70] For both they and their sons have married with their daughters, and the holy seed is mixed with the strange people of the land; and from the beginning of this matter the rulers and the great men have been partakers of this iniquity.

[71] And as soon as I had heard these things, I rent my

clothes, and the holy garment, and pulled off the hair from off my head and beard, and sat me down sad and very heavy.

[72] So all they that were then moved at the word of the Lord God of Israel assembled unto me, whilst I mourned for the iniquity: but I sat still full of heaviness until the evening sacrifice.

[73] Then rising up from the fast with my clothes and the holy garment rent, and bowing my knees, and stretching forth my hands unto the Lord,

[74] I said, O Lord, I am confounded and ashamed before thy face;

[75] For our sins are multiplied above our heads, and our ignorances have reached up unto heaven.

[76] For ever since the time of our fathers we have been and are in great sin, even unto this day.

[77] And for our sins and our fathers' we with our brethren and our kings and our priests were given up unto the kings of the earth, to the sword, and to captivity, and for a prey with shame, unto this day.

[78] And now in some measure hath mercy been shewed unto us from thee, O Lord, that there should be left us a root and a name in the place of thy sanctuary;

[79] And to discover unto us a light in the house of the Lord our God, and to give us food in the time of our servitude.

[80] Yea, when we were in bondage, we were not forsaken of our Lord; but he made us gracious before the kings of Persia, so that they gave us food;

[81] Yea, and honoured the temple of our Lord, and raised up the desolate Sion, that they have given us a sure abiding in Jewry and Jerusalem.

[82] And now, O Lord, what shall we say, having these things? for we have transgressed thy commandments, which thou gavest by the hand of thy servants the prophets, saying,

[83] That the land, which ye enter into to possess as an heritage, is a land polluted with the pollutions of the strangers of the land, and they have filled it with their uncleanness.

[84] Therefore now shall ye not join your daughters unto their sons, neither shall ye take their daughters unto your sons.

[85] Moreover ye shall never seek to have peace with them, that ye may be strong, and eat the good things of the land, and that ye may leave the inheritance of the land unto your children for evermore.

[86] And all that is befallen is done unto us for our wicked works and great sins; for thou, O Lord, didst make our sins light,

[87] And didst give unto us such a root: but we have turned back again to transgress thy law, and to mingle ourselves with the uncleanness of the nations of the land.

[88] Mightest not thou be angry with us to destroy us, till thou hadst left us neither root, seed, nor name?

[89] O Lord of Israel, thou art true: for we are left a root this day.

[90] Behold, now are we before thee in our iniquities, for we cannot stand any longer by reason of these things before thee.

[91] And as Esdras in his prayer made his confession, weeping, and lying flat upon the ground before the temple, there gathered unto him from Jerusalem a very great multitude of men and women and children: for there was great weeping among the multitude.

[92] Then Jechonias the son of Jeelus, one of the sons of Israel, called out, and said, O Esdras, we have sinned against the Lord God, we have married strange women of the nations of the land, and now is all Israel aloft.

[93] Let us make an oath to the Lord, that we will put away all our wives, which we have taken of the heathen, with their children,

[94] Like as thou hast decreed, and as many as do obey the law of the Lord.

[95] Arise and put in execution: for to thee doth this matter appertain, and we will be with thee: do valiantly.

[96] So Esdras arose, and took an oath of the chief of the priests and Levites of all Israel to do after these things; and so they sware.

1Esdr.9

[1] Then Esdras rising from the court of the temple went to the chamber of Joanan the son of Eliasib,

[2] And remained there, and did eat no meat nor drink water, mourning for the great iniquities of the multitude.

[3] And there was a proclamation in all Jewry and Jerusalem to all them that were of the captivity, that they should be gathered together at Jerusalem:

[4] And that whosoever met not there within two or three days according as the elders that bare rule appointed, their cattle should be seized to the use of the temple, and himself cast out from them that were of the captivity.

[5] And in three days were all they of the tribe of Judah and Benjamin gathered together at Jerusalem the twentieth day of the ninth month.

[6] And all the multitude sat trembling in the broad court of the temple because of the present foul weather.

[7] So Esdras arose up, and said unto them, Ye have transgressed the law in marrying strange wives, thereby to increase the sins of Israel.

[8] And now by confessing give glory unto the Lord God of our fathers,

[9] And do his will, and separate yourselves from the heathen of the land, and from the strange women.

[10] Then cried the whole multitude, and said with a loud voice, Like as thou hast spoken, so will we do.

[11] But forasmuch as the people are many, and it is foul weather, so that we cannot stand without, and this is not a work of a day or two, seeing our sin in these things is spread far:

[12] Therefore let the rulers of the multitude stay, and let all them of our habitations that have strange wives come at the time appointed,

[13] And with them the rulers and judges of every place, till we turn away the wrath of the Lord from us for this matter.

[14] Then Jonathan the son of Azael and Ezechias the son of Theocanus accordingly took this matter upon them: and Mosollam and Levis and Sabbatheus helped them.

[15] And they that were of the captivity did according to all these things.

[16] And Esdras the priest chose unto him the principal men of their families, all by name: and in the first day of the tenth month they sat together to examine the matter.

[17] So their cause that held strange wives was brought to an end in the first day of the first month.

[18] And of the priests that were come together, and had strange wives, there were found:

[19] Of the sons of Jesus the son of Josedec, and his brethren; Matthelas and Eleazar, and Joribus and Joadanus.

[20] And they gave their hands to put away their wives and to offer rams to make reconcilement for their errors.

[21] And of the sons of Emmer; Ananias, and Zabdeus, and Eanes, and Sameius, and Hiereel, and Azarias.

[22] And of the sons of Phaisur; Elionas, Massias Israel, and Nathanael, and Ocidelus and Talsas.

[23] And of the Levites; Jozabad, and Semis, and Colius, who was called Calitas, and Patheus, and Judas, and Jonas.

[24] Of the holy singers; Eleazurus, Bacchurus.

[25] Of the porters; Sallumus, and Tolbanes.

[26] Of them of Israel, of the sons of Phoros; Hiermas, and Eddias, and Melchias, and Maelus, and Eleazar, and Asibias, and Baanias.

[27] Of the sons of Ela; Matthanias, Zacharias, and Hierielus, and Hieremoth, and Aedias.

[28] And of the sons of Zamoth; Eliadas, Elisimus, Othonias, Jarimoth, and Sabatus, and Sardeus.

[29] Of the sons of Babai; Johannes, and Ananias and Josabad, and Amatheis.

[30] Of the sons of Mani; Olamus, Mamuchus, Jedeus, Jasubus, Jasael, and Hieremoth.

[31] And of the sons of Addi; Naathus, and Moosias, Lacunus, and Naidus, and Mathanias, and Sesthel, Balnuus, and Manasseas.

[32] And of the sons of Annas; Elionas and Aseas, and Melchias, and Sabbeus, and Simon Chosameus.

[33] And of the sons of Asom; Altaneus, and Matthias, and Baanaia, Eliphalet, and Manasses, and Semei.

[34] And of the sons of Maani; Jeremias, Momdis, Omaerus, Juel, Mabdai, and Pelias, and Anos, Carabasion, and Enasibus, and Mamnitanaimus, Eliasis, Bannus, Eliali, Samis, Selemias, Nathanias: and of the sons of Ozora; Sesis, Esril, Azaelus, Samatus, Zambis, Josephus.

[35] And of the sons of Ethma; Mazitias, Zabadaias, Edes, Juel, Banaias.

[36] All these had taken strange wives, and they put them away with their children.

[37] And the priests and Levites, and they that were of Israel, dwelt in Jerusalem, and in the country, in the first day of the seventh month: so the children of Israel were in their habitations.

[38] And the whole multitude came together with one accord into the broad place of the holy porch toward the east:

[39] And they spake unto Esdras the priest and reader, that he would bring the law of Moses, that was given of the Lord God of Israel.

[40] So Esdras the chief priest brought the law unto the whole multitude from man to woman, and to all the priests, to hear law in the first day of the seventh month.

[41] And he read in the broad court before the holy porch from morning unto midday, before both men and women; and the multitude gave heed unto the law.

[42] And Esdras the priest and reader of the law stood up upon a pulpit of wood, which was made for that purpose.

[43] And there stood up by him Mattathias, Sammus, Ananias, Azarias, Urias, Ezecias, Balasamus, upon the right hand:

[44] And upon his left hand stood Phaldaius, Misael, Melchias, Lothasubus, and Nabarias.

[45] Then took Esdras the book of the law before the multitude: for he sat honourably in the first place in the sight of them all.

[46] And when he opened the law, they stood all straight up. So Esdras blessed the Lord God most High, the God of hosts, Almighty.

[47] And all the people answered, Amen; and lifting up their hands they fell to the ground, and worshipped the Lord.

[48] Also Jesus, Anus, Sarabias, Adinus, Jacubus, Sabateas, Auteas, Maianeas, and Calitas, Asrias, and Joazabdus, and

Ananias, Biatas, the Levites, taught the law of the Lord, making them withal to understand it.

[49] Then spake Attharates unto Esdras the chief priest. and reader, and to the Levites that taught the multitude, even to all, saying,

[50] This day is holy unto the Lord; (for they all wept when they heard the law:)

[51] Go then, and eat the fat, and drink the sweet, and send part to them that have nothing;

[52] For this day is holy unto the Lord: and be not sorrowful; for the Lord will bring you to honour.

[53] So the Levites published all things to the people, saying, This day is holy to the Lord; be not sorrowful.

[54] Then went they their way, every one to eat and drink, and make merry, and to give part to them that had nothing, and to make great cheer;

[55] Because they understood the words wherein they were instructed, and for the which they had been assembled.

2Ezra.1

[1] The second book of the prophet Esdras, the son of Saraias, the son of Azarias, the son of Helchias, the son of Sadamias, the sou of Sadoc, the son of Achitob,

[2] The son of Achias, the son of Phinees, the son of Heli, the son of Amarias, the son of Aziei, the son of Marimoth, the son of And he spake unto the of Borith, the son of Abisei, the son of Phinees, the son of Eleazar,

[3] The son of Aaron, of the tribe of Levi; which was captive in the land of the Medes, in the reign of Artexerxes king of the Persians.

[4] And the word of the Lord came unto me, saying,

[5] Go thy way, and shew my people their sinful deeds, and their children their wickedness which they have done against me; that they may tell their children's children:

[6] Because the sins of their fathers are increased in them: for they have forgotten me, and have offered unto strange gods.

[7] Am not I even he that brought them out of the land of Egypt, from the house of bondage? but they have provoked me unto wrath, and despised my counsels.

[8] Pull thou off then the hair of thy head, and cast all evil upon them, for they have not been obedient unto my law, but it is a rebellious people.

[9] How long shall I forbear them, into whom I have done so much good?

[10] Many kings have I destroyed for their sakes; Pharaoh with his servants and all his power have I smitten down.

[11] All the nations have I destroyed before them, and in the east I have scattered the people of two provinces, even of Tyrus and Sidon, and have slain all their enemies.

[12] Speak thou therefore unto them, saying, Thus saith the Lord,

[13] I led you through the sea and in the beginning gave you a large and safe passage; I gave you Moses for a leader, and Aaron for a priest.

[14] I gave you light in a pillar of fire, and great wonders have I done among you; yet have ye forgotten me, saith the Lord.

[15] Thus saith the Almighty Lord, The quails were as a token to you; I gave you tents for your safeguard: nevertheless ye murmured there,

[16] And triumphed not in my name for the destruction of your enemies, but ever to this day do ye yet murmur.

[17] Where are the benefits that I have done for you? When ye were hungry and thirsty in the wilderness, did ye not cry unto me,

[18] Saying, Why hast thou brought us into this wilderness to kill us? it had been better for us to have served the Egyptians, than to die in this wilderness.

[19] Then had I pity upon your mournings, and gave you manna to eat; so ye did eat angels' bread.

[20] When ye were thirsty, did I not cleave the rock, and waters flowed out to your fill? for the heat I covered you with the leaves of the trees.

[21] I divided among you a fruitful land, I cast out the Canaanites, the Pherezites, and the Philistines, before you: what shall I yet do more for you? saith the Lord.

[22] Thus saith the Almighty Lord, When ye were in the wilderness, in the river of the Amorites, being athirst, and blaspheming my name,

[23] I gave you not fire for your blasphemies, but cast a tree in the water, and made the river sweet.

[24] What shall I do unto thee, O Jacob? thou, Juda, wouldest not obey me: I will turn me to other nations, and unto those will I give my name, that they may keep my statutes.

[25] Seeing ye have forsaken me, I will forsake you also; when ye desire me to be gracious unto you, I shall have no mercy upon you.

[26] Whensoever ye shall call upon me, I will not hear you: for ye have defiled your hands with blood, and your feet are swift to commit manslaughter.

[27] Ye have not as it were forsaken me, but your own selves, saith the Lord.

[28] Thus saith the Almighty Lord, Have I not prayed you as a father his sons, as a mother her daughters, and a nurse her young babes,

[29] That ye would be my people, and I should be your God; that ye would be my children, and I should be your father?

[30] I gathered you together, as a hen gathereth her chickens under her wings: but now, what shall I do unto you? I will cast you out from my face.

[31] When ye offer unto me, I will turn my face from you: for your solemn feastdays, your new moons, and your circumcisions, have I forsaken.

[32] I sent unto you my servants the prophets, whom ye have taken and slain, and torn their bodies in pieces, whose blood I will require of your hands, saith the Lord.

[33] Thus saith the Almighty Lord, Your house is desolate, I will cast you out as the wind doth stubble.

[34] And your children shall not be fruitful; for they have despised my commandment, and done the thing that is an evil before me.

[35] Your houses will I give to a people that shall come; which not having heard of me yet shall believe me; to whom I have shewed no signs, yet they shall do that I have commanded them.

[36] They have seen no prophets, yet they shall call their sins to remembrance, and acknowledge them.

[37] I take to witness the grace of the people to come, whose little ones rejoice in gladness: and though they have not seen me with bodily eyes, yet in spirit they believe the thing that I say.

[38] And now, brother, behold what glory; and see the people that come from the east:

[39] Unto whom I will give for leaders, Abraham, Isaac, and Jacob, Oseas, Amos, and Micheas, Joel, Abdias, and Jonas,

[40] Nahum, and Abacuc, Sophonias, Aggeus, Zachary, and Malachy, which is called also an angel of the Lord.

2Ezra.2

[1] Thus saith the Lord, I brought this people out of bondage, and I gave them my commandments by menservants the prophets; whom they would not hear, but despised my counsels.

[2] The mother that bare them saith unto them, Go your way, ye children; for I am a widow and forsaken.

[3] I brought you up with gladness; but with sorrow and heaviness have I lost you: for ye have sinned before the Lord your God, and done that thing that is evil before him.

[4] But what shall I now do unto you? I am a widow and forsaken: go your way, O my children, and ask mercy of the Lord.

[5] As for me, O father, I call upon thee for a witness over the mother of these children, which would not keep my covenant,

[6] That thou bring them to confusion, and their mother to a spoil, that there may be no offspring of them.

[7] Let them be scattered abroad among the heathen, let their names be put out of the earth: for they have despised my covenant.

[8] Woe be unto thee, Assur, thou that hidest the unrighteous in thee! O thou wicked people, remember what I did unto Sodom and Gomorrha;

[9] Whose land lieth in clods of pitch and heaps of ashes: even so also will I do unto them that hear me not, saith the Almighty Lord.

[10] Thus saith the Lord unto Esdras, Tell my people that I will give them the kingdom of Jerusalem, which I would have given unto Israel.

[11] Their glory also will I take unto me, and give these the everlasting tabernacles, which I had prepared for them.

[12] They shall have the tree of life for an ointment of sweet savour; they shall neither labour, nor be weary.

[13] Go, and ye shall receive: pray for few days unto you, that they may be shortened: the kingdom is already prepared for you: watch.

[14] Take heaven and earth to witness; for I have broken the evil in pieces, and created the good: for I live, saith the Lord.

[15] Mother, embrace thy children, and bring them up with gladness, make their feet as fast as a pillar: for I have chosen thee, saith the Lord.

[16] And those that be dead will I raise up again from their places, and bring them out of the graves: for I have known my name in Israel.

[17] Fear not, thou mother of the children: for I have chosen thee, saith the Lord.

[18] For thy help will I send my servants Esau and Jeremy, after whose counsel I have sanctified and prepared for thee twelve trees laden with divers fruits,

[19] And as many fountains flowing with milk and honey, and seven mighty mountains, whereupon there grow roses and lilies, whereby I will fill thy children with joy.

[20] Do right to the widow, judge for the fatherless, give to the poor, defend the orphan, clothe the naked,

[21] Heal the broken and the weak, laugh not a lame man to scorn, defend the maimed, and let the blind man come into the sight of my clearness.

[22] Keep the old and young within thy walls.

[23] Wheresoever thou findest the dead, take them and bury them, and I will give thee the first place in my resurrection.

[24] Abide still, O my people, and take thy rest, for thy quietness still come.

[25] Nourish thy children, O thou good nurse; stablish their feet.

[26] As for the servants whom I have given thee, there shall not one of them perish; for I will require them from among

thy number.

[27] Be not weary: for when the day of trouble and heaviness cometh, others shall weep and be sorrowful, but thou shalt be merry and have abundance.

[28] The heathen shall envy thee, but they shall be able to do nothing against thee, saith the Lord.

[29] My hands shall cover thee, so that thy children shall not see hell.

[30] Be joyful, O thou mother, with thy children; for I will deliver thee, saith the Lord.

[31] Remember thy children that sleep, for I shall bring them out of the sides of the earth, and shew mercy unto them: for I am merciful, saith the Lord Almighty.

[32] Embrace thy children until I come and shew mercy unto them: for my wells run over, and my grace shall not fail.

[33] I Esdras received a charge of the Lord upon the mount Oreb, that I should go unto Israel; but when I came unto them, they set me at nought, and despised the commandment of the Lord.

[34] And therefore I say unto you, O ye heathen, that hear and understand, look for your Shepherd, he shall give you everlasting rest; for he is nigh at hand, that shall come in the end of the world.

[35] Be ready to the reward of the kingdom, for the everlasting light shall shine upon you for evermore.

[36] Flee the shadow of this world, receive the joyfulness of your glory: I testify my Saviour openly.

[37] O receive the gift that is given you, and be glad, giving thanks unto him that hath led you to the heavenly kingdom.

[38] Arise up and stand, behold the number of those that be sealed in the feast of the Lord;

[39] Which are departed from the shadow of the world, and have received glorious garments of the Lord.

[40] Take thy number, O Sion, and shut up those of thine that are clothed in white, which have fulfilled the law of the Lord.

[41] The number of thy children, whom thou longedst for, is fulfilled: beseech the power of the Lord, that thy people, which have been called from the beginning, may be hallowed.

[42] I Esdras saw upon the mount Sion a great people, whom I could not number, and they all praised the Lord with songs.

[43] And in the midst of them there was a young man of a high stature, taller than all the rest, and upon every one of their heads he set crowns, and was more exalted; which I marvelled at greatly.

[44] So I asked the angel, and said, Sir, what are these?

[45] He answered and said unto me, These be they that have put off the mortal clothing, and put on the immortal, and have confessed the name of God: now are they crowned, and receive palms.

[46] Then said I unto the angel, What young person is it that crowneth them, and giveth them palms in their hands?

[47] So he answered and said unto me, It is the Son of God, whom they have confessed in the world. Then began I greatly to commend them that stood so stiffly for the name of the Lord.

[48] Then the angel said unto me, Go thy way, and tell my people what manner of things, and how great wonders of the Lord thy God, thou hast seen.

2Ezra.3

[1] In the thirtieth year after the ruin of the city I was in Babylon, and lay troubled upon my bed, and my thoughts came up over my heart:

[2] For I saw the desolation of Sion, and the wealth of them that dwelt at Babylon.

[3] And my spirit was sore moved, so that I began to speak words full of fear to the most High, and said,

[4] O Lord, who bearest rule, thou spakest at the beginning, when thou didst plant the earth, and that thyself alone, and commandedst the people,

[5] And gavest a body unto Adam without soul, which was the workmanship of thine hands, and didst breathe into him the breath of life, and he was made living before thee.

[6] And thou leadest him into paradise, which thy right hand had planted, before ever the earth came forward.

[7] And unto him thou gavest commandment to love thy way: which he transgressed, and immediately thou appointedst death in him and in his generations, of whom came nations, tribes, people, and kindreds, out of number.

[8] And every people walked after their own will, and did wonderful things before thee, and despised thy commandments.

[9] And again in process of time thou broughtest the flood upon those that dwelt in the world, and destroyedst them.

[10] And it came to pass in every of them, that as death was to Adam, so was the flood to these.

[11] Nevertheless one of them thou leftest, namely, Noah with his household, of whom came all righteous men.

[12] And it happened, that when they that dwelt upon the earth began to multiply, and had gotten them many children, and were a great people, they began again to be more ungodly than the first.

[13] Now when they lived so wickedly before thee, thou didst choose thee a man from among them, whose name was Abraham.

[14] Him thou lovedst, and unto him only thou shewedst thy will:

[15] And madest an everlasting covenant with him, promising him that thou wouldest never forsake his seed.

[16] And unto him thou gavest Isaac, and unto Isaac also thou gavest Jacob and Esau. As for Jacob, thou didst choose him to thee, and put by Esau: and so Jacob became a great multitude .

[17] And it came to pass, that when thou leadest his seed out of Egypt, thou broughtest them up to the mount Sinai.

[18] And bowing the heavens, thou didst set fast the earth, movedst the whole world, and madest the depths to tremble, and troubledst the men of that age.

[19] And thy glory went through four gates, of fire, and of earthquake, and of wind, and of cold; that thou mightest give the law unto the seed of Jacob, and diligence unto the generation of Israel.

[20] And yet tookest thou not away from them a wicked heart, that thy law might bring forth fruit in them.

[21] For the first Adam bearing a wicked heart transgressed, and was overcome; and so be all they that are born of him.

[22] Thus infirmity was made permanent; and the law (also) in the heart of the people with the malignity of the root; so that the good departed away, and the evil abode still.

[23] So the times passed away, and the years were brought to an end: then didst thou raise thee up a servant, called David:

[24] Whom thou commandedst to build a city unto thy name, and to offer incense and oblations unto thee therein.

[25] When this was done many years, then they that inhabited the city forsook thee,

[26] And in all things did even as Adam and all his generations had done: for they also had a wicked heart:

[27] And so thou gavest thy city over into the hands of thine enemies.

[28] Are their deeds then any better that inhabit Babylon, that they should therefore have the dominion over Sion?

[29] For when I came thither, and had seen impieties without number, then my soul saw many evildoers in this thirtieth year, so that my heart failed me.

[30] For I have seen how thou sufferest them sinning, and hast spared wicked doers: and hast destroyed thy people, and hast preserved thine enemies, and hast not signified it.

[31] I do not remember how this way may be left: Are they then of Babylon better than they of Sion?

[32] Or is there any other people that knoweth thee beside Israel? or what generation hath so believed thy covenants as Jacob?

[33] And yet their reward appeareth not, and their labour hath no fruit: for I have gone here and there through the heathen, and I see that they flow in wealth, and think not upon thy commandments.

[34] Weigh thou therefore our wickedness now in the balance, and their's also that dwell the world; and so shall thy name no where be found but in Israel.

[35] Or when was it that they which dwell upon the earth have not sinned in thy sight? or what people have so kept thy commandments?

[36] Thou shalt find that Israel by name hath kept thy precepts; but not the heathen.

2Ezra.4

[1] And the angel that was sent unto me, whose name was Uriel, gave me an answer,

[2] And said, Thy heart hath gone to far in this world, and thinkest thou to comprehend the way of the most High?

[3] Then said I, Yea, my lord. And he answered me, and said, I am sent to shew thee three ways, and to set forth three similitudes before thee:

[4] Whereof if thou canst declare me one, I will shew thee also the way that thou desirest to see, and I shall shew thee from whence the wicked heart cometh.

[5] And I said, Tell on, my lord. Then said he unto me, Go thy way, weigh me the weight of the fire, or measure me the blast of the wind, or call me again the day that is past.

[6] Then answered I and said, What man is able to do that, that thou shouldest ask such things of me?

[7] And he said unto me, If I should ask thee how great dwellings are in the midst of the sea, or how many springs are in the beginning of the deep, or how many springs are above the firmament, or which are the outgoings of paradise:

[8] Peradventure thou wouldest say unto me, I never went down into the deep, nor as yet into hell, neither did I ever climb up into heaven.

[9] Nevertheless now have I asked thee but only of the fire and wind, and of the day wherethrough thou hast passed, and of things from which thou canst not be separated, and yet canst thou give me no answer of them.

[10] He said moreover unto me, Thine own things, and such as are grown up with thee, canst thou not know;

[11] How should thy vessel then be able to comprehend the way of the Highest, and, the world being now outwardly corrupted to understand the corruption that is evident in my sight?

[12] Then said I unto him, It were better that we were not at all, than that we should live still in wickedness, and to

suffer, and not to know wherefore.

[13] He answered me, and said, I went into a forest into a plain, and the trees took counsel,

[14] And said, Come, let us go and make war against the sea that it may depart away before us, and that we may make us more woods.

[15] The floods of the sea also in like manner took counsel, and said, Come, let us go up and subdue the woods of the plain, that there also we may make us another country.

[16] The thought of the wood was in vain, for the fire came and consumed it.

[17] The thought of the floods of the sea came likewise to nought, for the sand stood up and stopped them.

[18] If thou wert judge now betwixt these two, whom wouldest thou begin to justify? or whom wouldest thou condemn?

[19] I answered and said, Verily it is a foolish thought that they both have devised, for the ground is given unto the wood, and the sea also hath his place to bear his floods.

[20] Then answered he me, and said, Thou hast given a right judgment, but why judgest thou not thyself also?

[21] For like as the ground is given unto the wood, and the sea to his floods: even so they that dwell upon the earth may understand nothing but that which is upon the earth: and he that dwelleth above the heavens may only understand the things that are above the height of the heavens.

[22] Then answered I and said, I beseech thee, O Lord, let me have understanding:

[23] For it was not my mind to be curious of the high things, but of such as pass by us daily, namely, wherefore Israel is given up as a reproach to the heathen, and for what cause the people whom thou hast loved is given over unto ungodly nations, and why the law of our forefathers is brought to nought, and the written covenants come to none effect,

[24] And we pass away out of the world as grasshoppers, and our life is astonishment and fear, and we are not worthy to obtain mercy.

[25] What will he then do unto his name whereby we are called? of these things have I asked.

[26] Then answered he me, and said, The more thou searchest, the more thou shalt marvel; for the world hasteth fast to pass away,

[27] And cannot comprehend the things that are promised to the righteous in time to come: for this world is full of unrighteousness and infirmities.

[28] But as concerning the things whereof thou askest me, I will tell thee; for the evil is sown, but the destruction thereof is not yet come.

[29] If therefore that which is sown be not turned upside down, and if the place where the evil is sown pass not away, then cannot it come that is sown with good.

[30] For the grain of evil seed hath been sown in the heart of Adam from the beginning, and how much ungodliness hath it brought up unto this time? and how much shall it yet bring forth until the time of threshing come?

[31] Ponder now by thyself, how great fruit of wickedness the grain of evil seed hath brought forth.

[32] And when the ears shall be cut down, which are without number, how great a floor shall they fill?

[33] Then I answered and said, How, and when shall these things come to pass? wherefore are our years few and evil?

[34] And he answered me, saying, Do not thou hasten above the most Highest: for thy haste is in vain to be above him, for thou hast much exceeded.

[35] Did not the souls also of the righteous ask question of these things in their chambers, saying, How long shall I hope on this fashion? when cometh the fruit of the floor of our reward?

[36] And unto these things Uriel the archangel gave them answer, and said, Even when the number of seeds is filled in you: for he hath weighed the world in the balance.

[37] By measure hath he measured the times; and by number hath he numbered the times; and he doth not move nor stir them, until the said measure be fulfilled.

[38] Then answered I and said, O Lord that bearest rule, even we all are full of impiety.

[39] And for our sakes peradventure it is that the floors of the righteous are not filled, because of the sins of them that dwell upon the earth.

[40] So he answered me, and said, Go thy way to a woman with child, and ask of her when she hath fulfilled her nine months, if her womb may keep the birth any longer within her.

[41] Then said I, No, Lord, that can she not. And he said unto me, In the grave the chambers of souls are like the womb of a woman:

[42] For like as a woman that travaileth maketh haste to escape the necessity of the travail: even so do these places haste to deliver those things that are committed unto them.

[43] From the beginning, look, what thou desirest to see, it shall be shewed thee.

[44] Then answered I and said, If I have found favour in thy sight, and if it be possible, and if I be meet therefore,

[45] Shew me then whether there be more to come than is past, or more past than is to come.

[46] What is past I know, but what is for to come I know not.

[47] And he said unto me, Stand up upon the right side, and I shall expound the similitude unto thee.

[48] So I stood, and saw, and, behold, an hot burning oven

passed by before me: and it happened that when the flame was gone by I looked, and, behold, the smoke remained still.

[49] After this there passed by before me a watery cloud, and sent down much rain with a storm; and when the stormy rain was past, the drops remained still.

[50] Then said he unto me, Consider with thyself; as the rain is more than the drops, and as the fire is greater than the smoke; but the drops and the smoke remain behind: so the quantity which is past did more exceed.

[51] Then I prayed, and said, May I live, thinkest thou, until that time? or what shall happen in those days?

[52] He answered me, and said, As for the tokens whereof thou askest me, I may tell thee of them in part: but as touching thy life, I am not sent to shew thee; for I do not know it.

2Ezra.5

[1] Nevertheless as coming the tokens, behold, the days shall come, that they which dwell upon earth shall be taken in a great number, and the way of truth shall be hidden, and the land shall be barren of faith.

[2] But iniquity shall be increased above that which now thou seest, or that thou hast heard long ago.

[3] And the land, that thou seest now to have root, shalt thou see wasted suddenly.

[4] But if the most High grant thee to live, thou shalt see after the third trumpet that the sun shall suddenly shine again in the night, and the moon thrice in the day:

[5] And blood shall drop out of wood, and the stone shall give his voice, and the people shall be troubled:

[6] And even he shall rule, whom they look not for that dwell upon the earth, and the fowls shall take their flight away together:

[7] And the Sodomitish sea shall cast out fish, and make a noise in the night, which many have not known: but they shall all hear the voice thereof.

[8] There shall be a confusion also in many places, and the fire shall be oft sent out again, and the wild beasts shall change their places, and menstruous women shall bring forth monsters:

[9] And salt waters shall be found in the sweet, and all friends shall destroy one another; then shall wit hide itself, and understanding withdraw itself into his secret chamber,

[10] And shall be sought of many, and yet not be found: then shall unrighteousness and incontinency be multiplied upon earth.

[11] One land also shall ask another, and say, Is righteousness that maketh a man righteous gone through thee? And it shall say, No.

[12] At the same time shall men hope, but nothing obtain: they shall labour, but their ways shall not prosper.

[13] To shew thee such tokens I have leave; and if thou wilt pray again, and weep as now, and fast even days, thou shalt hear yet greater things.

[14] Then I awaked, and an extreme fearfulness went through all my body, and my mind was troubled, so that it fainted.

[15] So the angel that was come to talk with me held me, comforted me, and set me up upon my feet.

[16] And in the second night it came to pass, that Salathiel the captain of the people came unto me, saying, Where hast thou been? and why is thy countenance so heavy?

[17] Knowest thou not that Israel is committed unto thee in the land of their captivity?

[18] Up then, and eat bread, and forsake us not, as the shepherd that leaveth his flock in the hands of cruel wolves.

[19] Then said I unto him, Go thy ways from me, and come not nigh me. And he heard what I said, and went from me.

[20] And so I fasted seven days, mourning and weeping, like as Uriel the angel commanded me.

[21] And after seven days so it was, that the thoughts of my heart were very grievous unto me again,

[22] And my soul recovered the spirit of understanding, and I began to talk with the most High again,

[23] And said, O Lord that bearest rule, of every wood of the earth, and of all the trees thereof, thou hast chosen thee one only vine:

[24] And of all lands of the whole world thou hast chosen thee one pit: and of all the flowers thereof one lily:

[25] And of all the depths of the sea thou hast filled thee one river: and of all builded cities thou hast hallowed Sion unto thyself:

[26] And of all the fowls that are created thou hast named thee one dove: and of all the cattle that are made thou hast provided thee one sheep:

[27] And among all the multitudes of people thou hast gotten thee one people: and unto this people, whom thou lovedst, thou gavest a law that is approved of all.

[28] And now, O Lord, why hast thou given this one people over unto many? and upon the one root hast thou prepared others, and why hast thou scattered thy only one people among many?

[29] And they which did gainsay thy promises, and believed not thy covenants, have trodden them down.

[30] If thou didst so much hate thy people, yet shouldest thou punish them with thine own hands.

[31] Now when I had spoken these words, the angel that

came to me the night afore was sent unto me,

[32] And said unto me, Hear me, and I will instruct thee; hearken to the thing that I say, and I shall tell thee more.

[33] And I said, Speak on, my Lord. Then said he unto me, Thou art sore troubled in mind for Israel's sake: lovest thou that people better than he that made them?

[34] And I said, No, Lord: but of very grief have I spoken: for my reins pain me every hour, while I labour to comprehend the way of the most High, and to seek out part of his judgment.

[35] And he said unto me, Thou canst not. And I said, Wherefore, Lord? whereunto was I born then? or why was not my mother's womb then my grave, that I might not have seen the travail of Jacob, and the wearisome toil of the stock of Israel?

[36] And he said unto me, Number me the things that are not yet come, gather me together the dross that are scattered abroad, make me the flowers green again that are withered,

[37] Open me the places that are closed, and bring me forth the winds that in them are shut up, shew me the image of a voice: and then I will declare to thee the thing that thou labourest to know.

[38] And I said, O Lord that bearest rule, who may know these things, but he that hath not his dwelling with men?

[39] As for me, I am unwise: how may I then speak of these things whereof thou askest me?

[40] Then said he unto me, Like as thou canst do none of these things that I have spoken of, even so canst thou not find out my judgment, or in the end the love that I have promised unto my people.

[41] And I said, Behold, O Lord, yet art thou nigh unto them that be reserved till the end: and what shall they do that have been before me, or we that be now, or they that shall come after us?

[42] And he said unto me, I will liken my judgment unto a ring: like as there is no slackness of the last, even so there is no swiftness of the first.

[43] So I answered and said, Couldest thou not make those that have been made, and be now, and that are for to come, at once; that thou mightest shew thy judgment the sooner?

[44] Then answered he me, and said, The creature may not haste above the maker; neither may the world hold them at once that shall be created therein.

[45] And I said, As thou hast said unto thy servant, that thou, which givest life to all, hast given life at once to the creature that thou hast created, and the creature bare it: even so it might now also bear them that now be present at once.

[46] And he said unto me, Ask the womb of a woman, and say unto her, If thou bringest forth children, why dost thou it not together, but one after another? pray her therefore to bring forth ten children at once.

[47] And I said, She cannot: but must do it by distance of time.

[48] Then said he unto me, Even so have I given the womb of the earth to those that be sown in it in their times.

[49] For like as a young child may not bring forth the things that belong to the aged, even so have I disposed the world which I created.

[50] And I asked, and said, Seeing thou hast now given me the way, I will proceed to speak before thee: for our mother, of whom thou hast told me that she is young, draweth now nigh unto age.

[51] He answered me, and said, Ask a woman that beareth children, and she shall tell thee.

[52] Say unto her, Wherefore are unto they whom thou hast now brought forth like those that were before, but less of stature?

[53] And she shall answer thee, They that be born in the the strength of youth are of one fashion, and they that are born in the time of age, when the womb faileth, are otherwise.

[54] Consider thou therefore also, how that ye are less of stature than those that were before you.

[55] And so are they that come after you less than ye, as the creatures which now begin to be old, and have passed over the strength of youth.

[56] Then said I, Lord, I beseech thee, if I have found favour in thy sight, shew thy servant by whom thou visitest thy creature.

2Ezra.6

[1] And he said unto me, In the beginning, when the earth was made, before the borders of the world stood, or ever the winds blew,

[2] Before it thundered and lightened, or ever the foundations of paradise were laid,

[3] Before the fair flowers were seen, or ever the moveable powers were established, before the innumerable multitude of angels were gathered together,

[4] Or ever the heights of the air were lifted up, before the measures of the firmament were named, or ever the chimneys in Sion were hot,

[5] And ere the present years were sought out, and or ever the inventions of them that now sin were turned, before they were sealed that have gathered faith for a treasure:

[6] Then did I consider these things, and they all were made through me alone, and through none other: by me also they shall be ended, and by none other.

[7] Then answered I and said, What shall be the parting asunder of the times? or when shall be the end of the first, and the beginning of it that followeth?

[8] And he said unto me, From Abraham unto Isaac, when Jacob and Esau were born of him, Jacob's hand held first the heel of Esau.

[9] For Esau is the end of the world, and Jacob is the beginning of it that followeth.

[10] The hand of man is betwixt the heel and the hand: other question, Esdras, ask thou not.

[11] I answered then and said, O Lord that bearest rule, if I have found favour in thy sight,

[12] I beseech thee, shew thy servant the end of thy tokens, whereof thou shewedst me part the last night.

[13] So he answered and said unto me, Stand up upon thy feet, and hear a mighty sounding voice.

[14] And it shall be as it were a great motion; but the place where thou standest shall not be moved.

[15] And therefore when it speaketh be not afraid: for the word is of the end, and the foundation of the earth is understood.

[16] And why? because the speech of these things trembleth and is moved: for it knoweth that the end of these things must be changed.

[17] And it happened, that when I had heard it I stood up upon my feet, and hearkened, and, behold, there was a voice that spake, and the sound of it was like the sound of many waters.

[18] And it said, Behold, the days come, that I will begin to draw nigh, and to visit them that dwell upon the earth,

[19] And will begin to make inquisition of them, what they be that have hurt unjustly with their unrighteousness, and when the affliction of Sion shall be fulfilled;

[20] And when the world, that shall begin to vanish away, shall be finished, then will I shew these tokens: the books shall be opened before the firmament, and they shall see all together:

[21] And the children of a year old shall speak with their voices, the women with child shall bring forth untimely children of three or four months old, and they shall live, and be raised up.

[22] And suddenly shall the sown places appear unsown, the full storehouses shall suddenly be found empty:

[23] And tha trumpet shall give a sound, which when every man heareth, they shall be suddenly afraid.

[24] At that time shall friends fight one against another like enemies, and the earth shall stand in fear with those that dwell therein, the springs of the fountains shall stand still, and in three hours they shall not run.

[25] Whosoever remaineth from all these that I have told thee shall escape, and see my salvation, and the end of your world.

[26] And the men that are received shall see it, who have not tasted death from their birth: and the heart of the inhabitants shall be changed, and turned into another meaning.

[27] For evil shall be put out, and deceit shall be quenched.

[28] As for faith, it shall flourish, corruption shall be overcome, and the truth, which hath been so long without fruit, shall be declared.

[29] And when he talked with me, behold, I looked by little and little upon him before whom I stood.

[30] And these words said he unto me; I am come to shew thee the time of the night to come.

[31] If thou wilt pray yet more, and fast seven days again, I shall tell thee greater things by day than I have heard.

[32] For thy voice is heard before the most High: for the Mighty hath seen thy righteous dealing, he hath seen also thy chastity, which thou hast had ever since thy youth.

[33] And therefore hath he sent me to shew thee all these things, and to say unto thee, Be of good comfort and fear not

[34] And hasten not with the times that are past, to think vain things, that thou mayest not hasten from the latter times.

[35] And it came to pass after this, that I wept again, and fasted seven days in like manner, that I might fulfil the three weeks which he told me.

[36] And in the eighth night was my heart vexed within me again, and I began to speak before the most High.

[37] For my spirit was greatly set on fire, and my soul was in distress.

[38] And I said, O Lord, thou spakest from the beginning of the creation, even the first day, and saidst thus; Let heaven and earth be made; and thy word was a perfect work.

[39] And then was the spirit, and darkness and silence were on every side; the sound of man's voice was not yet formed.

[40] Then commandedst thou a fair light to come forth of thy treasures, that thy work might appear.

[41] Upon the second day thou madest the spirit of the firmament, and commandedst it to part asunder, and to make a division betwixt the waters, that the one part might go up, and the other remain beneath.

[42] Upon the third day thou didst command that the waters should be gathered in the seventh part of the earth: six pats hast thou dried up, and kept them, to the intent that of these some being planted of God and tilled might serve thee.

[43] For as soon as thy word went forth the work was made.

[44] For immediately there was great and innumerable

fruit, and many and divers pleasures for the taste, and flowers of unchangeable colour, and odours of wonderful smell: and this was done the third day.

[45] Upon the fourth day thou commandedst that the sun should shine, and the moon give her light, and the stars should be in order:

[46] And gavest them a charge to do service unto man, that was to be made.

[47] Upon the fifth day thou saidst unto the seventh part, where the waters were gathered that it should bring forth living creatures, fowls and fishes: and so it came to pass.

[48] For the dumb water and without life brought forth living things at the commandment of God, that all people might praise thy wondrous works.

[49] Then didst thou ordain two living creatures, the one thou calledst Enoch, and the other Leviathan;

[50] And didst separate the one from the other: for the seventh part, namely, where the water was gathered together, might not hold them both.

[51] Unto Enoch thou gavest one part, which was dried up the third day, that he should dwell in the same part, wherein are a thousand hills:

[52] But unto Leviathan thou gavest the seventh part, namely, the moist; and hast kept him to be devoured of whom thou wilt, and when.

[53] Upon the sixth day thou gavest commandment unto the earth, that before thee it should bring forth beasts, cattle, and creeping things:

[54] And after these, Adam also, whom thou madest lord of all thy creatures: of him come we all, and the people also whom thou hast chosen.

[55] All this have I spoken before thee, O Lord, because thou madest the world for our sakes

[56] As for the other people, which also come of Adam, thou hast said that they are nothing, but be like unto spittle: and hast likened the abundance of them unto a drop that falleth from a vessel.

[57] And now, O Lord, behold, these heathen, which have ever been reputed as nothing, have begun to be lords over us, and to devour us.

[58] But we thy people, whom thou hast called thy firstborn, thy only begotten, and thy fervent lover, are given into their hands.

[59] If the world now be made for our sakes, why do we not possess an inheritance with the world? how long shall this endure?

2Ezra.7

[1] And when I had made an end of speaking these words, there was sent unto me the angel which had been sent unto me the nights afore:

[2] And he said unto me, Up, Esdras, and hear the words that I am come to tell thee.

[3] And I said, Speak on, my God. Then said he unto me, The sea is set in a wide place, that it might be deep and great.

[4] But put the case the entrance were narrow, and like a river;

[5] Who then could go into the sea to look upon it, and to rule it? if he went not through the narrow, how could he come into the broad?

[6] There is also another thing; A city is builded, and set upon a broad field, and is full of all good things:

[7] The entrance thereof is narrow, and is set in a dangerous place to fall, like as if there were a fire on the right hand, and on the left a deep water:

[8] And one only path between them both, even between the fire and the water, so small that there could but one man go there at once.

[9] If this city now were given unto a man for an inheritance, if he never shall pass the danger set before it, how shall he receive this inheritance?

[10] And I said, It is so, Lord. Then said he unto me, Even so also is Israel's portion.

[11] Because for their sakes I made the world: and when Adam transgressed my statutes, then was decreed that now is done.

[12] Then were the entrances of this world made narrow, full of sorrow and travail: they are but few and evil, full of perils,: and very painful.

[13] For the entrances of the elder world were wide and sure, and brought immortal fruit.

[14] If then they that live labour not to enter these strait and vain things, they can never receive those that are laid up for them.

[15] Now therefore why disquietest thou thyself, seeing thou art but a corruptible man? and why art thou moved, whereas thou art but mortal?

[16] Why hast thou not considered in thy mind this thing that is to come, rather than that which is present?

[17] Then answered I and said, O Lord that bearest rule, thou hast ordained in thy law, that the righteous should inherit these things, but that the ungodly should perish.

[18] Nevertheless the righteous shall suffer strait things, and hope for wide: for they that have done wickedly have suffered the strait things, and yet shall not see the wide.

[19] And he said unto me. There is no judge above God, and

none that hath understanding above the Highest.

[20] For there be many that perish in this life, because they despise the law of God that is set before them.

[21] For God hath given strait commandment to such as came, what they should do to live, even as they came, and what they should observe to avoid punishment.

[22] Nevertheless they were not obedient unto him; but spake against him, and imagined vain things;

[23] And deceived themselves by their wicked deeds; and said of the most High, that he is not; and knew not his ways:

[24] But his law have they despised, and denied his covenants; in his statutes have they not been faithful, and have not performed his works.

[25] And therefore, Esdras, for the empty are empty things, and for the full are the full things.

[26] Behold, the time shall come, that these tokens which I have told thee shall come to pass, and the bride shall appear, and she coming forth shall be seen, that now is withdrawn from the earth.

[27] And whosoever is delivered from the foresaid evils shall see my wonders.

[28] For my son Jesus shall be revealed with those that be with him, and they that remain shall rejoice within four hundred years.

[29] After these years shall my son Christ die, and all men that have life.

[30] And the world shall be turned into the old silence seven days, like as in the former judgments: so that no man shall remain.

[31] And after seven days the world, that yet awaketh not, shall be raised up, and that shall die that is corrupt

[32] And the earth shall restore those that are asleep in her, and so shall the dust those that dwell in silence, and the secret places shall deliver those souls that were committed unto them.

[33] And the most High shall appear upon the seat of judgment, and misery shall pass away, and the long suffering shall have an end:

[34] But judgment only shall remain, truth shall stand, and faith shall wax strong:

[35] And the work shall follow, and the reward shall be shewed, and the good deeds shall be of force, and wicked deeds shall bear no rule.

[36] Then said I, Abraham prayed first for the Sodomites, and Moses for the fathers that sinned in the wilderness:

[37] And Jesus after him for Israel in the time of Achan:

[38] And Samuel and David for the destruction: and Solomon for them that should come to the sanctuary:

[39] And Helias for those that received rain; and for the dead, that he might live:

[40] And Ezechias for the people in the time of Sennacherib: and many for many.

[41] Even so now, seeing corruption is grown up, and wickedness increased, and the righteous have prayed for the ungodly: wherefore shall it not be so now also?

[42] He answered me, and said, This present life is not the end where much glory doth abide; therefore have they prayed for the weak.

[43] But the day of doom shall be the end of this time, and the beginning of the immortality for to come, wherein corruption is past,

[44] Intemperance is at an end, infidelity is cut off, righteousness is grown, and truth is sprung up.

[45] Then shall no man be able to save him that is destroyed, nor to oppress him that hath gotten the victory.

[46] I answered then and said, This is my first and last saying, that it had been better not to have given the earth unto Adam: or else, when it was given him, to have restrained him from sinning.

[47] For what profit is it for men now in this present time to live in heaviness, and after death to look for punishment?

[48] O thou Adam, what hast thou done? for though it was thou that sinned, thou art not fallen alone, but we all that come of thee.

[49] For what profit is it unto us, if there be promised us an immortal time, whereas we have done the works that bring death?

[50] And that there is promised us an everlasting hope, whereas ourselves being most wicked are made vain?

[51] And that there are laid up for us dwellings of health and safety, whereas we have lived wickedly?

[52] And that the glory of the most High is kept to defend them which have led a wary life, whereas we have walked in the most wicked ways of all?

[53] And that there should be shewed a paradise, whose fruit endureth for ever, wherein is security and medicine, since we shall not enter into it?

[54] (For we have walked in unpleasant places.)

[55] And that the faces of them which have used abstinence shall shine above the stars, whereas our faces shall be blacker than darkness?

[56] For while we lived and committed iniquity, we considered not that we should begin to suffer for it after death.

[57] Then answered he me, and said, This is the condition of the battle, which man that is born upon the earth shall fight;

[58] That, if he be overcome, he shall suffer as thou hast said: but if he get the victory, he shall receive the thing that I say.

[59] For this is the life whereof Moses spake unto the people while he lived, saying, Choose thee life, that thou mayest live.

[60] Nevertheless they believed not him, nor yet the prophets after him, no nor me which have spoken unto them,

[61] That there should not be such heaviness in their destruction, as shall be joy over them that are persuaded to salvation.

[62] I answered then, and said, I know, Lord, that the most High is called merciful, in that he hath mercy upon them which are not yet come into the world,

[63] And upon those also that turn to his law;

[64] And that he is patient, and long suffereth those that have sinned, as his creatures;

[65] And that he is bountiful, for he is ready to give where it needeth;

[66] And that he is of great mercy, for he multiplieth more and more mercies to them that are present, and that are past, and also to them which are to come.

[67] For if he shall not multiply his mercies, the world would not continue with them that inherit therein.

[68] And he pardoneth; for if he did not so of his goodness, that they which have committed iniquities might be eased of them, the ten thousandth part of men should not remain living.

[69] And being judge, if he should not forgive them that are cured with his word, and put out the multitude of contentions,

[70] There should be very few left peradventure in an innumerable multitude.

2Ezra.8

[1] And he answered me, saying, The most High hath made this world for many, but the world to come for few.

[2] I will tell thee a similitude, Esdras; As when thou askest the earth, it shall say unto thee, that it giveth much mould whereof earthen vessels are made, but little dust that gold cometh of: even so is the course of this present world.

[3] There be many created, but few shall be saved.

[4] So answered I and said, Swallow then down, O my soul, understanding, and devour wisdom.

[5] For thou hast agreed to give ear, and art willing to prophesy: for thou hast no longer space than only to live.

[6] O Lord, if thou suffer not thy servant, that we may pray before thee, and thou give us seed unto our heart, and culture to our understanding, that there may come fruit of it; how shall each man live that is corrupt, who beareth the place of a man?

[7] For thou art alone, and we all one workmanship of thine hands, like as thou hast said.

[8] For when the body is fashioned now in the mother's womb, and thou givest it members, thy creature is preserved in fire and water, and nine months doth thy workmanship endure thy creature which is created in her.

[9] But that which keepeth and is kept shall both be preserved: and when the time cometh, the womb preserved delivereth up the things that grew in it.

[10] For thou hast commanded out of the parts of the body, that is to say, out of the breasts, milk to be given, which is the fruit of the breasts,

[11] That the thing which is fashioned may be nourished for a time, till thou disposest it to thy mercy.

[12] Thou broughtest it up with thy righteousness, and nurturedst it in thy law, and reformedst it with thy judgment.

[13] And thou shalt mortify it as thy creature, and quicken it as thy work.

[14] If therefore thou shalt destroy him which with so great labour was fashioned, it is an easy thing to be ordained by thy commandment, that the thing which was made might be preserved.

[15] Now therefore, Lord, I will speak; touching man in general, thou knowest best; but touching thy people, for whose sake I am sorry;

[16] And for thine inheritance, for whose cause I mourn; and for Israel, for whom I am heavy; and for Jacob, for whose sake I am troubled;

[17] Therefore will I begin to pray before thee for myself and for them: for I see the falls of us that dwell in the land.

[18] But I have heard the swiftness of the judge which is to come.

[19] Therefore hear my voice, and understand my words, and I shall speak before thee. This is the beginning of the words of Esdras, before he was taken up: and I said,

[20] O Lord, thou that dwellest in everlastingness which beholdest from above things in the heaven and in the air;

[21] Whose throne is inestimable; whose glory may not be comprehended; before whom the hosts of angels stand with trembling,

[22] Whose service is conversant in wind and fire; whose word is true, and sayings constant; whose commandment is strong, and ordinance fearful;

[23] Whose look drieth up the depths, and indignation maketh the mountains to melt away; which the truth witnesseth:

[24] O hear the prayer of thy servant, and give ear to the petition of thy creature.

[25] For while I live I will speak, and so long as I have

understanding I will answer.

[26] O look not upon the sins of thy people; but on them which serve thee in truth.

[27] Regard not the wicked inventions of the heathen, but the desire of those that keep thy testimonies in afflictions.

[28] Think not upon those that have walked feignedly before thee: but remember them, which according to thy will have known thy fear.

[29] Let it not be thy will to destroy them which have lived like beasts; but to look upon them that have clearly taught thy law.

[30] Take thou no indignation at them which are deemed worse than beasts; but love them that always put their trust in thy righteousness and glory.

[31] For we and our fathers do languish of such diseases: but because of us sinners thou shalt be called merciful.

[32] For if thou hast a desire to have mercy upon us, thou shalt be called merciful, to us namely, that have no works of righteousness.

[33] For the just, which have many good works laid up with thee, shall out of their own deeds receive reward.

[34] For what is man, that thou shouldest take displeasure at him? or what is a corruptible generation, that thou shouldest be so bitter toward it?

[35] For in truth them is no man among them that be born, but he hath dealt wickedly; and among the faithful there is none which hath not done amiss.

[36] For in this, O Lord, thy righteousness and thy goodness shall be declared, if thou be merciful unto them which have not the confidence of good works.

[37] Then answered he me, and said, Some things hast thou spoken aright, and according unto thy words it shall be.

[38] For indeed I will not think on the disposition of them which have sinned before death, before judgment, before destruction:

[39] But I will rejoice over the disposition of the righteous, and I will remember also their pilgrimage, and the salvation, and the reward, that they shall have.

[40] Like as I have spoken now, so shall it come to pass.

[41] For as the husbandman soweth much seed upon the ground, and planteth many trees, and yet the thing that is sown good in his season cometh not up, neither doth all that is planted take root: even so is it of them that are sown in the world; they shall not all be saved.

[42] I answered then and said, If I have found grace, let me speak.

[43] Like as the husbandman's seed perisheth, if it come not up, and receive not thy rain in due season; or if there come too much rain, and corrupt it:

[44] Even so perisheth man also, which is formed with thy hands, and is called thine own image, because thou art like unto him, for whose sake thou hast made all things, and likened him unto the husbandman's seed.

[45] Be not wroth with us but spare thy people, and have mercy upon thine own inheritance: for thou art merciful unto thy creature.

[46] Then answered he me, and said, Things present are for the present, and things to cometh for such as be to come.

[47] For thou comest far short that thou shouldest be able to love my creature more than I: but I have ofttimes drawn nigh unto thee, and unto it, but never to the unrighteous.

[48] In this also thou art marvellous before the most High:

[49] In that thou hast humbled thyself, as it becometh thee, and hast not judged thyself worthy to be much glorified among the righteous.

[50] For many great miseries shall be done to them that in the latter time shall dwell in the world, because they have walked in great pride.

[51] But understand thou for thyself, and seek out the glory for such as be like thee.

[52] For unto you is paradise opened, the tree of life is planted, the time to come is prepared, plenteousness is made ready, a city is builded, and rest is allowed, yea, perfect goodness and wisdom.

[53] The root of evil is sealed up from you, weakness and the moth is hid from you, and corruption is fled into hell to be forgotten:

[54] Sorrows are passed, and in the end is shewed the treasure of immortality.

[55] And therefore ask thou no more questions concerning the multitude of them that perish.

[56] For when they had taken liberty, they despised the most High, thought scorn of his law, and forsook his ways.

[57] Moreover they have trodden down his righteous,

[58] And said in their heart, that there is no God; yea, and that knowing they must die.

[59] For as the things aforesaid shalt receive you, so thirst and pain are prepared for them: for it was not his will that men should come to nought:

[60] But they which be created have defiled the name of him that made them, and were unthankful unto him which prepared life for them.

[61] And therefore is my judgment now at hand.

[62] These things have I not shewed unto all men, but unto thee, and a few like thee. Then answered I and said,

[63] Behold, O Lord, now hast thou shewed me the multitude of the wonders, which thou wilt begin to do in the last times: but at what time, thou hast not shewed me.

[1] He answered me then, and said, Measure thou the time diligently in itself: and when thou seest part of the signs past, which I have told thee before,

[2] Then shalt thou understand, that it is the very same time, wherein the Highest will begin to visit the world which he made.

[3] Therefore when there shall be seen earthquakes and uproars of the people in the world:

[4] Then shalt thou well understand, that the most High spake of those things from the days that were before thee, even from the beginning.

[5] For like as all that is made in the world hath a beginning and an end, and the end is manifest:

[6] Even so the times also of the Highest have plain beginnings in wonder and powerful works, and endings in effects and signs.

[7] And every one that shall be saved, and shall be able to escape by his works, and by faith, whereby ye have believed,

[8] Shall be preserved from the said perils, and shall see my salvation in my land, and within my borders: for I have sanctified them for me from the beginning.

[9] Then shall they be in pitiful case, which now have abused my ways: and they that have cast them away despitefully shall dwell in torments.

[10] For such as in their life have received benefits, and have not known me;

[11] And they that have loathed my law, while they had yet liberty, and, when as yet place of repentance was open unto them, understood not, but despised it;

[12] The same must know it after death by pain.

[13] And therefore be thou not curious how the ungodly shall be punished, and when: but enquire how the righteous shall be saved, whose the world is, and for whom the world is created.

[14] Then answered I and said,

[15] I have said before, and now do speak, and will speak it also hereafter, that there be many more of them which perish, than of them which shall be saved:

[16] Like as a wave is greater than a drop.

[17] And he answered me, saying, Like as the field is, so is also the seed; as the flowers be, such are the colours also; such as the workman is, such also is the work; and as the husbandman ls himself, so is his husbandry also: for it was the time of the world.

[18] And now when I prepared the world, which was not yet made, even for them to dwell in that now live, no man spake against me.

[19] For then every one obeyed: but now the manners of them which are created in this world that is made are corrupted by a perpetual seed, and by a law which is unsearchable rid themselves.

[20] So I considered the world, and, behold, there was peril because of the devices that were come into it.

[21] And I saw, and spared it greatly, and have kept me a grape of the cluster, and a plant of a great people.

[22] Let the multitude perish then, which was born in vain; and let my grape be kept, and my plant; for with great labour have I made it perfect.

[23] Nevertheless, if thou wilt cease yet seven days more, (but thou shalt not fast in them,

[24] But go into a field of flowers, where no house is builded, and eat only the flowers of the field; taste no flesh, drink no wine, but eat flowers only;

[25] And pray unto the Highest continually, then will I come and talk with thee.

[26] So I went my way into the field which is called Ardath, like as he commanded me; and there I sat among the flowers, and did eat of the herbs of the field, and the meat of the same satisfied me.

[27] After seven days I sat upon the grass, and my heart was vexed within me, like as before:

[28] And I opened my mouth, and began to talk before the most High, and said,

[29] O Lord, thou that shewest thyself unto us, thou wast shewed unto our fathers in the wilderness, in a place where no man treadeth, in a barren place, when they came out of Egypt.

[30] And thou spakest saying, Hear me, O Israel; and mark my words, thou seed of Jacob.

[31] For, behold, I sow my law in you, and it shall bring fruit in you, and ye shall be honoured in it for ever.

[32] But our fathers, which received the law, kept it not, and observed not thy ordinances: and though the fruit of thy law did not perish, neither could it, for it was thine;

[33] Yet they that received it perished, because they kept not the thing that was sown in them.

[34] And, lo, it ls a custom, when the ground hath received seed, or the sea a ship, or any vessel meat or drink, that, that being perished wherein it was sown or cast into,

[35] That thing also which was sown, or cast therein, or received, doth perish, and remaineth not with us: but with us it hath not happened so.

[36] For we that have received the law perish by sin, and our heart also which received it

[37] Notwithstanding the law perisheth not, but remaineth in his force.

[38] And when I spake these things in my heart, I looked back with mine eyes, and upon the right side I saw a

woman, and, behold, she mourned and wept with a loud voice, and was much grieved in heart, and her clothes were rent, and she had ashes upon her head.

[39] Then let I my thoughts go that I was in, and turned me unto her,

[40] And said unto her, Wherefore weepest thou? why art thou so grieved in thy mind?

[41] And she said unto me, Sir, let me alone, that I may bewail myself, and add unto my sorrow, for I am sore vexed in my mind, and brought very low.

[42] And I said unto her, What aileth thee? tell me.

[43] She said unto me, I thy servant have been barren, and had no child, though I had an husband thirty years,

[44] And those thirty years I did nothing else day and night, and every hour, but make my, prayer to the Highest.

[45] After thirty years God heard me thine handmaid, looked upon my misery, considered my trouble, and gave me a son: and I was very glad of him, so was my husband also, and all my neighbours: and we gave great honour unto the Almighty.

[46] And I nourished him with great travail.

[47] So when he grew up, and came to the time that he should have a wife, I made a feast.

2Ezra.10

[1] And it so came to pass, that when my son was entered into his wedding chamber, he fell down, and died.

[2] Then we all overthrew the lights, and all my neighbours rose up to comfort me: so I took my rest unto the second day at night.

[3] And it came to pass, when they had all left off to comfort me, to the end I might be quiet; then rose I up by night and fled, and came hither into this field, as thou seest.

[4] And I do now purpose not to return into the city, but here to stay, and neither to eat nor drink, but continually to mourn and to fast until I die.

[5] Then left I the meditations wherein I was, and spake to her in anger, saying,

[6] Thou foolish woman above all other, seest thou not our mourning, and what happeneth unto us?

[7] How that Sion our mother is full of all heaviness, and much humbled, mourning very sore?

[8] And now, seeing we all mourn and are sad, for we are all in heaviness, art thou grieved for one son?

[9] For ask the earth, and she shall tell thee, that it is she which ought to mourn for the fall of so many that grow upon her.

[10] For out of her came all at the first, and out of her shall all others come, and, behold, they walk almost all into destruction, and a multitude of them is utterly rooted out.

[11] Who then should make more mourning than she, that hath lost so great a multitude; and not thou, which art sorry but for one?

[12] But if thou sayest unto me, My lamentation is not like the earth's, because I have lost the fruit of my womb, which I brought forth with pains, and bare with sorrows;

[13] But the earth not so: for the multitude present in it according to the course of the earth is gone, as it came:

[14] Then say I unto thee, Like as thou hast brought forth with labour; even so the earth also hath given her fruit, namely, man, ever since the beginning unto him that made her.

[15] Now therefore keep thy sorrow to thyself, and bear with a good courage that which hath befallen thee.

[16] For if thou shalt acknowledge the determination of God to be just, thou shalt both receive thy son in time, and shalt be commended among women.

[17] Go thy way then into the city to thine husband.

[18] And she said unto me, That will I not do: I will not go into the city, but here will I die.

[19] So I proceeded to speak further unto her, and said,

[20] Do not so, but be counselled. by me: for how many are the adversities of Sion? be comforted in regard of the sorrow of Jerusalem.

[21] For thou seest that our sanctuary is laid waste, our altar broken down, our temple destroyed;

[22] Our psaltery is laid on the ground, our song is put to silence, our rejoicing is at an end, the light of our candlestick is put out, the ark of our covenant is spoiled, our holy things are defiled, and the name that is called upon us is almost profaned: our children are put to shame, our priests are burnt, our Levites are gone into captivity, our virgins are defiled, and our wives ravished; our righteous men carried away, our little ones destroyed, our young men are brought in bondage, and our strong men are become weak;

[23] And, which is the greatest of all, the seal of Sion hath now lost her honour; for she is delivered into the hands of them that hate us.

[24] And therefore shake off thy great heaviness, and put away the multitude of sorrows, that the Mighty may be merciful unto thee again, and the Highest shall give thee rest and ease from thy labour.

[25] And it came to pass while I was talking with her, behold, her face upon a sudden shined exceedingly, and her countenance glistered, so that I was afraid of her, and mused what it might be.

[26] And, behold, suddenly she made a great cry very fearful: so that the earth shook at the noise of the woman.

[27] And I looked, and, behold, the woman appeared unto me no more, but there was a city builded, and a large place shewed itself from the foundations: then was I afraid, and cried with a loud voice, and said,

[28] Where is Uriel the angel, who came unto me at the first? for he hath caused me to fall into many trances, and mine end is turned into corruption, and my prayer to rebuke.

[29] And as I was speaking these words behold, he came unto me, and looked upon me.

[30] And, lo, I lay as one that had been dead, and mine understanding was taken from me: and he took me by the right hand, and comforted me, and set me upon my feet, and said unto me,

[31] What aileth thee? and why art thou so disquieted? and why is thine understanding troubled, and the thoughts of thine heart?

[32] And I said, Because thou hast forsaken me, and yet I did according to thy words, and I went into the field, and, lo, I have seen, and yet see, that I am not able to express.

[33] And he said unto me, Stand up manfully, and I will advise thee.

[34] Then said I, Speak on, my lord, in me; only forsake me not, lest I die frustrate of my hope.

[35] For I have seen that I knew not, and hear that I do not know.

[36] Or is my sense deceived, or my soul in a dream?

[37] Now therefore I beseech thee that thou wilt shew thy servant of this vision.

[38] He answered me then, and said, Hear me, and I shall inform thee, and tell thee wherefore thou art afraid: for the Highest will reveal many secret things unto thee.

[39] He hath seen that thy way is right: for that thou sorrowest continually for thy people, and makest great lamentation for Sion.

[40] This therefore is the meaning of the vision which thou lately sawest:

[41] Thou sawest a woman mourning, and thou begannest to comfort her:

[42] But now seest thou the likeness of the woman no more, but there appeared unto thee a city builded.

[43] And whereas she told thee of the death of her son, this is the solution:

[44] This woman, whom thou sawest is Sion: and whereas she said unto thee, even she whom thou seest as a city builded,

[45] Whereas, I say, she said unto thee, that she hath been thirty years barren: those are the thirty years wherein there was no offering made in her.

[46] But after thirty years Solomon builded the city and offered offerings: and then bare the barren a son.

[47] And whereas she told thee that she nourished him with labour: that was the dwelling in Jerusalem.

[48] But whereas she said unto thee, That my son coming into his marriage chamber happened to have a fall, and died: this was the destruction that came to Jerusalem.

[49] And, behold, thou sawest her likeness, and because she mourned for her son, thou begannest to comfort her: and of these things which have chanced, these are to be opened unto thee.

[50] For now the most High seeth that thou art grieved unfeignedly, and sufferest from thy whole heart for her, so hath he shewed thee the brightness of her glory, and the comeliness of her beauty:

[51] And therefore I bade thee remain in the field where no house was builded:

[52] For I knew that the Highest would shew this unto thee.

[53] Therefore I commanded thee to go into the field, where no foundation of any building was.

[54] For in the place wherein the Highest beginneth to shew his city, there can no man's building be able to stand.

[55] And therefore fear not, let not thine heart be affrighted, but go thy way in, and see the beauty and greatness of the building, as much as thine eyes be able to see:

[56] And then shalt thou hear as much as thine ears may comprehend.

[57] For thou art blessed above many other, and art called with the Highest; and so are but few.

[58] But to morrow at night thou shalt remain here;

[59] And so shall the Highest shew thee visions of the high things, which the most High will do unto them that dwell upon the earth in the last days. So I slept that night and another, like as he commanded me.

2Ezra.11

[1] Then saw I a dream, and, behold, there came up from the sea an eagle, which had twelve feathered wings, and three heads.

[2] And I saw, and, behold, she spread her wings over all the earth, and all the winds of the air blew on her, and were gathered together.

[3] And I beheld, and out of her feathers there grew other contrary feathers; and they became little feathers and small.

[4] But her heads were at rest: the head in the midst was greater than the other, yet rested it with the residue.

[5] Moreover I beheld, and, lo, the eagle flew with her feathers, and reigned upon earth, and over them that dwelt therein.

[6] And I saw that all things under heaven were subject unto her, and no man spake against her, no, not one creature upon earth.

[7] And I beheld, and, lo, the eagle rose upon her talons, and spake to her feathers, saying,

[8] Watch not all at once: sleep every one in his own place, and watch by course:

[9] But let the heads be preserved for the last.

[10] And I beheld, and, lo, the voice went not out of her heads, but from the midst of her body.

[11] And I numbered her contrary feathers, and, behold, there were eight of them.

[12] And I looked, and, behold, on the right side there arose one feather, and reigned over all the earth;

[13] And so it was, that when it reigned, the end of it came, and the place thereof appeared no more: so the next following stood up. and reigned, and had a great time;

[14] And it happened, that when it reigned, the end of it came also, like as the first, so that it appeared no more.

[15] Then came there a voice unto it, and said,

[16] Hear thou that hast borne rule over the earth so long: this I say unto thee, before thou beginnest to appear no more,

[17] There shall none after thee attain unto thy time, neither unto the half thereof.

[18] Then arose the third, and reigned as the other before, and appeared no more also.

[19] So went it with all the residue one after another, as that every one reigned, and then appeared no more.

[20] Then I beheld, and, lo, in process of time the feathers that followed stood up upon the right side, that they might rule also; and some of them ruled, but within a while they appeared no more:

[21] For some of them were set up, but ruled not.

[22] After this I looked, and, behold, the twelve feathers appeared no more, nor the two little feathers:

[23] And there was no more upon the eagle's body, but three heads that rested, and six little wings.

[24] Then saw I also that two little feathers divided themselves from the six, and remained under the head that was upon the right side: for the four continued in their place.

[25] And I beheld, and, lo, the feathers that were under the wing thought to set up themselves and to have the rule.

[26] And I beheld, and, lo, there was one set up, but shortly it appeared no more.

[27] And the second was sooner away than the first.

[28] And I beheld, and, lo, the two that remained thought also in themselves to reign:

[29] And when they so thought, behold, there awaked one of the heads that were at rest, namely, it that was in the midst; for that was greater than the two other heads.

[30] And then I saw that the two other heads were joined with it.

[31] And, behold, the head was turned with them that were with it, and did eat up the two feathers under the wing that would have reigned.

[32] But this head put the whole earth in fear, and bare rule in it over all those that dwelt upon the earth with much oppression; and it had the governance of the world more than all the wings that had been.

[33] And after this I beheld, and, lo, the head that was in the midst suddenly appeared no more, like as the wings.

[34] But there remained the two heads, which also in like sort ruled upon the earth, and over those that dwelt therein.

[35] And I beheld, and, lo, the head upon the right side devoured it that was upon the left side.

[36] Then I head a voice, which said unto me, Look before thee, and consider the thing that thou seest.

[37] And I beheld, and lo, as it were a roaring lion chased out of the wood: and I saw that he sent out a man's voice unto the eagle, and said,

[38] Hear thou, I will talk with thee, and the Highest shall say unto thee,

[39] Art not thou it that remainest of the four beasts, whom I made to reign in my world, that the end of their times might come through them?

[40] And the fourth came, and overcame all the beasts that were past, and had power over the world with great fearfulness, and over the whole compass of the earth with much wicked oppression; and so long time dwelt he upon the earth with deceit.

[41] For the earth hast thou not judged with truth.

[42] For thou hast afflicted the meek, thou hast hurt the peaceable, thou hast loved liars, and destroyed the dwellings of them that brought forth fruit, and hast cast down the walls of such as did thee no harm.

[43] Therefore is thy wrongful dealing come up unto the Highest, and thy pride unto the Mighty.

[44] The Highest also hath looked upon the proud times, and, behold, they are ended, and his abominations are fulfilled.

[45] And therefore appear no more, thou eagle, nor thy horrible wings, nor thy wicked feathers nor thy malicious heads, nor thy hurtful claws, nor all thy vain body:

[46] That all the earth may be refreshed, and may return, being delivered from thy violence, and that she may hope for the judgment and mercy of him that made her.

[1] And it came to pass, whiles the lion spake these words unto the eagle, I saw,

[2] And, behold, the head that remained and the four wings appeared no more, and the two went unto it and set themselves up to reign, and their kingdom was small, and fill of uproar.

[3] And I saw, and, behold, they appeared no more, and the whole body of the eagle was burnt so that the earth was in great fear: then awaked I out of the trouble and trance of my mind, and from great fear, and said unto my spirit,

[4] Lo, this hast thou done unto me, in that thou searchest out the ways of the Highest.

[5] Lo, yet am I weary in my mind, and very weak in my spirit; and little strength is there in me, for the great fear wherewith I was afflicted this night.

[6] Therefore will I now beseech the Highest, that he will comfort me unto the end.

[7] And I said, Lord that bearest rule, if I have found grace before thy sight, and if I am justified with thee before many others, and if my prayer indeed be come up before thy face;

[8] Comfort me then, and shew me thy servant the interpretation and plain difference of this fearful vision, that thou mayest perfectly comfort my soul.

[9] For thou hast judged me worthy to shew me the last times.

[10] And he said unto me, This is the interpretation of the vision:

[11] The eagle, whom thou sawest come up from the sea, is the kingdom which was seen in the vision of thy brother Daniel.

[12] But it was not expounded unto him, therefore now I declare it unto thee.

[13] Behold, the days will come, that there shall rise up a kingdom upon earth, and it shall be feared above all the kingdoms that were before it.

[14] In the same shall twelve kings reign, one after another:

[15] Whereof the second shall begin to reign, and shall have more time than any of the twelve.

[16] And this do the twelve wings signify, which thou sawest.

[17] As for the voice which thou heardest speak, and that thou sawest not to go out from the heads but from the midst of the body thereof, this is the interpretation:

[18] That after the time of that kingdom there shall arise great strivings, and it shall stand in peril of failing: nevertheless it shall not then fall, but shall be restored again to his beginning.

[19] And whereas thou sawest the eight small under feathers sticking to her wings, this is the interpretation:

[20] That in him there shall arise eight kings, whose times shall be but small, and their years swift.

[21] And two of them shall perish, the middle time approaching: four shall be kept until their end begin to approach: but two shall be kept unto the end.

[22] And whereas thou sawest three heads resting, this is the interpretation:

[23] In his last days shall the most High raise up three kingdoms, and renew many things therein, and they shall have the dominion of the earth,

[24] And of those that dwell therein, with much oppression, above all those that were before them: therefore are they called the heads of the eagle.

[25] For these are they that shall accomplish his wickedness, and that shall finish his last end.

[26] And whereas thou sawest that the great head appeared no more, it signifieth that one of them shall die upon his bed, and yet with pain.

[27] For the two that remain shall be slain with the sword.

[28] For the sword of the one shall devour the other: but at the last shall he fall through the sword himself.

[29] And whereas thou sawest two feathers under the wings passing over the head that is on the right side;

[30] It signifieth that these are they, whom the Highest hath kept unto their end: this is the small kingdom and full of trouble, as thou sawest.

[31] And the lion, whom thou sawest rising up out of the wood, and roaring, and speaking to the eagle, and rebuking her for her unrighteousness with all the words which thou hast heard;

[32] This is the anointed, which the Highest hath kept for them and for their wickedness unto the end: he shall reprove them, and shall upbraid them with their cruelty.

[33] For he shall set them before him alive in judgment, and shall rebuke them, and correct them.

[34] For the rest of my people shall he deliver with mercy, those that have been pressed upon my borders, and he shall make them joyful until the coming of the day of judgment, whereof I have spoken unto thee from the the beginning.

[35] This is the dream that thou sawest, and these are the interpretations.

[36] Thou only hast been meet to know this secret of the Highest.

[37] Therefore write all these things that thou hast seen in a book, and hide them:

[38] And teach them to the wise of the people, whose hearts thou knowest may comprehend and keep these secrets.

[39] But wait thou here thyself yet seven days more, that it may be shewed thee, whatsoever it pleaseth the Highest to

declare unto thee. And with that he went his way.

[40] And it came to pass, when all the people saw that the seven days were past, and I not come again into the city, they gathered them all together, from the least unto the greatest, and came unto me, and said,

[41] What have we offended thee? and what evil have we done against thee, that thou forsakest us, and sittest here in this place?

[42] For of all the prophets thou only art left us, as a cluster of the vintage, and as a candle in a dark place, and as a haven or ship preserved from the tempest.

[43] Are not the evils which are come to us sufficient?

[44] If thou shalt forsake us, how much better had it been for us, if we also had been burned in the midst of Sion?

[45] For we are not better than they that died there. And they wept with a loud voice. Then answered I them, and said,

[46] Be of good comfort, O Israel; and be not heavy, thou house of Jacob:

[47] For the Highest hath you in remembrance, and the Mighty hath not forgotten you in temptation.

[48] As for me, I have not forsaken you, neither am I departed from you: but am come into this place, to pray for the desolation of Sion, and that I might seek mercy for the low estate of your sanctuary.

[49] And now go your way home every man, and after these days will I come unto you.

[50] So the people went their way into the city, like as I commanded them:

[51] But I remained still in the field seven days, as the angel commanded me; and did eat only in those days of the flowers of the field, and had my meat of the herbs

2Ezra.13

[1] And it came to pass after seven days, I dreamed a dream by night:

[2] And, lo, there arose a wind from the sea, that it moved all the waves thereof.

[3] And I beheld, and, lo, that man waxed strong with the thousands of heaven: and when he turned his countenance to look, all the things trembled that were seen under him.

[4] And whensoever the voice went out of his mouth, all they burned that heard his voice, like as the earth faileth when it feeleth the fire.

[5] And after this I beheld, and, lo, there was gathered together a multitude of men, out of number, from the four winds of the heaven, to subdue the man that came out of the sea

[6] But I beheld, and, lo, he had graved himself a great

mountain, and flew up upon it.

[7] But I would have seen the region or place whereout the hill was graven, and I could not.

[8] And after this I beheld, and, lo, all they which were gathered together to subdue him were sore afraid, and yet durst fight.

[9] And, lo, as he saw the violence of the multitude that came, he neither lifted up his hand, nor held sword, nor any instrument of war:

[10] But only I saw that he sent out of his mouth as it had been a blast of fire, and out of his lips a flaming breath, and out of his tongue he cast out sparks and tempests.

[11] And they were all mixed together; the blast of fire, the flaming breath, and the great tempest; and fell with violence upon the multitude which was prepared to fight, and burned them up every one, so that upon a sudden of an innumerable multitude nothing was to be perceived, but only dust and smell of smoke: when I saw this I was afraid.

[12] Afterward saw I the same man come down from the mountain, and call unto him another peaceable Multitude.

[13] And there came much people unto him, whereof some were glad, some were sorry, and some of them were bound, and other some brought of them that were offered: then was I sick through great fear, and I awaked, and said,

[14] Thou hast shewed thy servant these wonders from the beginning, and hast counted me worthy that thou shouldest receive my prayer:

[15] Shew me now yet the interpretation of this dream.

[16] For as I conceive in mine understanding, woe unto them that shall be left in those days and much more woe unto them that are not left behind!

[17] For they that were not left were in heaviness.

[18] Now understand I the things that are laid up in the latter days, which shall happen unto them, and to those that are left behind.

[19] Therefore are they come into great perils and many necessities, like as these dreams declare.

[20] Yet is it easier for him that is in danger to come into these things, than to pass away as a cloud out of the world, and not to see the things that happen in the last days. And he answered unto me, and said,

[21] The interpretation of the vision shall I shew thee, and I will open unto thee the thing that thou hast required.

[22] Whereas thou hast spoken of them that are left behind, this is the interpretation:

[23] He that shall endure the peril in that time hath kept himself: they that be fallen into danger are such as have works, and faith toward the Almighty.

[24] Know this therefore, that they which be left behind are more blessed than they that be dead.

[25] This is the meaning of the vision: Whereas thou sawest a man coming up from the midst of the sea:

[26] The same is he whom God the Highest hath kept a great season, which by his own self shall deliver his creature: and he shall order them that are left behind.

[27] And whereas thou sawest, that out of his mouth there came as a blast of wind, and fire, and storm;

[28] And that he held neither sword, nor any instrument of war, but that the rushing in of him destroyed the whole multitude that came to subdue him; this is the interpretation:

[29] Behold, the days come, when the most High will begin to deliver them that are upon the earth.

[30] And he shall come to the astonishment of them that dwell on the earth.

[31] And one shall undertake to fight against another, one city against another, one place against another, one people against another, and one realm against another.

[32] And the time shall be when these things shall come to pass, and the signs shall happen which I shewed thee before, and then shall my Son be declared, whom thou sawest as a man ascending.

[33] And when all the people hear his voice, every man shall in their own land leave the battle they have one against another.

[34] And an innumerable multitude shall be gathered together, as thou sawest them, willing to come, and to overcome him by fighting.

[35] But he shall stand upon the top of the mount Sion.

[36] And Sion shall come, and shall be shewed to all men, being prepared and builded, like as thou sawest the hill graven without hands.

[37] And this my Son shall rebuke the wicked inventions of those nations, which for their wicked life are fallen into the tempest;

[38] And shall lay before them their evil thoughts, and the torments wherewith they shall begin to be tormented, which are like unto a flame: and he shall destroy them without labour by the law which is like unto me.

[39] And whereas thou sawest that he gathered another peaceable multitude unto him;

[40] Those are the ten tribes, which were carried away prisoners out of their own land in the time of Osea the king, whom Salmanasar the king of Assyria led away captive, and he carried them over the waters, and so came they into another land.

[41] But they took this counsel among themselves, that they would leave the multitude of the heathen, and go forth into a further country, where never mankind dwelt,

[42] That they might there keep their statutes, which they never kept in their own land.

[43] And they entered into Euphrates by the narrow places of the river.

[44] For the most High then shewed signs for them, and held still the flood, till they were passed over.

[45] For through that country there was a great way to go, namely, of a year and a half: and the same region is called Arsareth.

[46] Then dwelt they there until the latter time; and now when they shall begin to come,

[47] The Highest shall stay the springs of the stream again, that they may go through: therefore sawest thou the multitude with peace.

[48] But those that be left behind of thy people are they that are found within my borders.

[49] Now when he destroyeth the multitude of the nations that are gathered together, he shall defend his people that remain.

[50] And then shall he shew them great wonders.

[51] Then said I, O Lord that bearest rule, shew me this: Wherefore have I seen the man coming up from the midst of the sea?

[52] And he said unto me, Like as thou canst neither seek out nor know the things that are in the deep of the sea: even so can no man upon earth see my Son, or those that be with him, but in the day time.

[53] This is the interpretation of the dream which thou sawest, and whereby thou only art here lightened.

[54] For thou hast forsaken thine own way, and applied thy diligence unto my law, and sought it.

[55] Thy life hast thou ordered in wisdom, and hast called understanding thy mother.

[56] And therefore have I shewed thee the treasures of the Highest: after other three days I will speak other things unto thee, and declare unto thee mighty and wondrous things.

[57] Then went I forth into the field, giving praise and thanks greatly unto the most High because of his wonders which he did in time;

[58] And because he governeth the same, and such things as fall in their seasons: and there I sat three days.

2Ezra.14

[1] And it came to pass upon the third day, I sat under an oak, and, behold, there came a voice out of a bush over against me, and said, Esdras, Esdras.

[2] And I said, Here am I, Lord And I stood up upon my feet.

[3] Then said he unto me, In the bush I did manifestly reveal myself unto Moses, and talked with him, when my people

served in Egypt:

[4] And I sent him and led my people out of Egypt, and brought him up to the mount of where I held him by me a long season,

[5] And told him many wondrous things, and shewed him the secrets of the times, and the end; and commanded him, saying,

[6] These words shalt thou declare, and these shalt thou hide.

[7] And now I say unto thee,

[8] That thou lay up in thy heart the signs that I have shewed, and the dreams that thou hast seen, and the interpretations which thou hast heard:

[9] For thou shalt be taken away from all, and from henceforth thou shalt remain with my Son, and with such as be like thee, until the times be ended.

[10] For the world hath lost his youth, and the times begin to wax old.

[11] For the world is divided into twelve parts, and the ten parts of it are gone already, and half of a tenth part:

[12] And there remaineth that which is after the half of the tenth part.

[13] Now therefore set thine house in order, and reprove thy people, comfort such of them as be in trouble, and now renounce corruption,

[14] Let go from thee mortal thoughts, cast away the burdens of man, put off now the weak nature,

[15] And set aside the thoughts that are most heavy unto thee, and haste thee to flee from these times.

[16] For yet greater evils than those which thou hast seen happen shall be done hereafter.

[17] For look how much the world shall be weaker through age, so much the more shall evils increase upon them that dwell therein.

[18] For the time is fled far away, and leasing is hard at hand: for now hasteth the vision to come, which thou hast seen.

[19] Then answered I before thee, and said,

[20] Behold, Lord, I will go, as thou hast commanded me, and reprove the people which are present: but they that shall be born afterward, who shall admonish them? thus the world is set in darkness, and they that dwell therein are without light.

[21] For thy law is burnt, therefore no man knoweth the things that are done of thee, or the work that shall begin.

[22] But if I have found grace before thee, send the Holy Ghost into me, and I shall write all that hath been done in the world since the beginning, which were written in thy law, that men may find thy path, and that they which will live in the latter days may live.

[23] And he answered me, saying, Go thy way, gather the people together, and say unto them, that they seek thee not for forty days.

[24] But look thou prepare thee many box trees, and take with thee Sarea, Dabria, Selemia, Ecanus, and Asiel, these five which are ready to write swiftly;

[25] And come hither, and I shall light a candle of understanding in thine heart, which shall not be put out, till the things be performed which thou shalt begin to write.

[26] And when thou hast done, some things shalt thou publish, and some things shalt thou shew secretly to the wise: to morrow this hour shalt thou begin to write.

[27] Then went I forth, as he commanded, and gathered all the people together, and said,

[28] Hear these words, O Israel.

[29] Our fathers at the beginning were strangers in Egypt, from whence they were delivered:

[30] And received the law of life, which they kept not, which ye also have transgressed after them.

[31] Then was the land, even the land of Sion, parted among you by lot: but your fathers, and ye yourselves, have done unrighteousness, and have not kept the ways which the Highest commanded you.

[32] And forasmuch as he is a righteous judge, he took from you in time the thing that he had given you.

[33] And now are ye here, and your brethren among you.

[34] Therefore if so be that ye will subdue your own understanding, and reform your hearts, ye shall be kept alive and after death ye shall obtain mercy.

[35] For after death shall the judgment come, when we shall live again: and then shall the names of the righteous be manifest, and the works of the ungodly shall be declared.

[36] Let no man therefore come unto me now, nor seek after me these forty days.

[37] So I took the five men, as he commanded me, and we went into the field, and remained there.

[38] And the next day, behold, a voice called me, saying, Esdras, open thy mouth, and drink that I give thee to drink.

[39] Then opened I my mouth, and, behold, he reached me a full cup, which was full as it were with water, but the colour of it was like fire.

[40] And I took it, and drank: and when I had drunk of it, my heart uttered understanding, and wisdom grew in my breast, for my spirit strengthened my memory:

[41] And my mouth was opened, and shut no more.

[42] The Highest gave understanding unto the five men, and they wrote the wonderful visions of the night that were told, which they knew not: and they sat forty days, and they wrote in the day, and at night they ate bread.

[43] As for me. I spake in the day, and I held not my tongue

by night.

[44] In forty days they wrote two hundred and four books.

[45] And it came to pass, when the forty days were filled, that the Highest spake, saying, The first that thou hast written publish openly, that the worthy and unworthy may read it:

[46] But keep the seventy last, that thou mayest deliver them only to such as be wise among the people:

[47] For in them is the spring of understanding, the fountain of wisdom, and the stream of knowledge.

[48] And I did so.

2Ezra.15

[1] Behold, speak thou in the ears of my people the words of prophecy, which I will put in thy mouth, saith the Lord:

[2] And cause them to be written in paper: for they are faithful and true.

[3] Fear not the imaginations against thee, let not the incredulity of them trouble thee, that speak against thee.

[4] For all the unfaithful shall die in their unfaithfulness.

[5] Behold, saith the Lord, I will bring plagues upon the world; the sword, famine, death, and destruction.

[6] For wickedness hath exceedingly polluted the whole earth, and their hurtful works are fulfilled.

[7] Therefore saith the Lord,

[8] I will hold my tongue no more as touching their wickedness, which they profanely commit, neither will I suffer them in those things, in which they wickedly exercise themselves: behold, the innocent and righteous blood crieth unto me, and the souls of the just complain continually.

[9] And therefore, saith the Lord, I will surely avenge them, and receive unto me all the innocent blood from among them.

[10] Behold, my people is led as a flock to the slaughter: I will not suffer them now to dwell in the land of Egypt:

[11] But I will bring them with a mighty hand and a stretched out arm, and smite Egypt with plagues, as before, and will destroy all the land thereof.

[12] Egypt shall mourn, and the foundation of it shall be smitten with the plague and punishment that God shall bring upon it.

[13] They that till the ground shall mourn: for their seeds shall fail through the blasting and hail, and with a fearful constellation.

[14] Woe to the world and them that dwell therein!

[15] For the sword and their destruction draweth nigh, and one people shall stand up and fight against another, and swords in their hands.

[16] For there shall be sedition among men, and invading one another; they shall not regard their kings nor princes, and the course of their actions shall stand in their power.

[17] A man shall desire to go into a city, and shall not be able.

[18] For because of their pride the cities shall be troubled, the houses shall be destroyed, and men shall be afraid.

[19] A man shall have no pity upon his neighbour, but shall destroy their houses with the sword, and spoil their goods, because of the lack of bread, and for great tribulation.

[20] Behold, saith God, I will call together all the kings of the earth to reverence me, which are from the rising of the sun, from the south, from the east, and Libanus; to turn themselves one against another, and repay the things that they have done to them.

[21] Like as they do yet this day unto my chosen, so will I do also, and recompense in their bosom. Thus saith the Lord God;

[22] My right hand shall not spare the sinners, and my sword shall not cease over them that shed innocent blood upon the earth.

[23] The fire is gone forth from his wrath, and hath consumed the foundations of the earth, and the sinners, like the straw that is kindled.

[24] Woe to them that sin, and keep not my commandments! saith the Lord.

[25] I will not spare them: go your way, ye children, from the power, defile not my sanctuary.

[26] For the Lord knoweth all them that sin against him, and therefore delivereth he them unto death and destruction.

[27] For now are the plagues come upon the whole earth and ye shall remain in them: for God shall not deliver you, because ye have sinned against him.

[28] Behold an horrible vision, and the appearance thereof from the east:

[29] Where the nations of the dragons of Arabia shall come out with many chariots, and the multitude of them shall be carried as the wind upon earth, that all they which hear them may fear and tremble.

[30] Also the Carmanians raging in wrath shall go forth as the wild boars of the wood, and with great power shall they come, and join battle with them, and shall waste a portion of the land of the Assyrians.

[31] And then shall the dragons have the upper hand, remembering their nature; and if they shall turn themselves, conspiring together in great power to persecute them,

[32] Then these shall be troubled bled, and keep silence through their power, and shall flee.

[33] And from the land of the Assyrians shall the enemy

besiege them, and consume some of them, and in their host shall be fear and dread, and strife among their kings.

[34] Behold clouds from the east and from the north unto the south, and they are very horrible to look upon, full of wrath and storm.

[35] They shall smite one upon another, and they shall smite down a great multitude of stars upon the earth, even their own star; and blood shall be from the sword unto the belly,

[36] And dung of men unto the camel's hough.

[37] And there shall be great fearfulness and trembling upon earth: and they that see the wrath shall be afraid, and trembling shall come upon them.

[38] And then shall there come great storms from the south, and from the north, and another part from the west.

[39] And strong winds shall arise from the east, and shall open it; and the cloud which he raised up in wrath, and the star stirred to cause fear toward the east and west wind, shall be destroyed.

[40] The great and mighty clouds shall be puffed up full of wrath, and the star, that they may make all the earth afraid, and them that dwell therein; and they shall pour out over every high and eminent place an horrible star,

[41] Fire, and hail, and flying swords, and many waters, that all fields may be full, and all rivers, with the abundance of great waters.

[42] And they shall break down the cities and walls, mountains and hills, trees of the wood, and grass of the meadows, and their corn.

[43] And they shall go stedfastly unto Babylon, and make her afraid.

[44] They shall come to her, and besiege her, the star and all wrath shall they pour out upon her: then shall the dust and smoke go up unto the heaven, and all they that be about her shall bewail her.

[45] And they that remain under her shall do service unto them that have put her in fear.

[46] And thou, Asia, that art partaker of the hope of Babylon, and art the glory of her person:

[47] Woe be unto thee, thou wretch, because thou hast made thyself like unto her; and hast decked thy daughters in whoredom, that they might please and glory in thy lovers, which have always desired to commit whoredom with thee.

[48] Thou hast followed her that is hated in all her works and inventions: therefore saith God,

[49] I will send plagues upon thee; widowhood, poverty, famine, sword, and pestilence, to waste thy houses with destruction and death.

[50] And the glory of thy Power shall be dried up as a flower, the heat shall arise that is sent over thee.

[51] Thou shalt be weakened as a poor woman with stripes, and as one chastised with wounds, so that the mighty and lovers shall not be able to receive thee.

[52] Would I with jealousy have so proceeded against thee, saith the Lord,

[53] If thou hadst not always slain my chosen, exalting the stroke of thine hands, and saying over their dead, when thou wast drunken,

[54] Set forth the beauty of thy countenance?

[55] The reward of thy whoredom shall be in thy bosom, therefore shalt thou receive recompence.

[56] Like as thou hast done unto my chosen, saith the Lord, even so shall God do unto thee, and shall deliver thee into mischief

[57] Thy children shall die of hunger, and thou shalt fall through the sword: thy cities shall be broken down, and all thine shall perish with the sword in the field.

[58] They that be in the mountains shall die of hunger, and eat their own flesh, and drink their own blood, for very hunger of bread, and thirst of water.

[59] Thou as unhappy shalt come through the sea, and receive plagues again.

[60] And in the passage they shall rush on the idle city, and shall destroy some portion of thy land, and consume part of thy glory, and shall return to Babylon that was destroyed.

[61] And thou shalt be cast down by them as stubble, and they shall be unto thee as fire;

[62] And shall consume thee, and thy cities, thy land, and thy mountains; all thy woods and thy fruitful trees shall they burn up with fire.

[63] Thy children shall they carry away captive, and, look, what thou hast, they shall spoil it, and mar the beauty of thy face.

2Ezra.16

[1] Woe be unto thee, Babylon, and Asia! woe be unto thee, Egypt and Syria!

[2] Gird up yourselves with cloths of sack and hair, bewail your children, and be sorry; for your destruction is at hand.

[3] A sword is sent upon you, and who may turn it back?

[4] A fire is sent among you, and who may quench it?

[5] Plagues are sent unto you, and what is he that may drive them away?

[6] May any man drive away an hungry lion in the wood? or may any one quench the fire in stubble, when it hath begun to burn?

[7] May one turn again the arrow that is shot of a strong archer?

[8] The mighty Lord sendeth the plagues and who is he that

can drive them away?

[9] A fire shall go forth from his wrath, and who is he that may quench it?

[10] He shall cast lightnings, and who shall not fear? he shall thunder, and who shall not be afraid?

[11] The Lord shall threaten, and who shall not be utterly beaten to powder at his presence?

[12] The earth quaketh, and the foundations thereof; the sea ariseth up with waves from the deep, and the waves of it are troubled, and the fishes thereof also, before the Lord, and before the glory of his power:

[13] For strong is his right hand that bendeth the bow, his arrows that he shooteth are sharp, and shall not miss, when they begin to be shot into the ends of the world.

[14] Behold, the plagues are sent, and shall not return again, until they come upon the earth.

[15] The fire is kindled, and shall not be put out, till it consume the foundation of the earth.

[16] Like as an arrow which is shot of a mighty archer returneth not backward: even so the plagues that shall be sent upon earth shall not return again.

[17] Woe is me! woe is me! who will deliver me in those days?

[18] The beginning of sorrows and great mournings; the beginning of famine and great death; the beginning of wars, and the powers shall stand in fear; the beginning of evils! what shall I do when these evils shall come?

[19] Behold, famine and plague, tribulation and anguish, are sent as scourges for amendment.

[20] But for all these things they shall not turn from their wickedness, nor be always mindful of the scourges.

[21] Behold, victuals shall be so good cheap upon earth, that they shall think themselves to be in good case, and even then shall evils grow upon earth, sword, famine, and great confusion.

[22] For many of them that dwell upon earth shall perish of famine; and the other, that escape the hunger, shall the sword destroy.

[23] And the dead shall be cast out as dung, and there shall be no man to comfort them: for the earth shall be wasted, and the cities shall be cast down.

[24] There shall be no man left to till the earth, and to sow it

[25] The trees shall give fruit, and who shall gather them?

[26] The grapes shall ripen, and who shall tread them? for all places shall be desolate of men:

[27] So that one man shall desire to see another, and to hear his voice.

[28] For of a city there shall be ten left, and two of the field, which shall hide themselves in the thick groves, and in the clefts of the rocks.

[29] As in an orchard of Olives upon every tree there are left three or four olives;

[30] Or as when a vineyard is gathered, there are left some clusters of them that diligently seek through the vineyard:

[31] Even so in those days there shall be three or four left by them that search their houses with the sword.

[32] And the earth shall be laid waste, and the fields thereof shall wax old, and her ways and all her paths shall grow full of thorns, because no man shall travel therethrough.

[33] The virgins shall mourn, having no bridegrooms; the women shall mourn, having no husbands; their daughters shall mourn, having no helpers.

[34] In the wars shall their bridegrooms be destroyed, and their husbands shall perish of famine.

[35] Hear now these things and understand them, ye servants of the Lord.

[36] Behold, the word of the Lord, receive it: believe not the gods of whom the Lord spake.

[37] Behold, the plagues draw nigh, and are not slack.

[38] As when a woman with child in the ninth month bringeth forth her son, with two or three hours of her birth great pains compass her womb, which pains, when the child cometh forth, they slack not a moment:

[39] Even so shall not the plagues be slack to come upon the earth, and the world shall mourn, and sorrows shall come upon it on every side.

[40] O my people, hear my word: make you ready to thy battle, and in those evils be even as pilgrims upon the earth.

[41] He that selleth, let him be as he that fleeth away: and he that buyeth, as one that will lose:

[42] He that occupieth merchandise, as he that hath no profit by it: and he that buildeth, as he that shall not dwell therein:

[43] He that soweth, as if he should not reap: so also he that planteth the vineyard, as he that shall not gather the grapes:

[44] They that marry, as they that shall get no children; and they that marry not, as the widowers.

[45] And therefore they that labour labour in vain:

[46] For strangers shall reap their fruits, and spoil their goods, overthrow their houses, and take their children captives, for in captivity and famine shall they get children.

[47] And they that occupy their merchandise with robbery, the more they deck their cities, their houses, their possessions, and their own persons:

[48] The more will I be angry with them for their sin, saith the Lord.

[49] Like as a whore envieth a right honest and virtuous woman:

[50] So shall righteousness hate iniquity, when she decketh herself, and shall accuse her to her face, when he cometh

that shall defend him that diligently searcheth out every sin upon earth.

[51] And therefore be ye not like thereunto, nor to the works thereof.

[52] For yet a little, and iniquity shall be taken away out of the earth, and righteousness shall reign among you.

[53] Let not the sinner say that he hath not sinned: for God shall burn coals of fire upon his head, which saith before the Lord God and his glory, I have not sinned.

[54] Behold, the Lord knoweth all the works of men, their imaginations, their thoughts, and their hearts:

[55] Which spake but the word, Let the earth be made; and it was made: Let the heaven be made; and it was created.

[56] In his word were the stars made, and he knoweth the number of them.

[57] He searcheth the deep, and the treasures thereof; he hath measured the sea, and what it containeth.

[58] He hath shut the sea in the midst of the waters, and with his word hath he hanged the earth upon the waters.

[59] He spreadeth out the heavens like a vault; upon the waters hath he founded it.

[60] In the desert hath he made springs of water, and pools upon the tops of the mountains, that the floods might pour down from the high rocks to water the earth.

[61] He made man, and put his heart in the midst of the body, and gave him breath, life, and understanding.

[62] Yea and the Spirit of Almighty God, which made all things, and searcheth out all hidden things in the secrets of the earth,

[63] Surely he knoweth your inventions, and what ye think in your hearts, even them that sin, and would hide their sin.

[64] Therefore hath the Lord exactly searched out all your works, and he will put you all to shame.

[65] And when your sins are brought forth, ye shall be ashamed before men, and your own sins shall be your accusers in that day.

[66] What will ye do? or how will ye hide your sins before God and his angels?

[67] Behold, God himself is the judge, fear him: leave off from your sins, and forget your iniquities, to meddle no more with them for ever: so shall God lead you forth, and deliver you from all trouble.

[68] For, behold, the burning wrath of a great multitude is kindled over you, and they shall take away certain of you, and feed you, being idle, with things offered unto idols.

[69] And they that consent unto them shall be had in derision and in reproach, and trodden under foot.

[70] For there shall be in every place, and in the next cities, a great insurrection upon those that fear the Lord.

[71] They shall be like mad men, sparing none, but still spoiling and destroying those that fear the Lord.

[72] For they shall waste and take away their goods, and cast them out of their houses.

[73] Then shall they be known, who are my chosen; and they shall be tried as the gold in the fire.

[74] Hear, O ye my beloved, saith the Lord: behold, the days of trouble are at hand, but I will deliver you from the same.

[75] Be ye not afraid neither doubt; for God is your guide,

[76] And the guide of them who keep my commandments and precepts, saith the Lord God: let not your sins weigh you down, and let not your iniquities lift up themselves.

[77] Woe be unto them that are bound with their sins, and covered with their iniquities like as a field is covered over with bushes, and the path thereof covered with thorns, that no man may travel through!

[78] It is left undressed, and is cast into the fire to be consumed therewith.

The Prophecy Of Jeremiah (Epistle Of Jeremiah)

EpJer.1

[1] Because of the sins which ye have committed before God, ye shall be led away captives into Babylon by Nabuchodonosor king of the Babylonians.

[2] So when ye be come unto Babylon, ye shall remain there many years, and for a long season, namely, seven generations: and after that I will bring you away peaceably from thence.

[3] Now shall ye see in Babylon gods of silver, and of gold, and of wood, borne upon shoulders, which cause the nations to fear.

[4] Beware therefore that ye in no wise be like to strangers, neither be ye and of them, when ye see the multitude before them and behind them, worshipping them.

[5] But say ye in your hearts, O Lord, we must worship thee.

[6] For mine angel is with you, and I myself caring for your souls.

[7] As for their tongue, it is polished by the workman, and they themselves are gilded and laid over with silver; yet are they but false, and cannot speak.

[8] And taking gold, as it were for a virgin that loveth to go gay, they make crowns for the heads of their gods.

[9] Sometimes also the priests convey from their gods gold and silver, and bestow it upon themselves.

[10] Yea, they will give thereof to the common harlots, and deck them as men with garments, [being] gods of silver, and gods of gold, and wood.

[11] Yet cannot these gods save themselves from rust and moth, though they be covered with purple raiment.

[12] They wipe their faces because of the dust of the temple, when there is much upon them.

[13] And he that cannot put to death one that offendeth him holdeth a sceptre, as though he were a judge of the country.

[14] He hath also in his right hand a dagger and an ax: but cannot deliver himself from war and thieves.

[15] Whereby they are known not to be gods: therefore fear them not.

[16] For like as a vessel that a man useth is nothing worth when it is broken; even so it is with their gods: when they be set up in the temple, their eyes be full of dust through the feet of them that come in.

[17] And as the doors are made sure on every side upon him that offendeth the king, as being committed to suffer death: even so the priests make fast their temples with doors, with locks, and bars, lest their gods be spoiled with robbers.

[18] They light them candles, yea, more than for themselves, whereof they cannot see one.

[19] They are as one of the beams of the temple, yet they say their hearts are gnawed upon by things creeping out of the earth; and when they eat them and their clothes, they feel it not.

[20] Their faces are blacked through the smoke that cometh out of the temple.

[21] Upon their bodies and heads sit bats, swallows, and birds, and the cats also.

[22] By this ye may know that they are no gods: therefore fear them not.

[23] Notwithstanding the gold that is about them to make them beautiful, except they wipe off the rust, they will not shine: for neither when they were molten did they feel it.

[24] The things wherein there is no breath are bought for a most high price.

[25] They are borne upon shoulders, having no feet whereby they declare unto men that they be nothing worth.

[26] They also that serve them are ashamed: for if they fall to the ground at any time, they cannot rise up again of themselves: neither, if one set them upright, can they move of themselves: neither, if they be bowed down, can they make themselves straight: but they set gifts before them as unto dead men.

[27] As for the things that are sacrificed unto them, their priests sell and abuse; in like manner their wives lay up part thereof in salt; but unto the poor and impotent they give nothing of it.

[28] Menstruous women and women in childbed eat their sacrifices: by these things ye may know that they are no gods: fear them not.

[29] For how can they be called gods? because women set meat before the gods of silver, gold, and wood.

[30] And the priests sit in their temples, having their clothes rent, and their heads and beards shaven, and nothing upon

their heads.

[31] They roar and cry before their gods, as men do at the feast when one is dead.

[32] The priests also take off their garments, and clothe their wives and children.

[33] Whether it be evil that one doeth unto them, or good, they are not able to recompense it: they can neither set up a king, nor put him down.

[34] In like manner, they can neither give riches nor money: though a man make a vow unto them, and keep it not, they will not require it.

[35] They can save no man from death, neither deliver the weak from the mighty.

[36] They cannot restore a blind man to his sight, nor help any man in his distress.

[37] They can shew no mercy to the widow, nor do good to the fatherless.

[38] Their gods of wood, and which are overlaid with gold and silver, are like the stones that be hewn out of the mountain: they that worship them shall be confounded.

[39] How should a man then think and say that they are gods, when even the Chaldeans themselves dishonour them?

[40] Who if they shall see one dumb that cannot speak, they bring him, and intreat Bel that he may speak, as though he were able to understand.

[41] Yet they cannot understand this themselves, and leave them: for they have no knowledge.

[42] The women also with cords about them, sitting in the ways, burn bran for perfume: but if any of them, drawn by some that passeth by, lie with him, she reproacheth her fellow, that she was not thought as worthy as herself, nor her cord broken.

[43] Whatsoever is done among them is false: how may it then be thought or said that they are gods?

[44] They are made of carpenters and goldsmiths: they can be nothing else than the workmen will have them to be.

[45] And they themselves that made them can never continue long; how should then the things that are made of them be gods?

[46] For they left lies and reproaches to them that come after.

[47] For when there cometh any war or plague upon them, the priests consult with themselves, where they may be hidden with them.

[48] How then cannot men perceive that they be no gods, which can neither save themselves from war, nor from plague?

[49] For seeing they be but of wood, and overlaid with silver and gold, it shall be known hereafter that they are false:

[50] And it shall manifestly appear to all nations and kings that they are no gods, but the works of men's hands, and that there is no work of God in them.

[51] Who then may not know that they are no gods?

[52] For neither can they set up a king in the land, nor give rain unto men.

[53] Neither can they judge their own cause, nor redress a wrong, being unable: for they are as crows between heaven and earth.

[54] Whereupon when fire falleth upon the house of gods of wood, or laid over with gold or silver, their priests will flee away, and escape; but they themselves shall be burned asunder like beams.

[55] Moreover they cannot withstand any king or enemies: how can it then be thought or said that they be gods?

[56] Neither are those gods of wood, and laid over with silver or gold, able to escape either from thieves or robbers.

[57] Whose gold, and silver, and garments wherewith they are clothed, they that are strong take, and go away withal: neither are they able to help themselves.

[58] Therefore it is better to be a king that sheweth his power, or else a profitable vessel in an house, which the owner shall have use of, than such false gods; or to be a door in an house, to keep such things therein, than such false gods. or a pillar of wood in a a palace, than such false gods.

[59] For sun, moon, and stars, being bright and sent to do their offices, are obedient.

[60] In like manner the lightning when it breaketh forth is easy to be seen; and after the same manner the wind bloweth in every country.

[61] And when God commandeth the clouds to go over the whole world, they do as they are bidden.

[62] And the fire sent from above to consume hills and woods doeth as it is commanded: but these are like unto them neither in shew nor power.

[63] Wherefore it is neither to be supposed nor said that they are gods, seeing, they are able neither to judge causes, nor to do good unto men.

[64] Knowing therefore that they are no gods, fear them not,

[65] For they can neither curse nor bless kings:

[66] Neither can they shew signs in the heavens among the heathen, nor shine as the sun, nor give light as the moon.

[67] The beasts are better than they: for they can get under a cover and help themselves.

[68] It is then by no means manifest unto us that they are gods: therefore fear them not.

[69] For as a scarecrow in a garden of cucumbers keepeth nothing: so are their gods of wood, and laid over with silver and gold.

[70] And likewise their gods of wood, and laid over with silver and gold, are like to a white thorn in an orchard, that every bird sitteth upon; as also to a dead body, that is east into the dark.

[71] And ye shall know them to be no gods by the bright purple that rotteth upon then: and they themselves afterward shall be eaten, and shall be a reproach in the country.

[72] Better therefore is the just man that hath none idols: for he shall be far from reproach.

Baruc

Bar.1

[1] And these are the words of the book, which Baruch the son of Nerias, the son of Maasias, the son of Sedecias, the son of Asadias, the son of Chelcias, wrote in Babylon,

[2] In the fifth year, and in the seventh day of the month, what time as the Chaldeans took Jerusalem, and burnt it with fire.

[3] And Baruch did read the words of this book in the hearing of Jechonias the son of Joachim king of Juda, and in the ears of all the people that came to hear the book,

[4] And in the hearing of the nobles, and of the king's sons, and in the hearing of the elders, and of all the people, from the lowest unto the highest, even of all them that dwelt at Babylon by the river Sud.

[5] Whereupon they wept, fasted, and prayed before the Lord.

[6] They made also a collection of money according to every man's power:

[7] And they sent it to Jerusalem unto Joachim the high priest, the son of Chelcias, son of Salom, and to the priests, and to all the people which were found with him at Jerusalem,

[8] At the same time when he received the vessels of the house of the Lord, that were carried out of the temple, to return them into the land of Juda, the tenth day of the month Sivan, namely, silver vessels, which Sedecias the son of Josias king of Jada had made,

[9] After that Nabuchodonosor king of Babylon had carried away Jechonias, and the princes, and the captives, and the mighty men, and the people of the land, from Jerusalem, and brought them unto Babylon.

[10] And they said, Behold, we have sent you money to buy

you burnt offerings, and sin offerings, and incense, and prepare ye manna, and offer upon the altar of the Lord our God;

[11] And pray for the life of Nabuchodonosor king of Babylon, and for the life of Balthasar his son, that their days may be upon earth as the days of heaven:

[12] And the Lord will give us strength, and lighten our eyes, and we shall live under the shadow of Nabuchodonosor king of Babylon, and under the shadow of Balthasar his son, and we shall serve them many days, and find favour in their sight.

[13] Pray for us also unto the Lord our God, for we have sinned against the Lord our God; and unto this day the fury of the Lord and his wrath is not turned from us.

[14] And ye shall read this book which we have sent unto you, to make confession in the house of the Lord, upon the feasts and solemn days.

[15] And ye shall say, To the Lord our God belongeth righteousness, but unto us the confusion of faces, as it is come to pass this day, unto them of Juda, and to the inhabitants of Jerusalem,

[16] And to our kings, and to our princes, and to our priests, and to our prophets, and to our fathers:

[17] For we have sinned before the Lord,

[18] And disobeyed him, and have not hearkened unto the voice of the Lord our God, to walk in the commandments that he gave us openly:

[19] Since the day that the Lord brought our forefathers out of the land of Egypt, unto this present day, we have been disobedient unto the Lord our God, and we have been negligent in not hearing his voice.

[20] Wherefore the evils cleaved unto us, and the curse, which the Lord appointed by Moses his servant at the time that he brought our fathers out of the land of Egypt, to give us a land that floweth with milk and honey, like as it is to see this day.

[21] Nevertheless we have not hearkened unto the voice of the Lord our God, according unto all the words of the prophets, whom he sent unto us:

[22] But every man followed the imagination of his own wicked heart, to serve strange gods, and to do evil in the sight of the Lord our God.

Bar.2

[1] Therefore the Lord hath made good his word, which he pronounced against us, and against our judges that judged Israel, and against our kings, and against our princes, and against the men of Israel and Juda,

[2] To bring upon us great plagues, such as never happened under the whole heaven, as it came to pass in Jerusalem, according to the things that were written in the law of Moses;

[3] That a man should eat the flesh of his own son, and the flesh of his own daughter.

[4] Moreover he hath delivered them to be in subjection to all the kingdoms that are round about us, to be as a reproach and desolation among all the people round about, where the Lord hath scattered them.

[5] Thus we were cast down, and not exalted, because we have sinned against the Lord our God, and have not been obedient unto his voice.

[6] To the Lord our God appertaineth righteousness: but unto us and to our fathers open shame, as appeareth this day.

[7] For all these plagues are come upon us, which the Lord hath pronounced against us

[8] Yet have we not prayed before the Lord, that we might turn every one from the imaginations of his wicked heart.

[9] Wherefore the Lord watched over us for evil, and the Lord hath brought it upon us: for the Lord is righteous in all his works which he hath commanded us.

[10] Yet we have not hearkened unto his voice, to walk in the commandments of the Lord, that he hath set before us.

[11] And now, O Lord God of Israel, that hast brought thy people out of the land of Egypt with a mighty hand, and high arm, and with signs, and with wonders, and with great power, and hast gotten thyself a name, as appeareth this day:

[12] O Lord our God, we have sinned, we have done ungodly, we have dealt unrighteously in all thine ordinances.

[13] Let thy wrath turn from us: for we are but a few left among the heathen, where thou hast scattered us.

[14] Hear our prayers, O Lord, and our petitions, and deliver us for thine own sake, and give us favour in the sight of them which have led us away:

[15] That all the earth may know that thou art the Lord our God, because Israel and his posterity is called by thy name.

[16] O Lord, look down from thine holy house, and consider us: bow down thine ear, O Lord, to hear us.

[17] Open thine eyes, and behold; for the dead that are in the graves, whose souls are taken from their bodies, will give unto the Lord neither praise nor righteousness:

[18] But the soul that is greatly vexed, which goeth stooping and feeble, and the eyes that fail, and the hungry soul, will give thee praise and righteousness, O Lord.

[19] Therefore we do not make our humble supplication before thee, O Lord our God, for the righteousness of our fathers, and of our kings.

[20] For thou hast sent out thy wrath and indignation upon

us, as thou hast spoken by thy servants the prophets, saying,

[21] Thus saith the Lord, Bow down your shoulders to serve the king of Babylon: so shall ye remain in the land that I gave unto your fathers.

[22] But if ye will not hear the voice of the Lord, to serve the king of Babylon,

[23] I will cause to cease out of the cites of Judah, and from without Jerusalem, the voice of mirth, and the voice of joy, the voice of the bridegroom, and the voice of the bride: and the whole land shall be desolate of inhabitants.

[24] But we would not hearken unto thy voice, to serve the king of Babylon: therefore hast thou made good the words that thou spakest by thy servants the prophets, namely, that the bones of our kings, and the bones of our fathers, should be taken out of their place.

[25] And, lo, they are cast out to the heat of the day, and to the frost of the night, and they died in great miseries by famine, by sword, and by pestilence.

[26] And the house which is called by thy name hast thou laid waste, as it is to be seen this day, for the wickedness of the house of Israel and the house of Juda.

[27] O Lord our God, thou hast dealt with us after all thy goodness, and according to all that great mercy of thine,

[28] As thou spakest by thy servant Moses in the day when thou didst command him to write the law before the children of Israel, saying,

[29] If ye will not hear my voice, surely this very great multitude shall be turned into a small number among the nations, where I will scatter them.

[30] For I knew that they would not hear me, because it is a stiffnecked people: but in the land of their captivities they shall remember themselves.

[31] And shall know that I am the Lord their God: for I will give them an heart, and ears to hear:

[32] And they shall praise me in the land of their captivity, and think upon my name,

[33] And return from their stiff neck, and from their wicked deeds: for they shall remember the way of their fathers, which sinned before the Lord.

[34] And I will bring them again into the land which I promised with an oath unto their fathers, Abraham, Isaac, and Jacob, and they shall be lords of it: and I will increase them, and they shall not be diminished.

[35] And I will make an everlasting covenant with them to be their God, and they shall be my people: and I will no more drive my people of Israel out of the land that I have given them.

Bar.3

[1] O Lord Almighty, God of Israel, the soul in anguish the troubled spirit, crieth unto thee.

[2] Hear, O Lord, and have mercy; ar thou art merciful: and have pity upon us, because we have sinned before thee.

[3] For thou endurest for ever, and we perish utterly.

[4] O Lord Almighty, thou God of Israel, hear now the prayers of the dead Israelites, and of their children, which have sinned before thee, and not hearkened unto the voice of thee their God: for the which cause these plagues cleave unto us.

[5] Remember not the iniquities of our forefathers: but think upon thy power and thy name now at this time.

[6] For thou art the Lord our God, and thee, O Lord, will we praise.

[7] And for this cause thou hast put thy fear in our hearts, to the intent that we should call upon thy name, and praise thee in our captivity: for we have called to mind all the iniquity of our forefathers, that sinned before thee.

[8] Behold, we are yet this day in our captivity, where thou hast scattered us, for a reproach and a curse, and to be subject to payments, according to all the iniquities of our fathers, which departed from the Lord our God.

[9] Hear, Israel, the commandments of life: give ear to understand wisdom.

[10] How happeneth it Israel, that thou art in thine enemies' land, that thou art waxen old in a strange country, that thou art defiled with the dead,

[11] That thou art counted with them that go down into the grave?

[12] Thou hast forsaken the fountain of wisdom.

[13] For if thou hadst walked in the way of God, thou shouldest have dwelled in peace for ever.

[14] Learn where is wisdom, where is strength, where is understanding; that thou mayest know also where is length of days, and life, where is the light of the eyes, and peace.

[15] Who hath found out her place? or who hath come into her treasures ?

[16] Where are the princes of the heathen become, and such as ruled the beasts upon the earth;

[17] They that had their pastime with the fowls of the air, and they that hoarded up silver and gold, wherein men trust, and made no end of their getting?

[18] For they that wrought in silver, and were so careful, and whose works are unsearchable,

[19] They are vanished and gone down to the grave, and others are come up in their steads.

[20] Young men have seen light, and dwelt upon the earth: but the way of knowledge have they not known,

[21] Nor understood the paths thereof, nor laid hold of it: their children were far off from that way.

[22] It hath not been heard of in Chanaan, neither hath it been seen in Theman.

[23] The Agarenes that seek wisdom upon earth, the merchants of Meran and of Theman, the authors of fables, and searchers out of understanding; none of these have known the way of wisdom, or remember her paths.

[24] O Israel, how great is the house of God! and how large is the place of his possession!

[25] Great, and hath none end; high, and unmeasurable.

[26] There were the giants famous from the beginning, that were of so great stature, and so expert in war.

[27] Those did not the Lord choose, neither gave he the way of knowledge unto them:

[28] But they were destroyed, because they had no wisdom, and perished through their own foolishness.

[29] Who hath gone up into heaven, and taken her, and brought her down from the clouds?

[30] Who hath gone over the sea, and found her, and will bring her for pure gold?

[31] No man knoweth her way, nor thinketh of her path.

[32] But he that knoweth all things knoweth her, and hath found her out with his understanding: he that prepared the earth for evermore hath filled it with fourfooted beasts:

[33] He that sendeth forth light, and it goeth, calleth it again, and it obeyeth him with fear.

[34] The stars shined in their watches, and rejoiced: when he calleth them, they say, Here we be; and so with cheerfulness they shewed light unto him that made them.

[35] This is our God, and there shall none other be accounted of in comparison of him

[36] He hath found out all the way of knowledge, and hath given it unto Jacob his servant, and to Israel his beloved.

[37] Afterward did he shew himself upon earth, and conversed with men.

Bar.4

[1] This is the book of the commandments of God, and the law that endureth for ever: all they that keep it shall come to life; but such as leave it shall die.

[2] Turn thee, O Jacob, and take hold of it: walk in the presence of the light thereof, that thou mayest be illuminated.

[3] Give not thine honour to another, nor the things that are profitable unto thee to a strange nation.

[4] O Israel, happy are we: for things that are pleasing to God are made known unto us.

[5] Be of good cheer, my people, the memorial of Israel.

[6] Ye were sold to the nations, not for [your] destruction: but because ye moved God to wrath, ye were delivered unto the enemies.

[7] For ye provoked him that made you by sacrificing unto devils, and not to God.

[8] Ye have forgotten the everlasting God, that brought you up; and ye have grieved Jerusalem, that nursed you.

[9] For when she saw the wrath of God coming upon you, she said, Hearken, O ye that dwell about Sion: God hath brought upon me great mourning;

[10] For I saw the captivity of my sons and daughters, which the Everlasting brought upon them.

[11] With joy did I nourish them; but sent them away with weeping and mourning.

[12] Let no man rejoice over me, a widow, and forsaken of many, who for the sins of my children am left desolate; because they departed from the law of God.

[13] They knew not his statutes, nor walked in the ways of his commandments, nor trod in the paths of discipline in his righteousness.

[14] Let them that dwell about Sion come, and remember ye the captivity of my sons and daughters, which the Everlasting hath brought upon them.

[15] For he hath brought a nation upon them from far, a shameless nation, and of a strange language, who neither reverenced old man, nor pitied child.

[16] These have carried away the dear beloved children of the widow, and left her that was alone desolate without daughters.

[17] But what can I help you?

[18] For he that brought these plagues upon you will deliver you from the hands of your enemies.

[19] Go your way, O my children, go your way: for I am left desolate.

[20] I have put off the clothing of peace, and put upon me the sackcloth of my prayer: I will cry unto the Everlasting in my days.

[21] Be of good cheer, O my children, cry unto the Lord, and he will deliver you from the power and hand of the enemies.

[22] For my hope is in the Everlasting, that he will save you; and joy is come unto me from the Holy One, because of the mercy which shall soon come unto you from the Everlasting our Saviour.

[23] For I sent you out with mourning and weeping: but God will give you to me again with joy and gladness for ever.

[24] Like as now the neighbours of Sion have seen your captivity: so shall they see shortly your salvation from our God which shall come upon you with great glory, and brightness of the Everlasting.

[25] My children, suffer patiently the wrath that is come upon you from God: for thine enemy hath persecuted thee; but shortly thou shalt see his destruction, and shalt tread upon his neck.

[26] My delicate ones have gone rough ways, and were taken away as a flock caught of the enemies.

[27] Be of good comfort, O my children, and cry unto God: for ye shall be remembered of him that brought these things upon you.

[28] For as it was your mind to go astray from God: so, being returned, seek him ten times more.

[29] For he that hath brought these plagues upon you shall bring you everlasting joy with your salvation.

[30] Take a good heart, O Jerusalem: for he that gave thee that name will comfort thee.

[31] Miserable are they that afflicted thee, and rejoiced at thy fall.

[32] Miserable are the cities which thy children served: miserable is she that received thy sons.

[33] For as she rejoiced at thy ruin, and was glad of thy fall: so shall she be grieved for her own desolation.

[34] For I will take away the rejoicing of her great multitude, and her pride shall be turned into mourning.

[35] For fire shall come upon her from the Everlasting, long to endure; and she shall be inhabited of devils for a great time.

[36] O Jerusalem, look about thee toward the east, and behold the joy that cometh unto thee from God.

[37] Lo, thy sons come, whom thou sentest away, they come gathered together from the east to the west by the word of the Holy One, rejoicing in the glory of God.

Bar.5

[1] Put off, O Jerusalem, the garment of mourning and affliction, and put on the comeliness of the glory that cometh from God for ever.

[2] Cast about thee a double garment of the righteousness which cometh from God; and set a diadem on thine head of the glory of the Everlasting.

[3] For God will shew thy brightness unto every country under heaven.

[4] For thy name shall be called of God for ever The peace of righteousness, and The glory of God's worship.

[5] Arise, O Jerusalem, and stand on high, and look about toward the east, and behold thy children gathered from the west unto the east by the word of the Holy One, rejoicing in the remembrance of God.

[6] For they departed from thee on foot, and were led away of their enemies: but God bringeth them unto thee exalted with glory, as children of the kingdom.

[7] For God hath appointed that every high hill, and banks of long continuance, should be cast down, and valleys filled up, to make even the ground, that Israel may go safely in the glory of God,

[8] Moreover even the woods and every sweetsmelling tree shall overshadow Israel by the commandment of God.

[9] For God shall lead Israel with joy in the light of his glory with the mercy and righteousness that cometh from him.

Additions Of The Book Of Esther

AddEsth.1

[1] Then Mardocheus said, God hath done these things.

[2] For I remember a dream which I saw concerning these matters, and nothing thereof hath failed.

[3] A little fountain became a river, and there was light, and the sun, and much water: this river is Esther, whom the king married, and made queen:

[4] And the two dragons are I and Aman.

[5] And the nations were those that were assembled to destroy the name of the Jews:

[6] And my nation is this Israel, which cried to God, and were saved: for the Lord hath saved his people, and the Lord hath delivered us from all those evils, and God hath wrought signs and great wonders, which have not been done among the Gentiles.

[7] Therefore hath he made two lots, one for the people of God, and another for all the Gentiles.

[8] And these two lots came at the hour, and time, and day of judgment, before God among all nations.

[9] So God remembered his people, and justified his inheritance.

[10] Therefore those days shall be unto them in the month Adar, the fourteenth and fifteenth day of the same month, with an assembly, and joy, and with gladness before God, according to the generations for ever among his people.

AddEsth.2

[1] In the fourth year of the reign of Ptolemeus and Cleopatra, Dositheus, who said he was a priest and Levite, and Ptolemeus his son, brought this epistle of Phurim, which they said was the same, and that Lysimachus the son of Ptolemeus, that was in Jerusalem, had interpreted it.

[2] In the second year of the reign of Artexerxes the great, in the first day of the month Nisan, Mardocheus the son of Jairus, the son of Semei, the son of Cisai, of the tribe of Benjamin, had a dream;

[3] Who was a Jew, and dwelt in the city of Susa, a great man, being a servitor in the king's court.

[4] He was also one of the captives, which Nabuchodonosor the king of Babylon carried from Jerusalem with Jechonias king of Judea; and this was his dream:

[5] Behold a noise of a tumult, with thunder, and earthquakes, and uproar in the land:

[6] And, behold, two great dragons came forth ready to fight, and their cry was great.

[7] And at their cry all nations were prepared to battle, that they might fight against the righteous people.

[8] And lo a day of darkness and obscurity, tribulation and anguish, affliction and great uproar, upon earth.

[9] And the whole righteous nation was troubled, fearing their own evils, and were ready to perish.

[10] Then they cried unto God, and upon their cry, as it were from a little fountain, was made a great flood, even much water.

[11] The light and the sun rose up, and the lowly were exalted, and devoured the glorious.

[12] Now when Mardocheus, who had seen this dream, and what God had determined to do, was awake, he bare this dream in mind, and until night by all means was desirous to know it.

AddEsth.3

[1] And Mardocheus took his rest in the court with Gabatha and Tharra, the two eunuchs of the king, and keepers of the palace.

[2] And he heard their devices, and searched out their purposes, and learned that they were about to lay hands upon Artexerxes the king; and so he certified the king of them.

[3] Then the king examined the two eunuchs, and after that they had confessed it, they were strangled.

[4] And the king made a record of these things, and Mardocheus also wrote thereof.

[5] So the king commanded, Mardocheus to serve in the court, and for this he rewarded him.

[6] Howbeit Aman the son of Amadathus the Agagite, who was in great honour with the king, sought to molest Mardocheus and his people because of the two eunuchs of the king.

AddEsth.4

[1] The copy of the letters was this: The great king Artexerxes writeth these things to the princes and governours that are under him from India unto Ethiopia in an hundred and seven and twenty provinces.

[2] After that I became lord over many nations and had dominion over the whole world, not lifted up with presumption of my authority, but carrying myself always with equity and mildness, I purposed to settle my subjects continually in a quiet life, and making my kingdom peaceable, and open for passage to the utmost coasts, to renew peace, which is desired of all men.

[3] Now when I asked my counsellors how this might be brought to pass, Aman, that excelled in wisdom among us, and was approved for his constant good will and steadfast fidelity, and had the honour of the second place in the kingdom,

[4] Declared unto us, that in all nations throughout the world there was scattered a certain malicious people, that had laws contrary to ail nations, and continually despised the commandments of kings, so as the uniting of our kingdoms, honourably intended by us cannot go forward.

[5] Seeing then we understand that this people alone is continually in opposition unto all men, differing in the strange manner of their laws, and evil affected to our state, working all the mischief they can that our kingdom may not be firmly established:

[6] Therefore have we commanded, that all they that are signified in writing unto you by Aman, who is ordained over the affairs, and is next unto us, shall all, with their wives and children, be utterly destroyed by the sword of their enemies, without all mercy and pity, the fourteenth day of the twelfth month Adar of this present year:

[7] That they, who of old and now also are malicious, may in one day with violence go into the grave, and so ever hereafter cause our affairs to be well settled, and without trouble.

[8] Then Mardocheus thought upon all the works of the Lord, and made his prayer unto him,

[9] Saying, O Lord, Lord, the King Almighty: for the whole world is in thy power, and if thou hast appointed to save Israel, there is no man that can gainsay thee:

[10] For thou hast made heaven and earth, and all the wondrous things under the heaven.

[11] Thou art Lord of all things, and and there is no man that can resist thee, which art the Lord.

[12] Thou knowest all things, and thou knowest, Lord, that it was neither in contempt nor pride, nor for any desire of glory, that I did not bow down to proud Aman.

[13] For I could have been content with good will for the salvation of Israel to kiss the soles of his feet.

[14] But I did this, that I might not prefer the glory of man above the glory of God: neither will I worship any but thee, O God, neither will I do it in pride.

[15] And now, O Lord God and King, spare thy people: for their eyes are upon us to bring us to nought; yea, they desire to destroy the inheritance, that hath been thine from the beginning.

[16] Despise not the portion, which thou hast delivered out of Egypt for thine own self.

[17] Hear my prayer, and be merciful unto thine inheritance: turn our sorrow into joy, that we may live, O Lord, and praise thy name: and destroy not the mouths of them that praise thee, O Lord.

[18] All Israel in like manner cried most earnestly unto the Lord, because their death was before their eyes.

AddEsth.5

[1] Queen Esther also, being in fear of death, resorted unto the Lord:

[2] And laid away her glorious apparel, and put on the garments of anguish and mourning: and instead of precious ointments, she covered her head with ashes and dung, and she humbled her body greatly, and all the places of her joy she filled with her torn hair.

[3] And she prayed unto the Lord God of Israel, saying, O my Lord, thou only art our King: help me, desolate woman, which have no helper but thee:

[4] For my danger is in mine hand.

[5] From my youth up I have heard in the tribe of my family that thou, O Lord, tookest Israel from among all people, and our fathers from all their predecessors, for a perpetual inheritance, and thou hast performed whatsoever thou didst promise them.

[6] And now we have sinned before thee: therefore hast thou given us into the hands of our enemies,

[7] Because we worshipped their gods: O Lord, thou art righteous.

[8] Nevertheless it satisfieth them not, that we are in bitter captivity: but they have stricken hands with their idols,

[9] That they will abolish the thing that thou with thy mouth hast ordained, and destroy thine inheritance, and stop the mouth of them that praise thee, and quench the glory of thy house, and of thine altar,

[10] And open the mouths of the heathen to set forth the praises of the idols, and to magnify a fleshly king for ever.

[11] O Lord, give not thy sceptre unto them that be nothing, and let them not laugh at our fall; but turn their device upon

themselves, and make him an example, that hath begun this against us.

[12] Remember, O Lord, make thyself known in time of our affliction, and give me boldness, O King of the nations, and Lord of all power.

[13] Give me eloquent speech in my mouth before the lion: turn his heart to hate him that fighteth against us, that there may be an end of him, and of all that are likeminded to him:

[14] But deliver us with thine hand, and help me that am desolate, and which have no other help but thee.

[15] Thou knowest all things, O Lord; thou knowest that I hate the glory of the unrighteous, and abhor the bed of the uncircumcised, and of all the heathen.

[16] Thou knowest my necessity: for I abhor the sign of my high estate, which is upon mine head in the days wherein I shew myself, and that I abhor it as a menstruous rag, and that I wear it not when I am private by myself.

[17] And that thine handmaid hath not eaten at Aman's table, and that I have not greatly esteemed the king's feast, nor drunk the wine of the drink offerings.

[18] Neither had thine handmaid any joy since the day that I was brought hither to this present, but in thee, O Lord God of Abraham.

[19] O thou mighty God above all, hear the voice of the forlorn and deliver us out of the hands of the mischievous, and deliver me out of my fear.

AddEsth.6

[1] And upon the third day, when she had ended her prayers, she laid away her mourning garments, and put on her glorious apparel.

[2] And being gloriously adorned, after she had called upon God, who is the beholder and saviour of all things, she took two maids with her:

[3] And upon the one she leaned, as carrying herself daintily;

[4] And the other followed, bearing up her train.

[5] And she was ruddy through the perfection of her beauty, and her countenance was cheerful and very amiable: but her heart was in anguish for fear.

[6] Then having passed through all the doors, she stood before the king, who sat upon his royal throne, and was clothed with all his robes of majesty, all glittering with gold and precious stones; and he was very dreadful.

[7] Then lifting up his countenance that shone with majesty, he looked very fiercely upon her: and the queen fell down, and was pale, and fainted, and bowed herself upon the head of the maid that went before her.

[8] Then God changed the spirit of the king into mildness, who in a fear leaped from his throne, and took her in his arms, till she came to herself again, and comforted her with loving words and said unto her,

[9] Esther, what is the matter? I am thy brother, be of good cheer:

[10] Thou shalt not die, though our our commandment be general: come near.

[11] And so he held up his golden sceptre, and laid it upon her neck,

[12] And embraced her, and said, Speak unto me.

[13] Then said she unto him, I saw thee, my lord, as an angel of God, and my heart was troubled for fear of thy majesty.

[14] For wonderful art thou, lord, and thy countenance is full of grace.

[15] And as she was speaking, she fell down for faintness.

[16] Then the king was troubled, and all his servants comforted her.

AddEsth.7

[1] The great king Artexerxes unto the princes and governors of an hundred and seven and twenty provinces from India unto Ethiopia, and unto all our faithful subjects, greeting.

[2] Many, the more often they are honoured with the great bounty of their gracious princes, the more proud they are waxen,

[3] And endeavour to hurt not our subjects only, but not being able to bear abundance, do take in hand to practise also against those that do them good:

[4] And take not only thankfulness away from among men, but also lifted up with the glorious words of lewd persons, that were never good, they think to escape the justice of God, that seeth all things and hateth evil.

[5] Oftentimes also fair speech of those, that are put in trust to manage their friends' affairs, hath caused many that are in authority to be partakers of innocent blood, and hath enwrapped them in remediless calamities:

[6] Beguiling with the falsehood and deceit of their lewd disposition the innocency and goodness of princes.

[7] Now ye may see this, as we have declared, not so much by ancient histories, as ye may, if ye search what hath been wickedly done of late through the pestilent behaviour of them that are unworthily placed in authority.

[8] And we must take care for the time to come, that our kingdom may be quiet and peaceable for all men,

[9] Both by changing our purposes, and always judging things that are evident with more equal proceeding.

[10] For Aman, a Macedonian, the son of Amadatha, being

indeed a stranger from the Persian blood, and far distant from our goodness, and as a stranger received of us,

[11] Had so far forth obtained the favour that we shew toward every nation, as that he was called our father, and was continually honoured of all the next person unto the king.

[12] But he, not bearing his great dignity, went about to deprive us of our kingdom and life:

[13] Having by manifold and cunning deceits sought of us the destruction, as well of Mardocheus, who saved our life, and continually procured our good, as also of blameless Esther, partaker of our kingdom, with their whole nation.

[14] For by these means he thought, finding us destitute of friends to have translated the kingdom of the Persians to the Macedonians.

[15] But we find that the Jews, whom this wicked wretch hath delivered to utter destruction, are no evildoers, but live by most just laws:

[16] And that they be children of the most high and most mighty, living God, who hath ordered the kingdom both unto us and to our progenitors in the most excellent manner.

[17] Wherefore ye shall do well not to put in execution the letters sent unto you by Aman the son of Amadatha.

[18] For he that was the worker of these things, is hanged at the gates of Susa with all his family: God, who ruleth all things, speedily rendering vengeance to him according to his deserts.

[19] Therefore ye shall publish the copy of this letter in all places, that the Jews may freely live after their own laws.

[20] And ye shall aid them, that even the same day, being the thirteenth day of the twelfth month Adar, they may be avenged on them, who in the time of their affliction shall set upon them.

[21] For Almighty God hath turned to joy unto them the day, wherein the chosen people should have perished.

[22] Ye shall therefore among your solemn feasts keep it an high day with all feasting:

[23] That both now and hereafter there may be safety to us and the well affected Persians; but to those which do conspire against us a memorial of destruction.

[24] Therefore every city and country whatsoever, which shall not do according to these things, shall be destroyed without mercy with fire and sword, and shall be made not only unpassable for men, but also most hateful to wild beasts and fowls for ever.

Psalm 151

151A (Hebrew)

A Hallelujah of David, Jesse's son.

[1] I was the smallest of my brothers,
  the youngest of my father's sons.
He made me shepherd of his flock,
  ruler over their young.

[2] My hands made a flute,
  my fingers a lyre.
Let me give glory to the Lord,
  I thought to myself.

[3] The mountains
cannot witness to God;
  the hills cannot proclaim him.
But the trees have cherished
my words,
  the flocks my deeds.

[4] Who can proclaim,
  who can announce,
  who can declare the Lord's deeds?
God has seen everything;
God has heard everything;
God has listened.

[5] God sent his prophet to anoint me;
  Samuel to make me great.
My brothers went out to meet him,
  handsome in form and appearance:

[6] Their stature tall,
  their hair beautiful,
  but the Lord God
  did not choose them.

[7] Instead, he sent and took me
from following the flock.
God anointed me with holy oil;
  God made me leader for his people,
  ruler over the children
  of his covenant.

151B (Hebrew and Syriac)

At the beginning of David's power after the prophet of God anointed him.

[1] I went out to attack the Philistine,
  who cursed me by his idols.

[2] But after I uncovered his own sword,
  I cut off his head.
So I removed the shame
from the Israelites.

151C (Greek)

This additional psalm is said to have been written by David when he fought Goliath in single combat.

[1] I was small among my brothers,
  and the youngest of my father's sons.
  I was shepherd of my father's sheep.

[2] My hands made a musical instrument;
  my fingers strung a lap harp.

[3] Who will tell my Lord?
  The Lord himself, the Lord hears me.

[4] The Lord himself sent his messenger,
  and took me away
  from my father's sheep.
  He put special oil on my forehead
  to anoint me.

[5] My brothers were good-looking and tall,
  but the Lord didn't take
  special pleasure in them.

[6] I went out to meet the Philistine,
  who cursed me by his idols.

[7] But I took his own sword out of its sheath
  and cut off his head.
So I removed the shame
from the Israelites.

The Wisdom Of Jesus Son Of Sirach (The Book Of Sirach or Ecclesiasticus)

Sir.1

[1] All wisdom cometh from the Lord, and is with him for ever.

[2] Who can number the sand of the sea, and the drops of rain, and the days of eternity?

[3] Who can find out the height of heaven, and the breadth of the earth, and the deep, and wisdom?

[4] Wisdom hath been created before all things, and the understanding of prudence from everlasting.

[5] The word of God most high is the fountain of wisdom; and her ways are everlasting commandments.

[6] To whom hath the root of wisdom been revealed? or who hath known her wise counsels?

[7] Unto whom hath the knowledge of wisdom been made manifest? and who hath understood her great experience?

[8] There is one wise and greatly to be feared, the Lord sitting upon his throne.

[9] He created her, and saw her, and numbered her, and poured her out upon all his works.

[10] She is with all flesh according to his gift, and he hath given her to them that love him.

[11] The fear of the Lord is honour, and glory, and gladness, and a crown of rejoicing.

[12] The fear of the Lord maketh a merry heart, and giveth joy, and gladness, and a long life.

[13] Whoso feareth the Lord, it shall go well with him at the last, and he shall find favour in the day of his death.

[14] To fear the Lord is the beginning of wisdom: and it was created with the faithful in the womb.

[15] She hath built an everlasting foundation with men, and she shall continue with their seed.

[16] To fear the Lord is fulness of wisdom, and filleth men with her fruits.

[17] She filleth all their house with things desirable, and the garners with her increase.

[18] The fear of the Lord is a crown of wisdom, making peace and perfect health to flourish; both which are the gifts of God: and it enlargeth their rejoicing that love him.

[19] Wisdom raineth down skill and knowledge of understanding standing, and exalteth them to honour that hold her fast.

[20] The root of wisdom is to fear the Lord, and the branches thereof are long life.

[21] The fear of the Lord driveth away sins: and where it is present, it turneth away wrath.

[22] A furious man cannot be justified; for the sway of his fury shall be his destruction.

[23] A patient man will tear for a time, and afterward joy shall spring up unto him.

[24] He will hide his words for a time, and the lips of many shall declare his wisdom.

[25] The parables of knowledge are in the treasures of wisdom: but godliness is an abomination to a sinner.

[26] If thou desire wisdom, keep the commandments, and the Lord shall give her unto thee.

[27] For the fear of the Lord is wisdom and instruction: and faith and meekness are his delight.

[28] Distrust not the fear of the Lord when thou art poor: and come not unto him with a double heart.

[29] Be not an hypocrite in the sight of men, and take good heed what thou speakest.

[30] Exalt not thyself, lest thou fall, and bring dishonour upon thy soul, and so God discover thy secrets, and cast thee down in the midst of the congregation, because thou camest not in truth to the fear of the Lord, but thy heart is full of deceit.

Sir.2

[1] My son, if thou come to serve the Lord, prepare thy soul for temptation.

[2] Set thy heart aright, and constantly endure, and make not haste in time of trouble.

[3] Cleave unto him, and depart not away, that thou mayest be increased at thy last end.

[4] Whatsoever is brought upon thee take cheerfully, and be patient when thou art changed to a low estate.

[5] For gold is tried in the fire, and acceptable men in the furnace of adversity.

[6] Believe in him, and he will help thee; order thy way aright, and trust in him.

[7] Ye that fear the Lord, wait for his mercy; and go not

aside, lest ye fall.

[8] Ye that fear the Lord, believe him; and your reward shall not fail.

[9] Ye that fear the Lord, hope for good, and for everlasting joy and mercy.

[10] Look at the generations of old, and see; did ever any trust in the Lord, and was confounded? or did any abide in his fear, and was forsaken? or whom did he ever despise, that called upon him?

[11] For the Lord is full of compassion and mercy, longsuffering, and very pitiful, and forgiveth sins, and saveth in time of affliction.

[12] Woe be to fearful hearts, and faint hands, and the sinner that goeth two ways!

[13] Woe unto him that is fainthearted! for he believeth not; therefore shall he not be defended.

[14] Woe unto you that have lost patience! and what will ye do when the Lord shall visit you?

[15] They that fear the Lord will not disobey his Word; and they that love him will keep his ways.

[16] They that fear the Lord will seek that which is well, pleasing unto him; and they that love him shall be filled with the law.

[17] They that fear the Lord will prepare their hearts, and humble their souls in his sight,

[18] Saying, We will fall into the hands of the Lord, and not into the hands of men: for as his majesty is, so is his mercy.

Sir.3

[1] Hear me your father, O children, and do thereafter, that ye may be safe.

[2] For the Lord hath given the father honour over the children, and hath confirmed the authority of the mother over the sons.

[3] Whoso honoureth his father maketh an atonement for his sins:

[4] And he that honoureth his mother is as one that layeth up treasure.

[5] Whoso honoureth his father shall have joy of his own children; and when he maketh his prayer, he shall be heard.

[6] He that honoureth his father shall have a long life; and he that is obedient unto the Lord shall be a comfort to his mother.

[7] He that feareth the Lord will honour his father, and will do service unto his parents, as to his masters.

[8] Honour thy father and mother both in word and deed, that a blessing may come upon thee from them.

[9] For the blessing of the father establisheth the houses of children; but the curse of the mother rooteth out foundations.

[10] Glory not in the dishonour of thy father; for thy father's dishonour is no glory unto thee.

[11] For the glory of a man is from the honour of his father; and a mother in dishonour is a reproach to the children.

[12] My son, help thy father in his age, and grieve him not as long as he liveth.

[13] And if his understanding fail, have patience with him; and despise him not when thou art in thy full strength.

[14] For the relieving of thy father shall not be forgotten: and instead of sins it shall be added to build thee up.

[15] In the day of thine affliction it shall be remembered; thy sins also shall melt away, as the ice in the fair warm weather.

[16] He that forsaketh his father is as a blasphemer; and he that angereth his mother is cursed: of God.

[17] My son, go on with thy business in meekness; so shalt thou be beloved of him that is approved.

[18] The greater thou art, the more humble thyself, and thou shalt find favour before the Lord.

[19] Many are in high place, and of renown: but mysteries are revealed unto the meek.

[20] For the power of the Lord is great, and he is honoured of the lowly.

[21] Seek not out things that are too hard for thee, neither search the things that are above thy strength.

[22] But what is commanded thee, think thereupon with reverence, for it is not needful for thee to see with thine eyes the things that are in secret.

[23] Be not curious in unnecessary matters: for more things are shewed unto thee than men understand.

[24] For many are deceived by their own vain opinion; and an evil suspicion hath overthrown their judgment.

[25] Without eyes thou shalt want light: profess not the knowledge therefore that thou hast not.

[26] A stubborn heart shall fare evil at the last; and he that loveth danger shall perish therein.

[27] An obstinate heart shall be laden with sorrows; and the wicked man shall heap sin upon sin.

[28] In the punishment of the proud there is no remedy; for the plant of wickedness hath taken root in him.

[29] The heart of the prudent will understand a parable; and an attentive ear is the desire of a wise man.

[30] Water will quench a flaming fire; and alms maketh an atonement for sins.

[31] And he that requiteth good turns is mindful of that which may come hereafter; and when he falleth, he shall find a stay.

Sir.4

[1] My son, defraud not the poor of his living, and make not the needy eyes to wait long.

[2] Make not an hungry soul sorrowful; neither provoke a man in his distress.

[3] Add not more trouble to an heart that is vexed; and defer not to give to him that is in need.

[4] Reject not the supplication of the afflicted; neither turn away thy face from a poor man.

[5] Turn not away thine eye from the needy, and give him none occasion to curse thee:

[6] For if he curse thee in the bitterness of his soul, his prayer shall be heard of him that made him.

[7] Get thyself the love of the congregation, and bow thy head to a great man.

[8] Let it not grieve thee to bow down thine ear to the poor, and give him a friendly answer with meekness.

[9] Deliver him that suffereth wrong from the hand of the oppressor; and be not fainthearted when thou sittest in judgment.

[10] Be as a father unto the fatherless, and instead of an husband unto their mother: so shalt thou be as the son of the most High, and he shall love thee more than thy mother doth.

[11] Wisdom exalteth her children, and layeth hold of them that seek her.

[12] He that loveth her loveth life; and they that seek to her early shall be filled with joy.

[13] He that holdeth her fast shall inherit glory; and wheresoever she entereth, the Lord will bless.

[14] They that serve her shall minister to the Holy One: and them that love her the Lord doth love.

[15] Whoso giveth ear unto her shall judge the nations: and he that attendeth unto her shall dwell securely.

[16] If a man commit himself unto her, he shall inherit her; and his generation shall hold her in possession.

[17] For at the first she will walk with him by crooked ways, and bring fear and dread upon him, and torment him with her discipline, until she may trust his soul, and try him by her laws.

[18] Then will she return the straight way unto him, and comfort him, and shew him her secrets.

[19] But if he go wrong, she will forsake him, and give him over to his own ruin.

[20] Observe the opportunity, and beware of evil; and be not ashamed when it concerneth thy soul.

[21] For there is a shame that bringeth sin; and there is a shame which is glory and grace.

[22] Accept no person against thy soul, and let not the reverence of any man cause thee to fall.

[23] And refrain not to speak, when there is occasion to do good, and hide not thy wisdom in her beauty.

[24] For by speech wisdom shall be known: and learning by the word of the tongue.

[25] In no wise speak against the truth; but be abashed of the error of thine ignorance.

[26] Be not ashamed to confess thy sins; and force not the course of the river.

[27] Make not thyself an underling to a foolish man; neither accept the person of the mighty.

[28] Strive for the truth unto death, and the Lord shall fight for thee.

[29] Be not hasty in thy tongue, and in thy deeds slack and remiss.

[30] Be not as a lion in thy house, nor frantick among thy servants.

[31] Let not thine hand be stretched out to receive, and shut when thou shouldest repay.

Sir.5

[1] Set thy heart upon thy goods; and say not, I have enough for my life.

[2] Follow not thine own mind and thy strength, to walk in the ways of thy heart:

[3] And say not, Who shall controul me for my works? for the Lord will surely revenge thy pride.

[4] Say not, I have sinned, and what harm hath happened unto me? for the Lord is longsuffering, he will in no wise let thee go.

[5] Concerning propitiation, be not without fear to add sin unto sin:

[6] And say not His mercy is great; he will be pacified for the multitude of my sins: for mercy and wrath come from him, and his indignation resteth upon sinners.

[7] Make no tarrying to turn to the Lord, and put not off from day to day: for suddenly shall the wrath of the Lord come forth, and in thy security thou shalt be destroyed, and perish in the day of vengeance.

[8] Set not thine heart upon goods unjustly gotten, for they shall not profit thee in the day of calamity.

[9] Winnow not with every wind, and go not into every way: for so doth the sinner that hath a double tongue.

[10] Be stedfast in thy understanding; and let thy word be the same.

[11] Be swift to hear; and let thy life be sincere; and with patience give answer.

[12] If thou hast understanding, answer thy neighbour; if not, lay thy hand upon thy mouth.

[13] Honour and shame is in talk: and the tongue of man is his fall.

[14] Be not called a whisperer, and lie not in wait with thy tongue: for a foul shame is upon the thief, and an evil condemnation upon the double tongue.

[15] Be not ignorant of any thing in a great matter or a small.

Sir.6

[1] Instead of a friend become not an enemy; for [thereby] thou shalt inherit an ill name, shame, and reproach: even so shall a sinner that hath a double tongue.

[2] Extol not thyself in the counsel of thine own heart; that thy soul be not torn in pieces as a bull [straying alone.]

[3] Thou shalt eat up thy leaves, and lose thy fruit, and leave thyself as a dry tree.

[4] A wicked soul shall destroy him that hath it, and shall make him to be laughed to scorn of his enemies.

[5] Sweet language will multiply friends: and a fairspeaking tongue will increase kind greetings.

[6] Be in peace with many: nevertheless have but one counsellor of a thousand.

[7] If thou wouldest get a friend, prove him first and be not hasty to credit him.

[8] For some man is a friend for his own occasion, and will not abide in the day of thy trouble.

[9] And there is a friend, who being turned to enmity, and strife will discover thy reproach.

[10] Again, some friend is a companion at the table, and will not continue in the day of thy affliction.

[11] But in thy prosperity he will be as thyself, and will be bold over thy servants.

[12] If thou be brought low, he will be against thee, and will hide himself from thy face.

[13] Separate thyself from thine enemies, and take heed of thy friends.

[14] A faithful friend is a strong defence: and he that hath found such an one hath found a treasure.

[15] Nothing doth countervail a faithful friend, and his excellency is invaluable.

[16] A faithful friend is the medicine of life; and they that fear the Lord shall find him.

[17] Whoso feareth the Lord shall direct his friendship aright: for as he is, so shall his neighbour be also.

[18] My son, gather instruction from thy youth up: so shalt thou find wisdom till thine old age.

[19] Come unto her as one that ploweth and soweth, and wait for her good fruits: for thou shalt not toil much in labouring about her, but thou shalt eat of her fruits right soon.

[20] She is very unpleasant to the unlearned: he that is without understanding will not remain with her.

[21] She will lie upon him as a mighty stone of trial; and he will cast her from him ere it be long.

[22] For wisdom is according to her name, and she is not manifest unto many.

[23] Give ear, my son, receive my advice, and refuse not my counsel,

[24] And put thy feet into her fetters, and thy neck into her chain.

[25] Bow down thy shoulder, and bear her, and be not grieved with her bonds.

[26] Come unto her with thy whole heart, and keep her ways with all thy power.

[27] Search, and seek, and she shall be made known unto thee: and when thou hast got hold of her, let her not go.

[28] For at the last thou shalt find her rest, and that shall be turned to thy joy.

[29] Then shall her fetters be a strong defence for thee, and her chains a robe of glory.

[30] For there is a golden ornament upon her, and her bands are purple lace.

[31] Thou shalt put her on as a robe of honour, and shalt put her about thee as a crown of joy.

[32] My son, if thou wilt, thou shalt be taught: and if thou wilt apply thy mind, thou shalt be prudent.

[33] If thou love to hear, thou shalt receive understanding: and if thou bow thine ear, thou shalt be wise,

[34] Stand in the multitude of the elders; and cleave unto him that is wise.

[35] Be willing to hear every godly discourse; and let not the parables of understanding escape thee.

[36] And if thou seest a man of understanding, get thee betimes unto him, and let thy foot wear the steps of his door.

[37] Let thy mind be upon the ordinances of the Lord and meditate continually in his commandments: he shall establish thine heart, and give thee wisdom at thine owns desire.

Sir.7

[1] Do no evil, so shall no harm come unto thee.

[2] Depart from the unjust, and iniquity shall turn away from thee.

[3] My son, sow not upon the furrows of unrighteousness, and thou shalt not reap them sevenfold.

[4] Seek not of the Lord preeminence, neither of the king the seat of honour.

[5] justify not thyself before the Lord; and boast not of thy wisdom before the king.

[6] Seek not to be judge, being not able to take away iniquity; lest at any time thou fear the person of the mighty, an stumblingblock in the way of thy uprightness.

[7] Offend not against the multitude of a city, and then thou shalt not cast thyself down among the people.

[8] Bind not one sin upon another; for in one thou shalt not be unpunished.

[9] Say not, God will look upon the multitude of my oblations, and when I offer to the most high God, he will accept it.

[10] Be not fainthearted when thou makest thy prayer, and neglect not to give alms.

[11] Laugh no man to scorn in the bitterness of his soul: for there is one which humbleth and exalteth.

[12] Devise not a lie against thy brother; neither do the like to thy friend.

[13] Use not to make any manner of lie: for the custom thereof is not good.

[14] Use not many words in a multitude of elders, and make not much babbling when thou prayest.

[15] Hate not laborious work, neither husbandry, which the most High hath ordained.

[16] Number not thyself among the multitude of sinners, but remember that wrath will not tarry long.

[17] Humble thyself greatly: for the vengeance of the ungodly is fire and worms.

[18] Change not a friend for any good by no means; neither a faithful brother for the gold of Ophir.

[19] Forego not a wise and good woman: for her grace is above gold.

[20] Whereas thy servant worketh truly, entreat him not evil. nor the hireling that bestoweth himself wholly for thee.

[21] Let thy soul love a good servant, and defraud him not of liberty.

[22] Hast thou cattle? have an eye to them: and if they be for thy profit, keep them with thee.

[23] Hast thou children? instruct them, and bow down their neck from their youth.

[24] Hast thou daughters? have a care of their body, and shew not thyself cheerful toward them.

[25] Marry thy daughter, and so shalt thou have performed a weighty matter: but give her to a man of understanding.

[26] Hast thou a wife after thy mind? forsake her not: but give not thyself over to a light woman.

[27] Honour thy father with thy whole heart, and forget not the sorrows of thy mother.

[28] Remember that thou wast begotten of them; and how canst thou recompense them the things that they have done for thee?

[29] Fear the Lord with all thy soul, and reverence his priests.

[30] Love him that made thee with all thy strength, and forsake not his ministers.

[31] Fear the Lord, and honor the priest; and give him his portion, as it is commanded thee; the firstfruits, and the trespass offering, and the gift of the shoulders, and the sacrifice of sanctification, and the firstfruits of the holy things.

[32] And stretch thine hand unto the poor, that thy blessing may be perfected.

[33] A gift hath grace in the sight of every man living; and for the dead detain it not.

[34] Fail not to be with them that weep, and mourn with them that mourn.

[35] Be not slow to visit the sick: fir that shall make thee to be beloved.

[36] Whatsoever thou takest in hand, remember the end, and thou shalt never do amiss.

Sir.8

[1] Strive not with a mighty man' lest thou fall into his hands.

[2] Be not at variance with a rich man, lest he overweigh thee: for gold hath destroyed many, and perverted the hearts of kings.

[3] Strive not with a man that is full of tongue, and heap not wood upon his fire.

[4] Jest not with a rude man, lest thy ancestors be disgraced.

[5] Reproach not a man that turneth from sin, but remember that we are all worthy of punishment.

[6] Dishonour not a man in his old age: for even some of us wax old.

[7] Rejoice not over thy greatest enemy being dead, but remember that we die all.

[8] Despise not the discourse of the wise, but acquaint thyself with their proverbs: for of them thou shalt learn instruction, and how to serve great men with ease.

[9] Miss not the discourse of the elders: for they also learned of their fathers, and of them thou shalt learn understanding, and to give answer as need requireth.

[10] Kindle not the coals of a sinner, lest thou be burnt with the flame of his fire.

[11] Rise not up [in anger] at the presence of an injurious person, lest he lie in wait to entrap thee in thy words

[12] Lend not unto him that is mightier than thyself; for if

thou lendest him, count it but lost.

[13] Be not surety above thy power: for if thou be surety, take care to pay it.

[14] Go not to law with a judge; for they will judge for him according to his honour.

[15] Travel not by the way with a bold fellow, lest he become grievous unto thee: for he will do according to his own will, and thou shalt perish with him through his folly.

[16] Strive not with an angry man, and go not with him into a solitary place: for blood is as nothing in his sight, and where there is no help, he will overthrow thee.

[17] Consult not with a fool; for he cannot keep counsel.

[18] Do no secret thing before a stranger; for thou knowest not what he will bring forth.

[19] Open not thine heart to every man, lest he requite thee with a shrewd turn.

Sir.9

[1] Be not jealous over the wife of thy bosom, and teach her not an evil lesson against thyself.

[2] Give not thy soul unto a woman to set her foot upon thy substance.

[3] Meet not with an harlot, lest thou fall into her snares.

[4] Use not much the company of a woman that is a singer, lest thou be taken with her attempts.

[5] Gaze not on a maid, that thou fall not by those things that are precious in her.

[6] Give not thy soul unto harlots, that thou lose not thine inheritance.

[7] Look not round about thee in the streets of the city, neither wander thou in the solitary place thereof.

[8] Turn away thine eye from a beautiful woman, and look not upon another's beauty; for many have been deceived by the beauty of a woman; for herewith love is kindled as a fire.

[9] Sit not at all with another man's wife, nor sit down with her in thine arms, and spend not thy money with her at the wine; lest thine heart incline unto her, and so through thy desire thou fall into destruction.

[10] Forsake not an old friend; for the new is not comparable to him: a new friend is as new wine; when it is old, thou shalt drink it with pleasure.

[11] Envy not the glory of a sinner: for thou knowest not what shall be his end.

[12] Delight not in the thing that the ungodly have pleasure in; but remember they shall not go unpunished unto their grave.

[13] Keep thee far from the man that hath power to kill; so shalt thou not doubt the fear of death: and if thou come unto him, make no fault, lest he take away thy life presently: remember that thou goest in the midst of snares, and that thou walkest upon the battlements of the city.

[14] As near as thou canst, guess at thy neighbour, and consult with the wise.

[15] Let thy talk be with the wise, and all thy communication in the law of the most High.

[16] And let just men eat and drink with thee; and let thy glorying be in the fear of the Lord.

[17] For the hand of the artificer the work shall be commended: and the wise ruler of the people for his speech.

[18] A man of an ill tongue is dangerous in his city; and he that is rash in his talk shall be hated.

Sir.10

[1] A wise judge will instruct his people; and the government of a prudent man is well ordered.

[2] As the judge of the people is himself, so are his officers; and what manner of man the ruler of the city is, such are all they that dwell therein.

[3] An unwise king destroyeth his people; but through the prudence of them which are in authority the city shall be inhabited.

[4] The power of the earth is in the hand of the Lord, and in due time he will set over it one that is profitable.

[5] In the hand of God is the prosperity of man: and upon the person of the scribe shall he lay his honour.

[6] Bear not hatred to thy neighbour for every wrong; and do nothing at all by injurious practices.

[7] Pride is hateful before God and man: and by both doth one commit iniquity.

[8] Because of unrighteous dealings, injuries, and riches got by deceit, the kingdom is translated from one people to another.

[9] Why is earth and ashes proud? There is not a more wicked thing than a covetous man: for such an one setteth his own soul to sale; because while he liveth he casteth away his bowels.

[10] The physician cutteth off a long disease; and he that is to day a king to morrow shall die.

[11] For when a man is dead, he shall inherit creeping things, beasts, and worms.

[12] The beginning of pride is when one departeth from God, and his heart is turned away from his Maker.

[13] For pride is the beginning of sin, and he that hath it shall pour out abomination: and therefore the Lord brought upon them strange calamities, and overthrew

them utterly.

[14] The Lord hath cast down the thrones of proud princes, and set up the meek in their stead.

[15] The Lord hath plucked up the roots of the proud nations, and planted the lowly in their place.

[16] The Lord overthrew countries of the heathen, and destroyed them to the foundations of the earth.

[17] He took some of them away, and destroyed them, and hath made their memorial to cease from the earth.

[18] Pride was not made for men, nor furious anger for them that are born of a woman.

[19] They that fear the Lord are a sure seed, and they that love him an honourable plant: they that regard not the law are a dishonourable seed; they that transgress the commandments are a deceivable seed.

[20] Among brethren he that is chief is honorable; so are they that fear the Lord in his eyes.

[21] The fear of the Lord goeth before the obtaining of authority: but roughness and pride is the losing thereof.

[22] Whether he be rich, noble, or poor, their glory is the fear of the Lord.

[23] It is not meet to despise the poor man that hath understanding; neither is it convenient to magnify a sinful man.

[24] Great men, and judges, and potentates, shall be honoured; yet is there none of them greater than he that feareth the Lord.

[25] Unto the servant that is wise shall they that are free do service: and he that hath knowledge will not grudge when he is reformed.

[26] Be not overwise in doing thy business; and boast not thyself in the time of thy distress.

[27] Better is he that laboureth, and aboundeth in all things, than he that boasteth himself, and wanteth bread.

[28] My son, glorify thy soul in meekness, and give it honour according to the dignity thereof.

[29] Who will justify him that sinneth against his own soul? and who will honour him that dishonoureth his own life?

[30] The poor man is honoured for his skill, and the rich man is honoured for his riches.

[31] He that is honoured in poverty, how much more in riches? and he that is dishonourable in riches, how much more in poverty?

Sir.11

[1] Wisdom lifteth up the head of him that is of low degree, and maketh him to sit among great men.

[2] Commend not a man for his beauty; neither abhor a man for his outward appearance.

[3] The bee is little among such as fly; but her fruit is the chief of sweet things.

[4] Boast not of thy clothing and raiment, and exalt not thyself in the day of honour: for the works of the Lord are wonderful, and his works among men are hidden.

[5] Many kings have sat down upon the ground; and one that was never thought of hath worn the crown.

[6] Many mighty men have been greatly disgraced; and the honourable delivered into other men's hands.

[7] Blame not before thou hast examined the truth: understand first, and then rebuke.

[8] Answer not before thou hast heard the cause: neither interrupt men in the midst of their talk.

[9] Strive not in a matter that concerneth thee not; and sit not in judgment with sinners.

[10] My son, meddle not with many matters: for if thou meddle much, thou shalt not be innocent; and if thou follow after, thou shalt not obtain, neither shalt thou escape by fleeing.

[11] There is one that laboureth, and taketh pains, and maketh haste, and is so much the more behind.

[12] Again, there is another that is slow, and hath need of help, wanting ability, and full of poverty; yet the eye of the Lord looked upon him for good, and set him up from his low estate,

[13] And lifted up his head from misery; so that many that saw from him is peace over all the

[14] Prosperity and adversity, life and death, poverty and riches, come of the Lord.

[15] Wisdom, knowledge, and understanding of the law, are of the Lord: love, and the way of good works, are from him.

[16] Error and darkness had their beginning together with sinners: and evil shall wax old with them that glory therein.

[17] The gift of the Lord remaineth with the ungodly, and his favour bringeth prosperity for ever.

[18] There is that waxeth rich by his wariness and pinching, and this his the portion of his reward:

[19] Whereas he saith, I have found rest, and now will eat continually of my goods; and yet he knoweth not what time shall come upon him, and that he must leave those things to others, and die.

[20] Be stedfast in thy covenant, and be conversant therein, and wax old in thy work.

[21] Marvel not at the works of sinners; but trust in the Lord, and abide in thy labour: for it is an easy thing in the sight of the Lord on the sudden to make a poor man rich.

[22] The blessing of the Lord is in the reward of the godly,

and suddenly he maketh his blessing flourish.

[23] Say not, What profit is there of my service? and what good things shall I have hereafter?

[24] Again, say not, I have enough, and possess many things, and what evil shall I have hereafter?

[25] In the day of prosperity there is a forgetfulness of affliction: and in the day of affliction there is no more remembrance of prosperity.

[26] For it is an easy thing unto the Lord in the day of death to reward a man according to his ways.

[27] The affliction of an hour maketh a man forget pleasure: and in his end his deeds shall be discovered.

[28] Judge none blessed before his death: for a man shall be known in his children.

[29] Bring not every man into thine house: for the deceitful man hath many trains.

[30] Like as a partridge taken [and kept] in a cage, so is the heart of the proud; and like as a spy, watcheth he for thy fall:

[31] For he lieth in wait, and turneth good into evil, and in things worthy praise will lay blame upon thee.

[32] Of a spark of fire a heap of coals is kindled: and a sinful man layeth wait for blood.

[33] Take heed of a mischievous man, for he worketh wickedness; lest he bring upon thee a perpetual blot.

[34] Receive a stranger into thine house, and he will disturb thee, and turn thee out of thine own.

Sir.12

[1] When thou wilt do good know to whom thou doest it; so shalt thou be thanked for thy benefits.

[2] Do good to the godly man, and thou shalt find a recompence; and if not from him, yet from the most High.

[3] There can no good come to him that is always occupied in evil, nor to him that giveth no alms.

[4] Give to the godly man, and help not a sinner.

[5] Do well unto him that is lowly, but give not to the ungodly: hold back thy bread, and give it not unto him, lest he overmaster thee thereby: for [else] thou shalt receive twice as much evil for all the good thou shalt have done unto him.

[6] For the most High hateth sinners, and will repay vengeance unto the ungodly, and keepeth them against the mighty day of their punishment.

[7] Give unto the good, and help not the sinner.

[8] A friend cannot be known in prosperity: and an enemy cannot be hidden in adversity.

[9] In the prosperity of a man enemies will be grieved: but in his adversity even a friend will depart.

[10] Never trust thine enemy: for like as iron rusteth, so is his wickedness.

[11] Though he humble himself, and go crouching, yet take good heed and beware of him, and thou shalt be unto him as if thou hadst wiped a lookingglass, and thou shalt know that his rust hath not been altogether wiped away.

[12] Set him not by thee, lest, when he hath overthrown thee, he stand up in thy place; neither let him sit at thy right hand, lest he seek to take thy seat, and thou at the last remember my words, and be pricked therewith.

[13] Who will pity a charmer that is bitten with a serpent, or any such as come nigh wild beasts?

[14] So one that goeth to a sinner, and is defiled with him in his sins, who will pity?

[15] For a while he will abide with thee, but if thou begin to fall, he will not tarry.

[16] An enemy speaketh sweetly with his lips, but in his heart he imagineth how to throw thee into a pit: he will weep with his eyes, but if he find opportunity, he will not be satisfied with blood.

[17] If adversity come upon thee, thou shalt find him there first; and though he pretend to help thee, yet shall he undermine thee.

[18] He will shake his head, and clap his hands, and whisper much, and change his countenance.

Sir.13

[1] He that toucheth pitch shall be defiled therewith; and he that hath fellowship with a proud man shall be like unto him.

[2] Burden not thyself above thy power while thou livest; and have no fellowship with one that is mightier and richer than thyself: for how agree the kettle and the earthen pot together? for if the one be smitten against the other, it shall be broken.

[3] The rich man hath done wrong, and yet he threateneth withal: the poor is wronged, and he must intreat also.

[4] If thou be for his profit, he will use thee: but if thou have nothing, he will forsake thee.

[5] If thou have any thing, he will live with thee: yea, he will make thee bare, and will not be sorry for it.

[6] If he have need of thee, he will deceive thee, and smile upon thee, and put thee in hope; he will speak thee fair, and say, What wantest thou?

[7] And he will shame thee by his meats, until he have drawn thee dry twice or thrice, and at the last he will laugh thee to scorn afterward, when he seeth thee, he will forsake thee, and shake his head at thee.

[8] Beware that thou be not deceived and brought down in

thy jollity.

[9] If thou be invited of a mighty man, withdraw thyself, and so much the more will he invite thee.

[10] Press thou not upon him, lest thou be put back; stand not far off, lest thou be forgotten.

[11] Affect not to be made equal unto him in talk, and believe not his many words: for with much communication will he tempt thee, and smiling upon thee will get out thy secrets:

[12] But cruelly he will lay up thy words, and will not spare to do thee hurt, and to put thee in prison.

[13] Observe, and take good heed, for thou walkest in peril of thy overthrowing: when thou hearest these things, awake in thy sleep.

[14] Love the Lord all thy life, and call upon him for thy salvation.

[15] Every beast loveth his like, and every man loveth his neighbor.

[16] All flesh consorteth according to kind, and a man will cleave to his like.

[17] What fellowship hath the wolf with the lamb? so the sinner with the godly.

[18] What agreement is there between the hyena and a dog? and what peace between the rich and the poor?

[19] As the wild ass is the lion's prey in the wilderness: so the rich eat up the poor.

[20] As the proud hate humility: so doth the rich abhor the poor.

[21] A rich man beginning to fall is held up of his friends: but a poor man being down is thrust away by his friends.

[22] When a rich man is fallen, he hath many helpers: he speaketh things not to be spoken, and yet men justify him: the poor man slipped, and yet they rebuked him too; he spake wisely, and could have no place.

[23] When a rich man speaketh, every man holdeth his tongue, and, look, what he saith, they extol it to the clouds: but if the poor man speak, they say, What fellow is this? and if he stumble, they will help to overthrow him.

[24] Riches are good unto him that hath no sin, and poverty is evil in the mouth of the ungodly.

[25] The heart of a man changeth his countenance, whether it be for good or evil: and a merry heart maketh a cheerful countenance.

[26] A cheerful countenance is a token of a heart that is in prosperity; and the finding out of parables is a wearisome labour of the mind.

Sir.14

[1] Blessed is the man that hath not slipped with his mouth, and is not pricked with the multitude of sins.

[2] Blessed is he whose conscience hath not condemned him, and who is not fallen from his hope in the Lord.

[3] Riches are not comely for a niggard: and what should an envious man do with money?

[4] He that gathereth by defrauding his own soul gathereth for others, that shall spend his goods riotously.

[5] He that is evil to himself, to whom will he be good? he shall not take pleasure in his goods.

[6] There is none worse than he that envieth himself; and this is a recompence of his wickedness.

[7] And if he doeth good, he doeth it unwillingly; and at the last he will declare his wickedness.

[8] The envious man hath a wicked eye; he turneth away his face, and despiseth men.

[9] A covetous man's eye is not satisfied with his portion; and the iniquity of the wicked drieth up his soul.

[10] A wicked eye envieth [his] bread, and he is a niggard at his table.

[11] My son, according to thy ability do good to thyself, and give the Lord his due offering.

[12] Remember that death will not be long in coming, and that the covenant of the grave is not shewed unto thee.

[13] Do good unto thy friend before thou die, and according to thy ability stretch out thy hand and give to him.

[14] Defraud not thyself of the good day, and let not the part of a good desire overpass thee.

[15] Shalt thou not leave thy travails unto another? and thy labours to be divided by lot?

[16] Give, and take, and sanctify thy soul; for there is no seeking of dainties in the grave.

[17] All flesh waxeth old as a garment: for the covenant from the beginning is, Thou shalt die the death.

[18] As of the green leaves on a thick tree, some fall, and some grow; so is the generation of flesh and blood, one cometh to an end, and another is born.

[19] Every work rotteth and consumeth away, and the worker thereof shall go withal.

[20] Blessed is the man that doth meditate good things in wisdom, and that reasoneth of holy things by his understanding. ing.

[21] He that considereth her ways in his heart shall also have understanding in her secrets.

[22] Go after her as one that traceth, and lie in wait in her ways.

[23] He that prieth in at her windows shall also hearken at

her doors.

[24] He that doth lodge near her house shall also fasten a pin in her walls.

[25] He shall pitch his tent nigh unto her, and shall lodge in a lodging where good things are.

[26] He shall set his children under her shelter, and shall lodge under her branches.

[27] By her he shall be covered from heat, and in her glory shall he dwell.

Sir.15

[1] He that feareth the Lord will do good, and he that hath the knowledge of the law shall obtain her.

[2] And as a mother shall she meet him, and receive him as a wife married of a virgin.

[3] With the bread of understanding shall she feed him, and give him the water of wisdom to drink.

[4] He shall be stayed upon her, and shall not be moved; and shall rely upon her, and shall not be confounded.

[5] She shall exalt him above his neighbours, and in the midst of the congregation shall she open his mouth.

[6] He shall find joy and a crown of gladness, and she shall cause him to inherit an everlasting name.

[7] But foolish men shall not attain unto her, and sinners shall not see her.

[8] For she is far from pride, and men that are liars cannot remember her.

[9] Praise is not seemly in the mouth of a sinner, for it was not sent him of the Lord.

[10] For praise shall be uttered in wisdom, and the Lord will prosper it.

[11] Say not thou, It is through the Lord that I fell away: for thou oughtest not to do the things that he hateth.

[12] Say not thou, He hath caused me to err: for he hath no need of the sinful man.

[13] The Lord hateth all abomination; and they that fear God love it not.

[14] He himself made man from the beginning, and left him in the hand of his counsel;

[15] If thou wilt, to keep the commandments, and to perform acceptable faithfulness.

[16] He hath set fire and water before thee: stretch forth thy hand unto whether thou wilt.

[17] Before man is life and death; and whether him liketh shall be given him.

[18] For the wisdom of the Lord is great, and he is mighty in power, and beholdeth all things:

[19] And his eyes are upon them that fear him, and he knoweth every work of man.

[20] He hath commanded no man to do wickedly, neither hath he given any man licence to sin.

Sir.16

[1] Desire not a multitude of unprofitable children, neither delight in ungodly sons.

[2] Though they multiply, rejoice not in them, except the fear of the Lord be with them.

[3] Trust not thou in their life, neither respect their multitude: for one that is just is better than a thousand; and better it is to die without children, than to have them that are ungodly.

[4] For by one that hath understanding shall the city be replenished: but the kindred of the wicked shall speedily become desolate.

[5] Many such things have I seen with mine eyes, and mine ear hath heard greater things than these.

[6] In the congregation of the ungodly shall a fire be kindled; and in a rebellious nation wrath is set on fire.

[7] He was not pacified toward the old giants, who fell away in the strength of their foolishness.

[8] Neither spared he the place where Lot sojourned, but abhorred them for their pride.

[9] He pitied not the people of perdition, who were taken away in their sins:

[10] Nor the six hundred thousand footmen, who were gathered together in the hardness of their hearts.

[11] And if there be one stiffnecked among the people, it is marvel if he escape unpunished: for mercy and wrath are with him; he is mighty to forgive, and to pour out displeasure.

[12] As his mercy is great, so is his correction also: he judgeth a man according to his works

[13] The sinner shall not escape with his spoils: and the patience of the godly shall not be frustrate.

[14] Make way for every work of mercy: for every man shall find according to his works.

[15] The Lord hardened Pharaoh, that he should not know him, that his powerful works might be known to the world.

[16] His mercy is manifest to every creature; and he hath separated his light from the darkness with an adamant.

[17] Say not thou, I will hide myself from the Lord: shall any remember me from above? I shall not be remembered among so many people: for what is my soul among such an infinite number of creatures?

[18] Behold, the heaven, and the heaven of heavens, the deep, and the earth, and all that therein is, shall be moved when he shall visit.

[19] The mountains also and foundations of the earth be shaken with trembling, when the Lord looketh upon them.

[20] No heart can think upon these things worthily: and who is able to conceive his ways?

[21] It is a tempest which no man can see: for the most part of his works are hid.

[22] Who can declare the works of his justice? or who can endure them? for his covenant is afar off, and the trial of all things is in the end.

[23] He that wanteth understanding will think upon vain things: and a foolish man erring imagineth follies.

[24] by son, hearken unto me, and learn knowledge, and mark my words with thy heart.

[25] I will shew forth doctrine in weight, and declare his knowledge exactly.

[26] The works of the Lord are done in judgment from the beginning: and from the time he made them he disposed the parts thereof.

[27] He garnished his works for ever, and in his hand are the chief of them unto all generations: they neither labour, nor are weary, nor cease from their works.

[28] None of them hindereth another, and they shall never disobey his word.

[29] After this the Lord looked upon the earth, and filled it with his blessings.

[30] With all manner of living things hath he covered the face thereof; and they shall return into it again.

Sir.17

[1] The Lord created man of the earth, and turned him into it again.

[2] He gave them few days, and a short time, and power also over the things therein.

[3] He endued them with strength by themselves, and made them according to his image,

[4] And put the fear of man upon all flesh, and gave him dominion over beasts and fowls.

[5] They received the use of the five operations of the Lord, and in the sixth place he imparted them understanding, and in the seventh speech, an interpreter of the cogitations thereof.]

[6] Counsel, and a tongue, and eyes, ears, and a heart, gave he them to understand.

[7] Withal he filled them with the knowledge of understanding, and shewed them good and evil.

[8] He set his eye upon their hearts, that he might shew them the greatness of his works.

[9] He gave them to glory in his marvellous acts for ever, that they might declare his works with understanding.

[10] And the elect shall praise his holy name.

[11] Beside this he gave them knowledge, and the law of life for an heritage.

[12] He made an everlasting covenant with them, and shewed them his judgments.

[13] Their eyes saw the majesty of his glory, and their ears heard his glorious voice.

[14] And he said unto them, Beware of all unrighteousness; and he gave every man commandment concerning his neighbour.

[15] Their ways are ever before him, and shall not be hid from his eyes.

[16] Every man from his youth is given to evil; neither could they make to themselves fleshy hearts for stony.

[17] For in the division of the nations of the whole earth he set a ruler over every people; but Israel is the Lord's portion:

[18] Whom, being his firstborn, he nourisheth with discipline, and giving him the light of his love doth not forsake him.

[19] Therefore all their works are as the sun before him, and his eyes are continually upon their ways.

[20] None of their unrighteous deeds are hid from him, but all their sins are before the Lord

[21] But the Lord being gracious and knowing his workmanship, neither left nor forsook them, but spared them.

[22] The alms of a man is as a signet with him, and he will keep the good deeds of man as the apple of the eye, and give repentance to his sons and daughters.

[23] Afterwards he will rise up and reward them, and render their recompence upon their heads.

[24] But unto them that repent, he granted them return, and comforted those that failed in patience.

[25] Return unto the Lord, and forsake thy sins, make thy prayer before his face, and offend less.

[26] Turn again to the most High, and turn away from iniquity: for he will lead thee out of darkness into the light of health, and hate thou abomination vehemently.

[27] Who shall praise the most High in the grave, instead of them which live and give thanks?

[28] Thanksgiving perisheth from the dead, as from one that is not: the living and sound in heart shall praise the Lord.

[29] How great is the lovingkindness of the Lord our God, and his compassion unto such as turn unto him in holiness!

[30] For all things cannot be in men, because the son of man is not immortal.

[31] What is brighter than the sun? yet the light thereof

faileth; and flesh and blood will imagine evil.

[32] He vieweth the power of the height of heaven; and all men are but earth and ashes.

Sir.18

[1] He that liveth for ever Hath created all things in general.

[2] The Lord only is righteous, and there is none other but he,

[3] Who governeth the world with the palm of his hand, and all things obey his will: for he is the King of all, by his power dividing holy things among them from profane.

[4] To whom hath he given power to declare his works? and who shall find out his noble acts?

[5] Who shall number the strength of his majesty? and who shall also tell out his mercies?

[6] As for the wondrous works of the Lord, there may nothing be taken from them, neither may any thing be put unto them, neither can the ground of them be found out.

[7] When a man hath done, then he beginneth; and when he leaveth off, then he shall be doubtful.

[8] What is man, and whereto serveth he? what is his good, and what is his evil?

[9] The number of a man's days at the most are an hundred years.

[10] As a drop of water unto the sea, and a gravelstone in comparison of the sand; so are a thousand years to the days of eternity.

[11] Therefore is God patient with them, and poureth forth his mercy upon them.

[12] He saw and perceived their end to be evil; therefore he multiplied his compassion.

[13] The mercy of man is toward his neighbour; but the mercy of the Lord is upon all flesh: he reproveth, and nurtureth, and teacheth and bringeth again, as a shepherd his flock.

[14] He hath mercy on them that receive discipline, and that diligently seek after his judgments.

[15] My son, blemish not thy good deeds, neither use uncomfortable words when thou givest any thing.

[16] Shall not the dew asswage the heat? so is a word better than a gift.

[17] Lo, is not a word better than a gift? but both are with a gracious man.

[18] A fool will upbraid churlishly, and a gift of the envious consumeth the eyes.

[19] Learn before thou speak, and use physick or ever thou be sick.

[20] Before judgment examine thyself, and in the day of visitation thou shalt find mercy.

[21] Humble thyself before thou be sick, and in the time of sins shew repentance.

[22] Let nothing hinder thee to pay thy vow in due time, and defer not until death to be justified.

[23] Before thou prayest, prepare thyself; and be not as one that tempteth the Lord.

[24] Think upon the wrath that shall be at the end, and the time of vengeance, when he shall turn away his face.

[25] When thou hast enough, remember the time of hunger: and when thou art rich, think upon poverty and need.

[26] From the morning until the evening the time is changed, and all things are soon done before the Lord.

[27] A wise man will fear in every thing, and in the day of sinning he will beware of offence: but a fool will not observe time.

[28] Every man of understanding knoweth wisdom, and will give praise unto him that found her.

[29] They that were of understanding in sayings became also wise themselves, and poured forth exquisite parables.

[30] Go not after thy lusts, but refrain thyself from thine appetites.

[31] If thou givest thy soul the desires that please her, she will make thee a laughingstock to thine enemies that malign thee.

[32] Take not pleasure in much good cheer, neither be tied to the expence thereof.

[33] Be not made a beggar by banqueting upon borrowing, when thou hast nothing in thy purse: for thou shalt lie in wait for thine own life, and be talked on.

Sir.19

[1] A labouring man that A is given to drunkenness shall not be rich: and he that contemneth small things shall fall by little and little.

[2] Wine and women will make men of understanding to fall away: and he that cleaveth to harlots will become impudent.

[3] Moths and worms shall have him to heritage, and a bold man shall be taken away.

[4] He that is hasty to give credit is lightminded; and he that sinneth shall offend against his own soul.

[5] Whoso taketh pleasure in wickedness shall be condemned: but he that resisteth pleasures crowneth his life.

[6] He that can rule his tongue shall live without strife; and he that hateth babbling shall have less evil.

[7] Rehearse not unto another that which is told unto thee,

and thou shalt fare never the worse.

[8] Whether it be to friend or foe, talk not of other men's lives; and if thou canst without offence, reveal them not.

[9] For he heard and observed thee, and when time cometh he will hate thee.

[10] If thou hast heard a word, let it die with thee; and be bold, it will not burst thee.

[11] A fool travaileth with a word, as a woman in labour of a child.

[12] As an arrow that sticketh in a man's thigh, so is a word within a fool's belly.

[13] Admonish a friend, it may be he hath not done it: and if he have done it, that he do it no more.

[14] Admonish thy friend, it may be he hath not said it: and if he have, that he speak it not again.

[15] Admonish a friend: for many times it is a slander, and believe not every tale.

[16] There is one that slippeth in his speech, but not from his heart; and who is he that hath not offended with his tongue?

[17] Admonish thy neighbour before thou threaten him; and not being angry, give place to the law of the most High.

[18] The fear of the Lord is the first step to be accepted [of him,] and wisdom obtaineth his love.

[19] The knowledge of the commandments of the Lord is the doctrine of life: and they that do things that please him shall receive the fruit of the tree of immortality.

[20] The fear of the Lord is all wisdom; and in all wisdom is the performance of the law, and the knowledge of his omnipotency.

[21] If a servant say to his master, I will not do as it pleaseth thee; though afterward he do it, he angereth him that nourisheth him.

[22] The knowledge of wickedness is not wisdom, neither at any time the counsel of sinners prudence.

[23] There is a wickedness, and the same an abomination; and there is a fool wanting in wisdom.

[24] He that hath small understanding, and feareth God, is better than one that hath much wisdom, and transgresseth the law of the most High.

[25] There is an exquisite subtilty, and the same is unjust; and there is one that turneth aside to make judgment appear; and there is a wise man that justifieth in judgment.

[26] There is a wicked man that hangeth down his head sadly; but inwardly he is full of deceit,

[27] Casting down his countenance, and making as if he heard not: where he is not known, he will do thee a mischief before thou be aware.

[28] And if for want of power he be hindered from sinning, yet when he findeth opportunity he will do evil.

[29] A man may be known by his look, and one that hath understanding by his countenance, when thou meetest him.

[30] A man's attire, and excessive laughter, and gait, shew what he is.

Sir.20

[1] There is a reproof that is not comely: again, some man holdeth his tongue, and he is wise.

[2] It is much better to reprove, than to be angry secretly: and he that confesseth his fault shall be preserved from hurt.

[3] How good is it, when thou art reproved, to shew repentance! for so shalt thou escape wilful sin.

[4] As is the lust of an eunuch to deflower a virgin; so is he that executeth judgment with violence.

[5] There is one that keepeth silence, and is found wise: and another by much babbling becometh hateful.

[6] Some man holdeth his tongue, because he hath not to answer: and some keepeth silence, knowing his time.

[7] A wise man will hold his tongue till he see opportunity: but a babbler and a fool will regard no time.

[8] He that useth many words shall be abhorred; and he that taketh to himself authority therein shall be hated.

[9] There is a sinner that hath good success in evil things; and there is a gain that turneth to loss.

[10] There is a gift that shall not profit thee; and there is a gift whose recompence is double.

[11] There is an abasement because of glory; and there is that lifteth up his head from a low estate.

[12] There is that buyeth much for a little, and repayeth it sevenfold.

[13] A wise man by his words maketh him beloved: but the graces of fools shall be poured out.

[14] The gift of a fool shall do thee no good when thou hast it; neither yet of the envious for his necessity: for he looketh to receive many things for one.

[15] He giveth little, and upbraideth much; he openeth his mouth like a crier; to day he lendeth, and to morrow will he ask it again: such an one is to be hated of God and man.

[16] The fool saith, I have no friends, I have no thank for all my good deeds, and they that eat my bread speak evil of me.

[17] How oft, and of how many shall he be laughed to scorn! for he knoweth not aright what it is to have; and it is all one unto him as if he had it not.

[18] To slip upon a pavement is better than to slip with the

tongue: so the fall of the wicked shall come speedily.

[19] An unseasonable tale will always be in the mouth of the unwise.

[20] A wise sentence shall be rejected when it cometh out of a fool's mouth; for he will not speak it in due season.

[21] There is that is hindered from sinning through want: and when he taketh rest, he shall not be troubled.

[22] There is that destroyeth his own soul through bashfulness, and by accepting of persons overthroweth himself.

[23] There is that for bashfulness promiseth to his friend, and maketh him his enemy for nothing.

[24] A lie is a foul blot in a man, yet it is continually in the mouth of the untaught.

[25] A thief is better than a man that is accustomed to lie: but they both shall have destruction to heritage.

[26] The disposition of a liar is dishonourable, and his shame is ever with him.

[27] A wise man shall promote himself to honour with his words: and he that hath understanding will please great men.

[28] He that tilleth his land shall increase his heap: and he that pleaseth great men shall get pardon for iniquity.

[29] Presents and gifts blind the eyes of the wise, and stop up his mouth that he cannot reprove.

[30] Wisdom that is hid, and treasure that is hoarded up, what profit is in them both?

[31] Better is he that hideth his folly than a man that hideth his wisdom.

[32] Necessary patience in seeking ing the Lord is better than he that leadeth his life without a guide.

Sir.21

[1] My son, hast thou sinned? do so no more, but ask pardon for thy former sins.

[2] Flee from sin as from the face of a serpent: for if thou comest too near it, it will bite thee: the teeth thereof are as the teeth of a lion, slaying the souls of men.

[3] All iniquity is as a two edged sword, the wounds whereof cannot be healed.

[4] To terrify and do wrong will waste riches: thus the house of proud men shall be made desolate.

[5] A prayer out of a poor man's mouth reacheth to the ears of God, and his judgment cometh speedily.

[6] He that hateth to be reproved is in the way of sinners: but he that feareth the Lord will repent from his heart.

[7] An eloquent man is known far and near; but a man of understanding knoweth when he slippeth.

[8] He that buildeth his house with other men's money is like one that gathereth himself stones for the tomb of his burial.

[9] The congregation of the wicked is like tow wrapped together: and the end of them is a flame of fire to destroy them.

[10] The way of sinners is made plain with stones, but at the end thereof is the pit of hell.

[11] He that keepeth the law of the Lord getteth the understanding thereof: and the perfection of the fear of the Lord is wisdom.

[12] He that is not wise will not be taught: but there is a wisdom which multiplieth bitterness.

[13] The knowledge of a wise man shall abound like a flood: and his counsel is like a pure fountain of life.

[14] The inner parts of a fool are like a broken vessel, and he will hold no knowledge as long as he liveth.

[15] If a skilful man hear a wise word, he will commend it, and add unto it: but as soon as one of no understanding heareth it, it displeaseth him, and he casteth it behind his back.

[16] The talking of a fool is like a burden in the way: but grace shall be found in the lips of the wise.

[17] They enquire at the mouth of the wise man in the congregation, and they shall ponder his words in their heart.

[18] As is a house that is destroyed, so is wisdom to a fool: and the knowledge of the unwise is as talk without sense.

[19] Doctrine unto fools is as fetters on the feet, and like manacles on the right hand.

[20] A fool lifteth up his voice with laughter; but a wise man doth scarce smile a little.

[21] Learning is unto a wise man as an ornament of gold, and like a bracelet upon his right arm.

[22] A foolish man's foot is soon in his [neighbour's] house: but a man of experience is ashamed of him.

[23] A fool will peep in at the door into the house: but he that is well nurtured will stand without.

[24] It is the rudeness of a man to hearken at the door: but a wise man will be grieved with the disgrace.

[25] The lips of talkers will be telling such things as pertain not unto them: but the words of such as have understanding are weighed in the balance.

[26] The heart of fools is in their mouth: but the mouth of the wise is in their heart.

[27] When the ungodly curseth Satan, he curseth his own soul.

[28] A whisperer defileth his own soul, and is hated wheresoever he dwelleth.

Sir.22

[1] A slothful man is compared to a filthy stone, and every one will hiss him out to his disgrace.

[2] A slothful man is compared to the filth of a dunghill: every man that takes it up will shake his hand.

[3] An evilnurtured man is the dishonour of his father that begat him: and a [foolish] daughter is born to his loss.

[4] A wise daughter shall bring an inheritance to her husband: but she that liveth dishonestly is her father's heaviness.

[5] She that is bold dishonoureth both her father and her husband, but they both shall despise her.

[6] A tale out of season [is as] musick in mourning: but stripes and correction of wisdom are never out of time.

[7] Whoso teacheth a fool is as one that glueth a potsherd together, and as he that waketh one from a sound sleep.

[8] He that telleth a tale to a fool speaketh to one in a slumber: when he hath told his tale, he will say, What is the matter?

[9] If children live honestly, and have wherewithal, they shall cover the baseness of their parents.

[10] But children, being haughty, through disdain and want of nurture do stain the nobility of their kindred.

[11] Weep for the dead, for he hath lost the light: and weep for the fool, for he wanteth understanding: make little weeping for the dead, for he is at rest: but the life of the fool is worse than death.

[12] Seven days do men mourn for him that is dead; but for a fool and an ungodly man all the days of his life.

[13] Talk not much with a fool, and go not to him that hath no understanding: beware of him, lest thou have trouble, and thou shalt never be defiled with his fooleries: depart from him, and thou shalt find rest, and never be disquieted with madness.

[14] What is heavier than lead? and what is the name thereof, but a fool?

[15] Sand, and salt, and a mass of iron, is easier to bear, than a man without understanding.

[16] As timber girt and bound together in a building cannot be loosed with shaking: so the heart that is stablished by advised counsel shall fear at no time.

[17] A heart settled upon a thought of understanding is as a fair plaistering on the wall of a gallery.

[18] Pales set on an high place will never stand against the wind: so a fearful heart in the imagination of a fool cannot stand against any fear.

[19] He that pricketh the eye will make tears to fall: and he that pricketh the heart maketh it to shew her knowledge.

[20] Whoso casteth a stone at the birds frayeth them away: and he that upbraideth his friend breaketh friendship.

[21] Though thou drewest a sword at thy friend, yet despair not: for there may be a returning [to favour.]

[22] If thou hast opened thy mouth against thy friend, fear not; for there may be a reconciliation: except for upbraiding, or pride, or disclosing of secrets, or a treacherous wound: for for these things every friend will depart.

[23] Be faithful to thy neighbour in his poverty, that thou mayest rejoice in his prosperity: abide stedfast unto him in the time of his trouble, that thou mayest be heir with him in his heritage: for a mean estate is not always to be contemned: nor the rich that is foolish to be had in admiration.

[24] As the vapour and smoke of a furnace goeth before the fire; so reviling before blood.

[25] I will not be ashamed to defend a friend; neither will I hide myself from him.

[26] And if any evil happen unto me by him, every one that heareth it will beware of him.

[27] Who shall set a watch before my mouth, and a seal of wisdom upon my lips, that I fall not suddenly by them, and that my tongue destroy me not?

Sir.23

[1] O Lord, Father and Governor of all my whole life, leave me not to their counsels, and let me not fall by them.

[2] Who will set scourges over my thoughts, and the discipline of wisdom over mine heart? that they spare me not for mine ignorances, and it pass not by my sins:

[3] Lest mine ignorances increase, and my sins abound to my destruction, and I fall before mine adversaries, and mine enemy rejoice over me, whose hope is far from thy mercy.

[4] O Lord, Father and God of my life, give me not a proud look, but turn away from thy servants always a haughty mind.

[5] Turn away from me vain hopes and concupiscence, and thou shalt hold him up that is desirous always to serve thee.

[6] Let not the greediness of the belly nor lust of the flesh take hold of me; and give not over me thy servant into an impudent mind.

[7] Hear, O ye children, the discipline of the mouth: he that keepeth it shall never be taken in his lips.

[8] The sinner shall be left in his foolishness: both the evil speaker and the proud shall fall thereby.

[9] Accustom not thy mouth to swearing; neither use thyself to the naming of the Holy One.

[10] For as a servant that is continually beaten shall not be without a blue mark: so he that sweareth and nameth God continually shall not be faultless.

[11] A man that useth much swearing shall be filled with iniquity, and the plague shall never depart from his house: if he shall offend, his sin shall be upon him: and if he acknowledge not his sin, he maketh a double offence: and if he swear in vain, he shall not be innocent, but his house shall be full of calamities.

[12] There is a word that is clothed about with death: God grant that it be not found in the heritage of Jacob; for all such things shall be far from the godly, and they shall not wallow in their sins.

[13] Use not thy mouth to intemperate swearing, for therein is the word of sin.

[14] Remember thy father and thy mother, when thou sittest among great men. Be not forgetful before them, and so thou by thy custom become a fool, and wish that thou hadst not been born, and curse they day of thy nativity.

[15] The man that is accustomed to opprobrious words will never be reformed all the days of his life.

[16] Two sorts of men multiply sin, and the third will bring wrath: a hot mind is as a burning fire, it will never be quenched till it be consumed: a fornicator in the body of his flesh will never cease till he hath kindled a fire.

[17] All bread is sweet to a whoremonger, he will not leave off till he die.

[18] A man that breaketh wedlock, saying thus in his heart, Who seeth me? I am compassed about with darkness, the walls cover me, and no body seeth me; what need I to fear? the most High will not remember my sins:

[19] Such a man only feareth the eyes of men, and knoweth not that the eyes of the Lord are ten thousand times brighter than the sun, beholding all the ways of men, and considering the most secret parts.

[20] He knew all things ere ever they were created; so also after they were perfected he looked upon them all.

[21] This man shall be punished in the streets of the city, and where he suspecteth not he shall be taken.

[22] Thus shall it go also with the wife that leaveth her husband, and bringeth in an heir by another.

[23] For first, she hath disobeyed the law of the most High; and secondly, she hath trespassed against her own husband; and thirdly, she hath played the whore in adultery, and brought children by another man.

[24] She shall be brought out into the congregation, and inquisition shall be made of her children.

[25] Her children shall not take root, and her branches shall bring forth no fruit.

[26] She shall leave her memory to be cursed, and her reproach shall not be blotted out.

[27] And they that remain shall know that there is nothing better than the fear of the Lord, and that there is nothing sweeter than to take heed unto the commandments of the Lord.

[28] It is great glory to follow the Lord, and to be received of him is long life.

Sir.24

[1] Wisdom shall praise herself, and shall glory in the midst of her people.

[2] In the congregation of the most High shall she open her mouth, and triumph before his power.

[3] I came out of the mouth of the most High, and covered the earth as a cloud.

[4] I dwelt in high places, and my throne is in a cloudy pillar.

[5] I alone compassed the circuit of heaven, and walked in the bottom of the deep.

[6] In the waves of the sea and in all the earth, and in every people and nation, I got a possession.

[7] With all these I sought rest: and in whose inheritance shall I abide?

[8] So the Creator of all things gave me a commandment, and he that made me caused my tabernacle to rest, and said, Let thy dwelling be in Jacob, and thine inheritance in Israel.

[9] He created me from the beginning before the world, and I shall never fail.

[10] In the holy tabernacle I served before him; and so was I established in Sion.

[11] Likewise in the beloved city he gave me rest, and in Jerusalem was my power.

[12] And I took root in an honourable people, even in the portion of the Lord's inheritance.

[13] I was exalted like a cedar in Libanus, and as a cypress tree upon the mountains of Hermon.

[14] I was exalted like a palm tree in En-gaddi, and as a rose plant in Jericho, as a fair olive tree in a pleasant field, and grew up as a plane tree by the water.

[15] I gave a sweet smell like cinnamon and aspalathus, and I yielded a pleasant odour like the best myrrh, as galbanum, and onyx, and sweet storax, and as the fume of frankincense in the tabernacle.

[16] As the turpentine tree I stretched out my branches, and my branches are the branches of honour and grace.

[17] As the vine brought I forth pleasant savour, and my flowers are the fruit of honour and riches.

[18] I am the mother of fair love, and fear, and knowledge, and holy hope: I therefore, being eternal, am given to all my children which are named of him.

[19] Come unto me, all ye that be desirous of me, and fill yourselves with my fruits.

[20] For my memorial is sweeter than honey, and mine inheritance than the honeycomb.

[21] They that eat me shall yet be hungry, and they that drink me shall yet be thirsty.

[22] He that obeyeth me shall never be confounded, and they that work by me shall not do amiss.

[23] All these things are the book of the covenant of the most high God, even the law which Moses commanded for an heritage unto the congregations of Jacob.

[24] Faint not to be strong in the Lord; that he may confirm you, cleave unto him: for the Lord Almighty is God alone, and beside him there is no other Saviour.

[25] He filleth all things with his wisdom, as Phison and as Tigris in the time of the new fruits.

[26] He maketh the understanding to abound like Euphrates, and as Jordan in the time of the harvest.

[27] He maketh the doctrine of knowledge appear as the light, and as Geon in the time of vintage.

[28] The first man knew her not perfectly: no more shall the last find her out.

[29] For her thoughts are more than the sea, and her counsels profounder than the great deep.

[30] I also came out as a brook from a river, and as a conduit into a garden.

[31] I said, I will water my best garden, and will water abundantly my garden bed: and, lo, my brook became a river, and my river became a sea.

[32] I will yet make doctrine to shine as the morning, and will send forth her light afar off.

[33] I will yet pour out doctrine as prophecy, and leave it to all ages for ever.

[34] Behold that I have not laboured for myself only, but for all them that seek wisdom.

Sir.25

[1] In three things I was beautified, and stood up beautiful both before God and men: the unity of brethren, the love of neighbours, a man and a wife that agree together.

[2] Three sorts of men my soul hateth, and I am greatly offended at their life: a poor man that is proud, a rich man that is a liar, and an old adulterer that doateth.

[3] If thou hast gathered nothing in thy youth, how canst thou find any thing in thine age?

[4] O how comely a thing is judgment for gray hairs, and for ancient men to know counsel!

[5] O how comely is the wisdom of old men, and understanding and counsel to men of honour.

[6] Much experience is the crown of old men, and the fear of God is their glory.

[7] There be nine things which I have judged in mine heart to be happy, and the tenth I will utter with my tongue: A man that hath joy of his children; and he that liveth to see the fall of his enemy:

[8] Well is him that dwelleth with a wife of understanding, and that hath not slipped with his tongue, and that hath not served a man more unworthy than himself:

[9] Well is him that hath found prudence, and he that speaketh in the ears of them that will hear:

[10] O how great is he that findeth wisdom! yet is there none above him that feareth the Lord.

[11] But the love of the Lord passeth all things for illumination: he that holdeth it, whereto shall he be likened?

[12] The fear of the Lord is the beginning of his love: and faith is the beginning of cleaving unto him.

[13] [Give me] any plague, but the plague of the heart: and any wickedness, but the wickedness of a woman:

[14] And any affliction, but the affliction from them that hate me: and any revenge, but the revenge of enemies.

[15] There is no head above the head of a serpent; and there is no wrath above the wrath of an enemy.

[16] I had rather dwell with a lion and a dragon, than to keep house with a wicked woman.

[17] The wickedness of a woman changeth her face, and darkeneth her countenance like sackcloth.

[18] Her husband shall sit among his neighbours; and when he heareth it shall sigh bitterly.

[19] All wickedness is but little to the wickedness of a woman: let the portion of a sinner fall upon her.

[20] As the climbing up a sandy way is to the feet of the aged, so is a wife full of words to a quiet man.

[21] Stumble not at the beauty of a woman, and desire her not for pleasure.

[22] A woman, if she maintain her husband, is full of anger, impudence, and much reproach.

[23] A wicked woman abateth the courage, maketh an heavy countenance and a wounded heart: a woman that will not comfort her husband in distress maketh weak hands and feeble knees.

[24] Of the woman came the beginning of sin, and through her we all die.

[25] Give the water no passage; neither a wicked woman liberty to gad abroad.

[26] If she go not as thou wouldest have her, cut her off from thy flesh, and give her a bill of divorce, and let her go.

Sir.26

[1] Blessed is the man that hath a virtuous wife, for the number of his days shall be double.

[2] A virtuous woman rejoiceth her husband, and he shall fulfil the years of his life in peace.

[3] A good wife is a good portion, which shall be given in the portion of them that fear the Lord.

[4] Whether a man be rich or poor, if he have a good heart toward the Lord, he shall at all times rejoice with a cheerful countenance.

[5] There be three things that mine heart feareth; and for the fourth I was sore afraid: the slander of a city, the gathering together of an unruly multitude, and a false accusation: all these are worse than death.

[6] But a grief of heart and sorrow is a woman that is jealous over another woman, and a scourge of the tongue which communicateth with all.

[7] An evil wife is a yoke shaken to and fro: he that hath hold of her is as though he held a scorpion.

[8] A drunken woman and a gadder abroad causeth great anger, and she will not cover her own shame.

[9] The whoredom of a woman may be known in her haughty looks and eyelids.

[10] If thy daughter be shameless, keep her in straitly, lest she abuse herself through overmuch liberty.

[11] Watch over an impudent eye: and marvel not if she trespass against thee.

[12] She will open her mouth, as a thirsty traveller when he hath found a fountain, and drink of every water near her: by every hedge will she sit down, and open her quiver against every arrow.

[13] The grace of a wife delighteth her husband, and her discretion will fatten his bones.

[14] A silent and loving woman is a gift of the Lord; and there is nothing so much worth as a mind well instructed.

[15] A shamefaced and faithful woman is a double grace, and her continent mind cannot be valued.

[16] As the sun when it ariseth in the high heaven; so is the beauty of a good wife in the ordering of her house.

[17] As the clear light is upon the holy candlestick; so is the beauty of the face in ripe age.

[18] As the golden pillars are upon the sockets of silver; so are the fair feet with a constant heart.

[19] My son, keep the flower of thine age sound; and give not thy strength to strangers.

[20] When thou hast gotten a fruitful possession through all the field, sow it with thine own seed, trusting in the goodness of thy stock.

[21] So thy race which thou leavest shall be magnified, having the confidence of their good descent.

[22] An harlot shall be accounted as spittle; but a married woman is a tower against death to her husband.

[23] A wicked woman is given as a portion to a wicked man: but a godly woman is given to him that feareth the Lord.

[24] A dishonest woman contemneth shame: but an honest woman will reverence her husband.

[25] A shameless woman shall be counted as a dog; but she that is shamefaced will fear the Lord.

[26] A woman that honoureth her husband shall be judged wise of all; but she that dishonoureth him in her pride shall be counted ungodly of all.

[27] A loud crying woman and a scold shall be sought out to drive away the enemies.

[28] There be two things that grieve my heart; and the third maketh me angry: a man of war that suffereth poverty; and men of understanding that are not set by; and one that returneth from righteousness to sin; the Lord prepareth such an one for the sword.

[29] A merchant shall hardly keep himself from doing wrong; and an huckster shall not be freed from sin.

Sir.27

[1] Many have sinned for a small matter; and he that seeketh for abundance will turn his eyes away.

[2] As a nail sticketh fast between the joinings of the stones; so doth sin stick close between buying and selling.

[3] Unless a man hold himself diligently in the fear of the Lord, his house shall soon be overthrown.

[4] As when one sifteth with a sieve, the refuse remaineth; so the filth of man in his talk.

[5] The furnace proveth the potter's vessels; so the trial of man is in his reasoning.

[6] The fruit declareth if the tree have been dressed; so is the utterance of a conceit in the heart of man.

[7] Praise no man before thou hearest him speak; for this is the trial of men.

[8] If thou followest righteousness, thou shalt obtain her, and put her on, as a glorious long robe.

[9] The birds will resort unto their like; so will truth return unto them that practise in her.

[10] As the lion lieth in wait for the prey; so sin for them that work iniquity.

[11] The discourse of a godly man is always with wisdom; but a fool changeth as the moon.

[12] If thou be among the indiscreet, observe the time; but be continually among men of understanding.

[13] The discourse of fools is irksome, and their sport is the wantonness of sin.

[14] The talk of him that sweareth much maketh the hair stand upright; and their brawls make one stop his ears.

[15] The strife of the proud is bloodshedding, and their revilings are grievous to the ear.

[16] Whoso discovereth secrets loseth his credit; and shall never find friend to his mind.

[17] Love thy friend, and be faithful unto him: but if thou betrayest his secrets, follow no more after him.

[18] For as a man hath destroyed his enemy; so hast thou lost the love of thy neighbor.

[19] As one that letteth a bird go out of his hand, so hast thou let thy neighbour go, and shalt not get him again

[20] Follow after him no more, for he is too far off; he is as a roe escaped out of the snare.

[21] As for a wound, it may be bound up; and after reviling there may be reconcilement: but he that betrayeth secrets is without hope.

[22] He that winketh with the eyes worketh evil: and he that knoweth him will depart from him.

[23] When thou art present, he will speak sweetly, and will admire thy words: but at the last he will writhe his mouth, and slander thy sayings.

[24] I have hated many things, but nothing like him; for the Lord will hate him.

[25] Whoso casteth a stone on high casteth it on his own head; and a deceitful stroke shall make wounds.

[26] Whoso diggeth a pit shall fall therein: and he that setteth a trap shall be taken therein.

[27] He that worketh mischief, it shall fall upon him, and he shall not know whence it cometh.

[28] Mockery and reproach are from the proud; but vengeance, as a lion, shall lie in wait for them.

[29] They that rejoice at the fall of the righteous shall be taken in the snare; and anguish shall consume them before they die.

[30] Malice and wrath, even these are abominations; and the sinful man shall have them both.

Sir.28

[1] He that revengeth shall find vengeance from the Lord, and he will surely keep his sins [in remembrance.]

[2] Forgive thy neighbour the hurt that he hath done unto thee, so shall thy sins also be forgiven when thou prayest.

[3] One man beareth hatred against another, and doth he seek pardon from the Lord?

[4] He sheweth no mercy to a man, which is like himself: and doth he ask forgiveness of his own sins?

[5] If he that is but flesh nourish hatred, who will intreat for pardon of his sins?

[6] Remember thy end, and let enmity cease; [remember] corruption and death, and abide in the commandments.

[7] Remember the commandments, and bear no malice to thy neighbour: [remember] the covenant of the Highest, and wink at ignorance.

[8] Abstain from strife, and thou shalt diminish thy sins: for a furious man will kindle strife,

[9] A sinful man disquieteth friends, and maketh debate among them that be at peace.

[10] As the matter of the fire is, so it burneth: and as a man's strength is, so is his wrath; and according to his riches his anger riseth; and the stronger they are which contend, the more they will be inflamed.

[11] An hasty contention kindleth a fire: and an hasty fighting sheddeth blood.

[12] If thou blow the spark, it shall burn: if thou spit upon it, it shall be quenched: and both these come out of thy mouth.

[13] Curse the whisperer and doubletongued: for such have destroyed many that were at peace.

[14] A backbiting tongue hath disquieted many, and driven them from nation to nation: strong cities hath it pulled down, and overthrown the houses of great men.

[15] A backbiting tongue hath cast out virtuous women, and deprived them of their labours.

[16] Whoso hearkeneth unto it shall never find rest, and never dwell quietly.

[17] The stroke of the whip maketh marks in the flesh: but the stroke of the tongue breaketh the bones.

[18] Many have fallen by the edge of the sword: but not so many as have fallen by the tongue.

[19] Well is he that is defended through the venom thereof; who hath not drawn the yoke thereof, nor hath been bound in her bands.

[20] For the yoke thereof is a yoke of iron, and the bands thereof are bands of brass.

[21] The death thereof is an evil death, the grave were better than it.

[22] It shall not have rule over them that fear God, neither shall they be burned with the flame thereof.

[23] Such as forsake the Lord shall fall into it; and it shall burn in them, and not be quenched; it shall be sent upon them as a lion, and devour them as a leopard.

[24] Look that thou hedge thy possession about with thorns, and bind up thy silver and gold,

[25] And weigh thy words in a balance, and make a door

and bar for thy mouth.

[26] Beware thou slide not by it, lest thou fall before him that lieth in wait.

Sir.29

[1] He that is merciful will lend unto his neighbour; and he that strengtheneth his hand keepeth the commandments.

[2] Lend to thy neighbour in time of his need, and pay thou thy neighbour again in due season.

[3] Keep thy word, and deal faithfully with him, and thou shalt always find the thing that is necessary for thee.

[4] Many, when a thing was lent them, reckoned it to be found, and put them to trouble that helped them.

[5] Till he hath received, he will kiss a man's hand; and for his neighbour's money he will speak submissly: but when he should repay, he will prolong the time, and return words of grief, and complain of the time.

[6] If he prevail, he shall hardly receive the half, and he will count as if he had found it: if not, he hath deprived him of his money, and he hath gotten him an enemy without cause: he payeth him with cursings and railings; and for honour he will pay him disgrace.

[7] Many therefore have refused to lend for other men's ill dealing, fearing to be defrauded.

[8] Yet have thou patience with a man in poor estate, and delay not to shew him mercy.

[9] Help the poor for the commandment's sake, and turn him not away because of his poverty.

[10] Lose thy money for thy brother and thy friend, and let it not rust under a stone to be lost.

[11] Lay up thy treasure according to the commandments of the most High, and it shall bring thee more profit than gold.

[12] Shut up alms in thy storehouses: and it shall deliver thee from all affliction.

[13] It shall fight for thee against thine enemies better than a mighty shield and strong spear.

[14] An honest man is surety for his neighbour: but he that is impudent will forsake him.

[15] Forget not the friendship of thy surety, for he hath given his life for thee.

[16] A sinner will overthrow the good estate of his surety:

[17] And he that is of an unthankful mind will leave him [in danger] that delivered him.

[18] Suretiship hath undone many of good estate, and shaken them as a wave of the sea: mighty men hath it driven from their houses, so that they wandered among strange nations.

[19] A wicked man transgressing the commandments of the Lord shall fall into suretiship: and he that undertaketh and followeth other men's business for gain shall fall into suits.

[20] Help thy neighbour according to thy power, and beware that thou thyself fall not into the same.

[21] The chief thing for life is water, and bread, and clothing, and an house to cover shame.

[22] Better is the life of a poor man in a mean cottage, than delicate fare in another man's house.

[23] Be it little or much, hold thee contented, that thou hear not the reproach of thy house.

[24] For it is a miserable life to go from house to house: for where thou art a stranger, thou darest not open thy mouth.

[25] Thou shalt entertain, and feast, and have no thanks: moreover thou shalt hear bitter words:

[26] Come, thou stranger, and furnish a table, and feed me of that thou hast ready.

[27] Give place, thou stranger, to an honourable man; my brother cometh to be lodged, and I have need of mine house.

[28] These things are grievous to a man of understanding; the upbraiding of houseroom, and reproaching of the lender.

Sir.30

[1] He that loveth his son causeth him oft to feel the rod, that he may have joy of him in the end.

[2] He that chastiseth his son shall have joy in him, and shall rejoice of him among his acquaintance.

[3] He that teacheth his son grieveth the enemy: and before his friends he shall rejoice of him.

[4] Though his father die, yet he is as though he were not dead: for he hath left one behind him that is like himself.

[5] While he lived, he saw and rejoiced in him: and when he died, he was not sorrowful.

[6] He left behind him an avenger against his enemies, and one that shall requite kindness to his friends.

[7] He that maketh too much of his son shall bind up his wounds; and his bowels will be troubled at every cry.

[8] An horse not broken becometh headstrong: and a child left to himself will be wilful.

[9] Cocker thy child, and he shall make thee afraid: play with him, and he will bring thee to heaviness.

[10] Laugh not with him, lest thou have sorrow with him, and lest thou gnash thy teeth in the end.

[11] Give him no liberty in his youth, and wink not at his follies.

[12] Bow down his neck while he is young, and beat him on

the sides while he is a child, lest he wax stubborn, and be disobedient unto thee, and so bring sorrow to thine heart.

[13] Chastise thy son, and hold him to labour, lest his lewd behaviour be an offence unto thee.

[14] Better is the poor, being sound and strong of constitution, than a rich man that is afflicted in his body.

[15] Health and good estate of body are above all gold, and a strong body above infinite wealth.

[16] There is no riches above a sound body, and no joy above the joy of the heart.

[17] Death is better than a bitter life or continual sickness.

[18] Delicates poured upon a mouth shut up are as messes of meat set upon a grave.

[19] What good doeth the offering unto an idol? for neither can it eat nor smell: so is he that is persecuted of the Lord.

[20] He seeth with his eyes and groaneth, as an eunuch that embraceth a virgin and sigheth.

[21] Give not over thy mind to heaviness, and afflict not thyself in thine own counsel.

[22] The gladness of the heart is the life of man, and the joyfulness of a man prolongeth his days.

[23] Love thine own soul, and comfort thy heart, remove sorrow far from thee: for sorrow hath killed many, and there is no profit therein.

[24] Envy and wrath shorten the life, and carefulness bringeth age before the time.

[25] A cheerful and good heart will have a care of his meat and diet.

Sir.31

[1] Watching for riches consumeth the flesh, and the care thereof driveth away sleep.

[2] Watching care will not let a man slumber, as a sore disease breaketh sleep,

[3] The rich hath great labour in gathering riches together; and when he resteth, he is filled with his delicates.

[4] The poor laboureth in his poor estate; and when he leaveth off, he is still needy.

[5] He that loveth gold shall not be justified, and he that followeth corruption shall have enough thereof.

[6] Gold hath been the ruin of many, and their destruction was present.

[7] It is a stumblingblock unto them that sacrifice unto it, and every fool shall be taken therewith.

[8] Blessed is the rich that is found without blemish, and hath not gone after gold.

[9] Who is he? and we will call him blessed: for wonderful things hath he done among his people.

[10] Who hath been tried thereby, and found perfect? then let him glory. Who might offend, and hath not offended? or done evil, and hath not done it?

[11] His goods shall be established, and the congregation shall declare his alms.

[12] If thou sit at a bountiful table, be not greedy upon it, and say not, There is much meat on it.

[13] Remember that a wicked eye is an evil thing: and what is created more wicked than an eye? therefore it weepeth upon every occasion.

[14] Stretch not thine hand whithersoever it looketh, and thrust it not with him into the dish.

[15] Judge not thy neighbour by thyself: and be discreet in every point.

[16] Eat as it becometh a man, those things which are set before thee; and devour note, lest thou be hated.

[17] Leave off first for manners' sake; and be not unsatiable, lest thou offend.

[18] When thou sittest among many, reach not thine hand out first of all.

[19] A very little is sufficient for a man well nurtured, and he fetcheth not his wind short upon his bed.

[20] Sound sleep cometh of moderate eating: he riseth early, and his wits are with him: but the pain of watching, and choler, and pangs of the belly, are with an unsatiable man.

[21] And if thou hast been forced to eat, arise, go forth, vomit, and thou shalt have rest.

[22] My son, hear me, and despise me not, and at the last thou shalt find as I told thee: in all thy works be quick, so shall there no sickness come unto thee.

[23] Whoso is liberal of his meat, men shall speak well of him; and the report of his good housekeeping will be believed.

[24] But against him that is a niggard of his meat the whole city shall murmur; and the testimonies of his niggardness shall not be doubted of.

[25] Shew not thy valiantness in wine; for wine hath destroyed many.

[26] The furnace proveth the edge by dipping: so doth wine the hearts of the proud by drunkeness.

[27] Wine is as good as life to a man, if it be drunk moderately: what life is then to a man that is without wine? for it was made to make men glad.

[28] Wine measurably drunk and in season bringeth gladness of the heart, and cheerfulness of the mind:

[29] But wine drunken with excess maketh bitterness of the mind, with brawling and quarrelling.

[30] Drunkenness increaseth the rage of a fool till he offend: it diminisheth strength, and maketh wounds.

[31] Rebuke not thy neighbour at the wine, and despise

him not in his mirth: give him no despiteful words, and press not upon him with urging him [to drink.]

Sir.32

[1] If thou be made the master [of a feast,] lift not thyself up, but be among them as one of the rest; take diligent care for them, and so sit down.

[2] And when thou hast done all thy office, take thy place, that thou mayest be merry with them, and receive a crown for thy well ordering of the feast.

[3] Speak, thou that art the elder, for it becometh thee, but with sound judgment; and hinder not musick.

[4] Pour not out words where there is a musician, and shew not forth wisdom out of time.

[5] A concert of musick in a banquet of wine is as a signet of carbuncle set in gold.

[6] As a signet of an emerald set in a work of gold, so is the melody of musick with pleasant wine.

[7] Speak, young man, if there be need of thee: and yet scarcely when thou art twice asked.

[8] Let thy speech be short, comprehending much in few words; be as one that knoweth and yet holdeth his tongue.

[9] If thou be among great men, make not thyself equal with them; and when ancient men are in place, use not many words.

[10] Before the thunder goeth lightning; and before a shamefaced man shall go favour.

[11] Rise up betimes, and be not the last; but get thee home without delay.

[12] There take thy pastime, and do what thou wilt: but sin not by proud speech.

[13] And for these things bless him that made thee, and hath replenished thee with his good things.

[14] Whoso feareth the Lord will receive his discipline; and they that seek him early shall find favour.

[15] He that seeketh the law shall be filled therewith: but the hypocrite will be offended thereat.

[16] They that fear the Lord shall find judgment, and shall kindle justice as a light.

[17] A sinful man will not be reproved, but findeth an excuse according to his will.

[18] A man of counsel will be considerate; but a strange and proud man is not daunted with fear, even when of himself he hath done without counsel.

[19] Do nothing without advice; and when thou hast once done, repent not.

[20] Go not in a way wherein thou mayest fall, and stumble not among the stones.

[21] Be not confident in a plain way.

[22] And beware of thine own children.

[23] In every good work trust thy own soul; for this is the keeping of the commandments.

[24] He that believeth in the Lord taketh heed to the commandment; and he that trusteth in him shall fare never the worse.

Sir.33

[1] There shall no evil happen unto him that feareth the Lord; but in temptation even again he will deliver him.

[2] A wise man hateth not the law; but he that is an hypocrite therein is as a ship in a storm.

[3] A man of understanding trusteth in the law; and the law is faithful unto him, as an oracle.

[4] Prepare what to say, and so thou shalt be heard: and bind up instruction, and then make answer.

[5] The heart of the foolish is like a cartwheel; and his thoughts are like a rolling axletree.

[6] A stallion horse is as a mocking friend, he neigheth under every one that sitteth upon him.

[7] Why doth one day excel another, when as all the light of every day in the year is of the sun?

[8] By the knowledge of the Lord they were distinguished: and he altered seasons and feasts.

[9] Some of them hath he made high days, and hallowed them, and some of them hath he made ordinary days.

[10] And all men are from the ground, and Adam was created of earth:

[11] In much knowledge the Lord hath divided them, and made their ways diverse.

[12] Some of them hath he blessed and exalted and some of them he sanctified, and set near himself: but some of them hath he cursed and brought low, and turned out of their places.

[13] As the clay is in the potter's hand, to fashion it at his pleasure: so man is in the hand of him that made him, to render to them as liketh him best.

[14] Good is set against evil, and life against death: so is the godly against the sinner, and the sinner against the godly.

[15] So look upon all the works of the most High; and there are two and two, one against another.

[16] I awaked up last of all, as one that gathereth after the grapegatherers: by the blessing of the Lord I profited, and tred my winepress like a gatherer of grapes.

[17] Consider that I laboured not for myself only, but for all them that seek learning.

[18] Hear me, O ye great men of the people, and hearken with your ears, ye rulers of the congregation.

[19] Give not thy son and wife, thy brother and friend, power over thee while thou livest, and give not thy goods to another: lest it repent thee, and thou intreat for the same again.

[20] As long as thou livest and hast breath in thee, give not thyself over to any.

[21] For better it is that thy children should seek to thee, than that thou shouldest stand to their courtesy.

[22] In all thy works keep to thyself the preeminence; leave not a stain in thine honour.

[23] At the time when thou shalt end thy days, and finish thy life, distribute thine inheritance.

[24] Fodder, a wand, and burdens, are for the ass; and bread, correction, and work, for a servant. .

[25] If thou set thy servant to labour, thou shalt find rest: but if thou let him go idle, he shall seek liberty.

[26] A yoke and a collar do bow the neck: so are tortures and torments for an evil servant.

[27] Send him to labour, that he be not idle; for idleness teacheth much evil.

[28] Set him to work, as is fit for him: if he be not obedient, put on more heavy fetters.

[29] But be not excessive toward any; and without discretion do nothing.

[30] If thou have a servant, let him be unto thee as thyself, because thou hast bought him with a price.

[31] If thou have a servant, entreat him as a brother: for thou hast need of him, as of thine own soul: if thou entreat him evil, and he run from thee, which way wilt thou go to seek him?

Sir.34

[1] The hopes of a man void of understanding are vain and false: and dreams lift up fools.

[2] Whoso regardeth dreams is like him that catcheth at a shadow, and followeth after the wind.

[3] The vision of dreams is the resemblance of one thing to another, even as the likeness of a face to a face.

[4] Of an unclean thing what can be cleansed? and from that thing which is false what truth can come?

[5] Divinations, and soothsayings, and dreams, are vain: and the heart fancieth, as a woman's heart in travail.

[6] If they be not sent from the most High in thy visitation, set not thy heart upon them.

[7] For dreams have deceived many, and they have failed that put their trust in them.

[8] The law shall be found perfect without lies: and wisdom is perfection to a faithful mouth.

[9] A man that hath travelled knoweth many things; and he that hath much experience will declare wisdom.

[10] He that hath no experience knoweth little: but he that hath travelled is full of prudence.

[11] When I travelled, I saw many things; and I understand more than I can express.

[12] I was ofttimes in danger of death: yet I was delivered because of these things.

[13] The spirit of those that fear the Lord shall live; for their hope is in him that saveth them.

[14] Whoso feareth the Lord shall not fear nor be afraid; for he is his hope.

[15] Blessed is the soul of him that feareth the Lord: to whom doth he look? and who is his strength?

[16] For the eyes of the Lord are upon them that love him, he is their mighty protection and strong stay, a defence from heat, and a cover from the sun at noon, a preservation from stumbling, and an help from falling.

[17] He raiseth up the soul, and lighteneth the eyes: he giveth health, life, and blessing.

[18] He that sacrificeth of a thing wrongfully gotten, his offering is ridiculous; and the gifts of unjust men are not accepted.

[19] The most High is not pleased with the offerings of the wicked; neither is he pacified for sin by the multitude of sacrifices.

[20] Whoso bringeth an offering of the goods of the poor doeth as one that killeth the son before his father's eyes.

[21] The bread of the needy is their life: he that defraudeth him thereof is a man of blood.

[22] He that taketh away his neighbour's living slayeth him; and he that defraudeth the labourer of his hire is a bloodshedder.

[23] When one buildeth, and another pulleth down, what profit have they then but labour?

[24] When one prayeth, and another curseth, whose voice will the Lord hear?

[25] He that washeth himself after the touching of a dead body, if he touch it again, what availeth his washing?

[26] So is it with a man that fasteth for his sins, and goeth again, and doeth the same: who will hear his prayer? or what doth his humbling profit him?

Sir.35

[1] He that keepeth the law bringeth offerings enough: he that taketh heed to the commandment offereth a peace offering.

[2] He that requiteth a goodturn offereth fine flour; and he that giveth alms sacrificeth praise.

[3] To depart from wickedness is a thing pleasing to the

Lord; and to forsake unrighteousness is a propitiation.

[4] Thou shalt not appear empty before the Lord.

[5] For all these things [are to be done] because of the commandment.

[6] The offering of the righteous maketh the altar fat, and the sweet savour thereof is before the most High.

[7] The sacrifice of a just man is acceptable. and the memorial thereof shall never be forgotten.

[8] Give the Lord his honour with a good eye, and diminish not the firstfruits of thine hands.

[9] In all thy gifts shew a cheerful countenance, and dedicate thy tithes with gladness.

[10] Give unto the most High according as he hath enriched thee; and as thou hast gotten, give with a cheerful eye.

[11] For the Lord recompenseth, and will give thee seven times as much.

[12] Do not think to corrupt with gifts; for such he will not receive: and trust not to unrighteous sacrifices; for the Lord is judge, and with him is no respect of persons.

[13] He will not accept any person against a poor man, but will hear the prayer of the oppressed.

[14] He will not despise the supplication of the fatherless; nor the widow, when she poureth out her complaint.

[15] Do not the tears run down the widow's cheeks? and is not her cry against him that causeth them to fall?

[16] He that serveth the Lord shall be accepted with favour, and his prayer shall reach unto the clouds.

[17] The prayer of the humble pierceth the clouds: and till it come nigh, he will not be comforted; and will not depart, till the most High shall behold to judge righteously, and execute judgment.

[18] For the Lord will not be slack, neither will the Mighty be patient toward them, till he have smitten in sunder the loins of the unmerciful, and repayed vengeance to the heathen; till he have taken away the multitude of the proud, and broken the sceptre of the unrighteous;

[19] Till he have rendered to every man according to his deeds, and to the works of men according to their devices; till he have judged the cause of his people, and made them to rejoice in his mercy.

[20] Mercy is seasonable in the time of affliction, as clouds of rain in the time of drought.

Sir.36

[1] Have mercy upon us, O Lord God of all, and behold us:

[2] And send thy fear upon all the nations that seek not after thee.

[3] Lift up thy hand against the strange nations, and let them see thy power.

[4] As thou wast sanctified in us before them: so be thou magnified among them before us.

[5] And let them know thee, as we have known thee, that there is no God but only thou, O God.

[6] Shew new signs, and make other strange wonders: glorify thy hand and thy right arm, that they may set forth thy wondrous works.

[7] Raise up indignation, and pour out wrath: take away the adversary, and destroy the enemy.

[8] Sake the time short, remember the covenant, and let them declare thy wonderful works.

[9] Let him that escapeth be consumed by the rage of the fire; and let them perish that oppress the people.

[10] Smite in sunder the heads of the rulers of the heathen, that say, There is none other but we.

[11] Gather all the tribes of Jacob together, and inherit thou them, as from the beginning.

[12] O Lord, have mercy upon the people that is called by thy name, and upon Israel, whom thou hast named thy firstborn.

[13] O be merciful unto Jerusalem, thy holy city, the place of thy rest.

[14] Fill Sion with thine unspeakable oracles, and thy people with thy glory:

[15] Give testimony unto those that thou hast possessed from the beginning, and raise up prophets that have been in thy name.

[16] Reward them that wait for thee, and let thy prophets be found faithful.

[17] O Lord, hear the prayer of thy servants, according to the blessing of Aaron over thy people, that all they which dwell upon the earth may know that thou art the Lord, the eternal God.

[18] The belly devoureth all meats, yet is one meat better than another.

[19] As the palate tasteth divers kinds of venison: so doth an heart of understanding false speeches.

[20] A froward heart causeth heaviness: but a man of experience will recompense him.

[21] A woman will receive every man, yet is one daughter better than another.

[22] The beauty of a woman cheereth the countenance, and a man loveth nothing better.

[23] If there be kindness, meekness, and comfort, in her tongue, then is not her husband like other men.

[24] He that getteth a wife beginneth a possession, a help like unto himself, and a pillar of rest.

[25] Where no hedge is, there the possession is spoiled: and he that hath no wife will wander up and down

mourning.

[26] Who will trust a thief well appointed, that skippeth from city to city? so [who will believe] a man that hath no house, and lodgeth wheresoever the night taketh him?

Sir.37

[1] Every friend saith, I am his friend also: but there is a friend, which is only a friend in name.

[2] Is it not a grief unto death, when a companion and friend is turned to an enemy?

[3] O wicked imagination, whence camest thou in to cover the earth with deceit?

[4] There is a companion, which rejoiceth in the prosperity of a friend, but in the time of trouble will be against him.

[5] There is a companion, which helpeth his friend for the belly, and taketh up the buckler against the enemy.

[6] Forget not thy friend in thy mind, and be not unmindful of him in thy riches.

[7] Every counsellor extolleth counsel; but there is some that counselleth for himself.

[8] Beware of a counsellor, and know before what need he hath; for he will counsel for himself; lest he cast the lot upon thee,

[9] And say unto thee, Thy way is good: and afterward he stand on the other side, to see what shall befall thee.

[10] Consult not with one that suspecteth thee: and hide thy counsel from such as envy thee.

[11] Neither consult with a woman touching her of whom she is jealous; neither with a coward in matters of war; nor with a merchant concerning exchange; nor with a buyer of selling; nor with an envious man of thankfulness; nor with an unmerciful man touching kindness; nor with the slothful for any work; nor with an hireling for a year of finishing work; nor with an idle servant of much business: hearken not unto these in any matter of counsel.

[12] But be continually with a godly man, whom thou knowest to keep the commandments of the Lord, whose, mind is according to thy mind, and will sorrow with thee, if thou shalt miscarry.

[13] And let the counsel of thine own heart stand: for there is no man more faithful unto thee than it.

[14] For a man's mind is sometime wont to tell him more than seven watchmen, that sit above in an high tower.

[15] And above all this pray to the most High, that he will direct thy way in truth.

[16] Let reason go before every enterprize, and counsel before every action.

[17] The countenance is a sign of changing of the heart.

[18] Four manner of things appear: good and evil, life and death: but the tongue ruleth over them continually.

[19] There is one that is wise and teacheth many, and yet is unprofitable to himself.

[20] There is one that sheweth wisdom in words, and is hated: he shall be destitute of all food.

[21] For grace is not given, him from the Lord, because he is deprived of all wisdom.

[22] Another is wise to himself; and the fruits of understanding are commendable in his mouth.

[23] A wise man instructeth his people; and the fruits of his understanding fail not.

[24] A wise man shall be filled with blessing; and all they that see him shall count him happy.

[25] The days of the life of man may be numbered: but the days of Israel are innumerable.

[26] A wise man shall inherit glory among his people, and his name shall be perpetual.

[27] My son, prove thy soul in thy life, and see what is evil for it, and give not that unto it.

[28] For all things are not profitable for all men, neither hath every soul pleasure in every thing.

[29] Be not unsatiable in any dainty thing, nor too greedy upon meats:

[30] For excess of meats bringeth sickness, and surfeiting will turn into choler.

[31] By surfeiting have many perished; but he that taketh heed prolongeth his life.

Sir.38

[1] Honour a physician with the honour due unto him for the uses which ye may have of him: for the Lord hath created him.

[2] For of the most High cometh healing, and he shall receive honour of the king.

[3] The skill of the physician shall lift up his head: and in the sight of great men he shall be in admiration.

[4] The Lord hath created medicines out of the earth; and he that is wise will not abhor them.

[5] Was not the water made sweet with wood, that the virtue thereof might be known?

[6] And he hath given men skill, that he might be honoured in his marvellous works.

[7] With such doth he heal [men,] and taketh away their pains.

[8] Of such doth the apothecary make a confection; and of his works there is no end; and from him is peace over all the earth,

[9] My son, in thy sickness be not negligent: but pray unto the Lord, and he will make thee whole.

[10] Leave off from sin, and order thine hands aright, and cleanse thy heart from all wickedness.

[11] Give a sweet savour, and a memorial of fine flour; and make a fat offering, as not being.

[12] Then give place to the physician, for the Lord hath created him: let him not go from thee, for thou hast need of him.

[13] There is a time when in their hands there is good success.

[14] For they shall also pray unto the Lord, that he would prosper that, which they give for ease and remedy to prolong life.

[15] He that sinneth before his Maker, let him fall into the hand of the physician.

[16] My son, let tears fall down over the dead, and begin to lament, as if thou hadst suffered great harm thyself; and then cover his body according to the custom, and neglect not his burial.

[17] Weep bitterly, and make great moan, and use lamentation, as he is worthy, and that a day or two, lest thou be evil spoken of: and then comfort thyself for thy heaviness.

[18] For of heaviness cometh death, and the heaviness of the heart breaketh strength.

[19] In affliction also sorrow remaineth: and the life of the poor is the curse of the heart.

[20] Take no heaviness to heart: drive it away, and member the last end.

[21] Forget it not, for there is no turning again: thou shalt not do him good, but hurt thyself.

[22] Remember my judgment: for thine also shall be so; yesterday for me, and to day for thee.

[23] When the dead is at rest, let his remembrance rest; and be comforted for him, when his Spirit is departed from him.

[24] The wisdom of a learned man cometh by opportunity of leisure: and he that hath little business shall become wise.

[25] How can he get wisdom that holdeth the plough, and that glorieth in the goad, that driveth oxen, and is occupied in their labours, and whose talk is of bullocks?

[26] He giveth his mind to make furrows; and is diligent to give the kine fodder.

[27] So every carpenter and workmaster, that laboureth night and day: and they that cut and grave seals, and are diligent to make great variety, and give themselves to counterfeit imagery, and watch to finish a work:

[28] The smith also sitting by the anvil, and considering the iron work, the vapour of the fire wasteth his flesh, and he fighteth with the heat of the furnace: the noise of the hammer and the anvil is ever in his ears, and his eyes look still upon the pattern of the thing that he maketh; he setteth his mind to finish his work, and watcheth to polish it perfectly:

[29] So doth the potter sitting at his work, and turning the wheel about with his feet, who is alway carefully set at his work, and maketh all his work by number;

[30] He fashioneth the clay with his arm, and boweth down his strength before his feet; he applieth himself to lead it over; and he is diligent to make clean the furnace:

[31] All these trust to their hands: and every one is wise in his work.

[32] Without these cannot a city be inhabited: and they shall not dwell where they will, nor go up and down:

[33] They shall not be sought for in publick counsel, nor sit high in the congregation: they shall not sit on the judges' seat, nor understand the sentence of judgment: they cannot declare justice and judgment; and they shall not be found where parables are spoken.

[34] But they will maintain the state of the world, and [all] their desire is in the work of their craft.

Sir.39

[1] But he that giveth his mind to the law of the most High, and is occupied in the meditation thereof, will seek out the wisdom of all the ancient, and be occupied in prophecies.

[2] He will keep the sayings of the renowned men: and where subtil parables are, he will be there also.

[3] He will seek out the secrets of grave sentences, and be conversant in dark parables.

[4] He shall serve among great men, and appear before princes: he will travel through strange countries; for he hath tried the good and the evil among men.

[5] He will give his heart to resort early to the Lord that made him, and will pray before the most High, and will open his mouth in prayer, and make supplication for his sins.

[6] When the great Lord will, he shall be filled with the spirit of understanding: he shall pour out wise sentences, and give thanks unto the Lord in his prayer.

[7] He shall direct his counsel and knowledge, and in his secrets shall he meditate.

[8] He shall shew forth that which he hath learned, and shall glory in the law of the covenant of the Lord.

[9] Many shall commend his understanding; and so long as the world endureth, it shall not be blotted out; his memorial shall not depart away, and his name shall live from generation to generation.

[10] Nations shall shew forth his wisdom, and the

congregation shall declare his praise.

[11] If he die, he shall leave a greater name than a thousand: and if he live, he shall increase it.

[12] Yet have I more to say, which I have thought upon; for I am filled as the moon at the full.

[13] Hearken unto me, ye holy children, and bud forth as a rose growing by the brook of the field:

[14] And give ye a sweet savour as frankincense, and flourish as a lily, send forth a smell, and sing a song of praise, bless the Lord in all his works.

[15] Magnify his name, and shew forth his praise with the songs of your lips, and with harps, and in praising him ye shall say after this manner:

[16] All the works of the Lord are exceeding good, and whatsoever he commandeth shall be accomplished in due season.

[17] And none may say, What is this? wherefore is that? for at time convenient they shall all be sought out: at his commandment the waters stood as an heap, and at the words of his mouth the receptacles of waters.

[18] At his commandment is done whatsoever pleaseth him; and none can hinder, when he will save.

[19] The works of all flesh are before him, and nothing can be hid from his eyes.

[20] He seeth from everlasting to everlasting; and there is nothing wonderful before him.

[21] A man need not to say, What is this? wherefore is that? for he hath made all things for their uses.

[22] His blessing covered the dry land as a river, and watered it as a flood.

[23] As he hath turned the waters into saltness: so shall the heathen inherit his wrath.

[24] As his ways are plain unto the holy; so are they stumblingblocks unto the wicked.

[25] For the good are good things created from the beginning: so evil things for sinners.

[26] The principal things for the whole use of man's life are water, fire, iron, and salt, flour of wheat, honey, milk, and the blood of the grape, and oil, and clothing.

[27] All these things are for good to the godly: so to the sinners they are turned into evil.

[28] There be spirits that are created for vengeance, which in their fury lay on sore strokes; in the time of destruction they pour out their force, and appease the wrath of him that made them.

[29] Fire, and hail, and famine, and death, all these were created for vengeance;

[30] Teeth of wild beasts, and scorpions, serpents, and the sword punishing the wicked to destruction.

[31] They shall rejoice in his commandment, and they shall be ready upon earth, when need is; and when their time is come, they shall not transgress his word.

[32] Therefore from the beginning I was resolved, and thought upon these things, and have left them in writing.

[33] All the works of the Lord are good: and he will give every needful thing in due season.

[34] So that a man cannot say, This is worse than that: for in time they shall all be well approved.

[35] And therefore praise ye the Lord with the whole heart and mouth, and bless the name of the Lord.

Sir.40

[1] Great travail is created for every man, and an heavy yoke is upon the sons of Adam, from the day that they go out of their mother's womb, till the day that they return to the mother of all things.

[2] Their imagination of things to come, and the day of death, [trouble] their thoughts, and [cause] fear of heart;

[3] From him that sitteth on a throne of glory, unto him that is humbled in earth and ashes;

[4] From him that weareth purple and a crown, unto him that is clothed with a linen frock.

[5] Wrath, and envy, trouble, and unquietness, fear of death, and anger, and strife, and in the time of rest upon his bed his night sleep, do change his knowledge.

[6] A little or nothing is his rest, and afterward he is in his sleep, as in a day of keeping watch, troubled in the vision of his heart, as if he were escaped out of a battle.

[7] When all is safe, he awaketh, and marvelleth that the fear was nothing.

[8] [Such things happen] unto all flesh, both man and beast, and that is sevenfold more upon sinners.

[9] Death, and bloodshed, strife, and sword, calamities, famine, tribulation, and the scourge;

[10] These things are created for the wicked, and for their sakes came the flood.

[11] All things that are of the earth shall turn to the earth again: and that which is of the waters doth return into the sea.

[12] All bribery and injustice shall be blotted out: but true dealing shall endure for ever.

[13] The goods of the unjust shall be dried up like a river, and shall vanish with noise, like a great thunder in rain.

[14] While he openeth his hand he shall rejoice: so shall transgressors come to nought.

[15] The children of the ungodly shall not bring forth many branches: but are as unclean roots upon a hard rock.

[16] The weed growing upon every water and bank of a river shall be pulled up before all grass.

[17] Bountifulness is as a most fruitful garden, and mercifulness endureth for ever.

[18] To labour, and to be content with that a man hath, is a sweet life: but he that findeth a treasure is above them both.

[19] Children and the building of a city continue a man's name: but a blameless wife is counted above them both.

[20] Wine and musick rejoice the heart: but the love of wisdom is above them both.

[21] The pipe and the psaltery make sweet melody: but a pleasant tongue is above them both.

[22] Thine eye desireth favour and beauty: but more than both corn while it is green.

[23] A friend and companion never meet amiss: but above both is a wife with her husband.

[24] Brethren and help are against time of trouble: but alms shall deliver more than them both.

[25] Gold and silver make the foot stand sure: but counsel is esteemed above them both.

[26] Riches and strength lift up the heart: but the fear of the Lord is above them both: there is no want in the fear of the Lord, and it needeth not to seek help.

[27] The fear of the Lord is a fruitful garden, and covereth him above all glory.

[28] My son, lead not a beggar's life; for better it is to die than to beg.

[29] The life of him that dependeth on another man's table is not to be counted for a life; for he polluteth himself with other men's meat: but a wise man well nurtured will beware thereof.

[30] Begging is sweet in the mouth of the shameless: but in his belly there shall burn a fire.

Sir.41

[1] O death, how bitter is the remembrance of thee to a man that liveth at rest in his possessions, unto the man that hath nothing to vex him, and that hath prosperity in all things: yea, unto him that is yet able to receive meat!

[2] O death, acceptable is thy sentence unto the needy, and unto him whose strength faileth, that is now in the last age, and is vexed with all things, and to him that despaireth, and hath lost patience!

[3] Fear not the sentence of death, remember them that have been before thee, and that come after; for this is the sentence of the Lord over all flesh.

[4] And why art thou against the pleasure of the most High? there is no inquisition in the grave, whether thou have lived ten, or an hundred, or a thousand years.

[5] The children of sinners are abominable children, and they that are conversant in the dwelling of the ungodly.

[6] The inheritance of sinners' children shall perish, and their posterity shall have a perpetual reproach.

[7] The children will complain of an ungodly father, because they shall be reproached for his sake.

[8] Woe be unto you, ungodly men, which have forsaken the law of the most high God! for if ye increase, it shall be to your destruction:

[9] And if ye be born, ye shall be born to a curse: and if ye die, a curse shall be your portion.

[10] All that are of the earth shall turn to earth again: so the ungodly shall go from a curse to destruction.

[11] The mourning of men is about their bodies: but an ill name of sinners shall be blotted out.

[12] Have regard to thy name; for that shall continue with thee above a thousand great treasures of gold.

[13] A good life hath but few days: but a good name endureth for ever.

[14] My children, keep discipline in peace: for wisdom that is hid, and a treasure that is not seen, what profit is in them both?

[15] A man that hideth his foolishness is better than a man that hideth his wisdom.

[16] Therefore be shamefaced according to my word: for it is not good to retain all shamefacedness; neither is it altogether approved in every thing.

[17] Be ashamed of whoredom before father and mother: and of a lie before a prince and a mighty man;

[18] Of an offence before a judge and ruler; of iniquity before a congregation and people; of unjust dealing before thy partner and friend;

[19] And of theft in regard of the place where thou sojournest, and in regard of the truth of God and his covenant; and to lean with thine elbow upon the meat; and of scorning to give and take;

[20] And of silence before them that salute thee; and to look upon an harlot;

[21] And to turn away thy face from thy kinsman; or to take away a portion or a gift; or to gaze upon another man's wife.

[22] Or to be overbusy with his maid, and come not near her bed; or of upbraiding speeches before friends; and after thou hast given, upbraid not;

[23] Or of iterating and speaking again that which thou hast heard; and of revealing of secrets.

[24] So shalt thou be truly shamefaced and find favour before all men.

Sir.42

[1] Of these things be not thou ashamed, and accept no person to sin thereby:

[2] Of the law of the most High, and his covenant; and of judgment to justify the ungodly;

[3] Of reckoning with thy partners and travellers; or of the gift of the heritage of friends;

[4] Of exactness of balance and weights; or of getting much or little;

[5] And of merchants' indifferent selling; of much correction of children; and to make the side of an evil servant to bleed.

[6] Sure keeping is good, where an evil wife is; and shut up, where many hands are.

[7] Deliver all things in number and weight; and put all in writing that thou givest out, or receivest in.

[8] Be not ashamed to inform the unwise and foolish, and the extreme aged that contendeth with those that are young: thus shalt thou be truly learned, and approved of all men living.

[9] The father waketh for the daughter, when no man knoweth; and the care for her taketh away sleep: when she is young, lest she pass away the flower of her age; and being married, lest she should be hated:

[10] In her virginity, lest she should be defiled and gotten with child in her father's house; and having an husband, lest she should misbehave herself; and when she is married, lest she should be barren.

[11] Keep a sure watch over a shameless daughter, lest she make thee a laughingstock to thine enemies, and a byword in the city, and a reproach among the people, and make thee ashamed before the multitude.

[12] Behold not every body's beauty, and sit not in the midst of women.

[13] For from garments cometh a moth, and from women wickedness.

[14] Better is the churlishness of a man than a courteous woman, a woman, I say, which bringeth shame and reproach.

[15] I will now remember the works of the Lord, and declare the things that I have seen: In the words of the Lord are his works.

[16] The sun that giveth light looketh upon all things, and the work thereof is full of the glory of the Lord.

[17] The Lord hath not given power to the saints to declare all his marvellous works, which the Almighty Lord firmly settled, that whatsoever is might be established for his glory.

[18] He seeketh out the deep, and the heart, and considereth their crafty devices: for the Lord knoweth all that may be known, and he beholdeth the signs of the world.

[19] He declareth the things that are past, and for to come, and revealeth the steps of hidden things.

[20] No thought escapeth him, neither any word is hidden from him.

[21] He hath garnished the excellent works of his wisdom, and he is from everlasting to everlasting: unto him may nothing be added, neither can he be diminished, and he hath no need of any counsellor.

[22] Oh how desirable are all his works! and that a man may see even to a spark.

[23] All these things live and remain for ever for all uses, and they are all obedient.

[24] All things are double one against another: and he hath made nothing imperfect.

[25] One thing establisheth the good or another: and who shall be filled with beholding his glory?

Sir.43

[1] The pride of the height, the clear firmament, the beauty of heaven, with his glorious shew;

[2] The sun when it appeareth, declaring at his rising a marvellous instrument, the work of the most High:

[3] At noon it parcheth the country, and who can abide the burning heat thereof?

[4] A man blowing a furnace is in works of heat, but the sun burneth the mountains three times more; breathing out fiery vapours, and sending forth bright beams, it dimmeth the eyes.

[5] Great is the Lord that made it; and at his commandment runneth hastily.

[6] He made the moon also to serve in her season for a declaration of times, and a sign of the world.

[7] From the moon is the sign of feasts, a light that decreaseth in her perfection.

[8] The month is called after her name, increasing wonderfully in her changing, being an instrument of the armies above, shining in the firmament of heaven;

[9] The beauty of heaven, the glory of the stars, an ornament giving light in the highest places of the Lord.

[10] At the commandment of the Holy One they will stand in their order, and never faint in their watches.

[11] Look upon the rainbow, and praise him that made it; very beautiful it is in the brightness thereof.

[12] It compasseth the heaven about with a glorious circle, and the hands of the most High have bended it.

[13] By his commandment he maketh the snow to fall

aplace, and sendeth swiftly the lightnings of his judgment.

[14] Through this the treasures are opened: and clouds fly forth as fowls.

[15] By his great power he maketh the clouds firm, and the hailstones are broken small.

[16] At his sight the mountains are shaken, and at his will the south wind bloweth.

[17] The noise of the thunder maketh the earth to tremble: so doth the northern storm and the whirlwind: as birds flying he scattereth the snow, and the falling down thereof is as the lighting of grasshoppers:

[18] The eye marvelleth at the beauty of the whiteness thereof, and the heart is astonished at the raining of it.

[19] The hoarfrost also as salt he poureth on the earth, and being congealed, it lieth on the top of sharp stakes.

[20] When the cold north wind bloweth, and the water is congealed into ice, it abideth upon every gathering together of water, and clotheth the water as with a breastplate.

[21] It devoureth the mountains, and burneth the wilderness, and consumeth the grass as fire.

[22] A present remedy of all is a mist coming speedily, a dew coming after heat refresheth.

[23] By his counsel he appeaseth the deep, and planteth islands therein.

[24] They that sail on the sea tell of the danger thereof; and when we hear it with our ears, we marvel thereat.

[25] For therein be strange and wondrous works, variety of all kinds of beasts and whales created.

[26] By him the end of them hath prosperous success, and by his word all things consist.

[27] We may speak much, and yet come short: wherefore in sum, he is all.

[28] How shall we be able to magnify him? for he is great above all his works.

[29] The Lord is terrible and very great, and marvellous is his power.

[30] When ye glorify the Lord, exalt him as much as ye can; for even yet will he far exceed: and when ye exalt him, put forth all your strength, and be not weary; for ye can never go far enough.

[31] Who hath seen him, that he might tell us? and who can magnify him as he is?

[32] There are yet hid greater things than these be, for we have seen but a few of his works.

[33] For the Lord hath made all things; and to the godly hath he given wisdom.

Sir.44

[1] Let us now praise famous men, and our fathers that begat us.

[2] The Lord hath wrought great glory by them through his great power from the beginning.

[3] Such as did bear rule in their kingdoms, men renowned for their power, giving counsel by their understanding, and declaring prophecies:

[4] Leaders of the people by their counsels, and by their knowledge of learning meet for the people, wise and eloquent are their instructions:

[5] Such as found out musical tunes, and recited verses in writing:

[6] Rich men furnished with ability, living peaceably in their habitations:

[7] All these were honoured in their generations, and were the glory of their times.

[8] There be of them, that have left a name behind them, that their praises might be reported.

[9] And some there be, which have no memorial; who are perished, as though they had never been; and are become as though they had never been born; and their children after them.

[10] But these were merciful men, whose righteousness hath not been forgotten.

[11] With their seed shall continually remain a good inheritance, and their children are within the covenant.

[12] Their seed standeth fast, and their children for their sakes.

[13] Their seed shall remain for ever, and their glory shall not be blotted out.

[14] Their bodies are buried in peace; but their name liveth for evermore.

[15] The people will tell of their wisdom, and the congregation will shew forth their praise.

[16] Enoch pleased the Lord, and was translated, being an example of repentance to all generations.

[17] Noah was found perfect and righteous; in the time of wrath he was taken in exchange [for the world;] therefore was he left as a remnant unto the earth, when the flood came.

[18] An everlasting covenant was made with him, that all flesh should perish no more by the flood.

[19] Abraham was a great father of many people: in glory was there none like unto him;

[20] Who kept the law of the most High, and was in covenant with him: he established the covenant in his flesh; and when he was proved, he was found faithful.

[21] Therefore he assured him by an oath, that he would

bless the nations in his seed, and that he would multiply him as the dust of the earth, and exalt his seed as the stars, and cause them to inherit from sea to sea, and from the river unto the utmost part of the land.

[22] With Isaac did he establish likewise [for Abraham his father's sake] the blessing of all men, and the covenant, And made it rest upon the head of Jacob. He acknowledged him in his blessing, and gave him an heritage, and divided his portions; among the twelve tribes did he part them.

Sir.45

[1] And he brought out of him a merciful man, which found favour in the sight of all flesh, even Moses, beloved of God and men, whose memorial is blessed.

[2] He made him like to the glorious saints, and magnified him, so that his enemies stood in fear of him.

[3] By his words he caused the wonders to cease, and he made him glorious in the sight of kings, and gave him a commandment for his people, and shewed him part of his glory.

[4] He sanctified him in his faithfuless and meekness, and chose him out of all men.

[5] He made him to hear his voice, and brought him into the dark cloud, and gave him commandments before his face, even the law of life and knowledge, that he might teach Jacob his covenants, and Israel his judgments.

[6] He exalted Aaron, an holy man like unto him, even his brother, of the tribe of Levi.

[7] An everlasting covenant he made with him and gave him the priesthood among the people; he beautified him with comely ornaments, and clothed him with a robe of glory.

[8] He put upon him perfect glory; and strengthened him with rich garments, with breeches, with a long robe, and the ephod.

[9] And he compassed him with pomegranates, and with many golden bells round about, that as he went there might be a sound, and a noise made that might be heard in the temple, for a memorial to the children of his people;

[10] With an holy garment, with gold, and blue silk, and purple, the work of the embroidere, with a breastplate of judgment, and with Urim and Thummim;

[11] With twisted scarlet, the work of the cunning workman, with precious stones graven like seals, and set in gold, the work of the jeweller, with a writing engraved for a memorial, after the number of the tribes of Israel.

[12] He set a crown of gold upon the mitre, wherein was engraved Holiness, an ornament of honour, a costly work, the desires of the eyes, goodly and beautiful.

[13] Before him there were none such, neither did ever any stranger put them on, but only his children and his children's children perpetually.

[14] Their sacrifices shall be wholly consumed every day twice continually.

[15] Moses consecrated him, and anointed him with holy oil: this was appointed unto him by an everlasting covenant, and to his seed, so long as the heavens should remain, that they should minister unto him, and execute the office of the priesthood, and bless the people in his name.

[16] He chose him out of all men living to offer sacrifices to the Lord, incense, and a sweet savour, for a memorial, to make reconciliation for his people.

[17] He gave unto him his commandments, and authority in the statutes of judgments, that he should teach Jacob the testimonies, and inform Israel in his laws.

[18] Strangers conspired together against him, and maligned him in the wilderness, even the men that were of Dathan's and Abiron's side, and the congregation of Core, with fury and wrath.

[19] This the Lord saw, and it displeased him, and in his wrathful indignation were they consumed: he did wonders upon them, to consume them with the fiery flame.

[20] But he made Aaron more honourable, and gave him an heritage, and divided unto him the firstfruits of the increase; especially he prepared bread in abundance:

[21] For they eat of the sacrifices of the Lord, which he gave unto him and his seed.

[22] Howbeit in the land of the people he had no inheritance, neither had he any portion among the people: for the Lord himself is his portion and inheritance.

[23] The third in glory is Phinees the son of Eleazar, because he had zeal in the fear of the Lord, and stood up with good courage of heart: when the people were turned back, and made reconciliation for Israel.

[24] Therefore was there a covenant of peace made with him, that he should be the chief of the sanctuary and of his people, and that he and his posterity should have the dignity of the priesthood for ever:

[25] According to the covenant made with David son of Jesse, of the tribe of Juda, that the inheritance of the king should be to his posterity alone: so the inheritance of Aaron should also be unto his seed.

[26] God give you wisdom in your heart to judge his people in righteousness, that their good things be not abolished, and that their glory may endure for ever.

Sir.46

[1] Jesus the son a Nave was valiant in the wars, and was the successor of Moses in prophecies, who according to his name was made great for the saving of the elect of God, and taking vengeance of the enemies that rose up against them, that he might set Israel in their inheritance.

[2] How great glory gat he, when he did lift up his hands, and stretched out his sword against the cities!

[3] Who before him so stood to it? for the Lord himself brought his enemies unto him.

[4] Did not the sun go back by his means? and was not one day as long as two?

[5] He called upon the most high Lord, when the enemies pressed upon him on every side; and the great Lord heard him.

[6] And with hailstones of mighty power he made the battle to fall violently upon the nations, and in the descent [of Beth-horon] he destroyed them that resisted, that the nations might know all their strength, because he fought in the sight of the Lord, and he followed the Mighty One.

[7] In the time of Moses also he did a work of mercy, he and Caleb the son of Jephunne, in that they withstood the congregation, and withheld the people from sin, and appeased the wicked murmuring.

[8] And of six hundred thousand people on foot, they two were preserved to bring them in to the heritage, even unto the land that floweth with milk and honey.

[9] The Lord gave strength also unto Caleb, which remained with him unto his old age: so that he entered upon the high places of the land, and his seed obtained it for an heritage:

[10] That all the children of Israel might see that it is good to follow the Lord.

[11] And concerning the judges, every one by name, whose heart went not a whoring, nor departed from the Lord, let their memory be blessed.

[12] Let their bones flourish out of their place, and let the name of them that were honoured be continued upon their children.

[13] Samuel, the prophet of the Lord, beloved of his Lord, established a kingdom, and anointed princes over his people.

[14] By the law of the Lord he judged the congregation, and the Lord had respect unto Jacob.

[15] By his faithfulness he was found a true prophet, and by his word he was known to be faithful in vision.

[16] He called upon the mighty Lord, when his enemies pressed upon him on every side, when he offered the sucking lamb.

[17] And the Lord thundered from heaven, and with a great noise made his voice to be heard.

[18] And he destroyed the rulers of the Tyrians, and all the princes cf the Philistines.

[19] And before his long sleep he made protestations in the sight of the Lord and his anointed, I have not taken any man's goods, so much as a shoe: and no man did accuse him.

[20] And after his death he prophesied, and shewed the king his end, and lifted up his voice from the earth in prophecy, to blot out the wickedness of the people.

Sir.47

[1] And after him rose up Nathan to prophesy in the time of David.

[2] As is the fat taken away from the peace offering, so was David chosen out of the children of Israel.

[3] He played with lions as with kids, and with bears as with lambs.

[4] Slew he not a giant, when he was yet but young? and did he not take away reproach from the people, when he lifted up his hand with the stone in the sling, and beat down the boasting of Goliath?

[5] For he called upon the most high Lord; and he gave him strength in his right hand to slay that mighty warrior, and set up the horn of his people.

[6] So the people honoured him with ten thousands, and praised him in the blessings of the Lord, in that he gave him a crown of glory.

[7] For he destroyed the enemies on every side, and brought to nought the Philistines his adversaries, and brake their horn in sunder unto this day.

[8] In all his works he praised the Holy One most high with words of glory; with his whole heart he sung songs, and loved him that made him.

[9] He set singers also before the altar, that by their voices they might make sweet melody, and daily sing praises in their songs.

[10] He beautified their feasts, and set in order the solemn times until the end, that they might praise his holy name, and that the temple might sound from morning.

[11] The Lord took away his sins, and exalted his horn for ever: he gave him a covenant of kings, and a throne of glory in Israel.

[12] After him rose up a wise son, and for his sake he dwelt at large.

[13] Solomon reigned in a peaceable time, and was honoured; for God made all quiet round about him, that he might build an house in his name, and prepare his

sanctuary for ever.

[14] How wise wast thou in thy youth and, as a flood, filled with understanding!

[15] Thy soul covered the whole earth, and thou filledst it with dark parables.

[16] Thy name went far unto the islands; and for thy peace thou wast beloved.

[17] The countries marvelled at thee for thy songs, and proverbs, and parables, and interpretations.

[18] By the name of the Lord God, which is called the Lord God of Israel, thou didst gather gold as tin and didst multiply silver as lead.

[19] Thou didst bow thy loins unto women, and by thy body thou wast brought into subjection.

[20] Thou didst stain thy honour, and pollute thy seed: so that thou broughtest wrath upon thy children, and wast grieved for thy folly.

[21] So the kingdom was divided, and out of Ephraim ruled a rebellious kingdom.

[22] But the Lord will never leave off his mercy, neither shall any of his works perish, neither will he abolish the posterity of his elect, and the seed of him that loveth him he will not take away: wherefore he gave a remnant unto Jacob, and out of him a root unto David.

[23] Thus rested Solomon with his fathers, and of his seed he left behind him Roboam, even the foolishness of the people, and one that had no understanding, who turned away the people through his counsel. There was also Jeroboam the son of Nebat, who caused Israel to sin, and shewed Ephraim the way of sin:

[24] And their sins were multiplied exceedingly, that they were driven out of the land.

[25] For they sought out all wickedness, till the vengeance came upon them.

Sir.48

[1] Then stood up Elias the prophet as fire, and his word burned like a lamp.

[2] He brought a sore famine upon them, and by his zeal he diminished their number.

[3] By the word of the Lord he shut up the heaven, and also three times brought down fire.

[4] O Elias, how wast thou honoured in thy wondrous deeds! and who may glory like unto thee!

[5] Who didst raise up a dead man from death, and his soul from the place of the dead, by the word of the most High:

[6] Who broughtest kings to destruction, and honorable men from their bed:

[7] Who heardest the rebuke of the Lord in Sinai, and in Horeb the judgment of vengeance:

[8] Who annointedst kings to take revenge, and prophets to succeed after him:

[9] Who was taken up in a whirlwind of fire, and in a chariot of fiery horses:

[10] Who wast ordained for reproofs in their times, to pacify the wrath of the Lord's judgment, before it brake forth into fury, and to turn the heart of the father unto the son, and to restore the tribes of Jacob.

[11] Blessed are they that saw thee, and slept in love; for we shall surely live.

[12] Elias it was, who was covered with a whirlwind: and Eliseus was filled with his spirit: whilst he lived, he was not moved with the presence of any prince, neither could any bring him into subjection.

[13] No word could overcome him; and after his death his body prophesied.

[14] He did wonders in his life, and at his death were his works marvellous.

[15] For all this the people repented not, neither departed they from their sins, till they were spoiled and carried out of their land, and were scattered through all the earth: yet there remained a small people, and a ruler in the house of David:

[16] Of whom some did that which was pleasing to God, and some multiplied sins.

[17] Ezekias fortified his city, and brought in water into the midst thereof: he digged the hard rock with iron, and made wells for waters.

[18] In his time Sennacherib came up, and sent Rabsaces, and lifted up his hand against Sion, and boasted proudly.

[19] Then trembled their hearts and hands, and they were in pain, as women in travail.

[20] But they called upon the Lord which is merciful, and stretched out their hands toward him: and immediately the Holy One heard them out of heaven, and delivered them by the ministry of Esay.

[21] He smote the host of the Assyrians, and his angel destroyed them.

[22] For Ezekias had done the thing that pleased the Lord, and was strong in the ways of David his father, as Esay the prophet, who was great and faithful in his vision, had commanded him.

[23] In his time the sun went backward, and he lengthened the king's life.

[24] He saw by an excellent spirit what should come to pass at the last, and he comforted them that mourned in Sion.

[25] He shewed what should come to pass for ever, and secret things or ever they came.

Sir.49

[1] The remembrance of Josias is like the composition of the perfume that is made by the art of the apothecary: it is sweet as honey in all mouths, and as musick at a banquet of wine.

[2] He behaved himself uprightly in the conversion of the people, and took away the abominations of iniquity.

[3] He directed his heart unto the Lord, and in the time of the ungodly he established the worship of God.

[4] All, except David and Ezekias and Josias, were defective: for they forsook the law of the most High, even the kings of Juda failed.

[5] Therefore he gave their power unto others, and their glory to a strange nation.

[6] They burnt the chosen city of the sanctuary, and made the streets desolate, according to the prophecy of Jeremias.

[7] For they entreated him evil, who nevertheless was a prophet, sanctified in his mother's womb, that he might root out, and afflict, and destroy; and that he might build up also, and plant.

[8] It was Ezekiel who saw the glorious vision, which was shewed him upon the chariot of the cherubims.

[9] For he made mention of the enemies under the figure of the rain, and directed them that went right.

[10] And of the twelve prophets let the memorial be blessed, and let their bones flourish again out of their place: for they comforted Jacob, and delivered them by assured hope.

[11] How shall we magnify Zorobabel? even he was as a signet on the right hand:

[12] So was Jesus the son of Josedec: who in their time builded the house, and set up an holy temple to the Lord, which was prepared for everlasting glory.

[13] And among the elect was Neemias, whose renown is great, who raised up for us the walls that were fallen, and set up the gates and the bars, and raised up our ruins again.

[14] But upon the earth was no man created like Enoch; for he was taken from the earth.

[15] Neither was there a young man born like Joseph, a governor of his brethren, a stay of the people, whose bones were regarded of the Lord.

[16] Sem and Seth were in great honour among men, and so was Adam above every living thing in creation.

Sir.50

[1] Simon the high priest, the son of Onias, who in his life repaired the house again, and in his days fortified the temple:

[2] And by him was built from the foundation the double height, the high fortress of the wall about the temple:

[3] In his days the cistern to receive water, being in compass as the sea, was covered with plates of brass:

[4] He took care of the temple that it should not fall, and fortified the city against besieging:

[5] How was he honoured in the midst of the people in his coming out of the sanctuary!

[6] He was as the morning star in the midst of a cloud, and as the moon at the full:

[7] As the sun shining upon the temple of the most High, and as the rainbow giving light in the bright clouds:

[8] And as the flower of roses in the spring of the year, as lilies by the rivers of waters, and as the branches of the frankincense tree in the time of summer:

[9] As fire and incense in the censer, and as a vessel of beaten gold set with all manner of precious stones:

[10] And as a fair olive tree budding forth fruit, and as a cypress tree which groweth up to the clouds.

[11] When he put on the robe of honour, and was clothed with the perfection of glory, when he went up to the holy altar, he made the garment of holiness honourable.

[12] When he took the portions out of the priests' hands, he himself stood by the hearth of the altar, compassed about, as a young cedar in Libanus; and as palm trees compassed they him round about.

[13] So were all the sons of Aaron in their glory, and the oblations of the Lord in their hands, before all the congregation of Israel.

[14] And finishing the service at the altar, that he might adorn the offering of the most high Almighty,

[15] He stretched out his hand to the cup, and poured of the blood of the grape, he poured out at the foot of the altar a sweetsmelling savour unto the most high King of all.

[16] Then shouted the sons of Aaron, and sounded the silver trumpets, and made a great noise to be heard, for a remembrance before the most High.

[17] Then all the people together hasted, and fell down to the earth upon their faces to worship their Lord God Almighty, the most High.

[18] The singers also sang praises with their voices, with great variety of sounds was there made sweet melody.

[19] And the people besought the Lord, the most High, by prayer before him that is merciful, till the solemnity of the

Lord was ended, and they had finished his service.

[20] Then he went down, and lifted up his hands over the whole congregation of the children of Israel, to give the blessing of the Lord with his lips, and to rejoice in his name.

[21] And they bowed themselves down to worship the second time, that they might receive a blessing from the most High.

[22] Now therefore bless ye the God of all, which only doeth wondrous things every where, which exalteth our days from the womb, and dealeth with us according to his mercy.

[23] He grant us joyfulness of heart, and that peace may be in our days in Israel for ever:

[24] That he would confirm his mercy with us, and deliver us at his time!

[25] There be two manner of nations which my heart abhorreth, and the third is no nation:

[26] They that sit upon the mountain of Samaria, and they that dwell among the Philistines, and that foolish people that dwell in Sichem.

[27] Jesus the son of Sirach of Jerusalem hath written in this book the instruction of understanding and knowledge, who out of his heart poured forth wisdom.

[28] Blessed is he that shall be exercised in these things; and he that layeth them up in his heart shall become wise.

[29] For if he do them, he shall be strong to all things: for the light of the Lord leadeth him, who giveth wisdom to the godly. Blessed be the name of the Lord for ever. Amen, Amen.

Sir.51

[A Prayer of Jesus the son of Sirach.][1] I will thank thee, O Lord and King, and praise thee, O God my Saviour: I do give praise unto thy name:

[2] For thou art my defender and helper, and has preserved my body from destruction, and from the snare of the slanderous tongue, and from the lips that forge lies, and has been mine helper against mine adversaries:

[3] And hast delivered me, according to the multitude of they mercies and greatness of thy name, from the teeth of them that were ready to devour me, and out of the hands of such as sought after my life, and from the manifold afflictions which I had;

[4] From the choking of fire on every side, and from the midst of the fire which I kindled not;

[5] From the depth of the belly of hell, from an unclean tongue, and from lying words.

[6] By an accusation to the king from an unrighteous

tongue my soul drew near even unto death, my life was near to the hell beneath.

[7] They compassed me on every side, and there was no man to help me: I looked for the succour of men, but there was none.

[8] Then thought I upon thy mercy, O Lord, and upon thy acts of old, how thou deliverest such as wait for thee, and savest them out of the hands of the enemies.

[9] Then lifted I up my supplications from the earth, and prayed for deliverance from death.

[10] I called upon the Lord, the Father of my Lord, that he would not leave me in the days of my trouble, and in the time of the proud, when there was no help.

[11] I will praise thy name continually, and will sing praises with thanksgiving; and so my prayer was heard:

[12] For thou savedst me from destruction, and deliveredst me from the evil time: therefore will I give thanks, and praise thee, and bless they name, O Lord.

[13] When I was yet young, or ever I went abroad, I desired wisdom openly in my prayer.

[14] I prayed for her before the temple, and will seek her out even to the end.

[15] Even from the flower till the grape was ripe hath my heart delighted in her: my foot went the right way, from my youth up sought I after her.

[16] I bowed down mine ear a little, and received her, and gat much learning.

[17] I profited therein, therefore will I ascribe glory unto him that giveth me wisdom.

[18] For I purposed to do after her, and earnestly I followed that which is good; so shall I not be confounded.

[19] My soul hath wrestled with her, and in my doings I was exact: I stretched forth my hands to the heaven above, and bewailed my ignorances of her.

[20] I directed my soul unto her, and I found her in pureness: I have had my heart joined with her from the beginning, therefore shall I not be foresaken.

[21] My heart was troubled in seeking her: therefore have I gotten a good possession.

[22] The Lord hath given me a tongue for my reward, and I will praise him therewith.

[23] Draw near unto me, ye unlearned, and dwell in the house of learning.

[24] Wherefore are ye slow, and what say ye to these things, seeing your souls are very thirsty?

[25] I opened my mouth, and said, Buy her for yourselves without money.

[26] Put your neck under the yoke, and let your soul receive instruction: she is hard at hand to find.

[27] Behold with your eyes, how that I have but little

labour, and have gotten unto me much rest.

[28] Get learning with a great sum of money, and get much gold by her.

[29] Let your soul rejoice in his mercy, and be not ashamed of his praise.

[30] Work your work betimes, and in his time he will give you your reward.

The Book Of Tobit

Tob.1

[1] The book of the words of Tobit, son of Tobiel, the son of Ananiel, the son of Aduel, the son of Gabael, of the seed of Asael, of the tribe of Nephthali;

[2] Who in the time of Enemessar king of the Assyrians was led captive out of Thisbe, which is at the right hand of that city, which is called properly Nephthali in Galilee above Aser.

[3] I Tobit have walked all the days of my life in the ways of truth and justice, and I did many almsdeeds to my brethren, and my nation, who came with me to Nineve, into the land of the Assyrians.

[4] And when I was in mine own country, in the land of Israel being but young, all the tribe of Nephthali my father fell from the house of Jerusalem, which was chosen out of all the tribes of Israel, that all the tribes should sacrifice there, where the temple of the habitation of the most High was consecrated and built for all ages.

[5] Now all the tribes which together revolted, and the house of my father Nephthali, sacrificed unto the heifer Baal.

[6] But I alone went often to Jerusalem at the feasts, as it was ordained unto all the people of Israel by an everlasting decree, having the firstfruits and tenths of increase, with that which was first shorn; and them gave I at the altar to the priests the children of Aaron.

[7] The first tenth part of all increase I gave to the sons of Aaron, who ministered at Jerusalem: another tenth part I sold away, and went, and spent it every year at Jerusalem:

[8] And the third I gave unto them to whom it was meet, as Debora my father's mother had commanded me, because I was left an orphan by my father.

[9] Furthermore, when I was come to the age of a man, I married Anna of mine own kindred, and of her I begat Tobias.

[10] And when we were carried away captives to Nineve, all my brethren and those that were of my kindred did eat of the bread of the Gentiles.

[11] But I kept myself from eating;

[12] Because I remembered God with all my heart.

[13] And the most High gave me grace and favour before Enemessar, so that I was his purveyor.

[14] And I went into Media, and left in trust with Gabael, the brother of Gabrias, at Rages a city of Media ten talents of silver.

[15] Now when Enemessar was dead, Sennacherib his son reigned in his stead; whose estate was troubled, that I could not go into Media.

[16] And in the time of Enemessar I gave many alms to my brethren, and gave my bread to the hungry,

[17] And my clothes to the naked: and if I saw any of my nation dead, or cast about the walls of Nineve, I buried him.

[18] And if the king Sennacherib had slain any, when he was come, and fled from Judea, I buried them privily; for in his wrath he killed many; but the bodies were not found, when they were sought for of the king.

[19] And when one of the Ninevites went and complained of me to the king, that I buried them, and hid myself; understanding that I was sought for to be put to death, I withdrew myself for fear.

[20] Then all my goods were forcibly taken away, neither was there any thing left me, beside my wife Anna and my son Tobias.

[21] And there passed not five and fifty days, before two of his sons killed him, and they fled into the mountains of Ararath; and Sarchedonus his son reigned in his stead; who appointed over his father's accounts, and over all his affairs, Achiacharus my brother Anael's son.

[22] And Achiacharus intreating for me, I returned to Nineve. Now Achiacharus was cupbearer, and keeper of the signet, and steward, and overseer of the accounts: and Sarchedonus appointed him next unto him: and he was my brother's son.

Tob.2

[1] Now when I was come home again, and my wife Anna was restored unto me, with my son Tobias, in the feast of Pentecost, which is the holy feast of the seven weeks, there was a good dinner prepared me, in the which I sat down to eat.

[2] And when I saw abundance of meat, I said to my son,

Go and bring what poor man soever thou shalt find out of our brethren, who is mindful of the Lord; and, lo, I tarry for thee.

[3] But he came again, and said, Father, one of our nation is strangled, and is cast out in the marketplace.

[4] Then before I had tasted of any meat, I started up, and took him up into a room until the going down of the sun.

[5] Then I returned, and washed myself, and ate my meat in heaviness,

[6] Remembering that prophecy of Amos, as he said, Your feasts shall be turned into mourning, and all your mirth into lamentation.

[7] Therefore I wept: and after the going down of the sun I went and made a grave, and buried him.

[8] But my neighbours mocked me, and said, This man is not yet afraid to be put to death for this matter: who fled away; and yet, lo, he burieth the dead again.

[9] The same night also I returned from the burial, and slept by the wall of my courtyard, being polluted and my face was uncovered:

[10] And I knew not that there were sparrows in the wall, and mine eyes being open, the sparrows muted warm dung into mine eyes, and a whiteness came in mine eyes: and I went to the physicians, but they helped me not: moreover Achiacharus did nourish me, until I went into Elymais.

[11] And my wife Anna did take women's works to do.

[12] And when she had sent them home to the owners, they paid her wages, and gave her also besides a kid.

[13] And when it was in my house, and began to cry, I said unto her, From whence is this kid? is it not stolen? render it to the owners; for it is not lawful to eat any thing that is stolen.

[14] But she replied upon me, It was given for a gift more than the wages. Howbeit I did not believe her, but bade her render it to the owners: and I was abashed at her. But she replied upon me, Where are thine alms and thy righteous deeds? behold, thou and all thy works are known.

Tob.3

[1] Then I being grieved did weep, and in my sorrow prayed, saying,

[2] O Lord, thou art just, and all thy works and all thy ways are mercy and truth, and thou judgest truly and justly for ever.

[3] Remember me, and look on me, punish me not for my sins and ignorances, and the sins of mg fathers, who have sinned before thee:

[4] For they obeyed not thy commandments: wherefore thou hast delivered us for a spoil, and unto captivity, and unto death, and for a proverb of reproach to all the nations among whom we are dispersed.

[5] And now thy judgments are many and true: deal with me according to my sins and my fathers': because we have not kept thy commandments, neither have walked in truth before thee.

[6] Now therefore deal with me as seemeth best unto thee, and command my spirit to be taken from me, that I may be dissolved, and become earth: for it is profitable for me to die rather than to live, because I have heard false reproaches, and have much sorrow: command therefore that I may now be delivered out of this distress, and go into the everlasting place: turn not thy face away from me.

[7] It came to pass the same day, that in Ecbatane a city of Media Sara the daughter of Raguel was also reproached by her father's maids;

[8] Because that she had been married to seven husbands, whom Asmodeus the evil spirit had killed, before they had lain with her. Dost thou not know, said they, that thou hast strangled thine husbands? thou hast had already seven husbands, neither wast thou named after any of them.

[9] Wherefore dost thou beat us for them? if they be dead, go thy ways after them, let us never see of thee either son or daughter.

[10] Whe she heard these things, she was very sorrowful, so that she thought to have strangled herself; and she said, I am the only daughter of my father, and if I do this, it shall be a reproach unto him, and I shall bring his old age with sorrow unto the grave.

[11] Then she prayed toward the window, and said, Blessed art thou, O Lord my God, and thine holy and glorious name is blessed and honourable for ever: let all thy works praise thee for ever.

[12] And now, O Lord, I set I mine eyes and my face toward thee,

[13] And say, Take me out of the earth, that I may hear no more the reproach.

[14] Thou knowest, Lord, that I am pure from all sin with man,

[15] And that I never polluted my name, nor the name of my father, in the land of my captivity: I am the only daughter of my father, neither hath he any child to be his heir, neither any near kinsman, nor any son of his alive, to whom I may keep myself for a wife: my seven husbands are already dead; and why should I live? but if it please not thee that I should die, command some regard to be had of me, and pity taken of me, that I hear no more reproach.

[16] So the prayers of them both were heard before the majesty of the great God.

[17] And Raphael was sent to heal them both, that is, to scale away the whiteness of Tobit's eyes, and to give Sara the daughter of Raguel for a wife to Tobias the son of Tobit; and to bind Asmodeus the evil spirit; because she belonged to Tobias by right of inheritance. The selfsame time came Tobit home, and entered into his house, and Sara the daughter of Raguel came down from her upper chamber.

Tob.4

[1] In that day Tobit remembered the money which he had committed to Gabael in Rages of Media,

[2] And said with himself, I have wished for death; wherefore do I not call for my son Tobias that I may signify to him of the money before I die?

[3] And when he had called him, he said, My son, when I am dead, bury me; and despise not thy mother, but honour her all the days of thy life, and do that which shall please her, and grieve her not.

[4] Remember, my son, that she saw many dangers for thee, when thou wast in her womb: and when she is dead, bury her by me in one grave.

[5] My son, be mindful of the Lord our God all thy days, and let not thy will be set to sin, or to transgress his commandments: do uprightly all thy life long, and follow not the ways of unrighteousness.

[6] For if thou deal truly, thy doings shall prosperously succeed to thee, and to all them that live justly.

[7] Give alms of thy substance; and when thou givest alms, let not thine eye be envious, neither turn thy face from any poor, and the face of God shall not be turned away from thee.

[8] If thou hast abundance give alms accordingly: if thou have but a little, be not afraid to give according to that little:

[9] For thou layest up a good treasure for thyself against the day of necessity.

[10] Because that alms do deliver from death, and suffereth not to come into darkness.

[11] For alms is a good gift unto all that give it in the sight of the most High.

[12] Beware of all whoredom, my son, and chiefly take a wife of the seed of thy fathers, and take not a strange woman to wife, which is not of thy father's tribe: for we are the children of the prophets, Noe, Abraham, Isaac, and Jacob: remember, my son, that our fathers from the beginning, even that they all married wives of their own kindred, and were blessed in their children, and their seed shall inherit the land.

[13] Now therefore, my son, love thy brethren, and despise not in thy heart thy brethren, the sons and daughters of thy people, in not taking a wife of them: for in pride is destruction and much trouble, and in lewdness is decay and great want: for lewdness is the mother of famine.

[14] Let not the wages of any man, which hath wrought for thee, tarry with thee, but give him it out of hand: for if thou serve God, he will also repay thee: be circumspect my son, in all things thou doest, and be wise in all thy conversation.

[15] Do that to no man which thou hatest: drink not wine to make thee drunken: neither let drunkenness go with thee in thy journey.

[16] Give of thy bread to the hungry, and of thy garments to them that are naked; and according to thine abundance give alms: and let not thine eye be envious, when thou givest alms.

[17] Pour out thy bread on the burial of the just, but give nothing to the wicked.

[18] Ask counsel of all that are wise, and despise not any counsel that is profitable.

[19] Bless the Lord thy God alway, and desire of him that thy ways may be directed, and that all thy paths and counsels may prosper: for every nation hath not counsel; but the Lord himself giveth all good things, and he humbleth whom he will, as he will; now therefore, my son, remember my commandments, neither let them be put out of thy mind.

[20] And now I signify this to they that I committed ten talents to Gabael the son of Gabrias at Rages in Media.

[21] And fear not, my son, that we are made poor: for thou hast much wealth, if thou fear God, and depart from all sin, and do that which is pleasing in his sight.

Tob.5

[1] Tobias then answered and said, Father, I will do all things which thou hast commanded me:

[2] But how can I receive the money, seeing I know him not?

[3] Then he gave him the handwriting, and said unto him, Seek thee a man which may go with thee, whiles I yet live, and I will give him wages: and go and receive the money.

[4] Therefore when he went to seek a man, he found Raphael that was an angel.

[5] But he knew not; and he said unto him, Canst thou go with me to Rages? and knowest thou those places well?

[6] To whom the angel said, I will go with thee, and I know

the way well: for I have lodged with our brother Gabael.

[7] Then Tobias said unto him, Tarry for me, till I tell my father.

[8] Then he said unto him, Go and tarry not. So he went in and said to his father, Behold, I have found one which will go with me. Then he said, Call him unto me, that I may know of what tribe he is, and whether he be a trusty man to go with thee.

[9] So he called him, and he came in, and they saluted one another.

[10] Then Tobit said unto him, Brother, shew me of what tribe and family thou art.

[11] To whom he said, Dost thou seek for a tribe or family, or an hired man to go with thy son? Then Tobit said unto him, I would know, brother, thy kindred and name.

[12] Then he said, I am Azarias, the son of Ananias the great, and of thy brethren.

[13] Then Tobit said, Thou art welcome, brother; be not now angry with me, because I have enquired to know thy tribe and thy family; for thou art my brother, of an honest and good stock: for I know Ananias and Jonathas, sons of that great Samaias, as we went together to Jerusalem to worship, and offered the firstborn, and the tenths of the fruits; and they were not seduced with the error of our brethren: my brother, thou art of a good stock.

[14] But tell me, what wages shall I give thee? wilt thou a drachm a day, and things necessary, as to mine own son?

[15] Yea, moreover, if ye return safe, I will add something to thy wages.

[16] So they were well pleased. Then said he to Tobias, Prepare thyself for the journey, and God send you a good journey. And when his son had prepared all things far the journey, his father said, Go thou with this man, and God, which dwelleth in heaven, prosper your journey, and the angel of God keep you company. So they went forth both, and the young man's dog with them.

[17] But Anna his mother wept, and said to Tobit, Why hast thou sent away our son? is he not the staff of our hand, in going in and out before us?

[18] Be not greedy to add money to money: but let it be as refuse in respect of our child.

[19] For that which the Lord hath given us to live with doth suffice us.

[20] Then said Tobit to her, Take no care, my sister; he shall return in safety, and thine eyes shall see him.

[21] For the good angel will keep him company, and his journey shall be prosperous, and he shall return safe.

[22] Then she made an end of weeping.

Tob.6

[1] And as they went on their journey, they came in the evening to the river Tigris, and they lodged there.

[2] And when the young man went down to wash himself, a fish leaped out of the river, and would have devoured him.

[3] Then the angel said unto him, Take the fish. And the young man laid hold of the fish, and drew it to land.

[4] To whom the angel said, Open the fish, and take the heart and the liver and the gall, and put them up safely.

[5] So the young man did as the angel commanded him; and when they had roasted the fish, they did eat it: then they both went on their way, till they drew near to Ecbatane.

[6] Then the young man said to the angel, Brother Azarias, to what use is the heart and the liver and the gal of the fish?

[7] And he said unto him, Touching the heart and the liver, if a devil or an evil spirit trouble any, we must make a smoke thereof before the man or the woman, and the party shall be no more vexed.

[8] As for the gall, it is good to anoint a man that hath whiteness in his eyes, and he shall be healed.

[9] And when they were come near to Rages,

[10] The angel said to the young man, Brother, to day we shall lodge with Raguel, who is thy cousin; he also hath one only daughter, named Sara; I will speak for her, that she may be given thee for a wife.

[11] For to thee doth the right of her appertain, seeing thou only art of her kindred.

[12] And the maid is fair and wise: now therefore hear me, and I will speak to her father; and when we return from Rages we will celebrate the marriage: for I know that Raguel cannot marry her to another according to the law of Moses, but he shall be guilty of death, because the right of inheritance doth rather appertain to thee than to any other.

[13] Then the young man answered the angel, I have heard, brother Azarias that this maid hath been given to seven men, who all died in the marriage chamber.

[14] And now I am the only son of my father, and I am afraid, lest if I go in unto her, I die, as the other before: for a wicked spirit loveth her, which hurteth no body, but those which come unto her; wherefore I also fear lest I die, and bring my father's and my mother's life because of me to the grave with sorrow: for they have no other son to bury them.

[15] Then the angel said unto him, Dost thou not remember the precepts which thy father gave thee, that

thou shouldest marry a wife of thine own kindred? wherefore hear me, O my brother; for she shall be given thee to wife; and make thou no reckoning of the evil spirit; for this same night shall she be given thee in marriage.

[16] And when thou shalt come into the marriage chamber, thou shalt take the ashes of perfume, and shalt lay upon them some of the heart and liver of the fish, and shalt make a smoke with it:

[17] And the devil shall smell it, and flee away, and never come again any more: but when thou shalt come to her, rise up both of you, and pray to God which is merciful, who will have pity on you, and save you: fear not, for she is appointed unto thee from the beginning; and thou shalt preserve her, and she shall go with thee. Moreover I suppose that she shall bear thee children. Now when Tobias had heard these things, he loved her, and his heart was effectually joined to her.

Tob.7

[1] And when they were come to Ecbatane, they came to the house of Raguel, and Sara met them: and after they had saluted one another, she brought them into the house.

[2] Then said Raguel to Edna his wife, How like is this young man to Tobit my cousin!

[3] And Raguel asked them, From whence are ye, brethren? To whom they said, We are of the sons of Nephthalim, which are captives in Nineve.

[4] Then he said to them, Do ye know Tobit our kinsman? And they said, We know him. Then said he, Is he in good health?

[5] And they said, He is both alive, and in good health: and Tobias said, He is my father.

[6] Then Raguel leaped up, and kissed him, and wept,

[7] And blessed him, and said unto him, Thou art the son of an honest and good man. But when he had heard that Tobit was blind, he was sorrowful, and wept.

[8] And likewise Edna his wife and Sara his daughter wept. Moreover they entertained them cheerfully; and after that they had killed a ram of the flock, they set store of meat on the table. Then said Tobias to Raphael, Brother Azarias, speak of those things of which thou didst talk in the way, and let this business be dispatched.

[9] So he communicated the matter with Raguel: and Raguel said to Tobias, Eat and drink, and make merry:

[10] For it is meet that thou shouldest marry my daughter: nevertheless I will declare unto thee the truth.

[11] I have given my daughter in marriage te seven men, who died that night they came in unto her: nevertheless for the present be merry. But Tobias said, I will eat

nothing here, till we agree and swear one to another.

[12] Raguel said, Then take her from henceforth according to the manner, for thou art her cousin, and she is thine, and the merciful God give you good success in all things.

[13] Then he called his daughter Sara, and she came to her father, and he took her by the hand, and gave her to be wife to Tobias, saying, Behold, take her after the law of Moses, and lead her away to thy father. And he blessed them;

[14] And called Edna his wife, and took paper, and did write an instrument of covenants, and sealed it.

[15] Then they began to eat.

[16] After Raguel called his wife Edna, and said unto her, Sister, prepare another chamber, and bring her in thither.

[17] Which when she had done as he had bidden her, she brought her thither: and she wept, and she received the tears of her daughter, and said unto her,

[18] Be of good comfort, my daughter; the Lord of heaven and earth give thee joy for this thy sorrow: be of good comfort, my daughter.

Tob.8

[1] And when they had supped, they brought Tobias in unto her.

[2] And as he went, he remembered the words of Raphael, and took the ashes of the perfumes, and put the heart and the liver of the fish thereupon, and made a smoke therewith.

[3] The which smell when the evil spirit had smelled, he fled into the utmost parts of Egypt, and the angel bound him.

[4] And after that they were both shut in together, Tobias rose out of the bed, and said, Sister, arise, and let us pray that God would have pity on us.

[5] Then began Tobias to say, Blessed art thou, O God of our fathers, and blessed is thy holy and glorious name for ever; let the heavens bless thee, and all thy creatures.

[6] Thou madest Adam, and gavest him Eve his wife for an helper and stay: of them came mankind: thou hast said, It is not good that man should be alone; let us make unto him an aid like unto himself.

[7] And now, O Lord, I take not this my sister for lush but uprightly: therefore mercifully ordain that we may become aged together.

[8] And she said with him, Amen.

[9] So they slept both that night. And Raguel arose, and went and made a grave,

[10] Saying, I fear lest he also be dead.

[11] But when Raguel was come into his house,

[12] He said unto his wife Edna. Send one of the maids, and let her see whether he be alive: if he be not, that we may bury him, and no man know it.

[13] So the maid opened the door, and went in, and found them both asleep,

[14] And came forth, and told them that he was alive.

[15] Then Raguel praised God, and said, O God, thou art worthy to be praised with all pure and holy praise; therefore let thy saints praise thee with all thy creatures; and let all thine angels and thine elect praise thee for ever.

[16] Thou art to be praised, for thou hast made me joyful; and that is not come to me which I suspected; but thou hast dealt with us according to thy great mercy.

[17] Thou art to be praised because thou hast had mercy of two that were the only begotten children of their fathers: grant them mercy, O Lord, and finish their life in health with joy and mercy.

[18] Then Raguel bade his servants to fill the grave.

[19] And he kept the wedding feast fourteen days.

[20] For before the days of the marriage were finished, Raguel had said unto him by an oath, that he should not depart till the fourteen days of the marriage were expired;

[21] And then he should take the half of his goods, and go in safety to his father; and should have the rest when I and my wife be dead.

Tob.9

[1] Then Tobias called Raphael, and said unto him,

[2] Brother Azarias, take with thee a servant, and two camels, and go to Rages of Media to Gabael, and bring me the money, and bring him to the wedding.

[3] For Raguel hath sworn that I shall not depart.

[4] But my father counteth the days; and if I tarry long, he will be very sorry.

[5] So Raphael went out, and lodged with Gabael, and gave him the handwriting: who brought forth bags which were sealed up, and gave them to him.

[6] And early in the morning they went forth both together, and came to the wedding: and Tobias blessed his wife.

Tob.10

[1] Now Tobit his father counted every day: and when the days of the journey were expired, and they came not,

[2] Then Tobit said, Are they detained? or is Gabael dead, and there is no man to give him the money?

[3] Therefore he was very sorry.

[4] Then his wife said unto him, My son is dead, seeing he stayeth long; and she began to wail him, and said,

[5] Now I care for nothing, my son, since I have let thee go, the light of mine eyes.

[6] To whom Tobit said, Hold thy peace, take no care, for he is safe.

[7] But she said, Hold thy peace, and deceive me not; my son is dead. And she went out every day into the way which they went, and did eat no meat on the daytime, and ceased not whole nights to bewail her son Tobias, until the fourteen days of the wedding were expired, which Raguel had sworn that he should spend there. Then Tobias said to Raguel, Let me go, for my father and my mother look no more to see me.

[8] But his father in law said unto him, Tarry with me, and I will send to thy father, and they shall declare unto him how things go with thee.

[9] But Tobias said, No; but let me go to my father.

[10] Then Raguel arose, and gave him Sara his wife, and half his goods, servants, and cattle, and money:

[11] And he blessed them, and sent them away, saying, The God of heaven give you a prosperous journey, my children.

[12] And he said to his daughter, Honour thy father and thy mother in law, which are now thy parents, that I may hear good report of thee. And he kissed her. Edna also said to Tobias, The Lord of heaven restore thee, my dear brother, and grant that I may see thy children of my daughter Sara before I die, that I may rejoice before the Lord: behold, I commit my daughter unto thee of special trust; where are do not entreat her evil.

Tob.11

[1] After these things Tobias went his way, praising God that he had given him a prosperous journey, and blessed Raguel and Edna his wife, and went on his way till they drew near unto Nineve.

[2] Then Raphael said to Tobias, Thou knowest, brother, how thou didst leave thy father:

[3] Let us haste before thy wife, and prepare the house.

[4] And take in thine hand the gall of the fish. So they went their way, and the dog went after them.

[5] Now Anna sat looking about toward the way for her son.

[6] And when she espied him coming, she said to his father, Behold, thy son cometh, and the man that went with him.

[7] Then said Raphael, I know, Tobias, that thy father will open his eyes.

[8] Therefore anoint thou his eyes with the gall, and being pricked therewith, he shall rub, and the whiteness shall fall

away, and he shall see thee.

[9] Then Anna ran forth, and fell upon the neck of her son, and said unto him, Seeing I have seen thee, my son, from henceforth I am content to die. And they wept both.

[10] Tobit also went forth toward the door, and stumbled: but his son ran unto him,

[11] And took hold of his father: and he strake of the gall on his fathers' eyes, saying, Be of good hope, my father.

[12] And when his eyes began to smart, he rubbed them;

[13] And the whiteness pilled away from the corners of his eyes: and when he saw his son, he fell upon his neck.

[14] And he wept, and said, Blessed art thou, O God, and blessed is thy name for ever; and blessed are all thine holy angels:

[15] For thou hast scourged, and hast taken pity on me: for, behold, I see my son Tobias. And his son went in rejoicing, and told his father the great things that had happened to him in Media.

[16] Then Tobit went out to meet his daughter in law at the gate of Nineve, rejoicing and praising God: and they which saw him go marvelled, because he had received his sight.

[17] But Tobias gave thanks before them, because God had mercy on him. And when he came near to Sara his daughter in law, he blessed her, saying, Thou art welcome, daughter: God be blessed, which hath brought thee unto us, and blessed be thy father and thy mother. And there was joy among all his brethren which were at Nineve.

[18] And Achiacharus, and Nasbas his brother's son, came:

[19] And Tobias' wedding was kept seven days with great joy.

Tob.12

[1] Then Tobit called his son Tobias, and said unto him, My son, see that the man have his wages, which went with thee, and thou must give him more.

[2] And Tobias said unto him, O father, it is no harm to me to give him half of those things which I have brought:

[3] For he hath brought me again to thee in safety, and made whole my wife, and brought me the money, and likewise healed thee.

[4] Then the old man said, It is due unto him.

[5] So he called the angel, and he said unto him, Take half of all that ye have brought and go away in safety.

[6] Then he took them both apart, and said unto them, Bless God, praise him, and magnify him, and praise him for the things which he hath done unto you in the sight of all that live. It is good to praise God, and exalt his name, and honourably to shew forth the works of God; therefore

be not slack to praise him.

[7] It is good to keep close the secret of a king, but it is honourable to reveal the works of God. Do that which is good, and no evil shall touch you.

[8] Prayer is good with fasting and alms and righteousness. A little with righteousness is better than much with unrighteousness. It is better to give alms than to lay up gold:

[9] For alms doth deliver from death, and shall purge away all sin. Those that exercise alms and righteousness shall be filled with life:

[10] But they that sin are enemies to their own life.

[11] Surely I will keep close nothing from you. For I said, It was good to keep close the secret of a king, but that it was honourable to reveal the works of God.

[12] Now therefore, when thou didst pray, and Sara thy daughter in law, I did bring the remembrance of your prayers before the Holy One: and when thou didst bury the dead, I was with thee likewise.

[13] And when thou didst not delay to rise up, and leave thy dinner, to go and cover the dead, thy good deed was not hid from me: but I was with thee.

[14] And now God hath sent me to heal thee and Sara thy daughter in law.

[15] I am Raphael, one of the seven holy angels, which present the prayers of the saints, and which go in and out before the glory of the Holy One.

[16] Then they were both troubled, and fell upon their faces: for they feared.

[17] But he said unto them, Fear not, for it shall go well with you; praise God therefore.

[18] For not of any favour of mine, but by the will of our God I came; wherefore praise him for ever.

[19] All these days I did appear unto you; but I did neither eat nor drink, but ye did see a vision.

[20] Now therefore give God thanks: for I go up to him that sent me; but write all things which are done in a book.

[21] And when they arose, they saw him no more.

[22] Then they confessed the great and wonderful works of God, and how the angel of the Lord had appeared unto them.

Tob.13

[1] Then Tobit wrote a prayer of rejoicing, and said, Blessed be God that liveth for ever, and blessed be his kingdom.

[2] For he doth scourge, and hath mercy: he leadeth down to hell, and bringeth up again: neither is there any that can avoid his hand.

[3] Confess him before the Gentiles, ye children of Israel: for he hath scattered us among them.

[4] There declare his greatness, and extol him before all the living: for he is our Lord, and he is the God our Father for ever.

[5] And he will scourge us for our iniquities, and will have mercy again, and will gather us out of all nations, among whom he hath scattered us.

[6] If ye turn to him with your whole heart, and with your whole mind, and deal uprightly before him, then will he turn unto you, and will not hide his face from you. Therefore see what he will do with you, and confess him with your whole mouth, and praise the Lord of might, and extol the everlasting King. In the land of my captivity do I praise him, and declare his might and majesty to a sinful nation. O ye sinners, turn and do justice before him: who can tell if he will accept you, and have mercy on you?

[7] I will extol my God, and my soul shall praise the King of heaven, and shall rejoice in his greatness.

[8] Let all men speak, and let all praise him for his righteousness.

[9] O Jerusalem, the holy city, he will scourge thee for thy children's works, and will have mercy again on the sons of the righteous.

[10] Give praise to the Lord, for he is good: and praise the everlasting King, that his tabernacle may be builded in thee again with joy, and let him make joyful there in thee those that are captives, and love in thee for ever those that are miserable.

[11] Many nations shall come from far to the name of the Lord God with gifts in their hands, even gifts to the King of heaven; all generations shall praise thee with great joy.

[12] Cursed are all they which hate thee, and blessed shall all be which love thee for ever.

[13] Rejoice and be glad for the children of the just: for they shall be gathered together, and shall bless the Lord of the just.

[14] O blessed are they which love thee, for they shall rejoice in thy peace: blessed are they which have been sorrowful for all thy scourges; for they shall rejoice for thee, when they have seen all thy glory, and shall be glad for ever.

[15] Let my soul bless God the great King.

[16] For Jerusalem shall be built up with sapphires and emeralds, and precious stone: thy walls and towers and battlements with pure gold.

[17] And the streets of Jerusalem shall be paved with beryl and carbuncle and stones of Ophir.

[18] And all her streets shall say, Alleluia; and they shall praise him, saying, Blessed be God, which hath extolled it for ever.

Tob.14

[1] So Tobit made an end of praising God.

[2] And he was eight and fifty years old when he lost his sight, which was restored to him after eight years: and he gave alms, and he increased in the fear of the Lord God, and praised him.

[3] And when he was very aged he called his son, and the sons of his son, and said to him, My son, take thy children; for, behold, I am aged, and am ready to depart out of this life.

[4] Go into Media my son, for I surely believe those things which Jonas the prophet spake of Nineve, that it shall be overthrown; and that for a time peace shall rather be in Media; and that our brethren shall lie scattered in the earth from that good land: and Jerusalem shall be desolate, and the house of God in it shall be burned, and shall be desolate for a time;

[5] And that again God will have mercy on them, and bring them again into the land, where they shall build a temple, but not like to the first, until the time of that age be fulfilled; and afterward they shall return from all places of their captivity, and build up Jerusalem gloriously, and the house of God shall be built in it for ever with a glorious building, as the prophets have spoken thereof.

[6] And all nations shall turn, and fear the Lord God truly, and shall bury their idols.

[7] So shall all nations praise the Lord, and his people shall confess God, and the Lord shall exalt his people; and all those which love the Lord God in truth and justice shall rejoice, shewing mercy to our brethren.

[8] And now, my son, depart out of Nineve, because that those things which the prophet Jonas spake shall surely come to pass.

[9] But keep thou the law and the commandments, and shew thyself merciful and just, that it may go well with thee.

[10] And bury me decently, and thy mother with me; but tarry no longer at Nineve. Remember, my son, how Aman handled Achiacharus that brought him up, how out of light he brought him into darkness, and how he rewarded him again: yet Achiacharus was saved, but the other had his reward: for he went down into darkness. Manasses gave alms, and escaped the snares of death which they had set for him: but Aman fell into the snare, and perished.

[11] Wherefore now, my son, consider what alms doeth, and how righteousness doth deliver. When he had said

these things, he gave up the ghost in the bed, being an hundred and eight and fifty years old; and he buried him honourably.

[12] And when Anna his mother was dead, he buried her with his father. But Tobias departed with his wife and children to Ecbatane to Raguel his father in law,

[13] Where he became old with honour, and he buried his father and mother in law honourably, and he inherited their substance, and his father Tobit's.

[14] And he died at Ecbatane in Media, being an hundred and seven and twenty years old.

[15] But before he died he heard of the destruction of Nineve, which was taken by Nabuchodonosor and Assuerus: and before his death he rejoiced over Nineve.

The Book Of Judith

Jdt.1

[1] In the twelfth year of the reign of Nabuchodonosor, who reigned in Nineve, the great city; in the days of Arphaxad, which reigned over the Medes in Ecbatane,

[2] And built in Ecbatane walls round about of stones hewn three cubits broad and six cubits long, and made the height of the wall seventy cubits, and the breadth thereof fifty cubits:

[3] And set the towers thereof upon the gates of it an hundred cubits high, and the breadth thereof in the foundation threescore cubits:

[4] And he made the gates thereof, even gates that were raised to the height of seventy cubits, and the breadth of them was forty cubits, for the going forth of his mighty armies, and for the setting in array of his footmen:

[5] Even in those days king Nabuchodonosor made war with king Arphaxad in the great plain, which is the plain in the borders of Ragau.

[6] And there came unto him all they that dwelt in the hill country, and all that dwelt by Euphrates, and Tigris and Hydaspes, and the plain of Arioch the king of the Elymeans, and very many nations of the sons of Chelod, assembled themselves to the battle.

[7] Then Nabuchodonosor king of the Assyrians sent unto all that dwelt in Persia, and to all that dwelt westward, and to those that dwelt in Cilicia, and Damascus, and Libanus, and Antilibanus, and to all that dwelt upon the sea coast,

[8] And to those among the nations that were of Carmel, and Galaad, and the higher Galilee, and the great plain of Esdrelom,

[9] And to all that were in Samaria and the cities thereof, and beyond Jordan unto Jerusalem, and Betane, and Chelus, and Kades, and the river of Egypt, and Taphnes, and Ramesse, and all the land of Gesem,

[10] Until ye come beyond Tanis and Memphis, and to all the inhabitants of Egypt, until ye come to the borders of Ethiopia.

[11] But all the inhabitants of the land made light of the commandment of Nabuchodonosor king of the Assyrians, neither went they with him to the battle; for they were not afraid of him: yea, he was before them as one man, and they sent away his ambassadors from them without effect, and with disgrace.

[12] Therefore Nabuchodonosor was very angry with all this country, and sware by his throne and kingdom, that he would surely be avenged upon all those coasts of Cilicia, and Damascus, and Syria, and that he would slay with the sword all the inhabitants of the land of Moab, and the children of Ammon, and all Judea, and all that were in Egypt, till ye come to the borders of the two seas.

[13] Then he marched in battle array with his power against king Arphaxad in the seventeenth year, and he prevailed in his battle: for he overthrew all the power of Arphaxad, and all his horsemen, and all his chariots,

[14] And became lord of his cities, and came unto Ecbatane, and took the towers, and spoiled the streets thereof, and turned the beauty thereof into shame.

[15] He took also Arphaxad in the mountains of Ragau, and smote him through with his darts, and destroyed him utterly that day.

[16] So he returned afterward to Nineve, both he and all his company of sundry nations being a very great multitude of men of war, and there he took his ease, and banqueted, both he and his army, an hundred and twenty days.

Jdt.2

[1] And in the eighteenth year, the two and twentieth day of the first month, there was talk in the house of Nabuchodonosor king of the Assyrians that he should, as he said, avenge himself on all the earth.

[2] So he called unto him all his officers, and all his nobles, and communicated with them his secret counsel, and concluded the afflicting of the whole earth out of his own mouth.

[3] Then they decreed to destroy all flesh, that did not obey the commandment of his mouth.

[4] And when he had ended his counsel, Nabuchodonosor king of the Assyrians called Holofernes the chief captain of his army, which was next unto him, and said unto him.

[5] Thus saith the great king, the lord of the whole earth,

Behold, thou shalt go forth from my presence, and take with thee men that trust in their own strength, of footmen an hundred and twenty thousand; and the number of horses with their riders twelve thousand.

[6] And thou shalt go against all the west country, because they disobeyed my commandment.

[7] And thou shalt declare unto that they prepare for me earth and water: for I will go forth in my wrath against them and will cover the whole face of the earth with the feet of mine army, and I will give them for a spoil unto them:

[8] So that their slain shall fill their valleys and brooks and the river shall be filled with their dead, till it overflow:

[9] And I will lead them captives to the utmost parts of all the earth.

[10] Thou therefore shalt go forth. and take beforehand for me all their coasts: and if they will yield themselves unto thee, thou shalt reserve them for me till the day of their punishment.

[11] But concerning them that rebel, let not thine eye spare them; but put them to the slaughter, and spoil them wheresoever thou goest.

[12] For as I live, and by the power of my kingdom, whatsoever I have spoken, that will I do by mine hand.

[13] And take thou heed that thou transgress none of the commandments of thy lord, but accomplish them fully, as I have commanded thee, and defer not to do them.

[14] Then Holofernes went forth from the presence of his lord, and called ail the governors and captains, and the officers of the army of Assur;

[15] And he mustered the chosen men for the battle, as his lord had commanded him, unto an hundred and twenty thousand, and twelve thousand archers on horseback;

[16] And he ranged them, as a great army is ordered for the war.

[17] And he took camels and asses for their carriages, a very great number; and sheep and oxen and goats without number for their provision:

[18] And plenty of victual for every man of the army, and very much gold and silver out of the king's house.

[19] Then he went forth and all his power to go before king Nabuchodonosor in the voyage, and to cover all the face of the earth westward with their chariots, and horsemen, and their chosen footmen.

[20] A great number also sundry countries came with them like locusts, and like the sand of the earth: for the multitude was without number.

[21] And they went forth of Nineve three days' journey toward the plain of Bectileth, and pitched from Bectileth near the mountain which is at the left hand of the upper Cilicia.

[22] Then he took all his army, his footmen, and horsemen and chariots, and went from thence into the hill country;

[23] And destroyed Phud and Lud, and spoiled all the children of Rasses, and the children of Israel, which were toward the wilderness at the south of the land of the Chellians.

[24] Then he went over Euphrates, and went through Mesopotamia, and destroyed all the high cities that were upon the river Arbonai, till ye come to the sea.

[25] And he took the borders of Cilicia, and killed all that resisted him, and came to the borders of Japheth, which were toward the south, over against Arabia.

[26] He compassed also all the children of Madian, and burned up their tabernacles, and spoiled their sheepcotes.

[27] Then he went down into the plain of Damascus in the time of wheat harvest, and burnt up all their fields, and destroyed their flocks and herds, also he spoiled their cities, and utterly wasted their countries, and smote all their young men with the edge of the sword.

[28] Therefore the fear and dread of him fell upon all the inhabitants of the sea coasts, which were in Sidon and Tyrus, and them that dwelt in Sur and Ocina, and all that dwelt in Jemnaan; and they that dwelt in Azotus and Ascalon feared him greatly.

Jdt.3

[1] So they sent ambassadors unto him to treat of peace, saying,

[2] Behold, we the servants of Nabuchodonosor the great king lie before thee; use us as shall be good in thy sight.

[3] Behold, our houses, and all our places, and all our fields of wheat, and flocks, and herds, and all the lodges of our tents lie before thy face; use them as it pleaseth thee.

[4] Behold, even our cities and the inhabitants thereof are thy servants; come and deal with them as seemeth good unto thee.

[5] So the men came to Holofernes, and declared unto him after this manner.

[6] Then came he down toward the sea coast, both he and his army, and set garrisons in the high cities, and took out of them chosen men for aid.

[7] So they and all the country round about received them with garlands, with dances, and with timbrels.

[8] Yet he did cast down their frontiers, and cut down their groves: for he had decreed to destroy all the gods of the land, that all nations should worship Nabuchodonosor only, and that all tongues and tribes should call upon him as god.

[9] Also he came over against Esdraelon near unto Judea, over against the great strait of Judea.

[10] And he pitched between Geba and Scythopolis, and there he tarried a whole month, that he might gather together all the carriages of his army.

Jdt.4

[1] Now the children of Israel, that dwelt in Judea, heard all that Holofernes the chief captain of Nabuchodonosor king of the Assyrians had done to the nations, and after what manner he had spoiled all their temples, and brought them to nought.

[2] Therefore they were exceedingly afraid of him, and were troubled for Jerusalem, and for the temple of the Lord their God:

[3] For they were newly returned from the captivity, and all the people of Judea were lately gathered together: and the vessels, and the altar, and the house, were sanctified after the profanation.

[4] Therefore they sent into all the coasts of Samaria, and the villages and to Bethoron, and Belmen, and Jericho, and to Choba, and Esora, and to the valley of Salem:

[5] And possessed themselves beforehand of all the tops of the high mountains, and fortified the villages that were in them, and laid up victuals for the provision of war: for their fields were of late reaped.

[6] Also Joacim the high priest, which was in those days in Jerusalem, wrote to them that dwelt in Bethulia, and Betomestham, which is over against Esdraelon toward the open country, near to Dothaim,

[7] Charging them to keep the passages of the hill country: for by them there was an entrance into Judea, and it was easy to stop them that would come up, because the passage was straight, for two men at the most.

[8] And the children of Israel did as Joacim the high priest had commanded them, with the ancients of all the people of Israel, which dwelt at Jerusalem.

[9] Then every man of Israel cried to God with great fervency, and with great vehemency did they humble their souls:

[10] Both they, and their wives and their children, and their cattle, and every stranger and hireling, and their servants bought with money, put sackcloth upon their loins.

[11] Thus every man and women, and the little children, and the inhabitants of Jerusalem, fell before the temple, and cast ashes upon their heads, and spread out their sackcloth before the face of the Lord: also they put sackcloth about the altar,

[12] And cried to the God of Israel all with one consent earnestly, that he would not give their children for a prey, and their wives for a spoil, and the cities of their inheritance to destruction, and the sanctuary to profanation and reproach, and for the nations to rejoice at.

[13] So God heard their prayers, and looked upon their afflictions: for the people fasted many days in all Judea and Jerusalem before the sanctuary of the Lord Almighty.

[14] And Joacim the high priest, and all the priests that stood before the Lord, and they which ministered unto the Lord, had their loins girt with sackcloth, and offered the daily burnt offerings, with the vows and free gifts of the people,

[15] And had ashes on their mitres, and cried unto the Lord with all their power, that he would look upon all the house of Israel graciously.

Jdt.5

[1] Then was it declared to Holofernes, the chief captain of the army of Assur, that the children of Israel had prepared for war, and had shut up the passages of the hill country, and had fortified all the tops of the high hills and had laid impediments in the champaign countries:

[2] Wherewith he was very angry, and called all the princes of Moab, and the captains of Ammon, and all the governors of the sea coast,

[3] And he said unto them, Tell me now, ye sons of Chanaan, who this people is, that dwelleth in the hill country, and what are the cities that they inhabit, and what is the multitude of their army, and wherein is their power and strength, and what king is set over them, or captain of their army;

[4] And why have they determined not to come and meet me, more than all the inhabitants of the west.

[5] Then said Achior, the captain of all the sons of Ammon, Let my lord now hear a word from the mouth of thy servant, and I will declare unto thee the truth concerning this people, which dwelleth near thee, and inhabiteth the hill countries: and there shall no lie come out of the mouth of thy servant.

[6] This people are descended of the Chaldeans:

[7] And they sojourned heretofore in Mesopotamia, because they would not follow the gods of their fathers, which were in the land of Chaldea.

[8] For they left the way of their ancestors, and worshipped the God of heaven, the God whom they knew: so they cast them out from the face of their gods, and they fled into Mesopotamia, and sojourned there many days.

[9] Then their God commanded them to depart from the place where they sojourned, and to go into the land of Chanaan: where they dwelt, and were increased with gold and silver, and with very much cattle.

[10] But when a famine covered all the land of Chanaan, they went down into Egypt, and sojourned there, while they were nourished, and became there a great multitude, so that one could not number their nation.

[11] Therefore the king of Egypt rose up against them, and dealt subtilly with them, and brought them low with labouring in brick, and made them slaves.

[12] Then they cried unto their God, and he smote all the land of Egypt with incurable plagues: so the Egyptians cast them out of their sight.

[13] And God dried the Red sea before them,

[14] And brought them to mount Sina, and Cades-Barne, and cast forth all that dwelt in the wilderness.

[15] So they dwelt in the land of the Amorites, and they destroyed by their strength all them of Esebon, and passing over Jordan they possessed all the hill country.

[16] And they cast forth before them the Chanaanite, the Pherezite, the Jebusite, and the Sychemite, and all the Gergesites, and they dwelt in that country many days.

[17] And whilst they sinned not before their God, they prospered, because the God that hateth iniquity was with them.

[18] But when they departed from the way which he appointed them, they were destroyed in many battles very sore, and were led captives into a land that was not their's, and the temple of their God was cast to the ground, and their cities were taken by the enemies.

[19] But now are they returned to their God, and are come up from the places where they were scattered, and have possessed Jerusalem, where their sanctuary is, and are seated in the hill country; for it was desolate.

[20] Now therefore, my lord and governor, if there be any error against this people, and they sin against their God, let us consider that this shall be their ruin, and let us go up, and we shall overcome them.

[21] But if there be no iniquity in their nation, let my lord now pass by, lest their Lord defend them, and their God be for them, and we become a reproach before all the world.

[22] And when Achior had finished these sayings, all the people standing round about the tent murmured, and the chief men of Holofernes, and all that dwelt by the sea side, and in Moab, spake that he should kill him.

[23] For, say they, we will not be afraid of the face of the children of Israel: for, lo, it is a people that have no strength nor power for a strong battle

[24] Now therefore, lord Holofernes, we will go up, and they shall be a prey to be devoured of all thine army.

Jdt.6

[1] And when the tumult of men that were about the council was ceased, Holofernes the chief captain of the army of Assur said unto Achior and all the Moabites before all the company of other nations,

[2] And who art thou, Achior, and the hirelings of Ephraim, that thou hast prophesied against us as to day, and hast said, that we should not make war with the people of Israel, because their God will defend them? and who is God but Nabuchodonosor?

[3] He will send his power, and will destroy them from the face of the earth, and their God shall not deliver them: but we his servants will destroy them as one man; for they are not able to sustain the power of our horses.

[4] For with them we will tread them under foot, and their mountains shall be drunken with their blood, and their fields shall be filled with their dead bodies, and their footsteps shall not be able to stand before us, for they shall utterly perish, saith king Nabuchodonosor, lord of all the earth: for he said, None of my words shall be in vain.

[5] And thou, Achior, an hireling of Ammon, which hast spoken these words in the day of thine iniquity, shalt see my face no more from this day, until I take vengeance of this nation that came out of Egypt.

[6] And then shall the sword of mine army, and the multitude of them that serve me, pass through thy sides, and thou shalt fall among their slain, when I return.

[7] Now therefore my servants shall bring thee back into the hill country, and shall set thee in one of the cities of the passages:

[8] And thou shalt not perish, till thou be destroyed with them.

[9] And if thou persuade thyself in thy mind that they shall be taken, let not thy countenance fall: I have spoken it, and none of my words shall be in vain.

[10] Then Holofernes commanded his servants, that waited in his tent, to take Achior, and bring him to Bethulia, and deliver him into the hands of the children of Israel.

[11] So his servants took him, and brought him out of the camp into the plain, and they went from the midst of the plain into the hill country, and came unto the fountains that were under Bethulia.

[12] And when the men of the city saw them, they took up their weapons, and went out of the city to the top of the hill: and every man that used a sling kept them from

coming up by casting of stones against them.

[13] Nevertheless having gotten privily under the hill, they bound Achior, and cast him down, and left him at the foot of the hill, and returned to their lord.

[14] But the Israelites descended from their city, and came unto him, and loosed him, and brought him to Bethulia, and presented him to the governors of the city:

[15] Which were in those days Ozias the son of Micha, of the tribe of Simeon, and Chabris the son of Gothoniel, and Charmis the son of Melchiel.

[16] And they called together all the ancients of the city, and all their youth ran together, and their women, to the assembly, and they set Achior in the midst of all their people. Then Ozias asked him of that which was done.

[17] And he answered and declared unto them the words of the council of Holofernes, and all the words that he had spoken in the midst of the princes of Assur, and whatsoever Holofernes had spoken proudly against the house of Israel.

[18] Then the people fell down and worshipped God, and cried unto God. saying,

[19] O Lord God of heaven, behold their pride, and pity the low estate of our nation, and look upon the face of those that are sanctified unto thee this day.

[20] Then they comforted Achior, and praised him greatly.

[21] And Ozias took him out of the assembly unto his house, and made a feast to the elders; and they called on the God of Israel all that night for help.

Jdt.7

[1] The next day Holofernes commanded all his army, and all his people which were come to take his part, that they should remove their camp against Bethulia, to take aforehand the ascents of the hill country, and to make war against the children of Israel.

[2] Then their strong men removed their camps in that day, and the army of the men of war was an hundred and seventy thousand footmen, and twelve thousand horsemen, beside the baggage, and other men that were afoot among them, a very great multitude.

[3] And they camped in the valley near unto Bethulia, by the fountain, and they spread themselves in breadth over Dothaim even to Belmaim, and in length from Bethulia unto Cynamon, which is over against Esdraelon.

[4] Now the children of Israel, when they saw the multitude of them, were greatly troubled, and said every one to his neighbour, Now will these men lick up the face of the earth; for neither the high mountains, nor the valleys, nor the hills, are able to bear their weight.

[5] Then every man took up his weapons of war, and when they had kindled fires upon their towers, they remained and watched all that night.

[6] But in the second day Holofernes brought forth all his horsemen in the sight of the children of Israel which were in Bethulia,

[7] And viewed the passages up to the city, and came to the fountains of their waters, and took them, and set garrisons of men of war over them, and he himself removed toward his people.

[8] Then came unto him all the chief of the children of Esau, and all the governors of the people of Moab, and the captains of the sea coast, and said,

[9] Let our lord now hear a word, that there be not an overthrow in thine army.

[10] For this people of the children of Israel do not trust in their spears, but in the height of the mountains wherein they dwell, because it is not easy to come up to the tops of their mountains.

[11] Now therefore, my lord, fight not against them in battle array, and there shall not so much as one man of thy people perish.

[12] Remain in thy camp, and keep all the men of thine army, and let thy servants get into their hands the fountain of water, which issueth forth of the foot of the mountain:

[13] For all the inhabitants of Bethulia have their water thence; so shall thirst kill them, and they shall give up their city, and we and our people shall go up to the tops of the mountains that are near, and will camp upon them, to watch that none go out of the city.

[14] So they and their wives and their children shall be consumed with fire, and before the sword come against them, they shall be overthrown in the streets where they dwell.

[15] Thus shalt thou render them an evil reward; because they rebelled, and met not thy person peaceably.

[16] And these words pleased Holofernes and all his servants, and he appointed to do as they had spoken.

[17] So the camp of the children of Ammon departed, and with them five thousand of the Assyrians, and they pitched in the valley, and took the waters, and the fountains of the waters of the children of Israel.

[18] Then the children of Esau went up with the children of Ammon, and camped in the hill country over against Dothaim: and they sent some of them toward the south, and toward the east over against Ekrebel, which is near unto Chusi, that is upon the brook Mochmur; and the rest of the army of the Assyrians camped in the plain, and covered the face of the whole land; and their tents and

carriages were pitched to a very great multitude.

[19] Then the children of Israel cried unto the Lord their God, because their heart failed, for all their enemies had compassed them round about, and there was no way to escape out from among them.

[20] Thus all the company of Assur remained about them, both their footmen, chariots, and horsemen, four and thirty days, so that all their vessels of water failed all the inhibitants of Bethulia.

[21] And the cisterns were emptied, and they had not water to drink their fill for one day; for they gave them drink by measure.

[22] Therefore their young children were out of heart, and their women and young men fainted for thirst, and fell down in the streets of the city, and by the passages of the gates, and there was no longer any strength in them.

[23] Then all the people assembled to Ozias, and to the chief of the city, both young men, and women, and children, and cried with a loud voice, and said before all the elders,

[24] God be judge between us and you: for ye have done us great injury, in that ye have not required peace of the children of Assur.

[25] For now we have no helper: but God hath sold us into their hands, that we should be thrown down before them with thirst and great destruction.

[26] Now therefore call them unto you, and deliver the whole city for a spoil to the people of Holofernes, and to all his army.

[27] For it is better for us to be made a spoil unto them, than to die for thirst: for we will be his servants, that our souls may live, and not see the death of our infants before our eyes, nor our wives nor our children to die.

[28] We take to witness against you the heaven and the earth, and our God and Lord of our fathers, which punisheth us according to our sins and the sins of our fathers, that he do not according as we have said this day.

[29] Then there was great weeping with one consent in the midst of the assembly; and they cried unto the Lord God with a loud voice.

[30] Then said Ozias to them, Brethren, be of good courage, let us yet endure five days, in the which space the Lord our God may turn his mercy toward us; for he will not forsake us utterly.

[31] And if these days pass, and there come no help unto us, I will do according to your word.

[32] And he dispersed the people, every one to their own charge; and they went unto the walls and towers of their city, and sent the women and children into their houses: and they were very low brought in the city.

Jdt.8

[1] Now at that time Judith heard thereof, which was the daughter of Merari, the son of Ox, the son of Joseph, the son of Ozel, the son of Elcia, the son of Ananias, the son of Gedeon, the son of Raphaim, the son of Acitho, the son of Eliu, the son of Eliab, the son of Nathanael, the son of Samael, the son of Salasadal, the son of Israel.

[2] And Manasses was her husband, of her tribe and kindred, who died in the barley harvest.

[3] For as he stood overseeing them that bound sheaves in the field, the heat came upon his head, and he fell on his bed, and died in the city of Bethulia: and they buried him with his fathers in the field between Dothaim and Balamo.

[4] So Judith was a widow in her house three years and four months.

[5] And she made her a tent upon the top of her house, and put on sackcloth upon her loins and ware her widow's apparel.

[6] And she fasted all the days of her widowhood, save the eves of the sabbaths, and the sabbaths, and the eves of the new moons, and the new moons and the feasts and solemn days of the house of Israel.

[7] She was also of a goodly countenance, and very beautiful to behold: and her husband Manasses had left her gold, and silver, and menservants and maidservants, and cattle, and lands; and she remained upon them.

[8] And there was none that gave her an ill word; ar she feared God greatly.

[9] Now when she heard the evil words of the people against the governor, that they fainted for lack of water; for Judith had heard all the words that Ozias had spoken unto them, and that he had sworn to deliver the city unto the Assyrians after five days;

[10] Then she sent her waitingwoman, that had the government of all things that she had, to call Ozias and Chabris and Charmis, the ancients of the city.

[11] And they came unto her, and she said unto them, Hear me now, O ye governors of the inhabitants of Bethulia: for your words that ye have spoken before the people this day are not right, touching this oath which ye made and pronounced between God and you, and have promised to deliver the city to our enemies, unless within these days the Lord turn to help you.

[12] And now who are ye that have tempted God this day, and stand instead of God among the children of men?

[13] And now try the Lord Almighty, but ye shall never know any thing.

[14] For ye cannot find the depth of the heart of man, neither can ye perceive the things that he thinketh: then

how can ye search out God, that hath made all these things, and know his mind, or comprehend his purpose? Nay, my brethren, provoke not the Lord our God to anger. [15] For if he will not help us within these five days, he hath power to defend us when he will, even every day, or to destroy us before our enemies. [16] Do not bind the counsels of the Lord our God: for God is not as man, that he may be threatened; neither is he as the son of man, that he should be wavering. [17] Therefore let us wait for salvation of him, and call upon him to help us, and he will hear our voice, if it please him. [18] For there arose none in our age, neither is there any now in these days neither tribe, nor family, nor people, nor city among us, which worship gods made with hands, as hath been aforetime. [19] For the which cause our fathers were given to the sword, and for a spoil, and had a great fall before our enemies. [20] But we know none other god, therefore we trust that he will not dispise us, nor any of our nation. [21] For if we be taken so, all Judea shall lie waste, and our sanctuary shall be spoiled; and he will require the profanation thereof at our mouth. [22] And the slaughter of our brethren, and the captivity of the country, and the desolation of our inheritance, will he turn upon our heads among the Gentiles, wheresoever we shall be in bondage; and we shall be an offence and a reproach to all them that possess us. [23] For our servitude shall not be directed to favour: but the Lord our God shall turn it to dishonour. [24] Now therefore, O brethren, let us shew an example to our brethren, because their hearts depend upon us, and the sanctuary, and the house, and the altar, rest upon us. [25] Moreover let us give thanks to the Lord our God, which trieth us, even as he did our fathers. [26] Remember what things he did to Abraham, and how he tried Isaac, and what happened to Jacob in Mesopotamia of Syria, when he kept the sheep of Laban his mother's brother. [27] For he hath not tried us in the fire, as he did them, for the examination of their hearts, neither hath he taken vengeance on us: but the Lord doth scourge them that come near unto him, to admonish them. [28] Then said Ozias to her, All that thou hast spoken hast thou spoken with a good heart, and there is none that may gainsay thy words. [29] For this is not the first day wherein thy wisdom is manifested; but from the beginning of thy days all the people have known thy understanding, because the disposition of thine heart is good. [30] But the people were very thirsty, and compelled us to do unto them as we have spoken, and to bring an oath upon ourselves, which we will not break. [31] Therefore now pray thou for us, because thou art a godly woman, and the Lord will send us rain to fill our cisterns, and we shall faint no more. [32] Then said Judith unto them, Hear me, and I will do a thing, which shall go throughout all generations to the children of our nation. [33] Ye shall stand this night in the gate, and I will go forth with my waitingwoman: and within the days that ye have promised to deliver the city to our enemies the Lord will visit Israel by mine hand. [34] But enquire not ye of mine act: for I will not declare it unto you, till the things be finished that I do. [35] Then said Ozias and the princes unto her, Go in peace, and the Lord God be before thee, to take vengeance on our enemies. [36] So they returned from the tent, and went to their wards.

Jdt.9

[1] Judith fell upon her face, and put ashes upon her head, and uncovered the sackcloth wherewith she was clothed; and about the time that the incense of that evening was offered in Jerusalem in the house of the Lord Judith cried with a loud voice, and said,
[2] O Lord God of my father Simeon, to whom thou gavest a sword to take vengeance of the strangers, who loosened the girdle of a maid to defile her, and discovered the thigh to her shame, and polluted her virginity to her reproach; for thou saidst, It shall not be so; and yet they did so:
[3] Wherefore thou gavest their rulers to be slain, so that they dyed their bed in blood, being deceived, and smotest the servants with their lords, and the lords upon their thrones;
[4] And hast given their wives for a prey, and their daughters to be captives, and all their spoils to be divided among thy dear children; which were moved with thy zeal, and abhorred the pollution of their blood, and called upon thee for aid: O God, O my God, hear me also a widow.
[5] For thou hast wrought not only those things, but also the things which fell out before, and which ensued after; thou hast thought upon the things which are now, and which are to come.
[6] Yea, what things thou didst determine were ready at hand, and said, Lo, we are here: for all thy ways are prepared, and thy judgments are in thy foreknowledge.

[7] For, behold, the Assyrians are multiplied in their power; they are exalted with horse and man; they glory in the strength of their footmen; they trust in shield, and spear, and bow, and sling; and know not that thou art the Lord that breakest the battles: the Lord is thy name.

[8] Throw down their strength in thy power, and bring down their force in thy wrath: for they have purposed to defile thy sanctuary, and to pollute the tabernacle where thy glorious name resteth and to cast down with sword the horn of thy altar.

[9] Behold their pride, and send thy wrath upon their heads: give into mine hand, which am a widow, the power that I have conceived.

[10] Smite by the deceit of my lips the servant with the prince, and the prince with the servant: break down their stateliness by the hand of a woman.

[11] For thy power standeth not in multitude nor thy might in strong men: for thou art a God of the afflicted, an helper of the oppressed, an upholder of the weak, a protector of the forlorn, a saviour of them that are without hope.

[12] I pray thee, I pray thee, O God of my father, and God of the inheritance of Israel, Lord of the heavens and earth, Creator of the waters, king of every creature, hear thou my prayer:

[13] And make my speech and deceit to be their wound and stripe, who have purposed cruel things against thy covenant, and thy hallowed house, and against the top of Sion, and against the house of the possession of thy children.

[14] And make every nation and tribe to acknowledge that thou art the God of all power and might, and that there is none other that protecteth the people of Israel but thou.

Jdt.10

[1] Now after that she had ceased to cry unto the God of Israel, and bad made an end of all these words.

[2] She rose where she had fallen down, and called her maid, and went down into the house in the which she abode in the sabbath days, and in her feast days,

[3] And pulled off the sackcloth which she had on, and put off the garments of her widowhood, and washed her body all over with water, and anointed herself with precious ointment, and braided the hair of her head, and put on a tire upon it, and put on her garments of gladness, wherewith she was clad during the life of Manasses her husband.

[4] And she took sandals upon her feet, and put about her her bracelets, and her chains, and her rings, and her earrings, and all her ornaments, and decked herself bravely, to allure the eyes of all men that should see her.

[5] Then she gave her maid a bottle of wine, and a cruse of oil, and filled a bag with parched corn, and lumps of figs, and with fine bread; so she folded all these things together, and laid them upon her.

[6] Thus they went forth to the gate of the city of Bethulia, and found standing there Ozias and the ancients of the city, Chabris and Charmis.

[7] And when they saw her, that her countenance was altered, and her apparel was changed, they wondered at her beauty very greatly, and said unto her.

[8] The God, the God of our fathers give thee favour, and accomplish thine enterprizes to the glory of the children of Israel, and to the exaltation of Jerusalem. Then they worshipped God.

[9] And she said unto them, Command the gates of the city to be opened unto me, that I may go forth to accomplish the things whereof ye have spoken with me. So they commanded the young men to open unto her, as she had spoken.

[10] And when they had done so, Judith went out, she, and her maid with her; and the men of the city looked after her, until she was gone down the mountain, and till she had passed the valley, and could see her no more.

[11] Thus they went straight forth in the valley: and the first watch of the Assyrians met her,

[12] And took her, and asked her, Of what people art thou? and whence comest thou? and whither goest thou? And she said, I am a woman of the Hebrews, and am fled from them: for they shall be given you to be consumed:

[13] And I am coming before Holofernes the chief captain of your army, to declare words of truth; and I will shew him a way, whereby he shall go, and win all the hill country, without losing the body or life of any one of his men.

[14] Now when the men heard her words, and beheld her countenance, they wondered greatly at her beauty, and said unto her,

[15] Thou hast saved thy life, in that thou hast hasted to come down to the presence of our lord: now therefore come to his tent, and some of us shall conduct thee, until they have delivered thee to his hands.

[16] And when thou standest before him, be not afraid in thine heart, but shew unto him according to thy word; and he will entreat thee well.

[17] Then they chose out of them an hundred men to accompany her and her maid; and they brought her to the tent of Holofernes.

[18] Then was there a concourse throughout all the camp:

for her coming was noised among the tents, and they came about her, as she stood without the tent of Holofernes, till they told him of her.

[19] And they wondered at her beauty, and admired the children of Israel because of her, and every one said to his neighbour, Who would despise this people, that have among them such women? surely it is not good that one man of them be left who being let go might deceive the whole earth.

[20] And they that lay near Holofernes went out, and all his servants and they brought her into the tent.

[21] Now Holofernes rested upon his bed under a canopy, which was woven with purple, and gold, and emeralds, and precious stones.

[22] So they shewed him of her; and he came out before his tent with silver lamps going before him.

[23] And when Judith was come before him and his servants they all marvelled at the beauty of her countenance; and she fell down upon her face, and did reverence unto him: and his servants took her up.

Jdt.11

[1] Then said Holofernes unto her, Woman, be of good comfort, fear not in thine heart: for I never hurt any that was willing to serve Nabuchodonosor, the king of all the earth.

[2] Now therefore, if thy people that dwelleth in the mountains had not set light by me, I would not have lifted up my spear against them: but they have done these things to themselves.

[3] But now tell me wherefore thou art fled from them, and art come unto us: for thou art come for safeguard; be of good comfort, thou shalt live this night, and hereafter:

[4] For none shall hurt thee, but entreat thee well, as they do the servants of king Nabuchodonosor my lord.

[5] Then Judith said unto him, Receive the words of thy servant, and suffer thine handmaid to speak in thy presence, and I will declare no lie to my lord this night.

[6] And if thou wilt follow the words of thine handmaid, God will bring the thing perfectly to pass by thee; and my lord shall not fail of his purposes.

[7] As Nabuchodonosor king of all the earth liveth, and as his power liveth, who hath sent thee for the upholding of every living thing: for not only men shall serve him by thee, but also the beasts of the field, and the cattle, and the fowls of the air, shall live by thy power under Nabuchodonosor and all his house.

[8] For we have heard of thy wisdom and thy policies, and it is reported in all the earth, that thou only art excellent in all the kingdom, and mighty in knowledge, and wonderful in feats of war.

[9] Now as concerning the matter, which Achior did speak in thy council, we have heard his words; for the men of Bethulia saved him, and he declared unto them all that he had spoken unto thee.

[10] Therefore, O lord and governor, respect not his word; but lay it up in thine heart, for it is true: for our nation shall not be punished, neither can sword prevail against them, except they sin against their God.

[11] And now, that my lord be not defeated and frustrate of his purpose, even death is now fallen upon them, and their sin hath overtaken them, wherewith they will provoke their God to anger whensoever they shall do that which is not fit to be done:

[12] For their victuals fail them, and all their water is scant, and they have determined to lay hands upon their cattle, and purposed to consume all those things, that God hath forbidden them to eat by his laws:

[13] And are resolved to spend the firstfruits of the the tenths of wine and oil, which they had sanctified, and reserved for the priests that serve in Jerusalem before the face of our God; the which things it is not lawful for any of the people so much as to touch with their hands.

[14] For they have sent some to Jerusalem, because they also that dwell there have done the like, to bring them a licence from the senate.

[15] Now when they shall bring them word, they will forthwith do it, and they shall be given to thee to be destroyed the same day.

[16] Wherefore I thine handmaid, knowing all this, am fled from their presence; and God hath sent me to work things with thee, whereat all the earth shall be astonished, and whosoever shall hear it.

[17] For thy servant is religious, and serveth the God of heaven day and night: now therefore, my lord, I will remain with thee, and thy servant will go out by night into the valley, and I will pray unto God, and he will tell me when they have committed their sins:

[18] And I will come and shew it unto thee: then thou shalt go forth with all thine army, and there shall be none of them that shall resist thee.

[19] And I will lead thee through the midst of Judea, until thou come before Jerusalem; and I will set thy throne in the midst thereof; and thou shalt drive them as sheep that have no shepherd, and a dog shall not so much as open his mouth at thee: for these things were told me according to my foreknowledge, and they were declared unto me, and I am sent to tell thee.

[20] Then her words pleased Holofernes and all his

servants; and they marvelled at her wisdom, and said,

[21] There is not such a woman from one end of the earth to the other, both for beauty of face, and wisdom of words.

[22] Likewise Holofernes said unto her. God hath done well to send thee before the people, that strength might be in our hands and destruction upon them that lightly regard my lord.

[23] And now thou art both beautiful in thy countenance, and witty in thy words: surely if thou do as thou hast spoken thy God shall be my God, and thou shalt dwell in the house of king Nabuchodonosor, and shalt be renowned through the whole earth.

Jdt.12

[1] Then he commanded to bring her in where his plate was set; and bade that they should prepare for her of his own meats, and that she should drink of his own wine.

[2] And Judith said, I will not eat thereof, lest there be an offence: but provision shall be made for me of the things that I have brought.

[3] Then Holofernes said unto her, If thy provision should fail, how should we give thee the like? for there be none with us of thy nation.

[4] Then said Judith unto him As thy soul liveth, my lord, thine handmaid shall not spend those things that I have, before the Lord work by mine hand the things that he hath determined.

[5] Then the servants of Holofernes brought her into the tent, and she slept till midnight, and she arose when it was toward the morning watch,

[6] And sent to Holofernes, saying, Let my lord now command that thine handmaid may go forth unto prayer.

[7] Then Holofernes commanded his guard that they should not stay her: thus she abode in the camp three days, and went out in the night into the valley of Bethulia, and washed herself in a fountain of water by the camp.

[8] And when she came out, she besought the Lord God of Israel to direct her way to the raising up of the children of her people.

[9] So she came in clean, and remained in the tent, until she did eat her meat at evening.

[10] And in the fourth day Holofernes made a feast to his own servants only, and called none of the officers to the banquet.

[11] Then said he to Bagoas the eunuch, who had charge over all that he had, Go now, and persuade this Hebrew woman which is with thee, that she come unto us, and eat and drink with us.

[12] For, lo, it will be a shame for our person, if we shall let such a woman go, not having had her company; for if we draw her not unto us, she will laugh us to scorn.

[13] Then went Bagoas from the presence of Holofernes, and came to her, and he said, Let not this fair damsel fear to come to my lord, and to be honoured in his presence, and drink wine, and be merry with us and be made this day as one of the daughters of the Assyrians, which serve in the house of Nabuchodonosor.

[14] Then said Judith unto him, Who am I now, that I should gainsay my lord? surely whatsoever pleaseth him I will do speedily, and it shall be my joy unto the day of my death.

[15] So she arose, and decked herself with her apparel and all her woman's attire, and her maid went and laid soft skins on the ground for her over against Holofernes, which she had received of Bagoas far her daily use, that she might sit and eat upon them.

[16] Now when Judith came in and sat down, Holofernes his heart was ravished with her, and his mind was moved, and he desired greatly her company; for he waited a time to deceive her, from the day that he had seen her.

[17] Then said Holofernes unto her, Drink now, and be merry with us.

[18] So Judith said, I will drink now, my lord, because my life is magnified in me this day more than all the days since I was born.

[19] Then she took and ate and drank before him what her maid had prepared.

[20] And Holofernes took great delight in her, and drank more wine than he had drunk at any time in one day since he was born.

Jdt.13

[1] Now when the evening was come, his servants made haste to depart, and Bagoas shut his tent without, and dismissed the waiters from the presence of his lord; and they went to their beds: for they were all weary, because the feast had been long.

[2] And Judith was left along in the tent, and Holofernes lying along upon his bed: for he was filled with wine.

[3] Now Judith had commanded her maid to stand without her bedchamber, and to wait for her. coming forth, as she did daily: for she said she would go forth to her prayers, and she spake to Bagoas according to the same purpose.

[4] So all went forth and none was left in the bedchamber, neither little nor great. Then Judith, standing by his bed, said in her heart, O Lord God of all power, look at this present upon the works of mine hands for the exaltation of Jerusalem.

[5] For now is the time to help thine inheritance, and to execute thine enterprizes to the destruction of the enemies which are risen against us.

[6] Then she came to the pillar of the bed, which was at Holofernes' head, and took down his fauchion from thence,

[7] And approached to his bed, and took hold of the hair of his head, and said, Strengthen me, O Lord God of Israel, this day.

[8] And she smote twice upon his neck with all her might, and she took away his head from him.

[9] And tumbled his body down from the bed, and pulled down the canopy from the pillars; and anon after she went forth, and gave Holofernes his head to her maid;

[10] And she put it in her bag of meat: so they twain went together according to their custom unto prayer: and when they passed the camp, they compassed the valley, and went up the mountain of Bethulia, and came to the gates thereof.

[11] Then said Judith afar off, to the watchmen at the gate, Open, open now the gate: God, even our God, is with us, to shew his power yet in Jerusalem, and his forces against the enemy, as he hath even done this day.

[12] Now when the men of her city heard her voice, they made haste to go down to the gate of their city, and they called the elders of the city.

[13] And then they ran all together, both small and great, for it was strange unto them that she was come: so they opened the gate, and received them, and made a fire for a light, and stood round about them.

[14] Then she said to them with a loud voice, Praise, praise God, praise God, I say, for he hath not taken away his mercy from the house of Israel, but hath destroyed our enemies by mine hands this night.

[15] So she took the head out of the bag, and shewed it, and said unto them, behold the head of Holofernes, the chief captain of the army of Assur, and behold the canopy, wherein he did lie in his drunkenness; and the Lord hath smitten him by the hand of a woman.

[16] As the Lord liveth, who hath kept me in my way that I went, my countenance hath deceived him to his destruction, and yet hath he not committed sin with me, to defile and shame me.

[17] Then all the people were wonderfully astonished, and bowed themselves and worshipped God, and said with one accord, Blessed be thou, O our God, which hast this day brought to nought the enemies of thy people.

[18] Then said Ozias unto her, O daughter, blessed art thou of the most high God above all the women upon the earth; and blessed be the Lord God, which hath created the heavens and the earth, which hath directed thee to the cutting off of the head of the chief of our enemies.

[19] For this thy confidence shall not depart from the heart of men, which remember the power of God for ever.

[20] And God turn these things to thee for a perpetual praise, to visit thee in good things because thou hast not spared thy life for the affliction of our nation, but hast revenged our ruin, walking a straight way before our God. And all the people said; So be it, so be it.

Jdt.14

[1] Then said Judith unto them, Hear me now, my brethren, and take this head, and hang it upon the highest place of your walls.

[2] And so soon as the morning shall appear, and the sun shall come forth upon the earth, take ye every one his weapons, and go forth every valiant man out of the city, and set ye a captain over them, as though ye would go down into the field toward the watch of the Assyrians; but go not down.

[3] Then they shall take their armour, and shall go into their camp, and raise up the captains of the army of Assur, and shall run to the tent of Holofernes, but shall not find him: then fear shall fall upon them, and they shall flee before your face.

[4] So ye, and all that inhabit the coast of Israel, shall pursue them, and overthrow them as they go.

[5] But before ye do these things, call me Achior the Ammonite, that he may see and know him that despised the house of Israel, and that sent him to us as it were to his death.

[6] Then they called Achior out of the house of Ozias; and when he was come, and saw the head of Holofernes in a man's hand in the assembly of the people, he fell down on his face, and his spirit failed.

[7] But when they had recovered him, he fell at Judith's feet, and reverenced her, and said, Blessed art thou in all the tabernacles of Juda, and in all nations, which hearing thy name shall be astonished.

[8] Now therefore tell me all the things that thou hast done in these days. Then Judith declared unto him in the midst of the people all that she had done, from the day that she went forth until that hour she spake unto them.

[9] And when she had left off speaking, the people shouted with a loud voice, and made a joyful noise in their city.

[10] And when Achior had seen all that the God of Israel had done, he believed in God greatly, and circumcised the flesh of his foreskin, and was joined unto the house of Israel unto this day.

[11] And as soon as the morning arose, they hanged the head of Holofernes upon the wall, and every man took his weapons, and they went forth by bands unto the straits of the mountain.

[12] But when the Assyrians saw them, they sent to their leaders, which came to their captains and tribunes, and to every one of their rulers.

[13] So they came to Holofernes' tent, and said to him that had the charge of all his things, Waken now our lord: for the slaves have been bold to come down against us to battle, that they may be utterly destroyed.

[14] Then went in Bagoas, and knocked at the door of the tent; for he thought that he had slept with Judith.

[15] But because none answered, he opened it, and went into the bedchamber, and found him cast upon the floor dead, and his head was taken from him.

[16] Therefore he cried with a loud voice, with weeping, and sighing, and a mighty cry, and rent his garments.

[17] After he went into the tent where Judith lodged: and when he found her not, he leaped out to the people, and cried,

[18] These slaves have dealt treacherously; one woman of the Hebrews hath brought shame upon the house of king Nabuchodonosor: for, behold, Holofernes lieth upon the ground without a head.

[19] When the captains of the Assyrians' army heard these words, they rent their coats and their minds were wonderfully troubled, and there was a cry and a very great noise throughout the camp.

Jdt.15

[1] And when they that were in the tents heard, they were astonished at the thing that was done.

[2] And fear and trembling fell upon them, so that there was no man that durst abide in the sight of his neighbour, but rushing out all together, they fled into every way of the plain, and of the hill country.

[3] They also that had camped in the mountains round about Bethulia fled away. Then the children of Israel, every one that was a warrior among them, rushed out upon them.

[4] Then sent Ozias to Betomasthem, and to Bebai, and Chobai, and Cola and to all the coasts of Israel, such as should tell the things that were done, and that all should rush forth upon their enemies to destroy them.

[5] Now when the children of Israel heard it, they all fell upon them with one consent, and slew them unto Chobai: likewise also they that came from Jerusalem, and from all the hill country, (for men had told them what things were done in the camp of their enemies) and they that were in Galaad, and in Galilee, chased them with a great slaughter, until they were past Damascus and the borders thereof.

[6] And the residue that dwelt at Bethulia, fell upon the camp of Assur, and spoiled them, and were greatly enriched.

[7] And the children of Israel that returned from the slaughter had that which remained; and the villages and the cities, that were in the mountains and in the plain, gat many spoils: for the multitude was very great.

[8] Then Joacim the high priest, and the ancients of the children of Israel that dwelt in Jerusalem, came to behold the good things that God had shewed to Israel, and to see Judith, and to salute her.

[9] And when they came unto her, they blessed her with one accord, and said unto her, Thou art the exaltation of Jerusalem, thou art the great glory of Israel, thou art the great rejoicing of our nation:

[10] Thou hast done all these things by thine hand: thou hast done much good to Israel, and God is pleased therewith: blessed be thou of the Almighty Lord for evermore. And all the people said, So be it.

[11] And the people spoiled the camp the space of thirty days: and they gave unto Judith Holofernes his tent, and all his plate, and beds, and vessels, and all his stuff: and she took it and laid it on her mule; and made ready her carts, and laid them thereon.

[12] Then all the women of Israel ran together to see her, and blessed her, and made a dance among them for her: and she took branches in her hand, and gave also to the women that were with her.

[13] And they put a garland of olive upon her and her maid that was with her, and she went before all the people in the dance, leading all the women: and all the men of Israel followed in their armour with garlands, and with songs in their mouths.

Jdt.16

[1] Then Judith began to sing this thanksgiving in all Israel, and all the people sang after her this song of praise.

[2] And Judith said, Begin unto my God with timbrels, sing unto my Lord with cymbals: tune unto him a new psalm: exalt him, and call upon his name.

[3] For God breaketh the battles: for among the camps in the midst of the people he hath delivered me out of the hands of them that persecuted me.

[4] Assur came out of the mountains from the north, he came with ten thousands of his army, the multitude whereof stopped the torrents, and their horsemen have

covered the hills.

[5] He bragged that he would burn up my borders, and kill my young men with the sword, and dash the sucking children against the ground, and make mine infants as a prey, and my virgins as a spoil.

[6] But the Almighty Lord hath disappointed them by the hand of a woman.

[7] For the mighty one did not fall by the young men, neither did the sons of the Titans smite him, nor high giants set upon him: but Judith the daughter of Merari weakened him with the beauty of her countenance.

[8] For she put off the garment of her widowhood for the exaltation of those that were oppressed in Israel, and anointed her face with ointment, and bound her hair in a tire, and took a linen garment to deceive him.

[9] Her sandals ravished his eyes, her beauty took his mind prisoner, and the fauchion passed through his neck.

[10] The Persians quaked at her boldness, and the Medes were daunted at her hardiness.

[11] Then my afflicted shouted for joy, and my weak ones cried aloud; but they were astonished: these lifted up their voices, but they were overthrown.

[12] The sons of the damsels have pierced them through, and wounded them as fugatives' children: they perished by the battle of the Lord.

[13] I will sing unto the Lord a new song: O Lord, thou art great and glorious, wonderful in strength, and invincible.

[14] Let all creatures serve thee: for thou spakest, and they were made, thou didst send forth thy spirit, and it created them, and there is none that can resist thy voice.

[15] For the mountains shall be moved from their foundations with the waters, the rocks shall melt as wax at thy presence: yet thou art merciful to them that fear thee.

[16] For all sacrifice is too little for a sweet savour unto thee, and all the fat is not sufficient for thy burnt offering: but he that feareth the Lord is great at all times.

[17] Woe to the nations that rise up against my kindred! the Lord Almighty will take vengeance of them in the day of judgment, in putting fire and worms in their flesh; and they shall feel them, and weep for ever.

[18] Now as soon as they entered into Jerusalem, they worshipped the Lord; and as soon as the people were purified, they offered their burnt offerings, and their free offerings, and their gifts.

[19] Judith also dedicated all the stuff of Holofernes, which the people had given her, and gave the canopy, which she had taken out of his bedchamber, for a gift unto the Lord.

[20] So the people continued feasting in Jerusalem before the sanctuary for the space of three months and Judith remained with them.

[21] After this time every one returned to his own inheritance, and Judith went to Bethulia, and remained in her own possession, and was in her time honourable in all the country.

[22] And many desired her, but none knew her all the days of her life, after that Manasses her husband was dead, and was gathered to his people.

[23] But she increased more and more in honour, and waxed old in her husband's house, being an hundred and five years old, and made her maid free; so she died in Bethulia: and they buried her in the cave of her husband Manasses.

[24] And the house of Israel lamented her seven days: and before she died, she did distribute her goods to all them that were nearest of kindred to Manasses her husband, and to them that were the nearest of her kindred.

[25] And there was none that made the children of Israel any more afraid in the days of Judith, nor a long time after her death.

Bel And The Dragon

Bel.1

[1] And king Astyages was gathered to his fathers, and Cyrus of Persia received his kingdom.

[2] And Daniel conversed with the king, and was honoured above all his friends.

[3] Now the Babylons had an idol, called Bel, and there were spent upon him every day twelve great measures of fine flour, and forty sheep, and six vessels of wine.

[4] And the king worshipped it and went daily to adore it: but Daniel worshipped his own God. And the king said unto him, Why dost not thou worship Bel?

[5] Who answered and said, Because I may not worship idols made with hands, but the living God, who hath created the heaven and the earth, and hath sovereignty over all flesh.

[6] Then said the king unto him, Thinkest thou not that Bel is a living God? seest thou not how much he eateth and drinketh every day?

[7] Then Daniel smiled, and said, O king, be not deceived: for this is but clay within, and brass without, and did never eat or drink any thing.

[8] So the king was wroth, and called for his priests, and said unto them, If ye tell me not who this is that devoureth these expences, ye shall die.

[9] But if ye can certify me that Bel devoureth them, then Daniel shall die: for he hath spoken blasphemy against Bel. And Daniel said unto the king, Let it be according to thy word.

[10] Now the priests of Bel were threescore and ten, beside their wives and children. And the king went with Daniel into the temple of Bel.

[11] So Bel's priests said, Lo, we go out: but thou, O king, set on the meat, and make ready the wine, and shut the door fast and seal it with thine own signet;

[12] And to morrow when thou comest in, if thou findest not that Bel hath eaten up all, we will suffer death: or else Daniel, that speaketh falsely against us.

[13] And they little regarded it: for under the table they had made a privy entrance, whereby they entered in continually, and consumed those things.

[14] So when they were gone forth, the king set meats before Bel. Now Daniel had commanded his servants to bring ashes, and those they strewed throughout all the temple in the presence of the king alone: then went they out, and shut the door, and sealed it with the king's signet, and so departed.

[15] Now in the night came the priests with their wives and children, as they were wont to do, and did eat and drinck up all.

[16] In the morning betime the king arose, and Daniel with him.

[17] And the king said, Daniel, are the seals whole? And he said, Yea, O king, they be whole.

[18] And as soon as he had opened the dour, the king looked upon the table, and cried with a loud voice, Great art thou, O Bel, and with thee is no deceit at all.

[19] Then laughed Daniel, and held the king that he should not go in, and said, Behold now the pavement, and mark well whose footsteps are these.

[20] And the king said, I see the footsteps of men, women, and children. And then the king was angry,

[21] And took the priests with their wives and children, who shewed him the privy doors, where they came in, and consumed such things as were upon the table.

[22] Therefore the king slew them, and delivered Bel into Daniel's power, who destroyed him and his temple.

[23] And in that same place there was a great dragon, which they of Babylon worshipped.

[24] And the king said unto Daniel, Wilt thou also say that this is of brass? lo, he liveth, he eateth and drinketh; thou canst not say that he is no living god: therefore worship him.

[25] Then said Daniel unto the king, I will worship the Lord my God: for he is the living God.

[26] But give me leave, O king, and I shall slay this dragon without sword or staff. The king said, I give thee leave.

[27] Then Daniel took pitch, and fat, and hair, and did seethe them together, and made lumps thereof: this he put in the dragon's mouth, and so the dragon burst in sunder : and Daniel said, Lo, these are the gods ye worship.

[28] When they of Babylon heard that, they took great indignation, and conspired against the king, saying, The

king is become a Jew, and he hath destroyed Bel, he hath slain the dragon, and put the priests to death.

[29] So they came to the king, and said, Deliver us Daniel, or else we will destroy thee and thine house.

[30] Now when the king saw that they pressed him sore, being constrained, he delivered Daniel unto them:

[31] Who cast him into the lions' den: where he was six days.

[32] And in the den there were seven lions, and they had given them every day two carcases, and two sheep: which then were not given to them, to the intent they might devour Daniel.

[33] Now there was in Jewry a prophet, called Habbacuc, who had made pottage, and had broken bread in a bowl, and was going into the field, for to bring it to the reapers.

[34] But the angel of the Lord said unto Habbacuc, Go, carry the dinner that thou hast into Babylon unto Daniel, who is in the lions' den.

[35] And Habbacuc said, Lord, I never saw Babylon; neither do I know where the den is.

[36] Then the angel of the Lord took him by the crown, and bare him by the hair of his head, and through the vehemency of his spirit set him in Babylon over the den.

[37] And Habbacuc cried, saying, O Daniel, Daniel, take the dinner which God hath sent thee.

[38] And Daniel said, Thou hast remembered me, O God: neither hast thou forsaken them that seek thee and love thee.

[39] So Daniel arose, and did eat: and the angel of the Lord set Habbacuc in his own place again immediately.

[40] Upon the seventh day the king went to bewail Daniel: and when he came to the den, he looked in, and behold, Daniel was sitting.

[41] Then cried the king with a loud voice, saying, Great art Lord God of Daniel, and there is none other beside thee.

[42] And he drew him out, and cast those that were the cause of his destruction into the den: and they were devoured in a moment before his face.

Susanna

Sus.1

[1] There dwelt a man in Babylon, called Joacim:

[2] And he took a wife, whose name was Susanna, the daughter of Chelcias, a very fair woman, and one that feared the Lord.

[3] Her parents also were righteous, and taught their daughter according to the law of Moses.

[4] Now Joacim was a great rich man, and had a fair garden joining unto his house: and to him resorted the Jews; because he was more honourable than all others.

[5] The same year were appointed two of the ancients of the people to be judges, such as the Lord spake of, that wickedness came from Babylon from ancient judges, who seemed to govern the people.

[6] These kept much at Joacim's house: and all that had any suits in law came unto them.

[7] Now when the people departed away at noon, Susanna went into her husband's garden to walk.

[8] And the two elders saw her going in every day, and walking; so that their lust was inflamed toward her.

[9] And they perverted their own mind, and turned away their eyes, that they might not look unto heaven, nor remember just judgments.

[10] And albeit they both were wounded with her love, yet durst not one shew another his grief.

[11] For they were ashamed to declare their lust, that they desired to have to do with her.

[12] Yet they watched diligently from day to day to see her.

[13] And the one said to the other, Let us now go home: for it is dinner time.

[14] So when they were gone out, they parted the one from the other, and turning back again they came to the same place; and after that they had asked one another the cause, they acknowledged their lust: then appointed they a time both together, when they might find her alone.

[15] And it fell out, as they watched a fit time, she went in as before with two maids only, and she was desirous to wash herself in the garden: for it was hot.

[16] And there was no body there save the two elders, that had hid themselves, and watched her.

[17] Then she said to her maids, Bring me oil and washing balls, and shut the garden doors, that I may wash me.

[18] And they did as she bade them, and shut the garden doors, and went out themselves at privy doors to fetch the things that she had commanded them: but they saw not the elders, because they were hid.

[19] Now when the maids were gone forth, the two elders rose up, and ran unto her, saying,

[20] Behold, the garden doors are shut, that no man can see us, and we are in love with thee; therefore consent unto us, and lie with us.

[21] If thou wilt not, we will bear witness against thee, that a young man was with thee: and therefore thou didst send away thy maids from thee.

[22] Then Susanna sighed, and said, I am straitened on every side: for if I do this thing, it is death unto me: and if I do it not I cannot escape your hands.

[23] It is better for me to fall into your hands, and not do it, than to sin in the sight of the Lord.

[24] With that Susanna cried with a loud voice: and the two elders cried out against her.

[25] Then ran the one, and opened the garden door.

[26] So when the servants of the house heard the cry in the garden, they rushed in at the privy door, to see what was done unto her.

[27] But when the elders had declared their matter, the servants were greatly ashamed: for there was never such a report made of Susanna.

[28] And it came to pass the next day, when the people were assembled to her husband Joacim, the two elders came also full of mischievous imagination against Susanna to put her to death;

[29] And said before the people, Send for Susanna, the daughter of Chelcias, Joacim's wife. And so they sent.

[30] So she came with her father and mother, her children, and all her kindred.

[31] Now Susanna was a very delicate woman, and beauteous to behold.

[32] And these wicked men commanded to uncover her face, (for she was covered) that they might be filled with her beauty.

[33] Therefore her friends and all that saw her wept.

[34] Then the two elders stood up in the midst of the people, and laid their hands upon her head.

[35] And she weeping looked up toward heaven: for her heart trusted in the Lord.

[36] And the elders said, As we walked in the garden alone, this woman came in with two maids, and shut the garden doors, and sent the maids away.

[37] Then a young man, who there was hid, came unto her, and lay with her.

[38] Then we that stood in a corner of the garden, seeing this wickedness, ran unto them.

[39] And when we saw them together, the man we could not hold: for he was stronger than we, and opened the door, and leaped out.

[40] But having taken this woman, we asked who the young man was, but she would not tell us: these things do we testify.

[41] Then the assembly believed them as those that were the elders and judges of the people: so they condemned her to death.

[42] Then Susanna cried out with a loud voice, and said, O everlasting God, that knowest the secrets, and knowest all things before they be:

[43] Thou knowest that they have borne false witness against me, and, behold, I must die; whereas I never did such things as these men have maliciously invented against me.

[44] And the Lord heard her voice.

[45] Therefore when she was led to be put to death, the Lord raised up the holy spirit of a young youth whose name was Daniel:

[46] Who cried with a loud voice, I am clear from the blood of this woman.

[47] Then all the people turned them toward him, and said, What mean these words that thou hast spoken?

[48] So he standing in the midst of them said, Are ye such fools, ye sons of Israel, that without examination or knowledge of the truth ye have condemned a daughter of Israel?

[49] Return again to the place of judgment: for they have borne false witness against her.

[50] Wherefore all the people turned again in haste, and the elders said unto him, Come, sit down among us, and shew it us, seeing God hath given thee the honour of an elder.

[51] Then said Daniel unto them, Put these two aside one far from another, and I will examine them.

[52] So when they were put asunder one from another, he called one of them, and said unto him, O thou that art waxen old in wickedness, now thy sins which thou hast committed aforetime are come to light.

[53] For thou hast pronounced false judgment and hast condemned the innocent and hast let the guilty go free; albeit the Lord saith, The innocent and righteous shalt thou not slay.

[54] Now then, if thou hast seen her, tell me, Under what tree sawest thou them companying together? Who answered, Under a mastick tree.

[55] And Daniel said, Very well; thou hast lied against thine own head; for even now the angel of God hath received the sentence of God to cut thee in two.

[56] So he put him aside, and commanded to bring the other, and said unto him, O thou seed of Chanaan, and not of Juda, beauty hath deceived thee, and lust hath perverted thine heart.

[57] Thus have ye dealt with the daughters of Israel, and they for fear companied with you: but the daughter of Juda would not abide your wickedness.

[58] Now therefore tell me, Under what tree didst thou take them companying together? Who answered, Under an holm tree.

[59] Then said Daniel unto him, Well; thou hast also lied against thine own head: for the angel of God waiteth with the sword to cut thee in two, that he may destroy you.

[60] With that all the assembly cried out with a loud voice, and praised God, who saveth them that trust in him.

[61] And they arose against the two elders, for Daniel had convicted them of false witness by their own mouth:

[62] And according to the law of Moses they did unto them in such sort as they maliciously intended to do to their neighbour: and they put them to death. Thus the innocent blood was saved the same day.

[63] Therefore Chelcias and his wife praised God for their daughter Susanna, with Joacim her husband, and all the kindred, because there was no dishonesty found in her.

[64] From that day forth was Daniel had in great reputation in the sight of the people.

APOCRYPHA ETHIOPIC PRAYERS

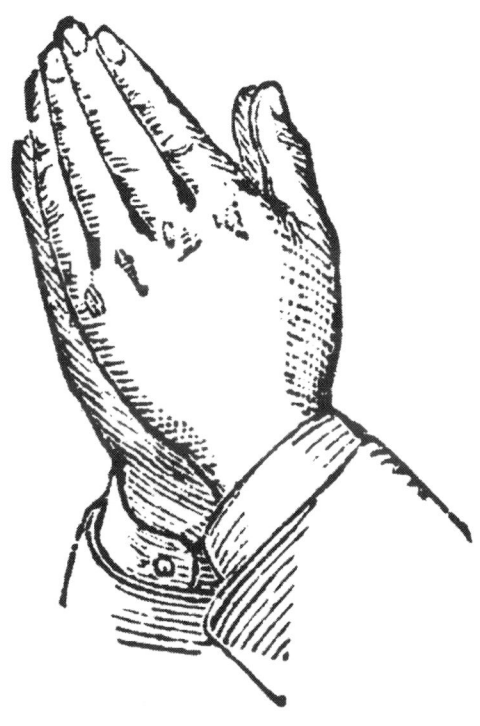

The Prayer Of Manasseh – King Of Judah

[1] Lord, Almighty God of our fathers, Abraham, Isaac, and Jacob, and of their righteous seed;

[2] Who hast made heaven and earth, with all the ornament thereof;

[3] Who hast bound the sea by the word of thy commandment;

[4] Whoho hast shut up the deep, and sealed it by thy terrible and glorious name; whom all men fear, and tremble before thy power;

[5] For the majesty of thy glory cannot be borne, and thine angry threatening toward sinners is importable: but thy merciful promise is unmeasurable and unsearchable;

[6] For thou art the most high Lord, of great compassion, longsuffering, very merciful, and repentest of the evils of men.

[7] Thou, O Lord, according to thy great goodness hast promised repentance and forgiveness to them that have sinned against thee: and of thine infinite mercies hast appointed repentance unto sinners, that they may be saved.

[8] Thou therefore, O Lord, that art the God of the just, hast not appointed repentance to the just, as to

[9] Abraham, and Isaac, and Jacob, which have not sinned against thee; but thou hast appointed repentance unto me that am a sinner: for I have sinned above the number of the sands of the sea.

[10] My transgressions, O Lord, are multiplied: my transgressions are multiplied, and I am not worthy to behold and see the height of heaven for the multitude of mine iniquities.

[11] I am bowed down with many iron bands, that I cannot life up mine head, neither have any release: for I have provoked thy wrath, and done evil before thee: I did not thy will, neither kept I thy commandments: I have set up abominations, and have multiplied offences.

[12] Now therefore I bow the knee of mine heart, beseeching thee of grace.

[13] I have sinned, O Lord, I have sinned, and I acknowledge mine iniquities: wherefore, I humbly beseech thee, forgive me, O Lord, forgive me, and destroy me not with mine iniquites.

[14] Be not angry with me for ever, by reserving evil for me; neither condemn me to the lower parts of the earth.

[15] For thou art the God, even the God of them that repent; and in me thou wilt shew all thy goodness: for thou wilt save me, that am unworthy, according to thy great mercy.

[16] Therefore I will praise thee for ever all the days of my life: for all the powers of the heavens do praise thee, and thine is the glory for ever and ever. Amen.

The Prayer Of Azariah

[1] And they walked in the midst of the fire, praising God, and blessing the Lord.

[2] Then Azarias stood up, and prayed on this manner; and opening his mouth in the midst of the fire said,

[3] Blessed art thou, O Lord God of our fathers: thy name is worthy to be praised and glorified for evermore:

[4] For thou art righteous in all the things that thou hast done to us: yea, true are all thy works, thy ways are right, and all thy judgments truth.

[5] In all the things that thou hast brought upon us, and upon the holy city of our fathers, even Jerusalem, thou hast executed true judgment: for according to truth and judgment didst thou bring all these things upon us because of our sins.

[6] For we have sinned and committed iniquity, departing from thee.

[7] In all things have we trespassed, and not obeyed thy commandments, nor kept them, neither done as thou hast commanded us, that it might go well with us.

[8] Wherefore all that thou hast brought upon us, and every thing that thou hast done to us, thou hast done in true judgment.

[9] And thou didst deliver us into the hands of lawless enemies, most hateful forsakers of God, and to an unjust king, and the most wicked in all the world.

[10] And now we cannot open our mouths, we are become a shame and reproach to thy servants; and to them that worship thee.

[11] Yet deliver us not up wholly, for thy name's sake, neither disannul thou thy covenant:

[12] And cause not thy mercy to depart from us, for thy beloved Abraham's sake, for thy servant Issac's sake, and for thy holy Israel's sake;

[13] To whom thou hast spoken and promised, that thou wouldest multiply their seed as the stars of heaven, and as the sand that lieth upon the seashore.

[14] For we, O Lord, are become less than any nation, and be kept under this day in all the world because of our sins.

[15] Neither is there at this time prince, or prophet, or leader, or burnt offering, or sacrifice, or oblation, or incense, or place to sacrifice before thee, and to find mercy.

[16] Nevertheless in a contrite heart and an humble spirit let us be accepted.

[17] Like as in the burnt offerings of rams and bullocks, and like as in ten thousands of fat lambs: so let our sacrifice be in thy sight this day, and grant that we may wholly go after thee: for they shall not be confounded that put their trust in thee.

[18] And now we follow thee with all our heart, we fear thee, and seek thy face.

[19] Put us not to shame: but deal with us after thy lovingkindness, and according to the multitude of thy mercies.

[20] Deliver us also according to thy marvellous works, and give glory to thy name, O Lord: and let all them that do thy servants hurt be ashamed;

[21] And let them be confounded in all their power and might, and let their strength be broken;

[22] And let them know that thou art God, the only God, and glorious over the whole world.

[23] And the king's servants, that put them in, ceased not to make the oven hot with rosin, pitch, tow, and small wood;

[24] So that the flame streamed forth above the furnace forty and nine cubits.

[25] And it passed through, and burned those Chaldeans it found about the furnace.

[26] But the angel of the Lord came down into the oven together with Azarias and his fellows, and smote the flame of the fire out of the oven;

[27] And made the midst of the furnace as it had been a moist whistling wind, so that the fire touched them not at all, neither hurt nor troubled them.

[28] Then the three, as out of one mouth, praised, glorified, and blessed, God in the furnace, saying,

[29] Blessed art thou, O Lord God of our fathers: and to be praised and exalted above all for ever.

[30] And blessed is thy glorious and holy name: and to be praised and exalted above all for ever.

[31] Blessed art thou in the temple of thine holy glory: and to be praised and glorified above all for ever.

[32] Blessed art thou that beholdest the depths, and sittest upon the cherubims: and to be praised and exalted above all for ever.

[33] Blessed art thou on the glorious throne of thy

kingdom: and to be praised and glorified above all for ever.

[34] Blessed art thou in the firmament of heaven: and above ail to be praised and glorified for ever.

[35] O all ye works of the Lord, bless ye the Lord : praise and exalt him above all for ever,

[36] O ye heavens, bless ye the Lord : praise and exalt him above all for ever.

[37] O ye angels of the Lord, bless ye the Lord: praise and exalt him above all for ever.

[38] O all ye waters that be above the heaven, bless ye the Lord: praise and exalt him above all for ever.

[39] O all ye powers of the Lord, bless ye the Lord: praise and exalt him above all for ever.

[40] O ye sun and moon, bless ye the Lord: praise and exalt him above all for ever.

[41] O ye stars of heaven, bless ye the Lord: praise and exalt him above all for ever.

[42] O every shower and dew, bless ye the Lord: praise and exalt him above all for ever.

[43] O all ye winds, bless ye the Lord: praise and exalt him above all for ever,

[44] O ye fire and heat, bless ye the Lord: praise and exalt him above all for ever.

[45] O ye winter and summer, bless ye the Lord: praise and exalt him above all for ever.

[46] o ye dews and storms of snow, bless ye the Lord: praise and exalt him above all for ever.

[47] O ye nights and days, bless ye the Lord: bless and exalt him above all for ever.

[48] O ye light and darkness, bless ye the Lord: praise and exalt him above all for ever.

[49] O ye ice and cold, bless ye the Lord: praise and exalt him above all for ever.

[50] O ye frost and snow, bless ye the Lord: praise and exalt him above all for ever.

[51] O ye lightnings and clouds, bless ye the Lord: praise and exalt him above all for ever.

[52] O let the earth bless the Lord: praise and exalt him above all for ever.

[53] O ye mountains and little hills, bless ye the Lord: praise and exalt him above all for ever.

[54] O all ye things that grow in the earth, bless ye the Lord: praise and exalt him above all for ever.

[55] O ye mountains, bless ye the Lord: Praise and exalt him above all for ever.

[56] O ye seas and rivers, bless ye the Lord: praise and exalt him above all for ever.

[57] O ye whales, and all that move in the waters, bless ye the Lord: praise and exalt him above all for ever.

[58] O all ye fowls of the air, bless ye the Lord: praise and exalt him above all for ever.

[59] O all ye beasts and cattle, bless ye the Lord: praise and exalt him above all for ever.

[60] O ye children of men, bless ye the Lord: praise and exalt him above all for ever.

[61] O Israel, bless ye the Lord: praise and exalt him above all for ever.

[62] O ye priests of the Lord, bless ye the Lord: praise and exalt him above all for ever.

[63] O ye servants of the Lord, bless ye the Lord: praise and exalt him above all for ever.

[64] O ye spirits and souls of the righteous, bless ye the Lord: praise and exalt him above all for ever.

[65] O ye holy and humble men of heart, bless ye the Lord: praise and exalt him above all for ever.

[66] O Ananias, Azarias, and Misael, bless ye the Lord: praise and exalt him above all for ever: far he hath delivered us from hell, and saved us from the hand of death, and delivered us out of the midst of the furnace and burning flame: even out of the midst of the fire hath he delivered us.

[67] O give thanks unto the Lord, because he is gracious: for his mercy endureth for ever.

[68] O all ye that worship the Lord, bless the God of gods, praise him, and give him thanks: for his mercy endureth for ever.

THANK YOU FOR READING THE ANCIENT ETHIOPIAN WRITINGS WE HAVE RELEASED.

If you liked our work and if you are interested in receiving other religious writings of history please let us know with appreciation.

It is important for us to get feedback and work on other translations, illustrated books and study guides of the ancient scriptures of history.

Made in the USA
Monee, IL
17 October 2023

44189825R00143